FRETBOARD BIOLOGY
COMPREHENSIVE GUITAR PROGRAM

"The Knowledge without the Colllege"™

LEVEL 4

This textbook accompanies
the Level 4 course at
Fretboardbiology.com

©2021 Joe Elliott. Please do not distribute or reproduce this material. This program represents a lifetime of work teaching guitar players like you how to be better musicians. If you think this program is great, please encourage your friends to sign up for the course and go through it with you. They will get more out of the program, and you will feel better knowing that you aren't hurting fellow artists by just giving away their work. Thank you.

Music Biology Publishing

Copyright © 2021 Joe Elliott

All rights reserved. Except as permitted under the U.S. Copyright Act of 1976, no part of this book may be reproduced in any manner whatsoever without written permission from the publisher, except in the case of brief quotations in critical articles or reviews.

The paper used in this publication meets the minimum requirements of the American National Standards for Information Services - Permanence of Paper for Printed Library Materials,
ANSI Z39.48-1984.

ISBN 13: 978-1-7362942-3-9

DEDICATION

I would like to dedicate this to all the great teachers out there who are passing along their knowledge and experience.

ACKNOWLEDGMENTS

In any project like this, it is hard to thank all of the people who have been instrumental in its development and success. I've been fortunate to have the support and friendship of many people along the way. I've somehow been wise enough to listen to those who know more than me, too. I encourage everyone to live that way.

I would like to start by thanking my wife, Eileen, for all the support, encouragement, and freedom to take on this monstrous project—and the faith that it would be a success—as well as all the years of putting up with the stresses of being married to a professional musician. My interest in music was fostered and supported by my parents, Jack and Marian Elliott, who always had a house full of big band and classical music, and my older siblings, Dave, Mary, and Dan, who exposed me to a lot of great music growing up like the Trashmen, The Beatles, The Stones, Sergio Mendes, Chicago, Sly, and Crosby, Stills, and Nash.

There were several people who were very influential in my development as a musician and educator that I would like to acknowledge: Fred Brush for showing so many great musicians to me in my formative years. Glen Johnston for exposing all of us "Montana Boys" to the real musicians in person at Montana State. Kent Erickson for drilling me on theory on our long road trips. Carl Schroeder for your unique way of getting your points across back in the day when I was in your classes in LA. You certainly shaped my way of teaching and managing a classroom. Keith Wyatt for the steady example of professionalism in guitar education. Combining great guitar talent with an organized mind is a great combination for any student. Scott Henderson for your relentless intolerance of mediocrity. You still scare me into working harder. Don Mock for being such an egoless sharer of your knowledge and gifts. You'll probably never know how many lives you affected with your pragmatic approach. Howard Roberts for all the lives you changed teaching guitar players real-world skills and shaping the most innovative guitar program that's ever existed. Bruce Buckingham for feeding me the right information at the right time. Eric Paschal for always finding the best in all your students. And Dan Gilbert for the energy you pumped into every class and the motivation to practice more than I've ever practiced.

For this project I was very fortunate to be surrounded by a team of amazing and intelligent musicians and specialty experts such as Ricky Peterson, Sean Nilson, Eliot Briggs, Bill Lafleur, Luke Elliott, Carter Elliott, John Krogh, Harry Chalmiers, Kevin Sullivan, Tony Axtell and the McNally Smith College of Music "guitar department in exile"—Tim Lyles, Paul Krueger, Chris Olson, Mike Salow, Dave Singley, and Eva Beneke—for test-driving this Fretboard Biology method for seven years.

None of this would have happened without the dedicated work of my business partner in the Fretboard Biology program, Todd Berntson, and his wife, Monique. There's a lot of skill and talent in that duo and it was only through Todd's insistence that this project was launched.

Lastly, I would like to thank all the great musicians and students I have had the pleasure to work with over the past 40 years.

TABLE OF CONTENTS

LEVEL 4 INTRODUCTION — 1

UNIT 1 — 3
- Theory - Modal Interchange, Inverted Intervals
- Fretboard Logic - Shell Voicings, Essential Chord Tones, Major and Minor Diatonic 3rd Shapes
- Rhythm Guitar - Introduction to Funk Rhythm Guitar
- Money Makers - Money Maker Licks using Diatonic 3rd Shapes
- Improvisation - Soloing with Modal Interchange
- Practice - Practice Routine Development

UNIT 2 — 33
- Theory - Analyzing Progressions with Modal Interchange
- Fretboard Logic - Shell Voicings, Diatonic 3rd Shapes
- Rhythm Guitar - Funk Rhythm Guitar
- Money Makers - Money Maker Licks using Diatonic 3rd Shapes
- Improvisation - Soloing with Modal Interchange
- Practice - Continue Practice Routine Development

UNIT 3 — 55
- Theory - Analyzing Triad Progressions with Modal Interchange
- Fretboard Logic - Root Maps, Root Map 1, Root Map Practice Progressions, Diatonic 4th Shapes, Common Tones in Major and Minor Pentatonic Scales
- Rhythm Guitar - Funk Rhythm Guitar
- Money Makers - Money Maker Licks using Diatonic 4th Shapes
- Improvisation - Soloing with Modal Interchange
- Practice - Continue Practice Routine Development

UNIT 4 — 81

- Theory - Analyzing 7th Chord Progressions with Modal Interchange
- Fretboard Logic - Root Map 2, Root Map 2 Shell Voicings, Root Map Practice Progressions, Diatonic 4th Shapes, Common Tones in Major and Natural Minor Scales
- Rhythm Guitar - Funk Rhythm Guitar
- Money Makers - Money Maker Licks using Diatonic 4th Shapes
- Improvisation - Soloing with Modal Interchange
- Practice - Continue Practice Routine Development

UNIT 5 — 101

- Theory - Continue Analyzing 7th Chord Progressions with Modal Interchange
- Fretboard Logic - Root Map 3, Root Map 3 Shell Voicings, Root Map Practice Progressions, Major and Minor Diatonic 5th Shapes, Common Tones in Major and Minor Pentatonic Scales
- Rhythm Guitar - Funk Rhythm Guitar, Funk Parts
- Money Makers - Money Maker Licks with Diatonic 5th Shapes
- Improvisation - Soloing with Modal Interchange
- Practice - Continue Practice Routine Development

UNIT 6 — 131

- Theory - Inversions, Voicings, Inverted Triads, Open and Closed Voicing, Ensemble Chords
- Fretboard Logic - Root Map 4, Root Map 4 Shell Voicings, Root Map Practice Progressions, Major and Minor Diatonic 5th Shapes, Common Tones in Major and Natural Minor Scales
- Rhythm Guitar - Classic R&B
- Money Makers - Money Maker Licks using Diatonic 5th Shapes
- Improvisation - Soloing with Modal Interchange
- Practice - Continue Practice Routine Development

UNIT 7 — 159

- Theory - Triad and 7th Chord Inversions, Writing Inversions on the Staff, Recognizing Inversions on the Staff
- Fretboard Logic - Inverted Open Chords, Major and Minor Diatonic 6th Shapes, Modal Interchange using Arpeggios
- Rhythm Guitar - Classic R&B
- Money Makers - Money Maker Licks using Diatonic 6th Shapes
- Improvisation - Soloing with Modal Interchange
- Practice - Continue Practice Routine Development

Fretboard Biology — Level 4: Table of Contents

UNIT 8 — 193
- Theory - Slash Chord Symbols, Using Inversions in Progressions
- Fretboard Logic - Chord Inversions in Progressions, Major and Minor Diatonic 7th Shapes, Using 7th Chord Arpeggios in progressions with Modal Interchange
- Rhythm Guitar - Classic R&B Groove in G
- Money Makers - Money Maker Licks using Diatonic 7th Shapes
- Improvisation - Soloing with Modal Interchange
- Practice - Continue Practice Routine Development

UNIT 9 — 225
- Theory - Analyzing Progressions with Inversions
- Fretboard Logic - Ensemble Chords, Octave Interval Shapes in Major, Patterns I-V Major and Minor In-Position Triad Arpeggios
- Rhythm Guitar - Classic R&B
- Money Makers - Using Octave Shapes in Major Keys
- Improvisation - Soloing with Modal Interchange
- Practice - Continue Practice Routine Development

UNIT 10 — 249
- Theory - Level 4 Summary
- Fretboard Logic - Octave Interval Shapes in Minor, Patterns I-V Major and Minor In-Position 7th Chord Arpeggios
- Rhythm Guitar - Classic R&B
- Money Makers - Using Octave Shapes in Minor Keys
- Improvisation - Soloing with Modal Interchange
- Practice - Continue Practice Routine Development

APPENDICES — 273
- Appendix 1: Family Tree
- Appendix 2: Table of Inverted Intervals
- Appendix 3: Shell Voicings
- Appendix 4: Root Maps
- Appendix 5: In-Position Arpeggios
- Appendix 6: Chord Chart

LEVEL 4 INTRODUCTION

Fretboard Biology Level 4 builds on the material in the previous levels. If you haven't completed those levels, go back and make sure that you are confident in all the material. In Level 4 you continue your study of Theory, Fretboard Logic, Rhythm Guitar, Improvisation, Money Makers, and Practice Techniques. Work at the pace that fits you.

What's in Level 4

- In the Theory modules, you will learn about modal interchange, which is the mix of major and minor tonalities. This includes harmonic analysis of progressions with modal interchange, and how to make good note choices. You will also learn about inverted chords and slash chords.
- In the Fretboard Logic modules, you will learn to superimpose major and minor pentatonic scales on top of one another, and the same with the seven-note major and Natural Minor scales. You will learn 7th-chord shell voicings from which all extended chords can be built. You will learn four root maps and how to use them. A root map is a tool for sight reading and transposition. You will learn the major and minor scales harmonized in 3rds, 4ths, 5ths, 6ths, and 7ths on all string sets. This prepares you for the Level 4 Money Maker modules.
- In the Improvisation modules, you will learn how to solo over progressions with modal interchange.
- In the Rhythm Guitar modules, you will study two styles: Funk and Classic R&B.
- In the Money Maker modules, you will learn guitar parts that use the major and minor scales harmonized in 3rds, 4ths, 5ths, 6ths, and 7ths in parts. You will also learn to use the major and minor scales played in octaves.

This is a progressive course. Each module in each level builds on the information from the previous one. You'll get the most out of the program by staying with the sequence.

Let's get started.

UNIT 1

Learning Modules

> **Theory** - Modal Interchange, Inverted Intervals

> **Fretboard Logic** - Shell Voicings, Essential Chord Tones, Major and Minor Scales harmonized with 3rd Shapes

> **Rhythm Guitar** - Introduction to Funk Rhythm Guitar

> **Money Makers** - Money Maker Parts using Diatonic 3rd Shapes

> **Improvisation** - Soloing with Modal Interchange

> **Practice** - Practice Routine Development

THEORY

Levels 1, 2, and 3 provided a solid foundation in diatonic harmony by teaching you the major and minor diatonic systems. You learned harmonic analysis with progressions made up of chords that are diatonic to the key. While there are songs that use only diatonic melody notes and chords, it is very common for songs to include non-diatonic notes and chords. In fact, it is so common that in many cases our ears don't really perceive these non-diatonic notes as outside the diatonic system.

You have learned one exception: In minor keys, the Vmi or Vmi7 chord is sometimes replaced by a chord with a major 3rd; that is, a Vma or V7 chord. Remember that the major 3rd of the V chord is the major 7th of the scale, and that is called the leading tone. When a V chord is a major triad or dominant 7, the attraction to the I chord is stronger because of the leading tone. In Level 1 you learned about relative and parallel keys. Let's review those definitions now.

Relative Keys

Relative keys share the same key signature. For example, C major and A minor are relative keys.

Parallel Keys

Parallel keys share the same tonic. For example, C major and C minor are parallel keys. Obviously, these two scales sound very different but they do share the same tonic or "tonal center".

Modal Interchange

We normally associate "happy" with major keys and "sad" with minor keys. It is common for the mood of a song to shift from happy to sad or Bluesy, or vice versa, without a change in the key center. This is done by using chords and melody notes borrowed from the parallel key. This concept is called modal interchange. In modal interchange, the tonal center (tonic) remains the same; the shift is between "parallel keys".

Here is how modal interchange works: When a major tonality is established in a song by means of a series of chords and melody notes all diatonic to the key, a momentary mood shift to sad is achieved by "borrowing" chords and melody notes from the parallel minor key. This is very common and you have heard this many times.

For a moment, consider the opposite: Consider a song that starts in a minor key and shifts to its parallel major. It is far less common for a song that begins in minor to have a momentary mood shift to major; that is, from sad to happy. It is a little more common for an entire passage of a song established in a minor key to shift to its parallel major key.

One more point about this idea: Often times, once a minor tonality is established, chords and melody notes are borrowed from other parallel minor scales like the Blues scale, harmonic minor, melodic minor, or the minor modes, Dorian and Phrygian. Specifically, this means that a song that starts in C minor might momentarily borrow melody notes and chords from C Blues, C harmonic minor, C melodic minor, C Dorian, or C Phrygian. This is discussed in great detail in Level 6. But for now our discussion of modal interchange will be about major keys borrowing from their parallel minor scale.

To study modal interchange, compare the C major scale to the C minor scale.

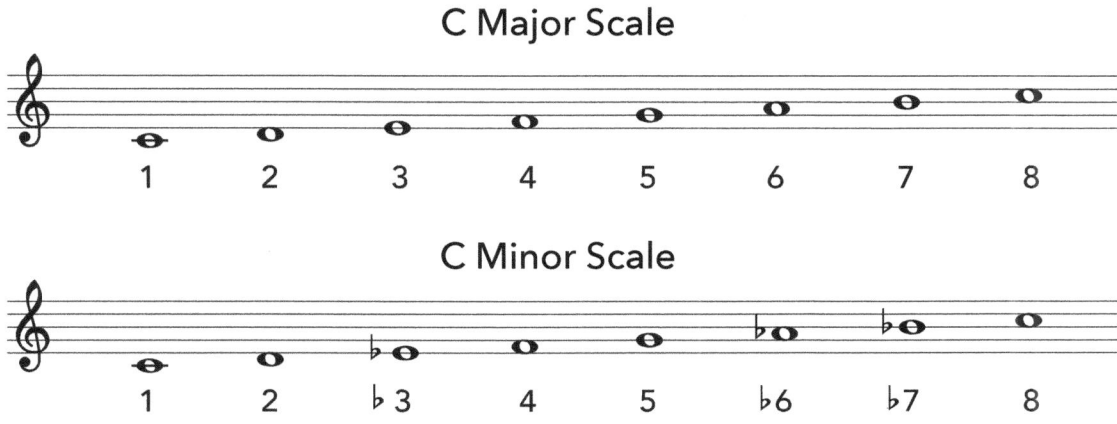

- Notice that the 1st, 2nd, 4th, and 5th scale degrees are the same.
- Notice that the 3rd, 6th, and 7th scale degrees are different.

Next, let's compare the harmonized major scale with the harmonized minor scale. Examine it first with triads and then with 7th chords.

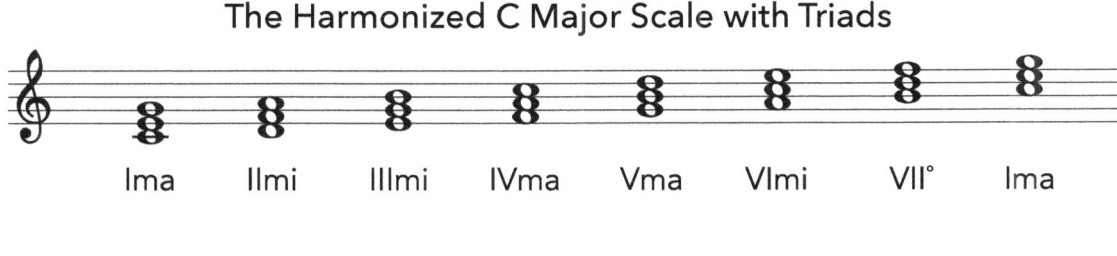

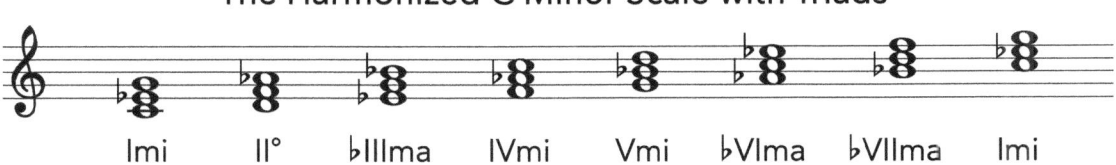

The Harmonized C Major Scale with 7th Chords

Ima7   IImi7   IIImi7   IVma7   V7   VImi7   VIImi7(♭5)

The Harmonized C Minor Scale with 7th Chords

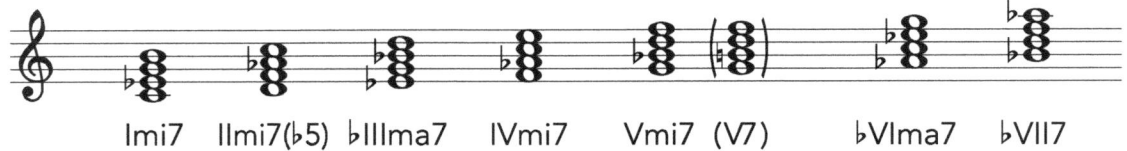

Imi7   IImi7(♭5)   ♭IIIma7   IVmi7   Vmi7 (V7)   ♭VIma7   ♭VII7

- Notice the chords that are built on the common scale degrees (I, II, IV, and V)
- Notice the chords that are built on scale degrees that are different (♭III, III, ♭VI, VI, ♭VII, and VII)

Look at this triad-based progression. Can you tell which chords belong to A major and which belong to A minor? The chords from A minor are borrowed.

Progression in A Major

Play the progression. How would you describe the mood change when the borrowed chords are played? The common description is that in triad progressions like this that use modal interchange, the mood shifts from a happy sound to a sad or Bluesy sound.

Next, look at this 7th chord-based progression. Which chords belong to C major? Which belong to C minor?

Progression in C Major

Cma7   Emi7   Fmi7   B♭7   Ami7   Dmi7   G7   Cma7

When you play this progression, how would you describe the mood change when the borrowed chords are played?

It is important to know why you are studying modal interchange. It informs you about the notes to use when writing melodies or soloing and it directly affects the notes you use when you embellish chords or write parts.

- If a song is in a major key, the note choices, in general, come from the major scale of the key.
- If a song in a major key borrows chords from the parallel minor key, the note choices for the duration of the borrowed chords come from the parallel minor scale.

Remember, with modal interchange the tonal center (tonic) remains the same, but there is a shift between parallel keys to create a shift in mood. You will study more about modal interchange throughout the Level 4 Theory modules.

Inverted Intervals

Intervals were introduced in the early levels but there is one more important dimension to add: inverted intervals. This topic has unique relevance for guitarists because of how important shapes are to understanding the fretboard.

To invert an interval, place the bottom note of an interval one octave higher. Then measure the distance from the note that is now lower than the note that has been moved up one octave.

Inverted Interval: P4 to P5

(move the lower note up one octave)

For example, here is C and F above it. The interval is a perfect 4th. To invert it, move C up an octave. Next, measure the distance from F up to C. That interval is a perfect 5th.

Conclusion? An inverted perfect 4th is a perfect 5th.

Inverted Interval: Ma2 to Mi7

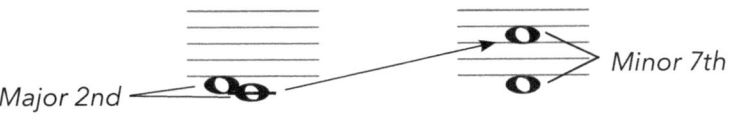

(move the lower note up one octave)

Look at another example. C to D is a major 2nd. To invert it, place the bottom note, C, up an octave. The distance from D up to C is a minor 7th.

Conclusion? An inverted major 2nd is a minor 7th.

Table of Inverted Intervals

INTERVAL	→	INVERSION
Mi2	Mi2 → Ma7	Ma7
Ma2	Ma2 → Mi7	Mi7
Mi3	Mi3 → Ma6	Ma6
Ma3	Ma3 → Mi6	Mi6
P4	P4 → P5	P5
A4	A4 → D5	D5
D5	D5 → A4	A4
P5	P5 → P4	P4
Mi6	Mi6 → Ma3	Ma3
Ma6	Ma6 → Mi3	Mi3
Mi7	Mi7 → Ma2	Ma2
Ma7	Ma7 → Mi2	Mi2
P8	P8 → Unison	Unison

Look at the table of inverted intervals above. There are a couple of characteristics to point out. First, notice that if you add the two numbers in each pair of inverted intervals the total is nine. Second, notice that the qualities flip:

- Minor intervals become major intervals.
- Major intervals become minor intervals.

- Diminished intervals become augmented intervals.
- Augmented intervals become diminished intervals.
- Perfect intervals stay perfect intervals.

Why is it important to understand inverted intervals? Guitarists see the fretboard as a big matrix of shapes. You learn all of the scales, chords, arpeggios, and intervals as shapes. And when you voice chords, you place the components of the chord – the root, 3rd, and 5th – on the fretboard in a variety of arrangements called voicings.

Examine this C triad. It is in root position and in closed voicing. From the bottom up it is root, 3rd, and 5th (1). Add the root again at the top of the voicing: root, 3rd, 5th, and root (2).

C Triad Voicings

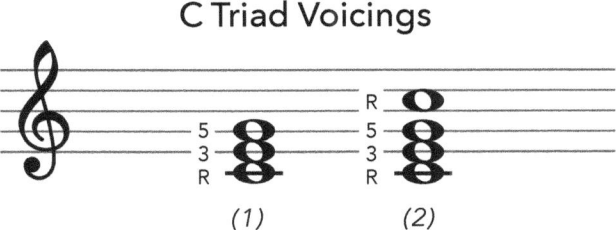

(1)   (2)

Next, measure some of the internal intervals. What is the interval from the 3rd of the chord to the root voiced on top?

C Triad Internal Intervals

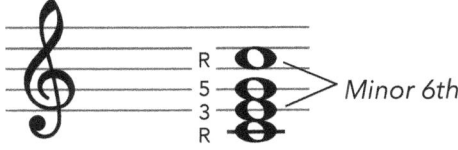

It is a major 3rd from the root at the bottom of the chord to the 3rd, but it is a minor 6th from the major 3rd of the chord to the root voiced on top.

Let's look at another. From the root at the bottom of the chord to the 5th it is a perfect 5th. What is the interval from the 5th of the chord to the root voiced at the top?

C Triad Internal Intervals

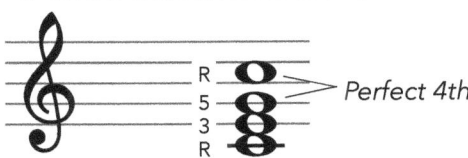

It is a perfect 5th from the root at the bottom of the chord to the 5th, but it is a perfect 4th from the perfect 5th of the chord to the root voiced on top.

Inverted intervals have real significance as you work through the major and minor scales harmonized in 3rds, 4ths, 5ths, and 6ths in the Fretboard Logic modules in this Level. Study every interval's inversion. Do the exercises and study the table of inverted intervals.

FRETBOARD LOGIC

Through Levels 1, 2, and 3 you have learned the big picture of how the fretboard is organized. Your knowledge is organized within the Family Tree and we will add more to it in the coming levels.

The focus in the Level 4 Fretboard Logic modules is in four areas:

1. The use of shell voicings to comp through chord progressions by number, or what is called chord "function". For this you will learn "root maps". This makes it possible to play through progressions efficiently without looking at the fretboard. It also is an important skill for transposing in real time. Transposing is moving a song written or normally played in one key to a new key.
2. Inverted chord voicings and how to read the chord symbols for them using slash chord notation.
3. Blending the scales and arpeggios of parallel keys. This facilitates playing through changes where modal interchange occurs.
4. In the category of interval shapes, you will use your knowledge of 3rds, 4ths, 5th, 6ths, and 7ths to work to play the major and minor scales harmonized with dyads. This sounds more complicated than it is. Interesting textures for rhythm guitar parts, fills, and solos can be created by harmonizing the major and minor scales in 3rds, 4ths, 5th, 6ths, and 7ths. You already used some of these shapes in the Money Maker modules of Level 3. Level 4 takes a more comprehensive look at how all the shapes fit together on the fretboard.

We begin with a discussion about shell voicings. Using the word "shell" should remind you of the pentatonic shells and why they are called shells. "Shell" implies a framework that can be used to build other things, and that's exactly how you learned the pentatonic scales. You can build major, minor, and Blues scales from pentatonic shells.

Shell Voicings

The word "shell" used with "voicing", as in "shell voicing", implies a chord framework that can be used to build other chord voicings. That's exactly what is meant here. The focus in this Level will be on learning just the shells for now and using them to move through chord progressions. The study of building upon them comes later in Fretboard Biology. Shell voicings contain the essential chord tones of a 7th chord.

Essential chord tones are the notes of a chord that must be played to represent the quality of the chord. You might be asking yourself, "don't all the notes of a 7th chord need to be played in order for it to sound like itself?" The answer is no.

Each 7th chord contains a 3rd, 5th, and 7th above the root. The quality of a 7th chord is determined by the quality of its 3rd, 5th, and 7th.

- A major 7th chord contains a Ma3, P5, and Ma7.
- A dominant 7th chord contains a Ma3, P5, and Mi7.
- A minor 7th chord contains a Mi3, P5, and Mi7.
- A minor 7(♭5) chord contains a Mi3, D5, and Mi7.

But in each chord, the 5th is NOT essential. That means the root, 3rd, and 7th are the essential chord tones.

Play each of these chords on a C root in Pattern IV. Play each chord first with the 5th and then without. When you hear the chord without the 5th, there is nothing noticeable about its absence. Omitting the 5th does not affect how you perceive the chord.

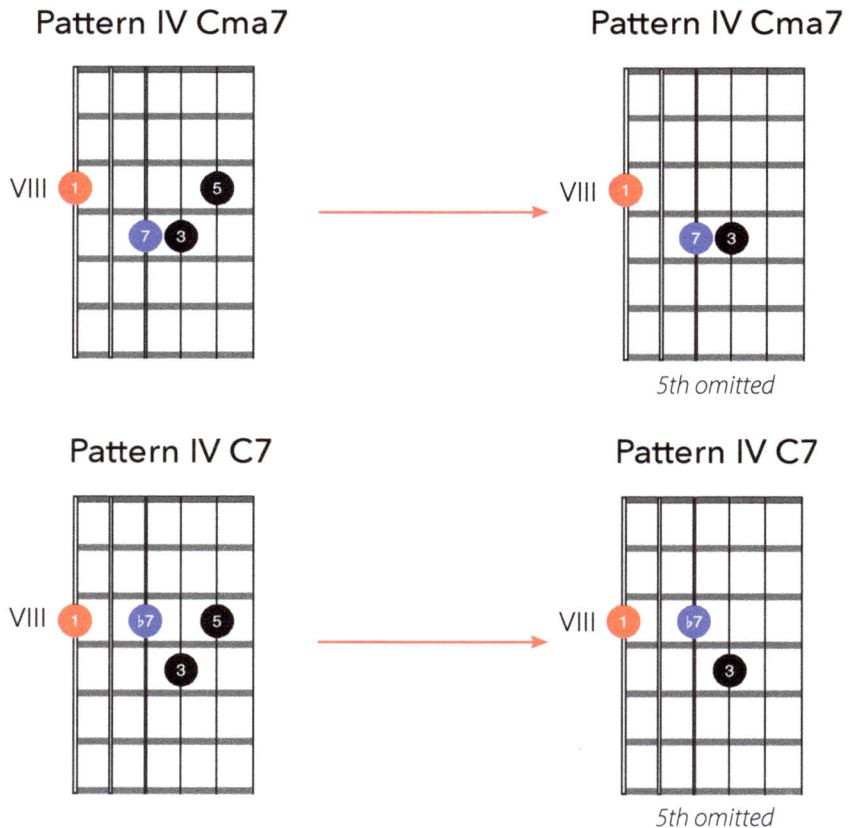

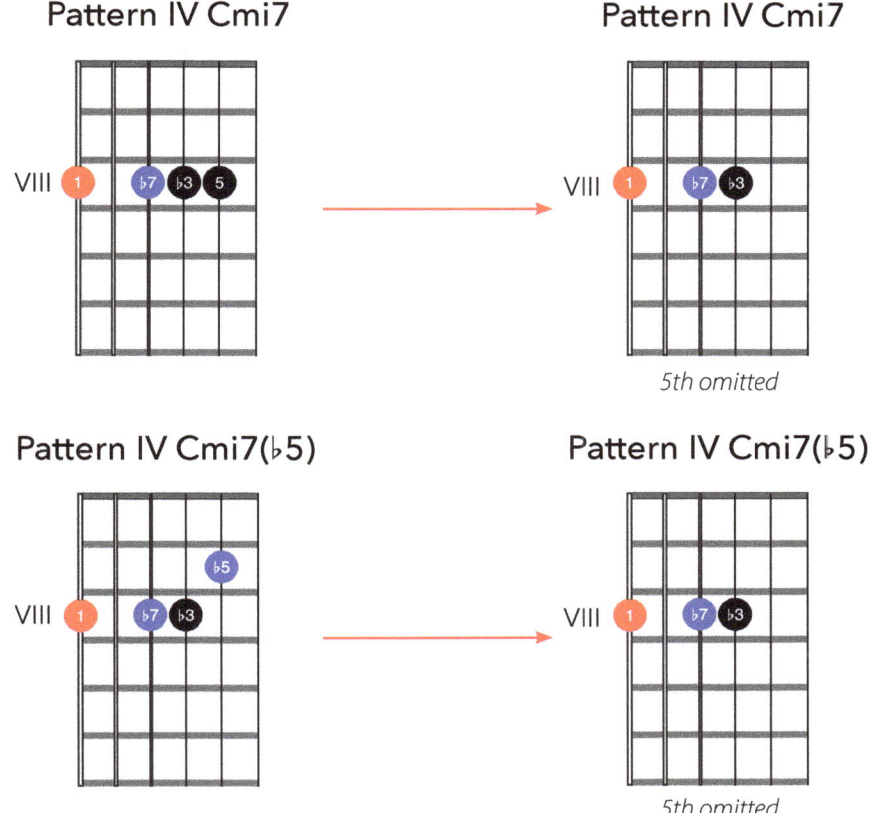

It is interesting to note that (♭5) is part of the name of a minor 7(♭5) chord and while its absence is probably more noticeable than the 5ths in the other chords, in the context of a key, it can still be left out of the voicing.

The reason for learning voicings with no 5th is to "make room" for other chord tones you will add to the shell voicing to make more colorful and elaborate chords. These additional chord tones are called "extensions" and we will study them in great detail in a coming level. By leaving out the 5th, you will be able to use the finger and string that were used to play the 5th to play another note, such as an extension. You have four fingers and 7th chords have four notes. Clearly, it is difficult to add any additional notes if you don't have enough fingers to play them.

The shell voicings also have a leaner sound. The 5th is in the "overtone" series of the root – that means you hear it implied when you hear the root. This means that the 7th chord sounds full and complete even without the 5th.

You will study four shell voicings in this module and four more in the next. The shell voicings in this module are based in Pattern IV and you will be happy to hear that you already know them. Because the first four are really just Pattern IV voicings, they have 6th-string roots and we will call them that – 6th-string shell voicings.

Here is a Pattern IV Cma7 chord with the chord tones labeled. Pay special attention to the strings where the root, 3rd, 5th, and 7th are located:

- The root is on the 6th string
- The Ma7 is on the 4th string
- The Ma3 is on the 3rd string and
- The P5 is on the 2nd string

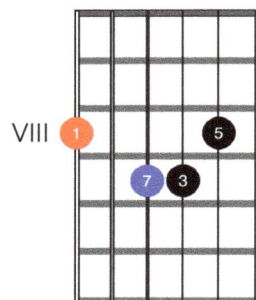
Pattern IV Cma7

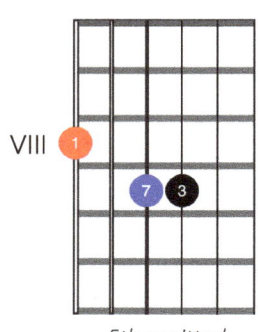
Pattern IV Cma7

5th omitted

Here is a Pattern IV C7 chord with the chord tones labeled. Again, pay special attention to the strings where the root, 3rd, 5th, and 7th are located:

Notice that:

- The root is on the 6th string
- The Mi7 is on the 4th string
- The Ma3 is on the 3rd string
- The P5 is on the 2nd string

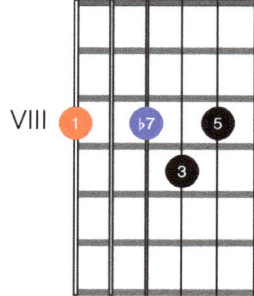
Pattern IV C7

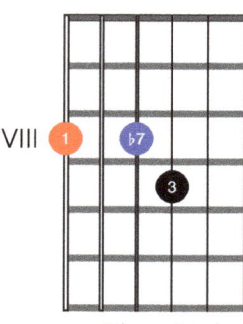
Pattern IV C7

5th omitted

Here is a Pattern IV Cmi7 chord with the chord tones labeled. Again, pay special attention to the strings where the root, 3rd, 5th, and 7th are located:

- The root is on the 6th string
- The Mi7th is on the 4th string
- The Mi3rd is on the 3rd string
- The P5th is on the 2nd string

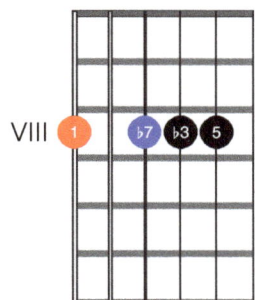
Pattern IV Cmi7

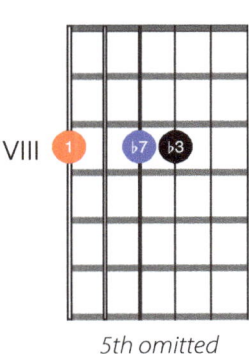
Pattern IV Cmi7

5th omitted

Here is a Pattern IV Cmi7(♭5) chord with the chord tones labeled. Again, pay special attention to the strings where the root, 3rd, 5th, and 7th are located:

- The root is on the 6th string
- The Mi7th is on the 4th string
- The Mi3rd is on the 3rd string
- The D5th is on the 2nd string

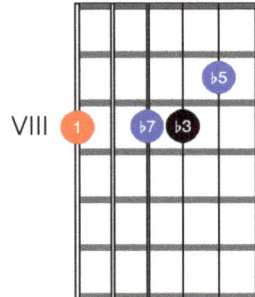
Pattern IV Cmi7(♭5)

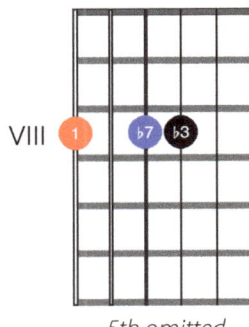
Pattern IV Cmi7(♭5)

5th omitted

Notice that in all four voicings the 7th is on the 4th string and the 3rd is on the 3rd string.

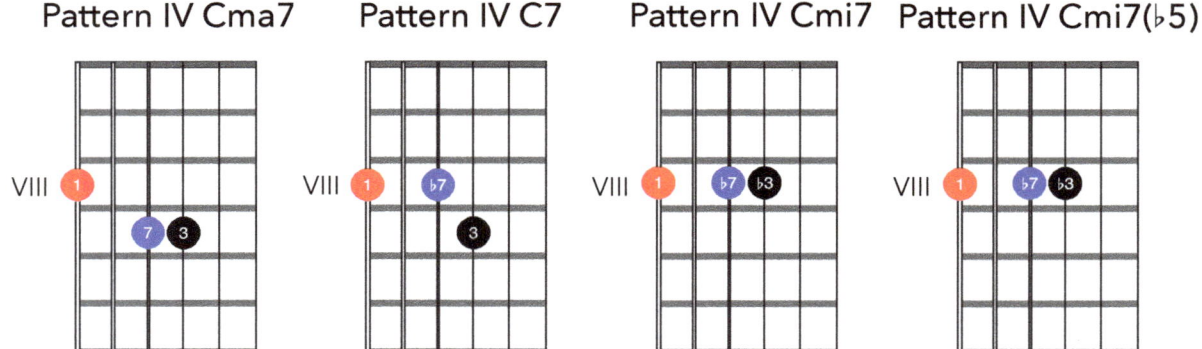

You now know a 6th-string root shell voicing for each type of 7th chord found in the major and minor diatonic systems.

These are the characteristics that are common to all of them:

- The root is on the 6th string
- The 7th is on the 4th string
- The 3rd is on the 3rd string

It is worth noting that in many situations where there is a bass player and 7th chords are used, the guitarist or keyboard player can also leave out the root voiced as the lowest note. In many cases this actually sounds better. The 6th-string root is in a lower register near where the bass player is playing and too many notes in the same range can make the rhythm section sound muddy.

It is also worth noting that the 3rd and 7th of the voicings are on the middle strings which means they are in the middle register. Think about the spectrum of notes in a band from lowest to highest. The bass player is at the bottom and the lead part – whether it be vocals or another instrument – is usually in the high-middle register to high register. Arrangements sound best when the spectrum of low to high is balanced. Filling out the middle register is important. Memorize these four shell voicings and their chord tones.

Intervals

In the Level 3 Money Maker modules you learned to use a variety of intervals and played them as double stops. Level 4 takes a more comprehensive look at all of the simple interval shapes as they relate to the diatonic scales.

Interval shapes played along two-string sets are a common source for improvised or planned melodies as well as background fills. They can be played as double stops (harmonic intervals) or separately (melodic intervals). The most commonly used intervals are 3rds, 4ths, 5ths, and 6ths. This module delves into 3rds.

Diatonic 3rd Shapes in Major

For demonstration purposes, start in the key of D major. Consider the notes along the 2nd string as the "scale degrees" starting with D at the 3rd fret. Play the D scale along the 2nd string: D, E, F#, G, A, B, C#, and D.

D Major Scale on the 2nd String

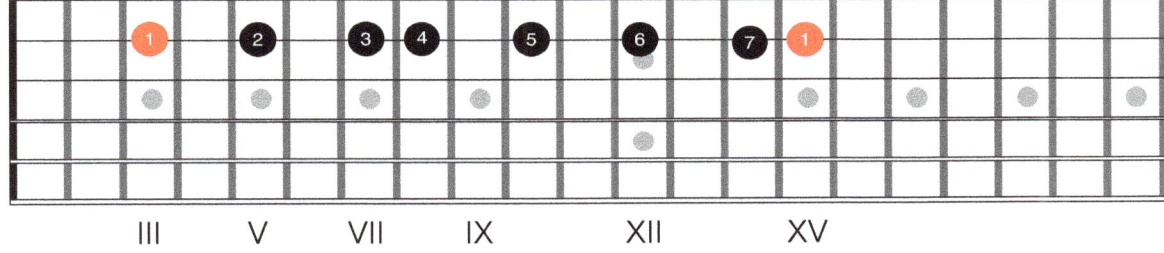

Here are the Diatonic 3rd shapes for the D major scale shown along the 2nd and 1st strings. When using 3rds, think of the lower of the two notes as the melodic guide.

Diatonic 3rds on the 2nd and 1st Strings in Major

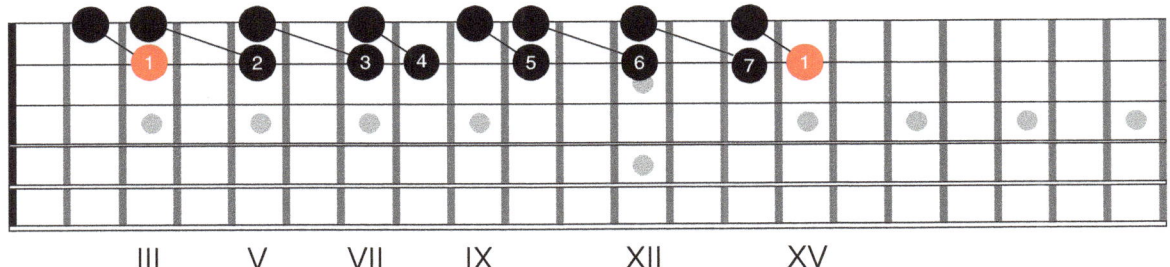

Here is a hint: Think of the quality of the chord built on each scale degree to determine whether it should be a major or minor 3rd: major 3rd, minor 3rd, minor 3rd, major 3rd, major 3rd, minor 3rd, and minor 3rd (because the VII is diminished and has a minor 3rd). This works for any major key. Track the scale along the 2nd string.

This set of shapes for the major scale works for the strings that are a 4th apart.

- The 2nd and 1st strings

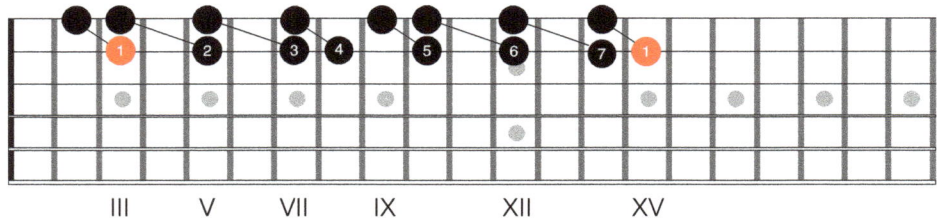

- NOT the 3rd and 2nd strings because they are a 3rd apart.
- The 4th and 3rd strings.

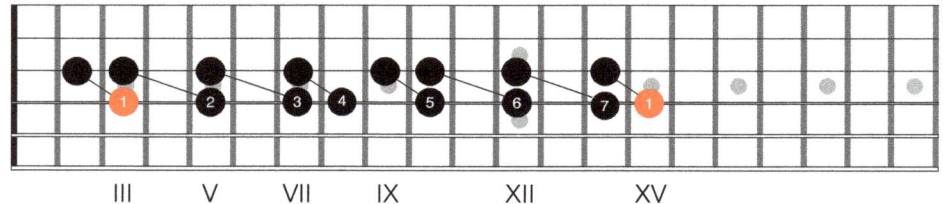

- The 5th and 4th strings.

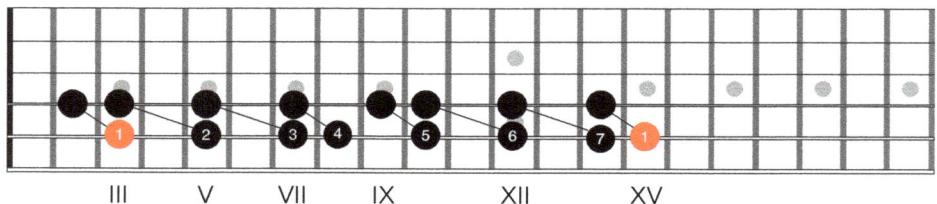

- The 6th and 5th strings.

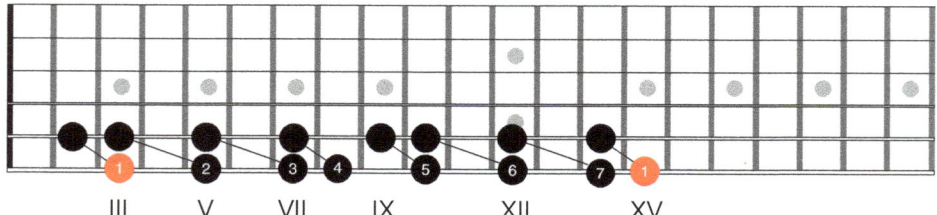

Diatonic 3rd Shapes in Minor

Now look at the key of D minor. Consider the notes along the 2nd string as the "scale degrees" starting with D at the 3rd fret. Play the D minor scale along the 2nd string: D, E, F, G, A, B♭, C, and D.

D Minor Scale on the 2nd String

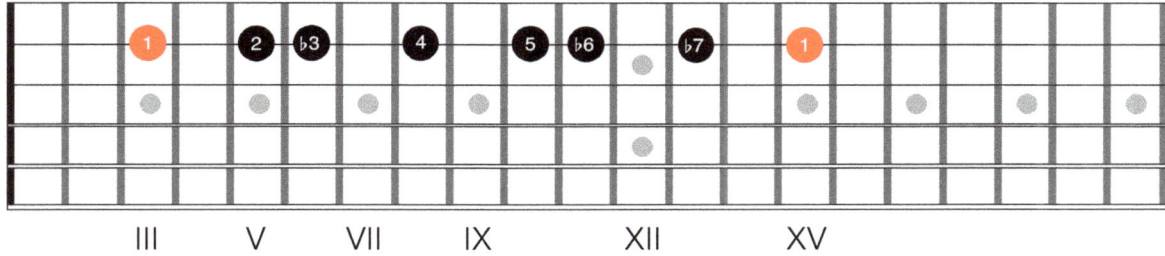

Here are the diatonic 3rd shapes for the D minor scale shown along the 1st and 2nd strings. When using 3rds, think of the lower of the two notes as the melodic guide.

Diatonic 3rds on the 2nd and 1st Strings in Minor

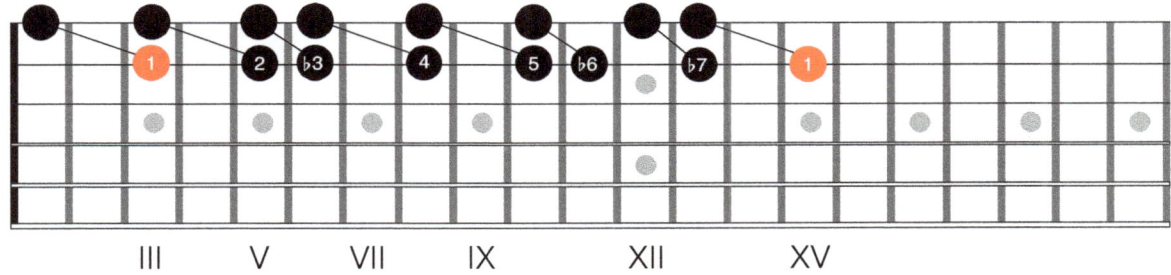

Here is the same hint: Think of the quality of the chord built on each scale degree to find the correct 3rd: minor 3rd, minor 3rd (because the II is diminished and has a minor 3rd), major 3rd, minor 3rd, minor 3rd, major 3rd, and major 3rd. This works for any minor key. Track the scale along the 2nd string.

This set of shapes for the major scale works for the strings that are a 4th apart.

- The 2nd and 1st strings.

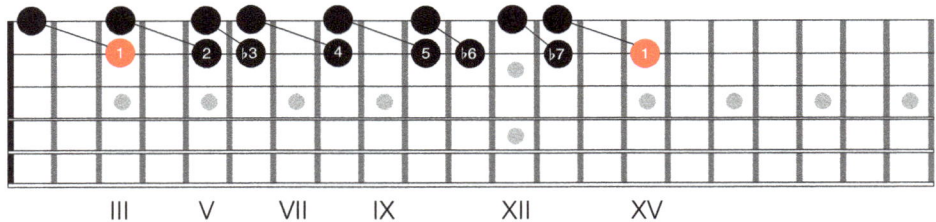

- NOT the 3rd and 2nd strings because they are a 3rd apart.
- The 4th and 3rd strings.

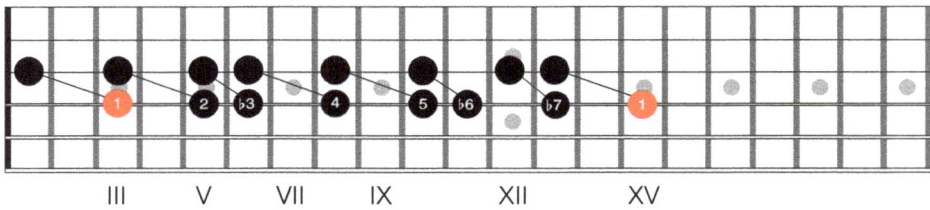

- The 5th and 4th strings.

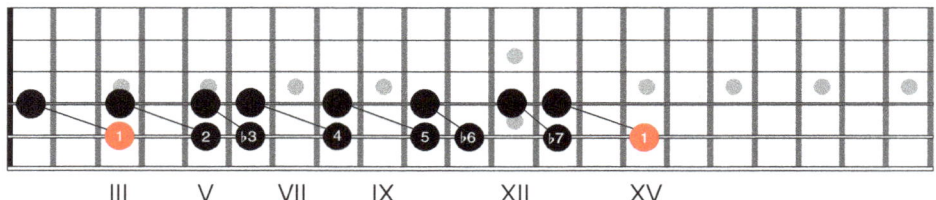

- The 6th and 5th strings.

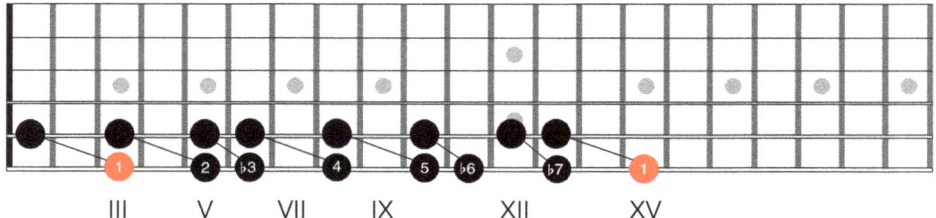

In the Level 4 Money Maker modules, you will put these intervals to work in some simple examples.

RHYTHM GUITAR

Funk Rhythm Guitar

The next series of units discuss how to play Funk rhythm guitar. Funk evolved from R&B and Soul music. The line between Funk and its R&B is not very clear so many of the elements you will study in the R&B units apply in Funk and vice versa. The guitar parts in this series are derived from classic songs by artists like James Brown, Sly and the Family Stone, The Isley Brothers, Parliament, The Average White Band, Prince, and Earth, Wind and Fire. These artists' songs all incorporate signature guitar parts.

Funk grooves are established by strong and interlocking drum and bass parts. Guitar parts are repetitive and are often riff-based, using single lines, chords, or a combination of the two. In some of the classic Funk repertoire, the harmony is simple and is based on one or two chord vamps. There are many examples of Funk music with more complex harmony but the attention here will be on one or two chord vamps so you can keep your focus on the groove. Remember that all of these Rhythm modules are intended to introduce you to the basics of a particular genre. As with all the genres, it is important to listen and learn as many parts and songs as possible.

Funk is all about the groove and requires a great rhythm section. Generally, drums are in the forefront with a dominant kick and snare pattern: the kick drum on or around beats 1 and 3 and the snare on or around beats 2 and 4, the back-beat. There are exceptions to this, but for our purposes the grooves will be pretty conventional. The bass guitar parts are also usually repetitive, both rhythmically and melodically, and are in sync with the kick drum pattern. Keyboard parts can range from pads to more complex syncopated parts and there are often multiple parts. Guitars are also usually repetitive percussion-like or moving chordal parts.

Funk Groove #1

In this module we'll learn a phrase that mimics a James Brown classic. Look at the complete part and then at the individual chords.

Funk Groove #1 in D

This is based on a chord called D9 which is derived from a Pattern II D7 barre chord. It is voiced on the top four strings.

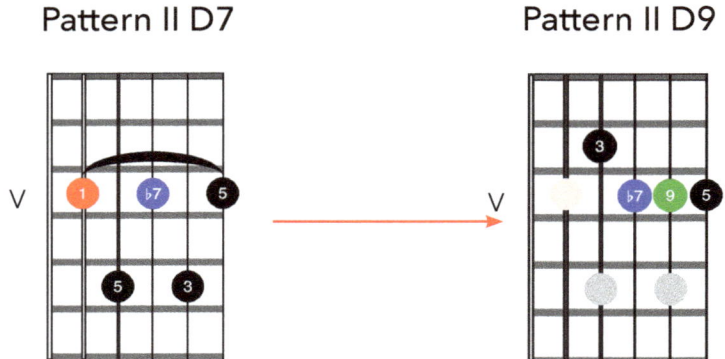

To play a Pattern II D9 chord:
- Start by playing an F#, which is the 3rd of the chord, with your 1st finger at the 4th fret of the 4th string.
- Barre across the 3rd, 2nd, and 1st strings at the 5th fret with your 2nd finger.
- C at the 5th fret of the 3rd string is the ♭7.
- E at the 5th fret of the 2nd string is the 9th.
- A at the 5th fret of the 1st string is the 5th.

Notice the "ghost" of the Pattern 2 barre chord for your reference.

Use this voicing for the first three attacks. They are:
- on beat one
- on the last 16th of beat one
- on beat three

For the attack on beat four, keep all your fingers in place but add B, which is the 13th (or 6th) on the 1st string at the 7th fret with your 4th finger.

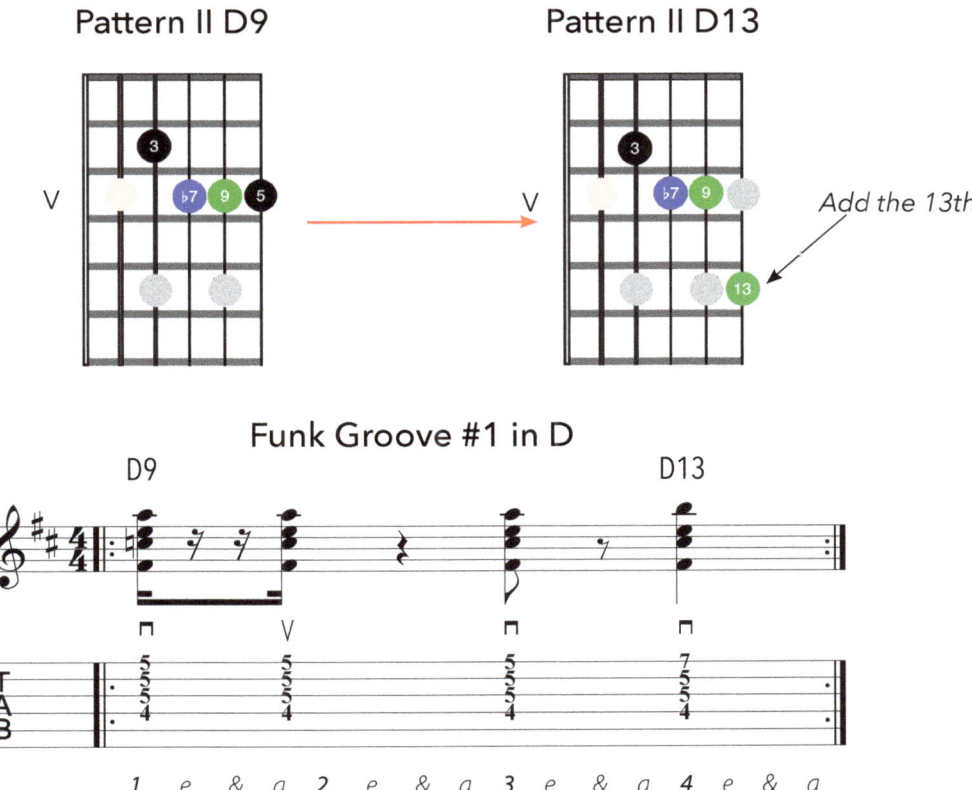

Use a clean sound with no effects (other than a little reverb). Strive for perfect execution and time. Your tone should be round but crisp so it cuts, but not painful to the listener. On a Strat, Tele, or Les Paul, I suggest the neck pickup.

Here is the part with the chord voicing and pick direction.

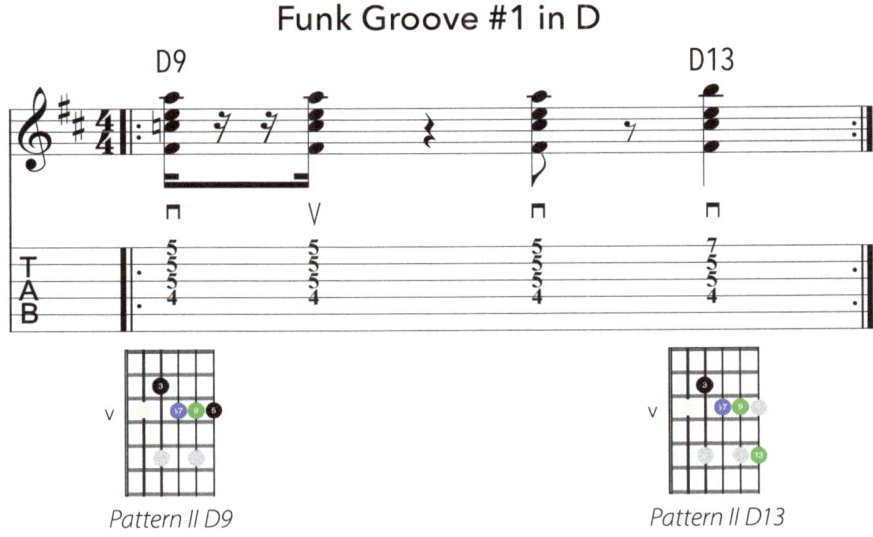

Proper Pick Direction is Critical

Proper 16th-note pick direction is critical to maintaining a steady groove, so coordinate your pick direction according to the rules. Here's a reminder: When a 16th note is the smallest note in a measure:

- The attack on the beat is played with a downstroke.
- The attack on the second 16th note of the beat is an upstroke.
- The attack on the third 16th note of the beat is a downstroke.
- The attack on the fourth 16th note of the beat is an upstroke.

Stay true to this or the groove will suffer. When playing this part:

- The attack on beat one is a crisp and short downstroke and it usually helps to keep the constant 16th-note movement in your picking hand, which means to make the upstroke motion on the second 16th – but miss the strings.
- Then make the downstroke motion on the third 16th – but miss the strings.
- Then the fourth 16th is played with an upstroke. It is also helpful to make the downstroke motion for beat two even though you are not touching the strings with your pick. It really helps with timing. I generally keep the 16th-note down-up-down-up motion going regardless of whether I'm making contact with the strings or not.
- Beat three is a crisp downstroke followed by the up-down-up motion, missing the strings.
- Beat four is a downstroke and is sustained for the whole beat.

Don't assume this part is easy. That is one of the biggest follies I see when teaching this subject. Guitarists think they have it down, but they miss the subtleties of the groove. You must record yourself playing this part. The challenge will be playing the fourth 16th note of beat one with the right feel. Listen to the recorded example and then practice, record, and listen until it feels right. Some Funk parts don't seem difficult on the surface but to get them to feel right is the a challenge. Don't take it lightly.

Funk guitar parts are generally repetitive and are an important part of the total rhythm section sound. The subtleties of the groove and feel are critical. This is a typical kind of part. Log it away for future use in other songs.

MONEY MAKERS

In Level 3 you learned that Money Makers are short licks, fills, and musical ideas that every guitar player should know. You can think of Money Makers as standard vocabulary. The examples you learned are based in and around the Pattern III major pentatonic and Pattern IV minor pentatonic shells. Level 4 takes a different approach to the idea of Money Makers. Instead of pentatonic-based ideas, you will learn ways to apply the information about scales harmonized in intervals that you learn in the Fretboard Logic modules.

Many guitarists explore little bits of the scales harmonized in intervals but rarely the whole picture. But it is worth the effort because a more complete understanding of all the interval shapes exponentially expands the number of solo, fill, and comping options you have. In the Level 4 Fretboard Logic modules you will learn fingerings for the major and minor scales harmonized on two-string sets. You will work with 3rds, 4ths, 5ths, 6ths, 7ths, and octaves. Each of these intervals has a distinct personality and can be applied when soloing, creating fills, or playing hooky background parts. But first you need to know them.

In Units 1 and 2 you will work with 3rds in both major and minor keys starting with the string sets that are 4th apart and then those that are a 3rd apart. This Unit starts with strings that are a 4th apart and you will learn two examples: one in a major key and one in a minor key.

Diatonic 3rds in a Major Key

This eight-bar progression is a very low-key and low-tempo progression to make it easy to experiment with the shapes.

Progression in E Major

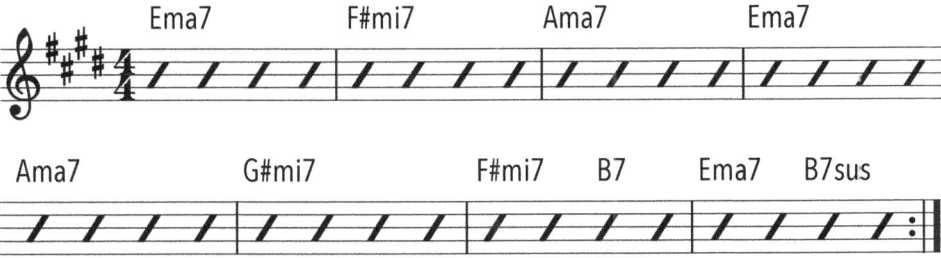

Over this progression, play the major scale on string set 2 and 1, harmonized in 3rds.

Diatonic 3rds on the 2nd and 1st Strings in Major

Here is a part that uses 3rds for you to practice.

Diatonic 3rds in E

The adjective you use to describe how 3rds sound when used in this way is up to you, but I am certain you will recognize a characteristic "personality" they have. 3rds have a unique sound. 4ths, 5ths, 6ths and 7ths each have a unique personality as well. It is your job to learn them and have them in your toolbox.

Play around with this progression using some of your own ideas that use 3rd shapes. This part same part could be used for any of the string sets that are a 4th apart: string sets 3 and 4, 4 and 5, and 5 and 6, although the lower in the register they are, the more unusable they become. Experiment and see for yourself.

Diatonic 3rds in a Minor Key

Next, work in a minor key. Here is an eight-bar progression over which the part will be played. This is another a very low-key track at a slow tempo so it's easy to experiment with the shapes.

Progression in E Minor

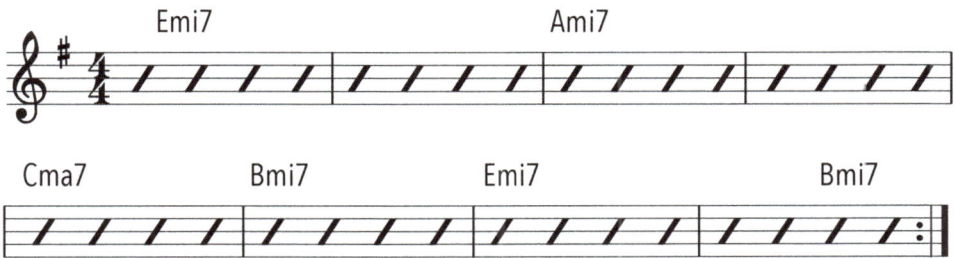

Review the minor scale harmonized in 3rds along the 2nd and 1st strings that you learned in the Fretboard Logic module.

When adjacent strings are harmonized in 3rds, use the lower of the two notes to track the scale. So first, play the E minor scale on the 2nd string only.

Diatonic 3rds on the 2nd and 1st Strings in Minor

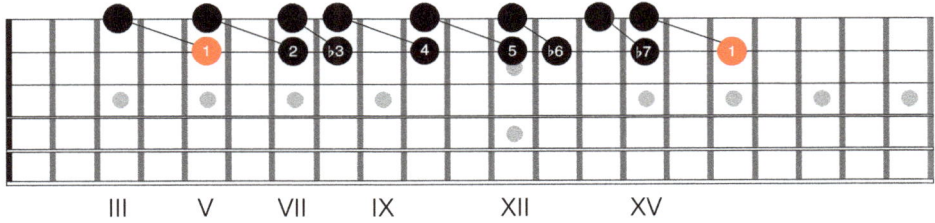

Next, here is a part that fits over this progression.

Diatonic 3rds in Emi

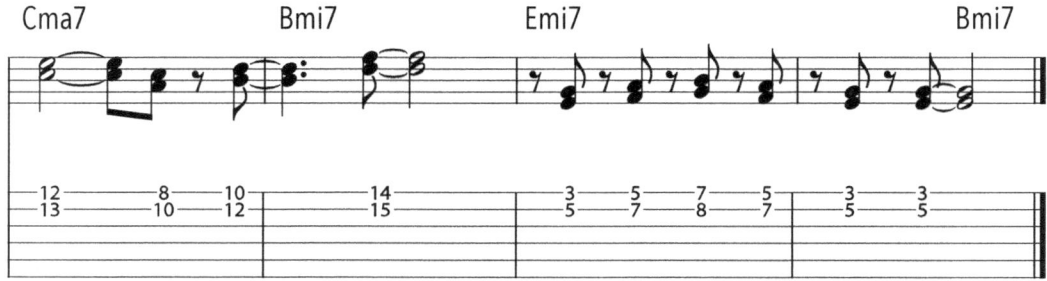

Again, note the "personality" of 3rds, but this time in a minor key. Play around with some of your own ideas using these 3rd shapes. This part could also be used for string sets 3 and 4, 4 and 5, and 5 and 6, but the lower in the register they are, the more unusable they become. Experiment and see for yourself.

Remember that these ideas are transposable to all minor keys!

IMPROVISATION

Soloing over progressions that have borrowed chords – that is, modal interchange – is the focus of the Level 4 Improvisation modules. Modal interchange is also the focus of Level 4 Theory. It is important because it directly affects the notes you use when soloing. If a song is in a major key, you know your note choices come from the major scale of the key. However, if a song in a major key borrows chords from the parallel minor key, you use notes from the parallel minor scale on those borrowed chords. It's that simple.

Take a look at this two-chord progression in A major.

Progression in A Major

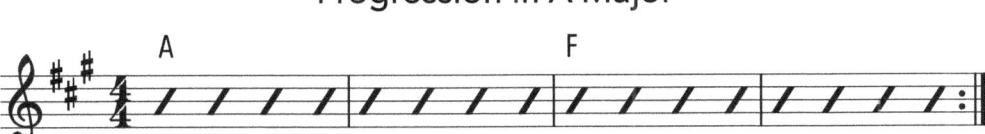

A is the Ima chord. The F chord is not diatonic to A major. F is a borrowed chord from A minor, the parallel minor, so an A minor-sounding scale is the appropriate sound. F is the bVIma chord in A minor. Because the tonic doesn't change in this progression, it does not modulate. It just borrows a chord from the relative minor. This is modal interchange.

As an improviser, it's best to navigate through modal interchange using pentatonic scales to start. You need to know which pentatonic scale to play over each of these chords. A major pentatonic works over the A, but it won't work over the F because F is from the parallel minor. The F chord is borrowed from A minor so the A minor pentatonic scale is an appropriate choice there. You will need to switch back and forth between the two:

- A major pentatonic on A
- A minor pentatonic on F

There will be a lot of time devoted to this topic over the next few modules but for now, use the simplest approach. You will use the two shapes most guitarists use when they first learn to solo. Those are the Pattern III A major pentatonic scale on A and the Pattern IV A minor pentatonic scale on F. Again, that's because the F chord comes from A minor.

To improvise over this progression, first play a few notes from the two scale shapes just mentioned: Pattern III A major pentatonic over the A, and Pattern IV A minor pentatonic over the F. Then, solo, moving between scales at the appropriate time.

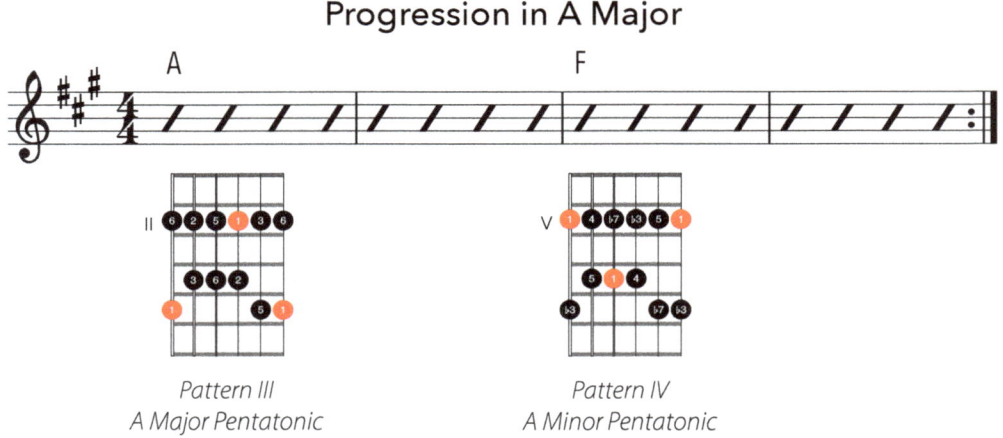

Pattern III
A Major Pentatonic

Pattern IV
A Minor Pentatonic

When I was about 13 or 14, a friend showed me the Pattern IV minor pentatonic scale. Not long after that I figured out that I could slide the shape down three frets and it sounded major. Using this same general shape and moving it around was my primary way of soloing growing up and beyond, and it still works well to this day. Don't be too proud to use this. There is a lot of good music in those shapes.

Don't forget the money makers learned in Level 3. The progressions in Level 4 are a great place to use them. Think about it: You need the A major sound on the A chord and A minor sound on F. Remember that the first five Money Maker modules were based around Pattern III major pentatonic scale. And later, the Unit 6 Money Maker module was all about Pattern IV minor pentatonic and Blues. The Blues scale usually sounds great on the chords borrowed from minor.

Try mixing in a few of the money makers you learned in Level 3 with the pentatonic scales. Have fun and spend some time soloing over this. Stick with your major and minor pentatonic shells and a few money makers for now.

Level 4 Unit 1 • Improv Demo

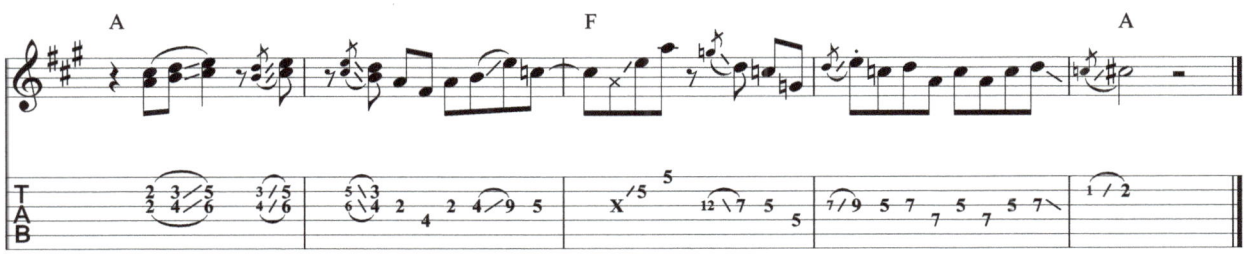

PRACTICE

Theory

- ❑ Go to the tabs below the Theory video on the website and complete the quiz.
- ❑ Understand the concepts of modal interchange.
- ❑ Learn the inversion of each interval.

Fretboard Logic

- ❑ Learn the shell voicings for the Pattern VI 7th chord shapes.
- ❑ Learn the major and minor diatonic 3rd shapes on the string sets that are a 4th apart.

Rhythm Guitar

- ❑ Learn the basics of Funk rhythm guitar.
- ❑ Practice playing Funk Groove #1 parts in D.

Money Makers

- ❑ Practice playing major and minor 3rd parts over a progression.

Improvisation

- ❑ Practice playing solos over an A major progression with modal interchange.

UNIT 2

Learning Modules

> **Theory** - Analyzing Progressions with Modal Interchange

> **Fretboard Logic** - Shell Voicings, Major and Minor Scales harmonized with 3rd Shapes

> **Rhythm Guitar** - Funk Rhythm Guitar

> **Money Makers** - Money Maker Parts using Diatonic 3rd Shapes

> **Improvisation** - Soloing with Modal Interchange

> **Practice** - Continue Practice Routine Development

THEORY

In the last unit you learned about modal interchange. Modal interchange occurs when a song shifts momentarily from a major key to its parallel minor and then back. With modal interchange, melody notes and chords are borrowed from the parallel minor key. It is important to review why you are studying this. When playing a song with modal interchange, the borrowed chords have a critical impact on what notes fit in a solo or written part. If a song is in a major key only, your note choices generally come from the major scale of the key. If a song in a major key borrows chords from the parallel minor key, note choices for the borrowed chords come from the parallel minor scale (for the duration of those borrowed chords only).

Musicians need to recognize modal interchange in progressions and make note choices accordingly. There is a good chance you have already encountered this and have figured it out by ear. But let's make certain you know why. Start by analyzing progressions where modal interchange occurs, beginning with a triad progression.

Take a look at the progression below. This progression will require a slight adjustment to the method of harmonic analysis you have used up until now. First, analyze all the chords that are easy to fit into one key – call these chords the "low-hanging fruit".

Progression in C Major

The last chord is C. The final chord is often a good place to start when locating the key center of a song. The first and last chords are C, and if they are the tonic chords then F fits nicely as IVma. But what about F minor? It certainly isn't diatonic to C major. Save its analysis for last because it doesn't seem to be a diatonic chord. Here are some questions to consider:

- Could it be from the parallel key?
- What is C major's parallel minor? It's C minor, right?
- Is there an F minor chord in C minor? Yes, IVmi.

What is happening here when the chord changes from F to F minor? Modal interchange. The first C chord and F chord are diatonic to C major. F minor is borrowed from the parallel C minor scale. Then, the last chord is C major – back to the major key.

Does the progression modulate; that is, does it change keys? Not really. The tonic never changes. The tonic is C through the entire progression, but there is a temporary shift to C minor.

Progression in C Major

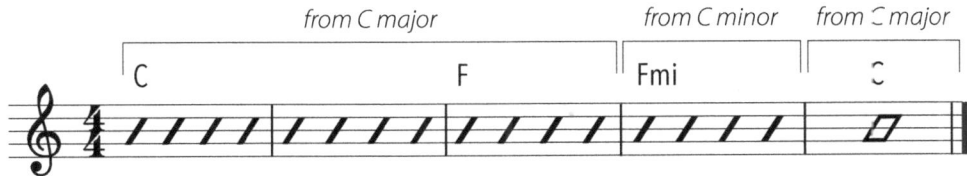

The progression has a happy mood while the C and F chords are played. The mood shifts to sad or kind of Bluesy on F minor and then returns to a happier mood on C major. This is modal interchange.

It is important to know how to label chords borrowed from the parallel minor scale. It is simple: Write the Roman numeral of the root and then the quality. This progression would be labeled like this:

Progression in C Major

The graphic below shows how to label all of the chords that can be borrowed from the parallel minor scale. To do this, compare the harmonized major and minor scales like in Unit 1. And for now, work with triads only.

Harmonized Triad Chords

MAJOR:	Ima	IImi	IIImi	IVma	Vma	VImi	VIIdim
	C	Dmi	Emi	F	G	Ami	B°
MINOR:	Imi	IIdim	♭IIIma	IVmi	Vmi	♭VIma	♭VIIma
	Cmi	D°	E♭	Fmi	Gmi	A♭	B♭

Notice that the I, II, IV, and V chords are built on the same roots in parallel major and minor scales. Take a closer look at what happens in modal interchange:

- If a progression borrows the I chord from the parallel minor scale it is labeled Imi.
- If a progression borrows the II chord from the parallel minor scale it is labeled IIdim.

- If a progression borrows the III chord from the parallel minor scale it is labeled ♭IIIma. Why ♭III? Because the III chord in a minor key is built on the minor 3rd (♭3) of the scale, whereas the III chord in a major key is built on the major 3rd scale degree. In a situation where modal interchange occurs, the ♭III chord is appearing in an otherwise major context. The distinction must be made from the diatonic III chord which would be IIImi.
- If a progression borrows the IV chord from the parallel minor scale it is labeled IVmi.
- If a progression borrows the V chord from the parallel minor scale it is labeled Vmi.
- If a progression borrows the VI chord from the parallel minor scale it is labeled ♭VIma. Why ♭VI? Because the VI chord in a minor key is built on the minor 6th (♭6) of the scale, whereas the VI chord in major key is built on the major 6th scale degree. In a situation where modal interchange is occurring, the ♭VI chord is appearing in an otherwise major context. The distinction must be made from the diatonic VI chord which would be VImi.
- If a progression borrows the VII chord from the parallel minor scale it is labeled ♭VIIma. Why ♭VII? Because the VII chord in a minor key is built on the minor 7th (♭7) of the scale, whereas a VII chord in a major key is built on the major 7th scale degree. In a situation where modal interchange is occurring, the ♭VII chord is appearing in an otherwise major context. The distinction must be made from the diatonic VI chord which would be VIIdim.

Let's take a look at a few progressions with borrowed chords.

In this progression D dim is labeled IIdim (II°). The diatonic II chord is Dmi.

Progression 1 in C Major

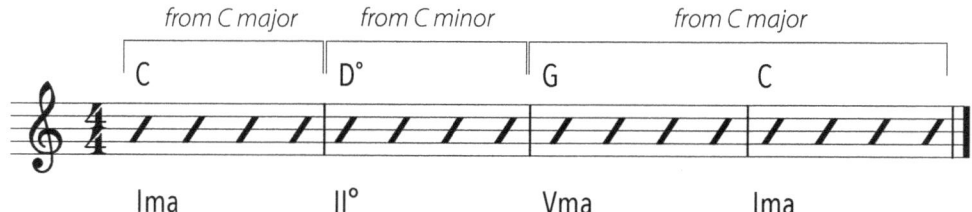

In this progression E♭ is labeled ♭IIIma. The diatonic III chord is Emi.

Progression 2 in C Major

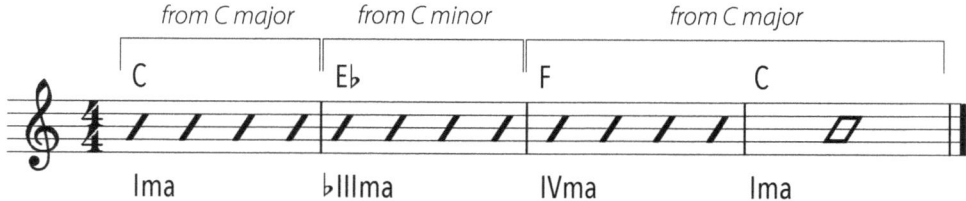

In this progression Fmi is labeled IVmi. The diatonic IV chord is F.

Progression 3 in C Major

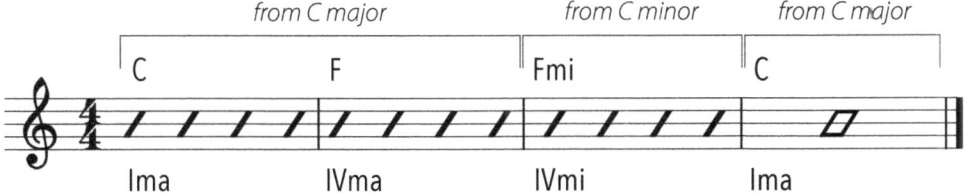

In this progression Gmi is labeled Vmi. The diatonic V chord is G.

Progression 4 in C Major

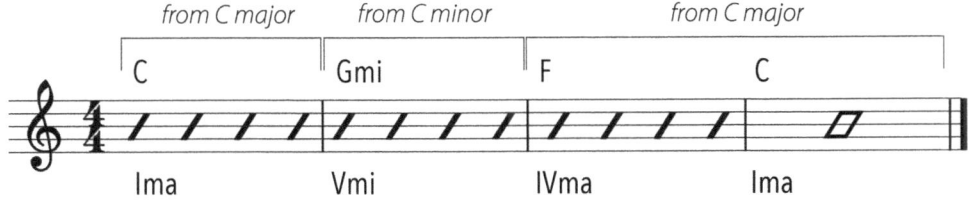

In this progression A♭ is labeled ♭VIma. The diatonic VI chord is Ami.

Progression 5 in C Major

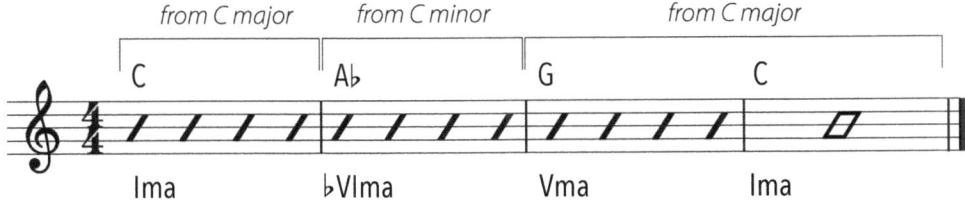

In this progression B♭ is labeled ♭VIIma. The diatonic VII chord is Bdim.

Progression 6 in C Major

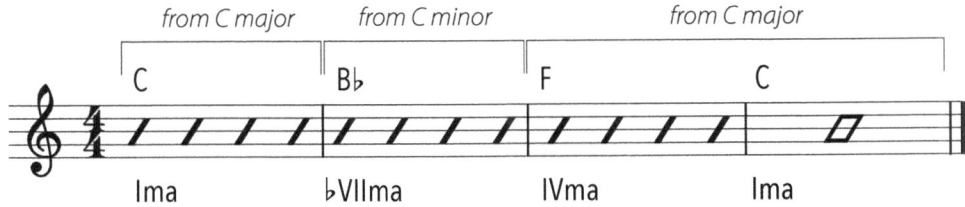

Acquaint yourself with this so you will be ready to analyze triad progressions with modal interchange in the next unit.

FRETBOARD LOGIC

In the last unit you learned about shell voicings and learned the four that are built on 6th-string roots. You learned that essential chord tones are the notes of a chord that must be played for its quality to be heard. The root, 3rd, and 7th are essential chord tones and the 5th is not: The 5th can be left out of a 7th chord voicing and it sounds fine.

Shell voicings are important because there are other chord tones called extensions that can be added to make more colorful and elaborate chords. We will study them in great detail in a future level. By leaving out the 5th, a finger and string are made available to play another note, such as an extension. And don't forget that shell voicings also have a clearer and less cluttered sound. The four shell voicings you will learn in this module have a 5th-string root and they sit on the line between Patterns I and II.

Shell Voicings

Here are the four 5th-string root shell voicings. Pay special attention the string on which each chord tone is played.

Major 7 Shell Voicing

Here is a 5th-string root major 7 shell voicing.

- The root is on the 5th string
- The Ma3 is on the 4th string
- The Ma7 is on the 3rd string

Major 7 Shell Voicing

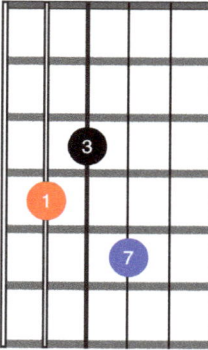

Dominant 7 Shell Voicing

Here is a 5th-string root dominant 7 shell voicing.
- The root is on the 5th string
- The Ma3 is on the 4th string
- The Mi7 is on the 3rd string

Dominant 7 Shell Voicing

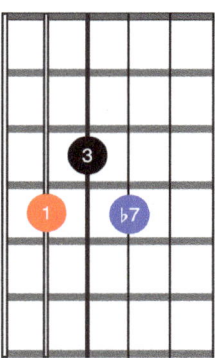

Minor 7 Shell Voicing

Here is a 5th-string root minor 7 shell voicing.
- The root is on the 5th string
- The Mi3 is on the 4th string
- The Mi7 is on the 3rd string

Minor 7 Shell Voicing

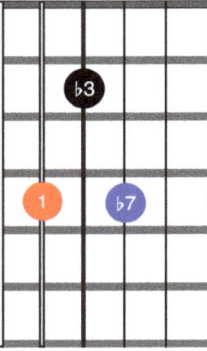

Minor 7(♭5) Shell Voicing

Here is a 5th-string root minor 7(♭5) shell voicing.

- The root is on the 5th string
- The Mi3 is on the 4th string
- The Mi7 is on the 3rd string

Minor 7(♭5) Shell Voicing

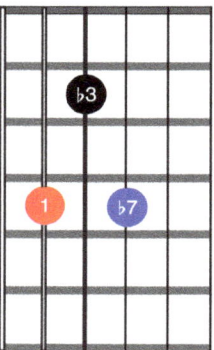

It is interesting to note that (♭5) is part of the name of a minor 7(♭5) chord and while it's probably more noticeable than the 5ths in the other chords, in the context of a key it can still be left out of the voicing.

| Major 7 | Dominant 7 | Minor 7 | Minor 7(♭5) |

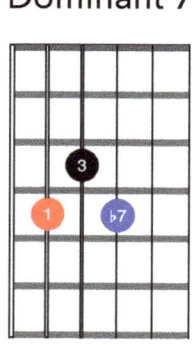 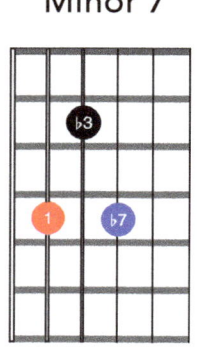 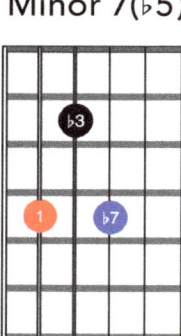

You now know a 5th-string root shell voicing for each type of 7th chord found in the major and minor diatonic systems.

Notice these characteristics that are common to all of them.

- The root is on the 5th string
- The 3rd is on the 4th string
- The 7th is on the 3rd string

In the last unit you learned that in situations where there is a bass player, the guitarist can leave out the root on the 5th string and it often sounds better. It is also worth noting that the 3rd and 7th of these voicings are on the middle strings, which means they are in the middle register. You will also recall from the last unit that with 6th-string shell voicings, the 7th is on the 4th string and the 3rd is on the 3rd string. With 5th-string shell voicings it is just the opposite: The 3rd is on the 4th string and the 7th is on the 3rd string.

That sets up an interesting way to work through chords when switching between 6th-string and 5th-string shell voicings. And in both cases the 3rds and 7ths stay in the middle register. Memorize these four 5th-string root shell voicings and the chord tones.

Intervals

The last unit started a more comprehensive study of all of the simple interval shapes as they relate to the diatonic scales. You learned the major and minor scales harmonized in 3rds along string sets 2 and 1, 4 and 3, 5 and 4, and 6 and 5. In this module you will look at the major and minor scales harmonized in 3rds along the 3rd and 2nd strings.

Diatonic 3rd Shapes in Major

For demonstration purposes, we will use the key of A major. Consider the notes along the 3rd string as the "scale degrees" starting with A at the 2nd fret. Play the A scale along the 3rd string: A, B, C#, D, E, F#, G#, and A.

A Major Scale on the 3rd String

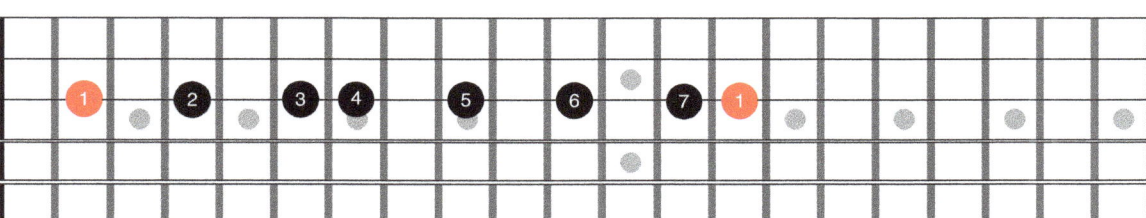

Here are the diatonic 3rd shapes for the A major scale shown along the 3rd and 2nd strings. When playing scales in 3rds, think of the lower of the two notes as the melodic guide.

Diatonic 3rds on 3rd and 2nd Strings in Major

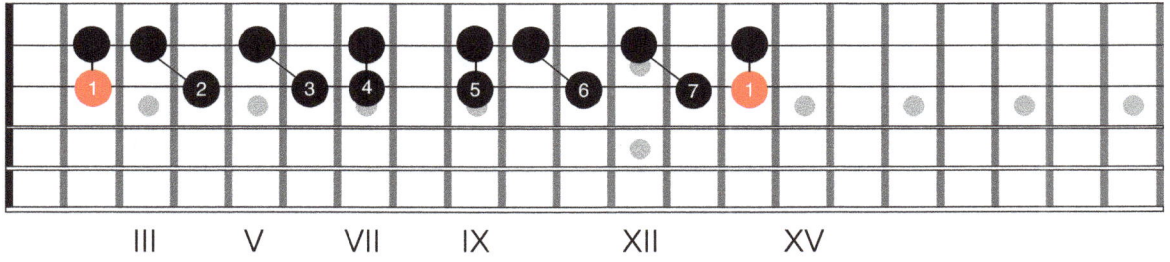

Here is a hint: Think of the quality of the chord built on each scale degree to determine whether it's a major or minor 3rd: major 3rd, minor 3rd, minor 3rd, major 3rd, major 3rd, minor 3rd, minor 3rd (because the VII is diminished and has a minor 3rd). This works for any major key. Track the scale along the 3rd string.

Diatonic 3rd Shapes in Minor

Look at the key of A minor. Consider the notes along the 3rd string as the "scale degrees" starting with A at the 2nd fret. Play the A minor scale along the 3rd string: A, B, C, D, E, F, G, A.

A Minor Scale on the 2nd String

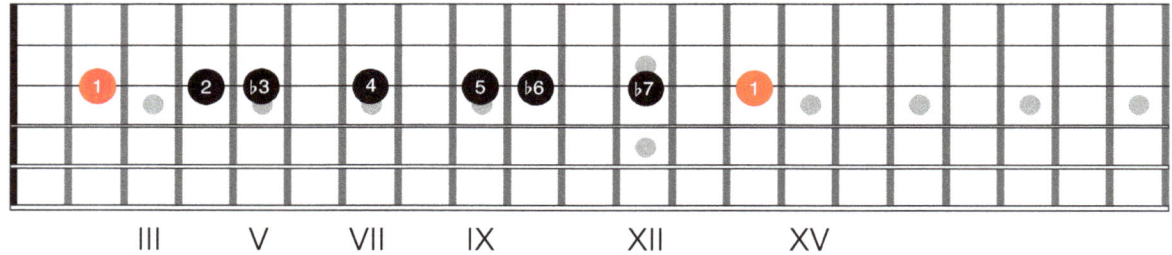

Here are the diatonic 3rd shapes for the A minor scale shown along the 3rd and 2nd strings. And again, when playing scales in 3rds, think of the lower of the two notes as the melodic guide.

Diatonic 3rds on 3rd and 2nd Strings in Minor

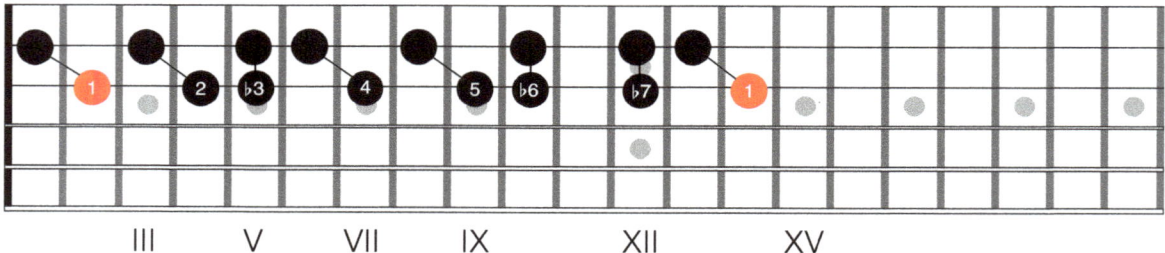

As before, think of the quality of the chord built on each scale degree to find the correct 3rd: minor 3rd, minor 3rd (because the II is diminished and has a minor 3rd), major 3rd, minor 3rd, minor 3rd, major 3rd, and major 3rd. This works for any minor key. Track the scale along the 3rd string.

You will put these intervals to work in the Money Maker modules.

RHYTHM GUITAR

Funk Groove #2

In this module you will learn a part played on an E dominant 7 chord phrase. There are two distinct parts. Part 1 is derived from a Sly and the Family Stone classic. This four-bar phrase combines a simple bass-like riff on the lower strings and uses the same dominant 9 chord voicing used in Unit 1. Part 2 is a percussive popcorn part. Before going into each of the parts individually, let's see at what they look like together.

This groove has a 16th-note subdivision. Follow the rules of pick direction. When in doubt, get your picking hand going in non-stop 16th notes: down-up-down-up.

Funk Groove #2 in E

Part 1

Part 1 is a four-bar phrase. It begins with the interval of a minor 7th played as a double stop.

Part 1 – 1st Phrase

- While playing open E, which is the tonic, also fret the ♭7, D, with your 1st finger at the 5th fret of the 5th string. This is a downstroke.

- On the "and" of 1, play the open E along with its octave, E, fretted with your 3rd finger at the 7th fret of the 5th string. This is a downstroke, too.

- On beat two, the first three 6ths are "scratches" which means there is no pitch, just the 5th string or more muted to make only a percussive sound. Mute by releasing the pressure in your fretting hand. The fourth 16th is the ♭3, G, played with your 1st finger at the 5th fret of the 4th string. This is tied over to an 8th note on beat three.

- On the "and" of 3, return to E at the 7th fret of the 5th string with your 3rd finger and a downstroke.

- On beat four, the first three 6ths are scratches again. The fourth 16th note is an open E and the ♭7 again, that's D with your 1st finger at the 5th fret of the 5th string. This is tied over to an 8th note on beat one of the next measure.

Fretboard Biology — Level 4 • Unit 2: Rhythm Guitar — 45

Part 1 – 2nd Phrase

- On the "and" of 1, play the open E along with its octave, E, fretted with your 3rd finger at the 7th fret of the 5th string. This is a downstroke.
- There is a rest on beat two. Beat three begins with an 8th note rest, but on the "and" fret F# with a downstroke and with your 2nd finger.
- On the fourth 16th, slide to G at the 3rd fret, also using your 2nd finger.
- On beat four, play the tonic, E, at the 2nd fret of the 4th string with your 1st finger.

That completes the first half of the phrase.

Part 1 – 3rd and 4th Phrases

For the second half of the phrase, much is the same:

- The third measure through beat one of the fourth measure is identical to the first measure.
- Beat three begins with an 8th-note rest, but on the "and" strum an E9 with a downstroke and the last 16th with an upstroke.
- Then play beat four with a downstroke.

The challenge is getting a strumming effect while keeping to just the lower strings.

Part 2

Part 2 uses the popcorn technique introduced in earlier units. This part uses two notes from the scale: the ♭7 and 6, that's D and C#, on the 3rd string. While Part 1 is a four-bar phrase, Part 2 is actually a two-bar phrase played twice. Proper pick direction is crucial for playing this part with good time and feel.

Part 2 – 1st Phrase

Go to 6th position and place your 1st finger at the 6th fret, C#, of the 3rd string. Place your 2nd finger at the 7th fret, D, of the 3rd string. These are the only two notes for this part.

- For the first two 16ths of beat one, play D with a downstroke and then an upstroke.
- On the "and", play C# with a downstroke.
- On the first 16th of beat two, play a D again with a downstroke.
- On the fourth 16th of beat two, play a D again with an upstroke.
- The first 16th of beat three is a rest, but make the downstroke motion.
- Play D on the second 16th with an upstroke.
- Play C# on the "and" with a downstroke and then D again on the fourth 16th with an upstroke.
- Beat four starts with a rest for the first three 16ths, but make the down-up-down motion without striking the string.
- Play D on the fourth 16th with an upstroke.

I recommend keeping the 16th-note subdivision motion with your picking hand even during rests.

Part 2 – 2nd Phrase

- Beat one starts with a 16th rest, but make the motion and miss the string.
- Play D on the second 16th with an upstroke and then C# on the "and" with a downstroke.
- On beat two, play D on the beat with a downstroke.
- On beat three and the second 16th, play D with downstroke, then an upstroke.
- On the "and", play C# with a downstroke.
- On beat four, play D on the beat with a downstroke.

These two parts work well together and don't interfere with each other. There is some rhythmic overlap but it is coordinated. In some places, Part 2 plays where Part 1 leaves space. They are mostly in different registers, too: Part 1 is low and part 2 is more in the middle.

Popcorn parts are an important arranging tool for Funk tunes; they are used as sort of a pitched percussion instrument. It is common for popcorn parts to be written around the b7 and 6th of dominant chords. Remember this popcorn part so you can re-purpose it in some other song.

Again, some Funk parts don't seem difficult on the surface but to get them to feel right is the biggest challenge. Proper pick direction is really important. These are typical kinds of parts. Log them away for future use in other songs.

MONEY MAKERS

In Unit 1 you learned parts for two progressions: one in a major key and one in a minor key. They use 3rds from the harmonized major and minor scales. The parts are for strings a 4th apart. They are written specifically for string set 1 and 2. However, they could also be used for string sets 3 and 4, 4 and 5, and 5 and 6, although the lower in register they are, the more unusable they become.

This Unit works with string set 2 and 3. These strings are a 3rd apart so the shapes will be different. Review the major scale harmonized in 3rds along the 3rd and 2nd strings that you learned in the Unit 2 Fretboard Logic Module.

Diatonic 3rds in a Major Key

Let's use the same E major progression that we used in the previous module for this example.

Progression in E Major

| Ema7 | F#mi7 | Ama7 | Ema7 |
| Ama7 | G#mi7 | F#mi7 B7 | Ema7 B7sus |

Over this progression, play the major scale on string set 3 and 2, harmonized in 3rds.

Diatonic 3rds on 3rd and 2nd Strings in Major

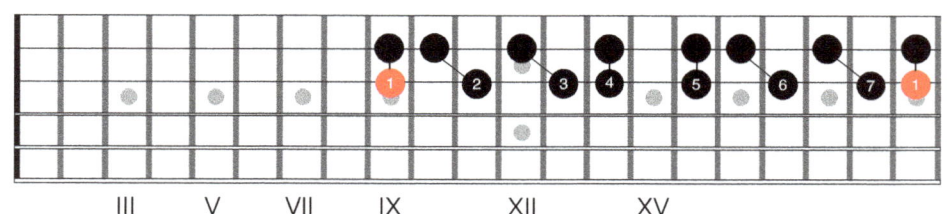

This can be played in any key. Again, you will recall that when adjacent strings are harmonized in 3rds, use the lower of the two notes to track the scale.

Here is the part. It's the same examples as Unit 1, but this time on string set 3 and 2.

Again, note the characteristic "personality" of 3rds. Test some of your own ideas using these 3rds shapes.

Diatonic 3rds in E

Diatonic 3rds in a Minor Key

Next, work in a minor key. Review the minor scale harmonized in 3rds along the 3rd and 2nd strings that you learned in the Fretboard Logic Module. Here is the progression over which the example will be played.

Review the minor scale harmonized in 3rds along the 2nd and 1st strings that we learned in the Fretboard Logic Module. It was demonstrated in the key of A minor.

Progression in E Minor

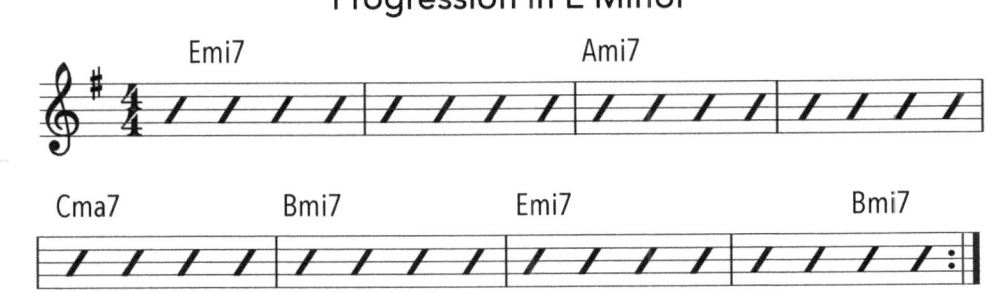

This can be played in any key. Remember, when adjacent strings are harmonized in 3rds, use the lower of the two notes to track the scale.

Diatonic 3rds on 3rd and 2nd Strings in Minor

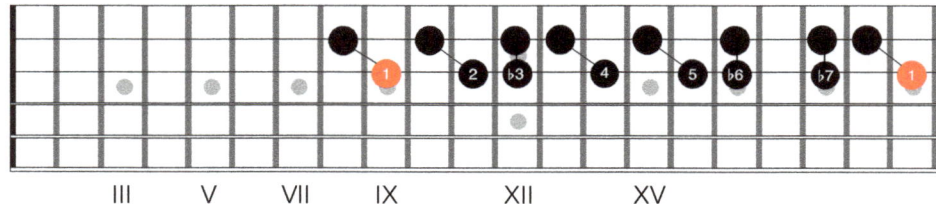

Now here is the part.

Again, note the "personality" of 3rds, but this time in a minor key. Experiment with some of your own ideas using these 3rds shapes. Remember that these ideas are transposable to all minor keys.

Diatonic 3rds in Emi

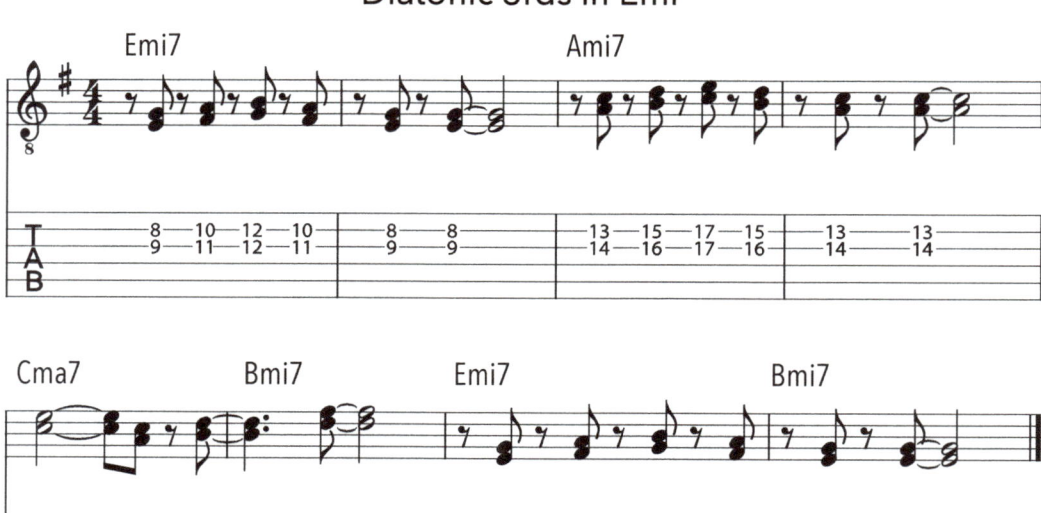

IMPROVISATION

This module goes deeper into soloing over progressions that have borrowed chords. Modal interchange is very common and directly affects the notes you use when soloing. It requires and deserves a lot of attention.

If a song is in a major key, the note choices come from the major scale of the key. But if a song in a major key borrows chords from the parallel minor key, use notes from the parallel minor scale on the borrowed chords.

Here is a four-bar chord progression in C major.

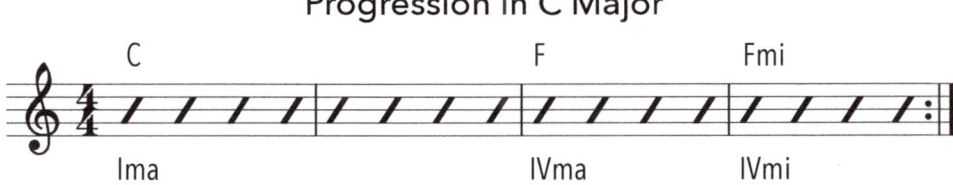

C is the Ima chord. F is the diatonic IVma chord. Fmi, however, is not diatonic to C major. Fmi is a borrowed chord. It is borrowed from C minor, the parallel minor. It is the IVmi chord in the key of C minor. You can play pentatonic scales and money makers over this progression as you did in the last unit, and I encourage you to do so to at first. Pentatonics are always a good way to get familiar with a new progression. But in this module, expand your options and use full seven-note scales.

Approach this similarly to the last unit. Use the Pattern III C major scale for the C and F chords and the Pattern IV C minor scale on the F minor chord. Again, this is because F minor chord is from C minor. You will need to switch back and forth between the two:

- Pattern III C major pentatonic over C and F.
- Pattern IV C minor pentatonic over F minor.

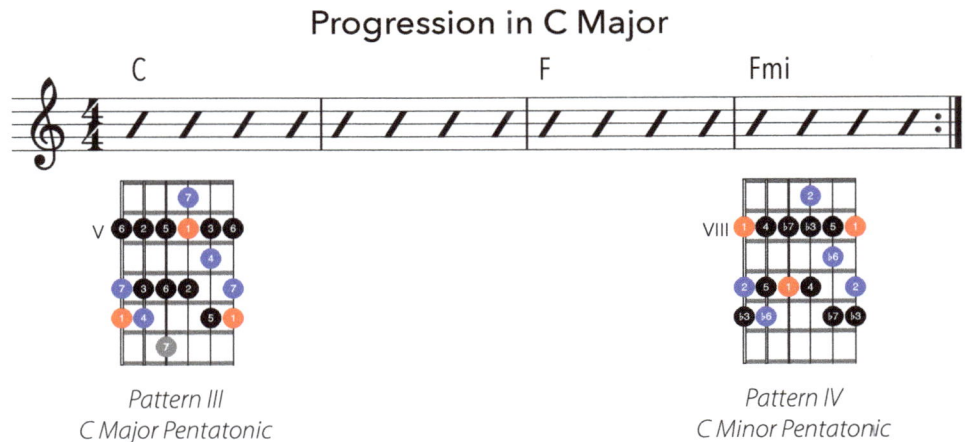

Pattern III
C Major Pentatonic

Pattern IV
C Minor Pentatonic

Level 4 Unit 2 • Improv Demo

PRACTICE

Theory

- ☐ Go to the tabs below the Theory video on the website and complete the quiz.
- ☐ Learn how to analyze progressions that have modal interchange.

Fretboard Logic

- ☐ Learn the shapes for the most common shell voicings.
- ☐ Learn the major and minor diatonic 3rd shapes on the 2nd and 3rd strings.

Rhythm Guitar

- ☐ Practice playing Funk Groove #2 parts in E.

Money Makers

- ☐ Practice playing major and minor diatonic 3rd parts over a progression.

Improvisation

- ☐ Practice playing solos over a C major progression with modal interchange.

UNIT 3

Learning Modules

> **Theory** - Analyzing Triad Progressions with Modal Interchange

> **Fretboard Logic** - Root Maps, Root Map 1, Root Map Practice Progressions, Major and Minor Scales Harmonized with 4th Shapes, Common Tones in Major and Minor Pentatonic Scales

> **Rhythm Guitar** - Funk Rhythm Guitar

> **Money Makers** - Money Maker Parts using Diatonic 4th Shapes

> **Improvisation** - Soloing with Modal Interchange

> **Practice** - Continue Practice Routine Development

THEORY

In the last unit, you learned how to identify, analyze, and label borrowed chords. In this module, you will use your new skill to analyze triad-based progressions in a few different keys. Here are the steps to take:

- First, analyze and label all the chords that are diatonic to the key; the low-hanging fruit.
- Next, if there are chords that are not diatonic, examine the parallel minor key and determine whether the non-diatonic chords came from there. If so, label them according to the information in the last unit (IIdim, ♭IIIma, IVmi, Vmi, ♭VIma, or ♭VIIma).

Here are a few progressions to analyze.

Progression in G Major

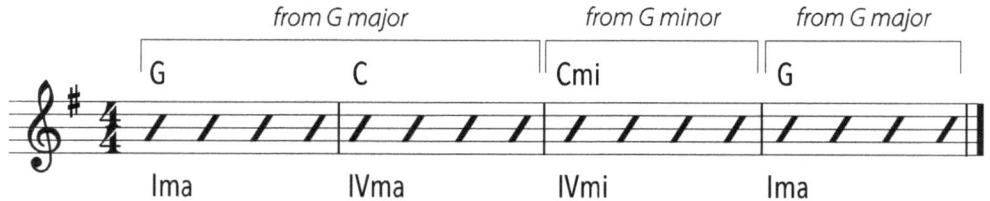

In this progression, notice that the last chord is G. You know from previous units that the final chord is often a good place to start when locating the key center of a song. The first and last chords of this progression are G and if they are the tonic chords, then C fits nicely as the IV major.

- But what about Cmi? It is not diatonic to G. Could it be from the parallel key?
- What is G major's parallel minor? It is G minor.
- Is there Cmi in G minor? Yes, it's IVmi.

What is happening here? Modal interchange.

- Cmi is borrowed from the key of G minor.
- G and C are diatonic to G major.
- Cmi is borrowed from the parallel G minor scale.
- The last chord is G, back to the major key.

Does the progression modulate; that is, does it change keys? No. The tonic never changes. The tonic is G throughout the entire progression. Do you hear the mood shift momentarily on Cmi? Play it and listen again.

Here is another example.

Progression in E Major

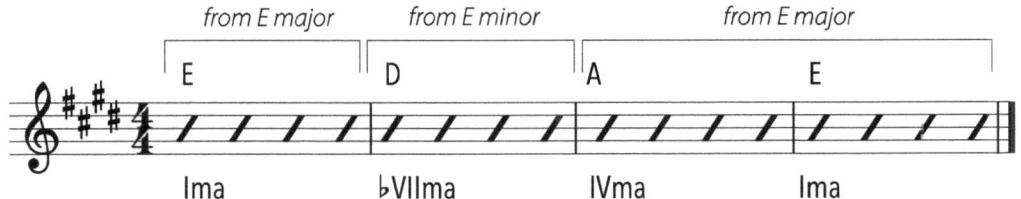

In this progression the last chord is E and you know the last chord is often the I chord. The first and last chords are E and let's assume they are the tonic chords.

- What about D? It isn't diatonic to E. Could it be from the parallel key?
- What is E major's parallel minor? It is E minor.
- Is there a D in E minor? Yes. It is ♭VII.

Again, this is modal interchange.

- D is borrowed from the key of E minor.
- A fits nicely as the IVma It is diatonic to E major.
- E and A are diatonic to E major.
- D is borrowed from the parallel E minor scale.

The tonic is E throughout the entire progression. The mood shifts momentarily on the D, but the progression does not change keys. So while there is modal interchange, the progression does not modulate.

Here is another example.

In this progression the last chord is D. Assume it is the tonic chord.

Progression in D Major

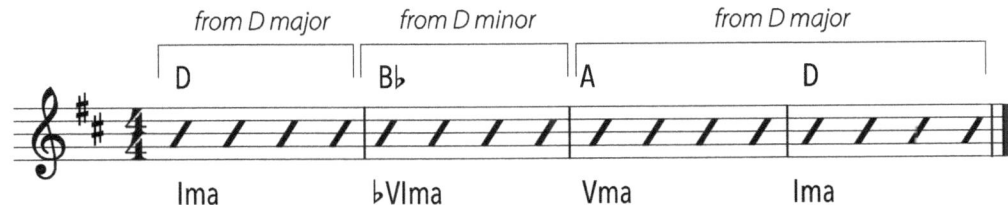

- But what about B♭? It isn't diatonic to D.
- What is D major's parallel key? D major's parallel minor is D minor.
- Is there a B♭ in D minor? Yes. It is ♭VI.

Again, this is modal interchange.
- B♭ is borrowed from the key of D minor.
- The A fits nicely as Vma It's diatonic to D major.
- D and A are diatonic to D major.
- B♭ is borrowed from the parallel D minor scale.

Here is another example.

Progression in C Major

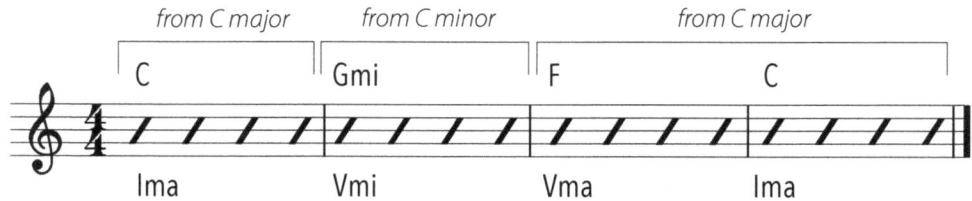

In this progression the last chord is C. Assume it is the tonic.
- But what about Gmi? It is not diatonic to C. Is it from the parallel key? C major's parallel minor is C minor.
- Is there a Gmi in C minor? Yes, it's Vmi.

This is modal interchange.
- The tonic stays the same.
- Gmi is borrowed temporarily from the key of C minor.
- F is the diatonic IVma chord in C major.

Here is another example.

Progression in F Major

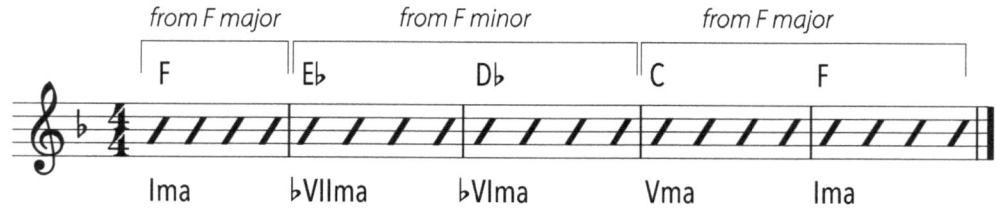

In this progression, the last chord is F. Assume that it is the I chord in the key of F major.
- But what about E♭? It isn't diatonic to F. Is from the parallel key? F major's parallel minor is F minor.

- Is there an E♭ chord in F minor? Yes, it's ♭VIIma.
- So, E♭ is borrowed from the key of F minor.
- What about D♭? It isn't diatonic to F. Is it also from F major's parallel minor, F minor?
- Is there an D♭ in F minor? Yes, it's ♭VIma.

Again, this is modal interchange.
- C is the diatonic Vma chord in F major. F and C are diatonic to F major.
- E♭ and D♭ are borrowed from the parallel F minor scale.

Here is another example.

In this progression the last chord is B. Assume that it's the I chord.

Progression in B Major

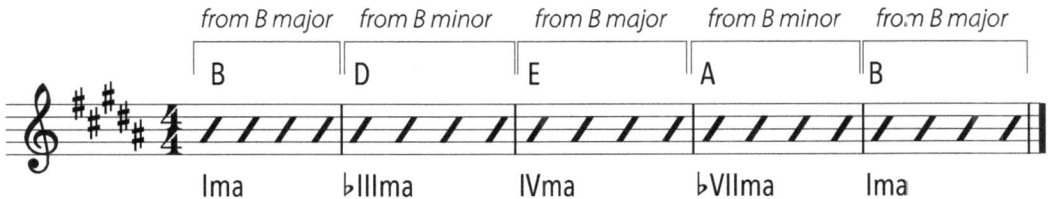

- But what about D? It isn't diatonic to B. It is from B minor. It is ♭IIIma borrowed from the key of B minor.
- E is the diatonic IVma chord in B major.
- What about A? It isn't diatonic to B major. It is from B minor as well. It is ♭VIIma, borrowed from the key of B minor.
- B and E are diatonic to B major. D and A are borrowed from the parallel B minor scale.

Look at one more example.

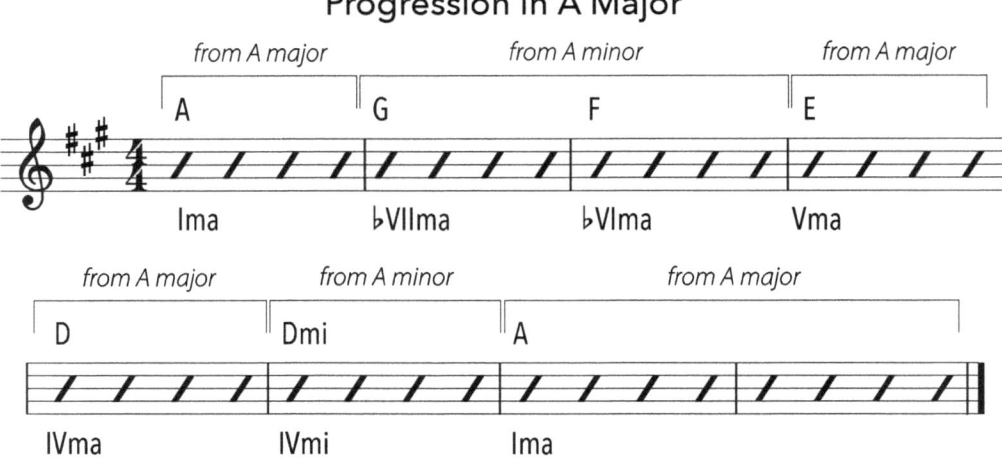

In this progression the last chord is A. Assume that it is the I chord.
- But what about G? It isn't diatonic to A. It is ♭VIIma from A minor.
- What about F? It isn't diatonic to A, either. It's ♭VIma from A minor.
- E is the diatonic Vma chord in A major.
- D is the diatonic IVma chord in A major.
- What about Dmi? It isn't diatonic to A major. It's IVmi borrowed from the key of A minor.

Once again, this is modal interchange.
- A, D, and E are diatonic to A major.
- G, F, and Dmi are borrowed from the parallel A minor scale.

You should know how to analyze triad-based progressions with borrowed chords.

FRETBOARD LOGIC

Root Maps

It is common in rehearsals and recording sessions or on gigs for the chord changes of a song to be communicated verbally through the use of the chord numbers. A leader might say something like, "on the verse, the chord changes are I, V, VI, IV, and it's in the key of G." So, what would be expected of you?

First of all, you weren't given music to read, and were not given chord names. You were only given the key and the numbers of the chords: I, V, VI, IV. Because you know the harmonized major scale, you could eventually figure out that in the key of G, the I chord is G, the V chord is D, the VI chord is Emi, and the IV is C. But the leader did not communicate with you that way. The leader didn't say the chords are G, D, Emi, C. The leader said I, V, VI, IV in G. What do you do?

In this module you will learn how to play chords by number using what is called a "root map".

Root Map

A root map is a scale pattern built on the 6th and 5th strings used to play the shell voicings of a harmonized scale by number.

There are several benefits of using root maps:

- If the chords are communicated by number, and if you have a map of where the roots of the diatonic chords are, you can easily find each of the chords in any key. This will be the main focus in this module.
- By knowing each chord's function, you can take advantage of things like substitution of chords within the chord family or improvising with the arpeggios of other chords in the family.
- Another benefit is transposition. To transpose a song means to move the tonic of a song from the written or original key to a new key. Transposition is the act of changing the key.

Imagine this common scenario where your band wants to learn a popular song and the original recording is in the key of G. The chords are: G, D, Emi, and C. Everyone in the band learns the song but they also learn the chords by number: I, V, VI, IV. If your singer can't hit the high notes and asks the band to change to a lower key, like F, you have a quick way to see where the roots of the chords by number, so transposition is instantaneous if you know the numbers of the chords.

In the key of F, the progression I, V, VI, IV is F, C, Dmi, B♭. If you have a visual root map, which is merely a pattern, you can just transpose to the new location on the fretboard without having to think about it using the numbers. So G, D, Emi, and C (I, V, VI, IV) from the song's original key of G becomes F, C, Dmi, B♭ in the new key of F.

After you have played a lot of songs with diatonic chords, patterns of where the roots are will emerge within keys over time. It just happens. But you can accelerate getting that skill with a simple root map system.

You will learn four root maps over the next four modules. Here they are:
- For major keys, based on a Ima7 chord shell voicing on the 6th string.
- For minor keys, based on a Imi7 chord shell voicing on the 6th string.
- For major keys, based on a Ima7 chord shell voicing on the 5th string.
- For minor keys, based on a Imi7 chord shell voicing on the 5th string.

Root Map 1

Begin with the root map for major keys referenced to a 6th-string root I major chord. This is Root Map 1 and it can be moved to any location and therefore any key on the 6th string.

Root Map 1

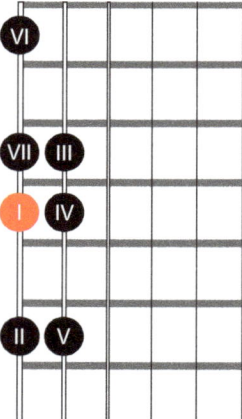

This is basically the lower part of a Pattern IV major scale shape with the addition of the 6th scale degree on the 6th string below the tonic and 7th scale degree. And notice the pattern is written with Roman numerals to correspond to the chords built on each scale degree.

Next, here are the shell voicings that are to be played with each root on the root map.

Root Map 1 Shell Voicings

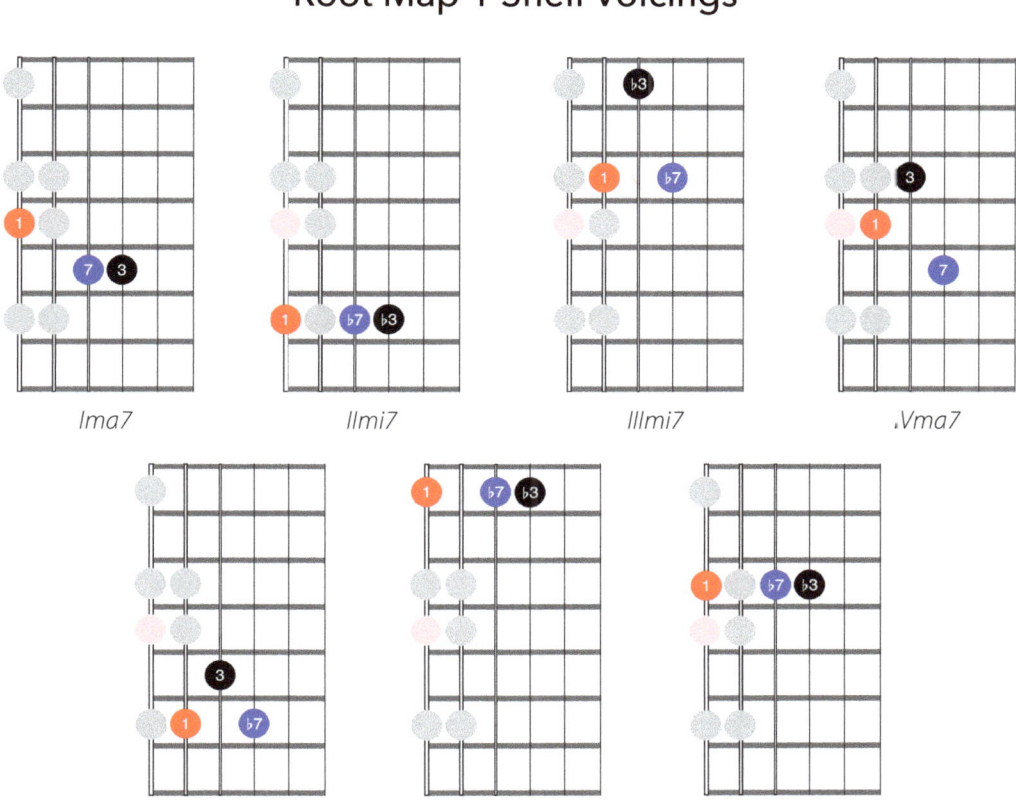

Ima7   *IImi7*   *IIImi7*   *IVma7*

V7   *VImi7*   *VIImi7(♭5)*

Regardless of the key, the map and associated shell voicings stay the same. Just move it to the key where you want to play.

Using Root Maps with Barre Chords

It's very important to know that full Pattern IV and II major and minor barre chords can be used with the root maps as well. Remember there is no barre chord for VIImi7(♭5) in major and IImi7(♭5) in minor. This is rarely an issue because these chords are seldom used in triad-based progressions.

I urge you to practice this root map and the next three you learn with barre chords as well as the shell voicings.

Root Map Exercise

In the exercise below, read the chord progressions that are written using only Roman numerals. Pick any key, go to that location on the fretboard, and play through the progression. Practice this in several keys and keep the tempo slow. It is more important to be accurate than fast. Be sure to use both shell voicings and barre chords.

Shell Voicing Practice Progressions - Root Map 1

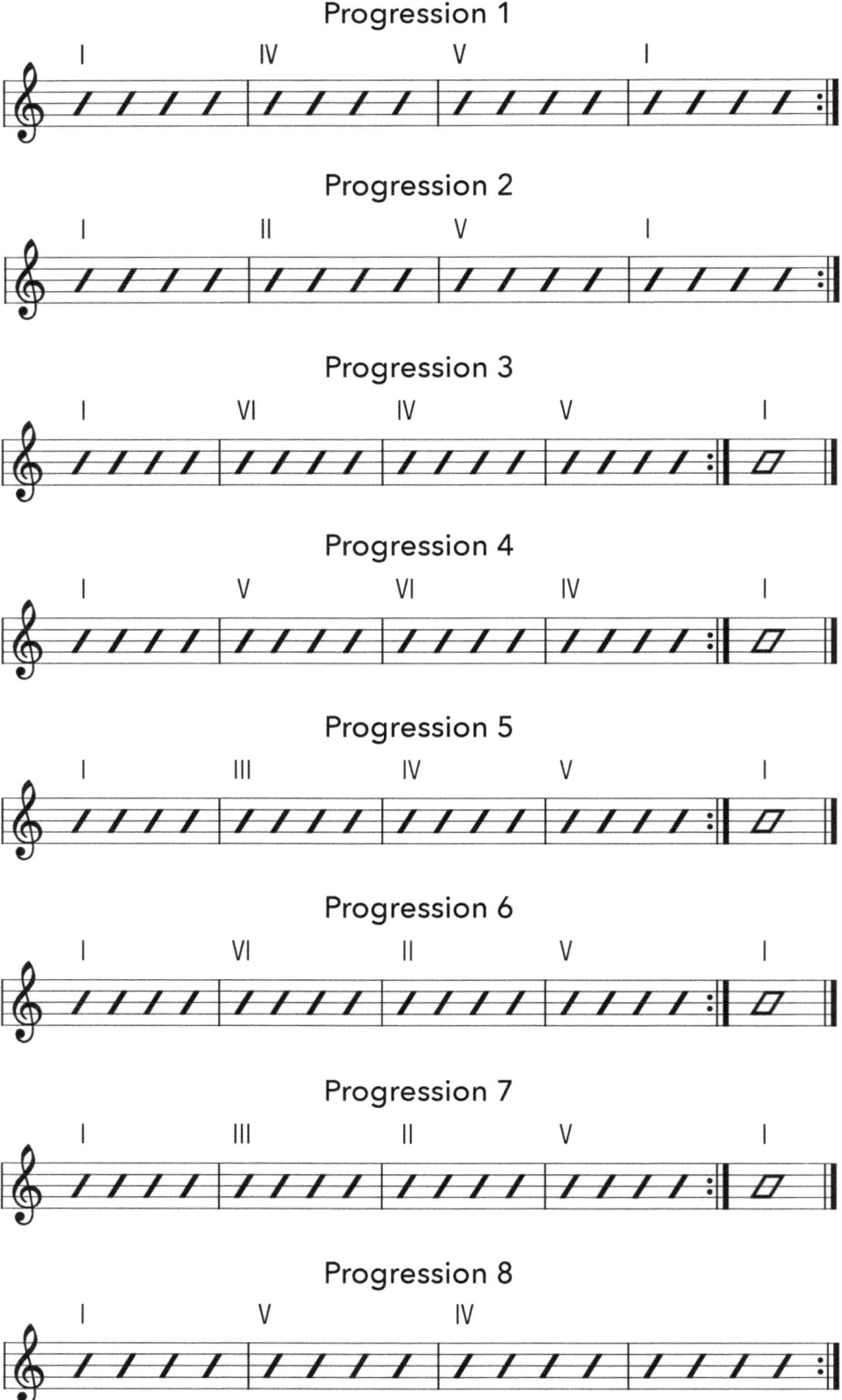

Using Roman numerals I through VII, write your own progressions, too. Pick a key, set your metronome at a slow tempo and play each chord for one measure. The point is to get comfortable with the root map and shell voicings.

Intervals

You have learned the diatonic 3rd shapes along adjacent strings as they relate to the diatonic major and minor scales. Interval shapes played along adjacent strings are a common source for improvised or planned melodies as well as background fills. This module focuses on 4ths.

The scale is tracked differently with 4ths as compared to 3rds. Read carefully. *When using 4ths, think of the higher of the two notes as the melodic guide.* The lower note, which is a 4th below, is the same as a note a 5th above the note on the 1st string. Remember the discussion about inverted intervals in the Unit 1 Theory Module. If you are unclear about inverted intervals, review that module. It is important to this and future modules.

Diatonic 4th Shapes in Major

For demonstration purposes, start in the key of G major. Consider the notes along the 1st string as the "scale degrees" starting with G at the 3rd fret. Play the G scale along the 1st string: G, A, B, C, D, E, F#, and G.

G Major Scale on the 1st String

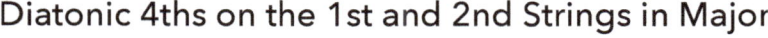

Next, play the note a diatonic 4th lower than each scale degree on the 2nd string. Remember when playing scales in 4ths, think of the higher of the two notes as the melodic guide. The note a 4th below is actually the 5th (above).

Diatonic 4ths on the 1st and 2nd Strings in Major

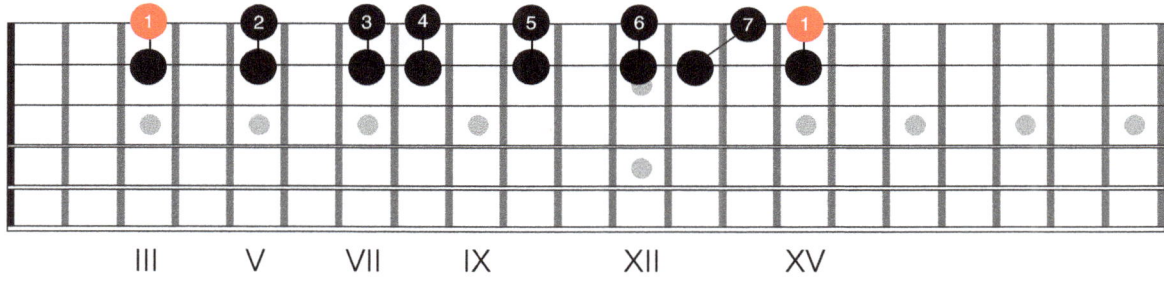

Here is a hint: Think of the quality of the 5th in the chord built on each scale degree to determine whether the 4th should be a perfect 4th or augmented 4th. They will all be perfect 5ths, which means a 4th below, except for the 7th scale degree which will be a diminished 5th which is an augmented 4th below. This works for any major key. Track the scale along the 1st string.

This set of shapes for the major scale works for the strings that are a 4th apart.

- The 1st and 2nd strings

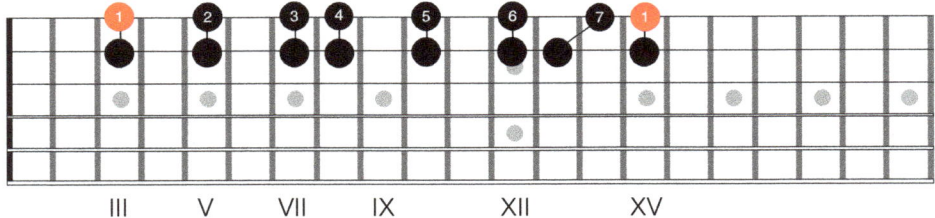

- NOT the 2nd and 3rd strings. They are a 3rd apart.
- The 3rd and 4th strings.

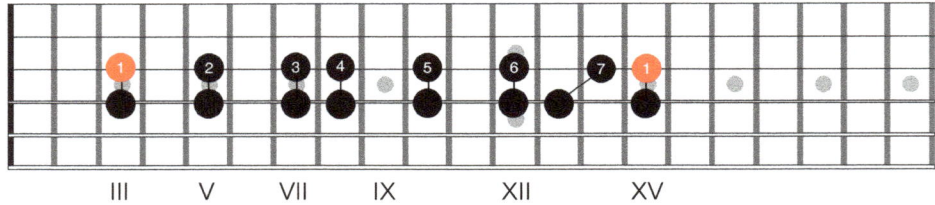

- The 4th and 5th strings.

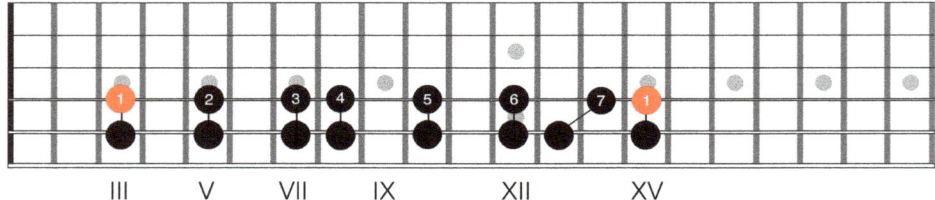

- The 5th and 6th strings.

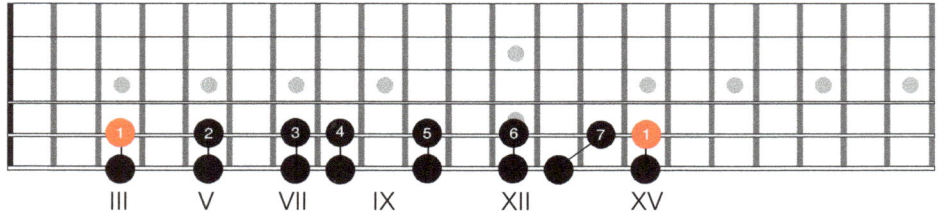

Diatonic 4th Shapes in Minor

Next look at the key of G minor. Consider the notes along the 1st string as the "scale degrees" starting with G at the 3rd fret. Play the G minor scale along the 1st string: G, A, B♭, C, D, E♭, F, G.

G Minor Scale on the 1st String

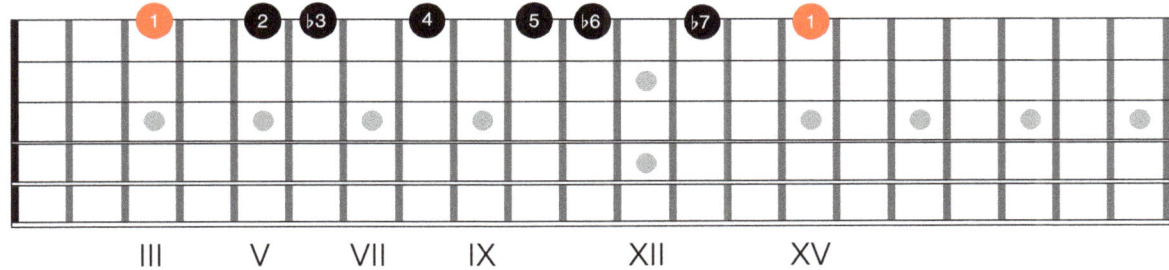

Here are the notes a diatonic 4th lower than each scale degree on the 2nd string. When playing scales in 4ths, think of the higher of the two notes as the melodic guide.

Diatonic 4ths on the 1st and 2nd Strings in Minor

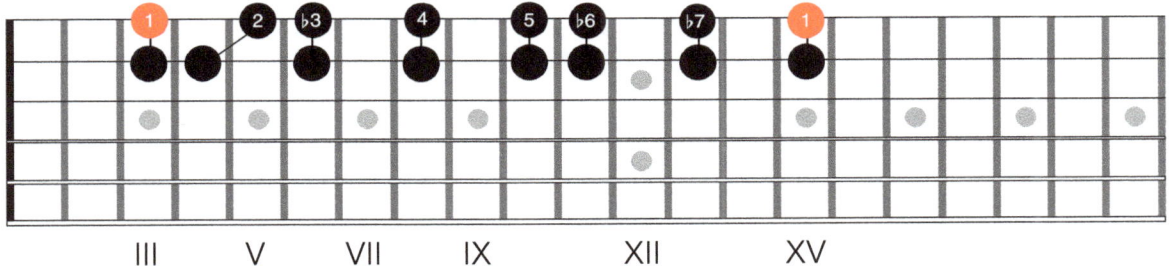

Here is a hint: Think of the quality of the 5th in the chord built on each scale degree to determine whether it should be a perfect or augmented 4th. They will all be perfect 5ths, which means a 4th below, except for the 2nd scale degree which will be a diminished 5th which is an augmented 4th below. This works for any minor key. Track the scale along the 1st string.

This set of shapes for the major scale works for the strings that are a 4th apart.

- The 1st and 2nd strings.

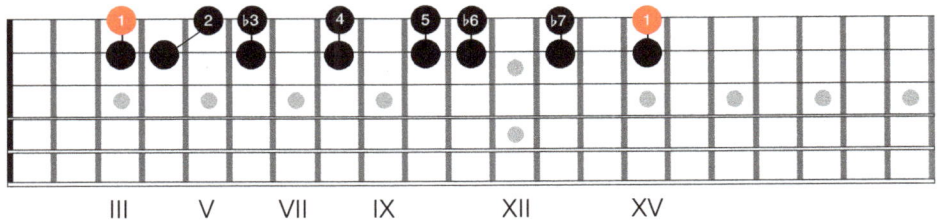

- NOT the 2nd and 3rd strings. They are a 3rd apart.
- The 3rd and 4th strings.

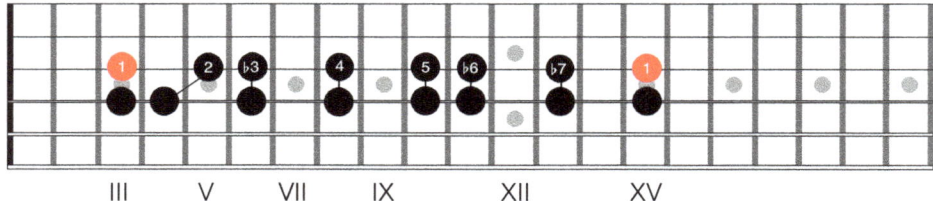

- The 4th and 5th strings.

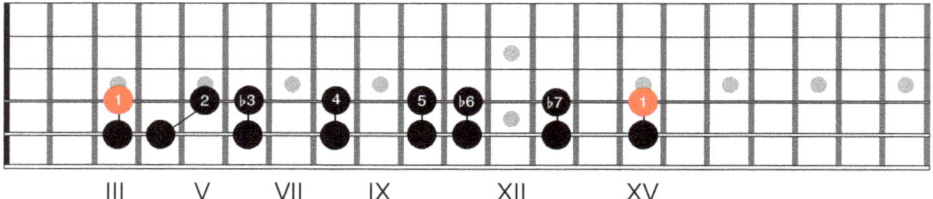

- The 5th and 6th strings.

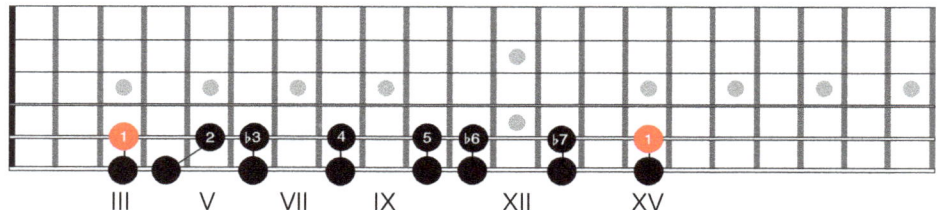

In the Money Maker modules, you will put these intervals to work in some simple examples.

Scales

You have soloed over progressions that shifted between parallel major and minor in the first two Level 4 Improvisation modules. In Unit 1 you were instructed to move your hand from Pattern III A major pentatonic to Pattern IV A minor pentatonic. These shapes resemble each other but are three frets apart.

Try a different approach. Locate the Pattern III major pentatonic scale again which places you in 2nd position, and then Pattern III minor pentatonic, which is also in 2nd position. The goal in this module is simple: You need to see both the major and minor pentatonic shells in the exact same location. The goal is to stay in position. Identify what notes are common between them and what notes are not.

This can be accomplished by seeing them side-by-side on paper and also on the fretboard, as well as playing each one, one step at at time.

Fretboard Biology
Level 4 • Unit 3: Fretboard Logic

Here are the two pentatonic shells side-by-side.

Pattern III Major Pentatonic   **Pattern III Minor Pentatonic**

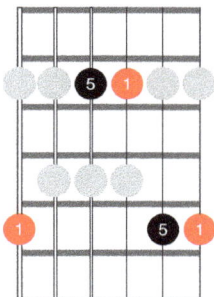   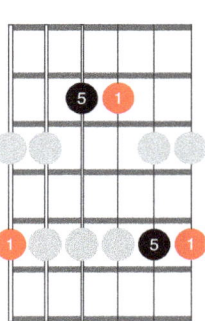

Here is how they look on the staff:

Common Tones in Major and Minor Pentatonic Scales

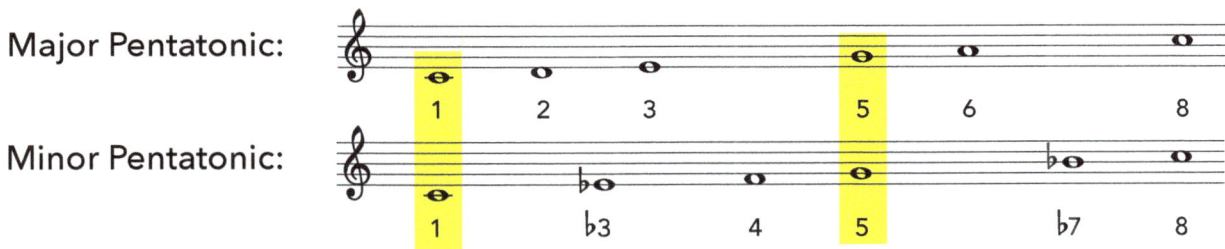

The common notes are 1 and 5. You can exploit these as common tones. The notes that are different are your opportunity to define the change from major to minor when soloing. Use this information in the Improvisation module for this Unit.

Before moving on, be sure you understand the logic of learning root maps and make sure to memorize Root Map 1. Practice playing progressions using this root map in different keys. Make sure you know the major and minor scales harmonized in 4ths along string sets 1 and 2, 3 and 4, 4 and 5, and 5 and 6. Finally, be sure you understand the similarities and differences between parallel major and minor pentatonic shells so that you can use them when soloing in progressions with modal interchange.

RHYTHM GUITAR

Funk Groove #3

In this module you will learn a two-bar rhythm guitar phrase in the key of E Dorian Minor. The Dorian mode has not been formally introduced but here is a simple and quick explanation: The Dorian mode (or Dorian scale) can be created by adding a major 2nd and major 6th to a minor pentatonic scale. Another popular way to think about it is as a Natural Minor scale with a major 6th instead of a minor 6th. That is all you need to know for now.

There are two different guitar parts. Part 1 uses chords and Part 2 is a percussive popcorn part. The example has a 16th-note subdivision so follow the rules of pick direction.

Funk Groove #3 in Emi

Part 1

Part 1 uses two chords, Emi9, which is a derivative of Emi7, and A13, which is a derivative of A7. I suggest the neck pickup for most guitars but as always, experiment for yourself.

The voicing of Emi9 is played by placing your 1st finger at the 5th fret of the 4th string. Place your 3rd finger at the 7th fret of the 3rd string. Place your 4th finger at the 7th fret of the 2nd string.

The voicing of A13 is played by placing your 1st finger at the 5th fret of the 4th string. Place your 2nd finger at the 6th fret of the 3rd string. Place your 3rd finger at the 7th fret of the 2nd string.

Part 1 – 1st Phrase

- On beat one of measure one, play Emi9 with a downstroke.
- On the second 16th note, play an upstroke.
- On the "and" of beat two, play Emi9 again with a downstroke.
- On the fourth 16th note, play an upstroke.

The rhythm for the second measure is the same but played with the A13 chord.

Part 2

Part 2 uses the popcorn technique. It uses a little "box" from the minor pentatonic scale. The box is from Pattern II E minor pentatonic on the 3rd and 4th strings in 7th position. When playing this part, assign your 1st finger to the 7th fret playing the minor 7th, D, on the 3rd string and the 4th, A, on the 4th string.

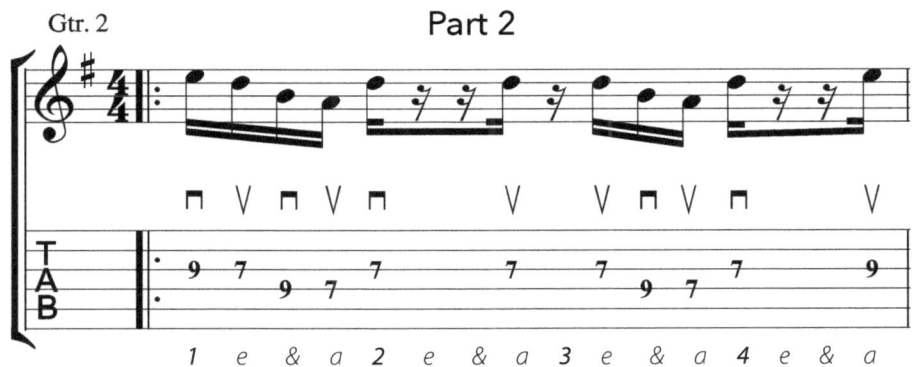

Assign your 3rd finger the 9th fret playing the tonic, E on the 3rd string and the 5th, B, on the 4th string. This box approach is very common for popcorn parts in minor keys. Log this away as part of your vocabulary.

Pattern II Pentatonic Scale

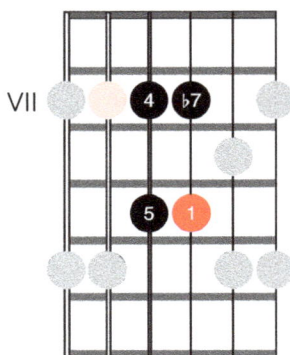

Follow the 16th-note pick-direction rules as shown in the example. I suggest the bridge/middle combination pickup setting for Strat-style guitars and for other guitars, experiment to find a dry sound that leans more treble than round.

Experiment with different degrees of muting. Start by fully fretting the notes and gradually release pressure until you are barely hearing the pitches. Having control of fretting-hand pressure is important for playing expressively. There are occasions when a song may call for almost complete muting. Popcorn parts serve not only as a repetitive background line but also as a percussion-type part.

These two parts work well together and don't interfere with each other rhythmically. For the most part, Part 2 is played where Part 1 leaves space. Even though they both occupy the same general register, the rhythmic, tonal, and textural differences make them compatible. These are typical Funk rhythm guitar parts. Log them away for future use in other songs.

Remember that popcorn parts are an important arranging tool for Funk tunes. This box approach using the tonic, ♭7, 5th, and 4th is very common for popcorn parts in minor keys.

When two or more guitars are being used in a rhythm section, it's wise to have them stay out of each other's way. As always, proper pick direction is really important.

MONEY MAKERS

In Units 1 and 2 you learned parts that use 3rds from the harmonized major and minor scales. You learned examples in both major and minor keys. In Units 3 and 4 you will work with 4ths from both the harmonized major and minor keys. This unit addresses the string sets that are a 4th apart. You'll learn one in example major and one in minor.

Diatonic 4ths in a Major Key

The first progression is major and in the key of B♭. This eight-bar progression is a very low-key progression at a slow tempo to make it easy to experiment with the shapes.

Progression in B♭ Major

Review the major scale harmonized in 4ths along the 1st and 2nd strings that you learned in the Fretboard Logic Module. It's shown here in the key of B♭.

Diatonic 4ths on the 1st and 2nd Strings in Major

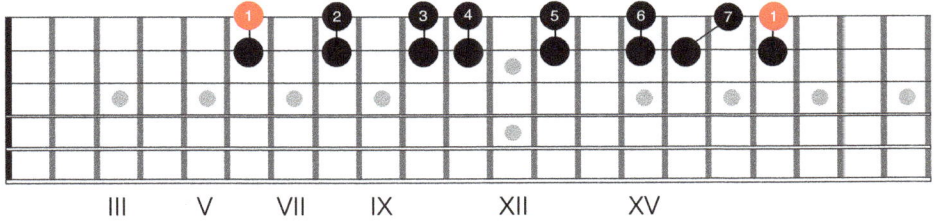

This part can be played in any key. Keep in mind that when adjacent strings are harmonized in 4ths, use the higher of the two notes to track the scale.

Here is the part.

Diatonic 4ths in B♭

Note the characteristic "personality" of 4ths. Experiment with some of your own ideas using these 4th shapes. This part can be used for string sets 3 and 4, 4 and 5, and 5 and 6.

Diatonic 4ths in a Minor Key

This example is in a minor key. Here is medium-tempo Rock track. It's a four-bar progression in G minor.

Progression in G Minor

Review the minor scale harmonized in 4ths along the 1st and 2nd strings that you learned in the Fretboard Logic Module. It's shown here in the key of G minor.

Diatonic 4ths on the 1st and 2nd Strings in Minor

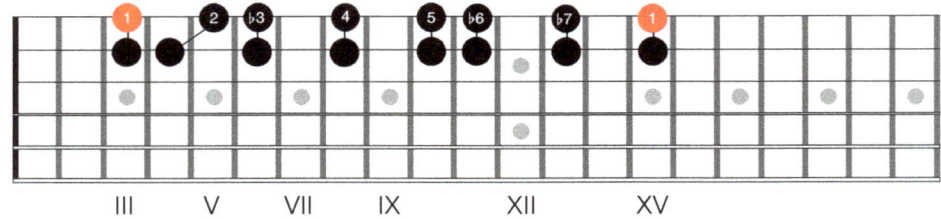

Remember, when adjacent strings are harmonized in 4ths, use the higher of the two notes to track the scale.

Here is the part.

Diatonic 4ths in G Minor

Again, note the characteristic "personality" of 4ths, now in a minor key. Test some of your own ideas using these 4ths shapes.

This part could also be used for string sets 3 and 4, 4 and 5, and 5 and 6, but as before, the lower they are in register, the more unusable they become. Experiment and see for yourself. Remember that these ideas are transposable to all minor keys!

IMPROVISATION

In this module you will learn a more physically efficient approach to playing over progressions with modal interchange. You will learn to stay "in position". You learned to be physically efficient with chord tones by organizing the arpeggios from the harmonized major and minor scales in position. That helps you stay in one area of the fretboard. What you learn in this module should feel familiar because the goal here is to be physically efficient and not have to move your hand very far, or at all.

Here is a four-bar chord progression in A major. It has the sound of an old R&B progression.

Progression in A Major

Ima   bIIIma   IVma   bVIIma

When analyzing this progression, it's clear that A is Ima and D is IVma, but C and G are not diatonic to A major. C is a borrowed chord. It's bIIIma in the parallel key of A minor. G is not diatonic to A major, either. It is a borrowed chord, too, and it's bVII7 in A minor. There are two borrowed chords, but A still remains the tonic throughout this progression.

The objective in this module is to stay in position while soloing. For the sake of this exercise, keep it simple and solo using pentatonic shells only.

- Over A, use Pattern III A major pentatonic.

- Over C, stay in position this time and use the Pattern III A minor pentatonic scale. This is different than Modules 1 and 2 where you shifted to a new position for the borrowed chords. By using Pattern III shapes for both the major and minor pentatonic scales, it is possible to stay in position.

- The D chord is back in A major. You can use the Pattern III A major pentatonic shell. But the A minor pentatonic scale is also an optional scale because the IV chord in Blues is a based on a major triad. So on D, which is IV major, you have two choices, A major or A minor pentatonic, and it is acceptable to blend the two.

- Over the G, stay in position and again use the Pattern III A minor pentatonic scale. You need to shift in and out of the parallel minor scale twice within four bars.

First play a few notes from each scale for each chord to get comfortable. Then improvise using the appropriate scale for each chord.

- Pattern III A major pentatonic over A and D.
- Pattern III A minor pentatonic over C and G.

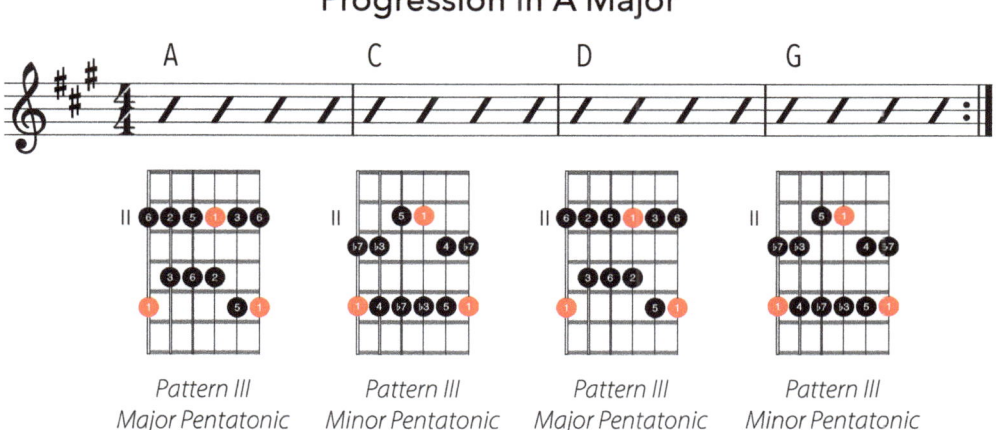

Common Tones

It is always good to know which notes are common to both parallel scales. 1 and 5 are common to both parallel major and minor pentatonic shells. You can exploit these common tones by playing them through all the chords or use them to pivot and change direction.

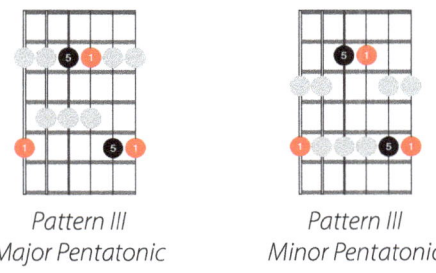

Level 4 Unit 3 • Improv Demo

PRACTICE

Theory

- ❏ Go to the tabs below the Theory video on the website and complete the quiz.
- ❏ Practice analyzing triad progressions with modal interchange.

Fretboard Logic

- ❏ Learn Root Map 1 and the associated shell voicings.
- ❏ Learn the major and minor diatonic 4th shapes on string sets that are a 4th apart.
- ❏ Learn the common tones in the major and minor pentatonic scales.

Rhythm Guitar

- ❏ Practice Funk Groove #3, paying special attention to pick direction.

Money Makers

- ❏ Practice playing major and minor diatonic 4th parts over an A major progression.

Improvisation

- ❏ Practice playing solos over an A major progression with modal interchange.

UNIT 4

Learning Modules

> **Theory** - Introduction to Analyzing 7th Chord Progressions with Modal Interchange

> **Fretboard Logic** - Root Map 2, Root Map 2 Shell Voicings, Root Map Practice Progressions, Major and Minor Diatonic Scales Harmonized with 4th Shapes, Common Tones in Major and Natural Minor Scales

> **Rhythm Guitar** - Funk Rhythm Guitar, Funk Groove #4

> **Money Makers** - Money Maker Parts using Diatonic 4th Shapes

> **Improvisation** - Soloing with Modal Interchange

> **Practice** - Continue Practice Routine Development

THEORY

In recent modules you learned how to identify, analyze, and label borrowed chords in triad-based progressions. Next you will learn how to identify, analyze, and label borrowed chords in 7th chord-based progressions.

Look at the comparison of the C major scale and its parallel minor again.

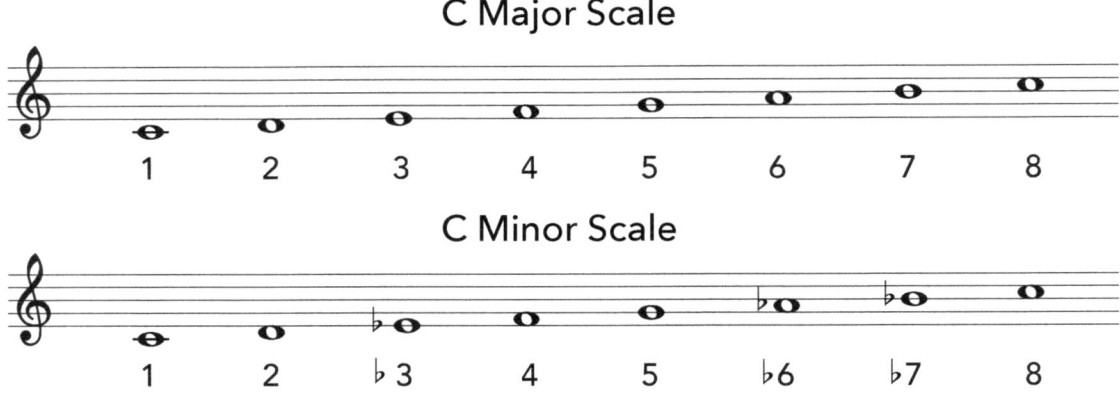

It is important to learn to label all of the 7th chords that can be borrowed from the parallel minor scale. To do this, compare the harmonized major and minor scales, but this time, with 7th chords.

Harmonized with 7th Chords

MAJOR:	Ima7	IImi7		IIImi7	IVma7	V7		VImi7		VIImi7(♭5)
	Cma7	Dmi7		Emi7	Fma7	G7		Ami7		Bmi7(♭5)
MINOR:	Imi7	IImi7(♭5)	♭IIIma7		IVmi7	Vmi7	♭VIma7		♭VII7	
	Cmi7	Dmi7(♭5)	E♭ma7		Fmi7	Gmi7	A♭ma7		B♭7	

Labeling 7th chords borrowed from the parallel minor is similar to labeling borrowed triads. Write the Roman numeral of the root and then the quality.

- If a progression borrows the II chord from the parallel minor scale it is labeled IImi7(♭5).
- If a progression borrows the III chord from the parallel minor scale it is labeled ♭IIIma7 because the III chord in a minor key is built on the minor 3rd of the scale. In a situation where modal interchange is occurring, the ♭IIIma7 chord is appearing in an otherwise major context. The distinction must be made from the diatonic III chord which would be IIImi7.
- If a progression borrows the IV chord from the parallel minor scale it is labeled IVmi7.

- If a progression borrows the V chord from the parallel minor scale it is labeled Vmi7.
- If a progression borrows the VI chord from the parallel minor scale it is labeled ♭VIma7 because the VI chord in a minor key is built on the minor 6th of the scale. In a situation with modal interchange, the ♭VIma7 chord is appearing in an otherwise major context. The distinction must be made from the diatonic VI chord which would be VImi7.
- If a progression borrows the VII chord from the parallel minor scale it is labeled ♭VII7 because the VII chord in a minor key is built on the minor 7th of the scale. With modal interchange, the ♭VII7 chord is in an otherwise major context. The distinction must be made from the diatonic VI chord which would be VIImi7(♭5).

Analyze these progressions with 7th chords using the same process as with triads.

Progression in C Major

First, analyze all the chords that are easy to fit into a single key; the low-hanging fruit.
- The last chord is often a good place to start when identifying the key center of a song, so assume it is Ima7. The first and last chord is Cma7.
- Fma7 fits as the IVma7 chord in C.
- What about Fmi7? It isn't diatonic to C major.
- It is from C minor. It's IVmi7 in C minor.

Progression in C Major

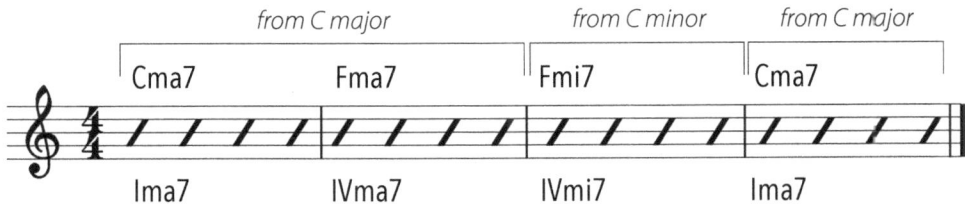

This is modal interchange.
- Fmi7 is borrowed from the key of C minor.
- Cma7 and the Fma7 are diatonic to C major.
- Fmi7 is borrowed from the parallel C minor scale. The last chord is Cma7, returning to the major key.

Does the progression modulate? No. The tonic doesn't change. The tonic is C through the entire progression. But there is a mood shift momentarily on Fmi7. Play the progression and pay attention to the shift in mood when this major progression borrows from its relative minor. The progression is happy and positive during Cma7 and Fma7. The mood shifts to sad or melancholy on Fmi7 and then returns to happy on C maj7. This is modal interchange.

Here are some other examples where progressions borrow chords from their parallel minor.

In this progression Dmi7(♭5) is labeled IIDmi7(♭5). The diatonic II chord is Dmi7.

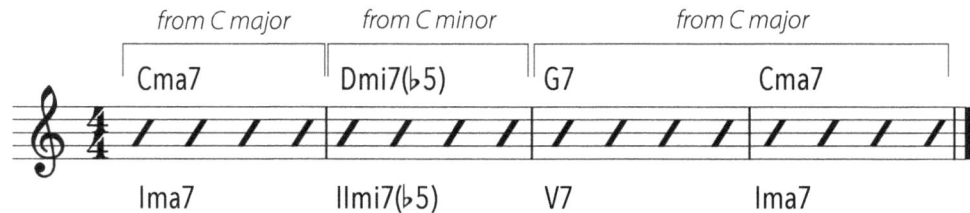

In this progression E♭ma7 is labeled ♭IIIma7. The diatonic III chord is Emi7.

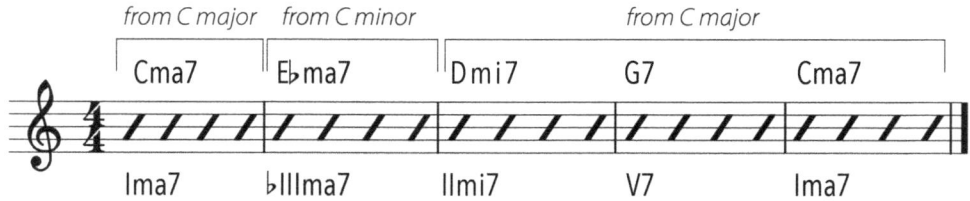

In this progression Fmi7 is labeled IVmi7. The diatonic IV chord is Fma7.

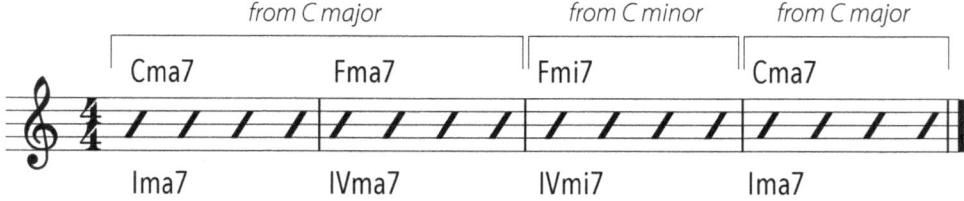

In this progression Gmi7 is labeled Vmi7. The diatonic V chord is G7.

Progression in C Major

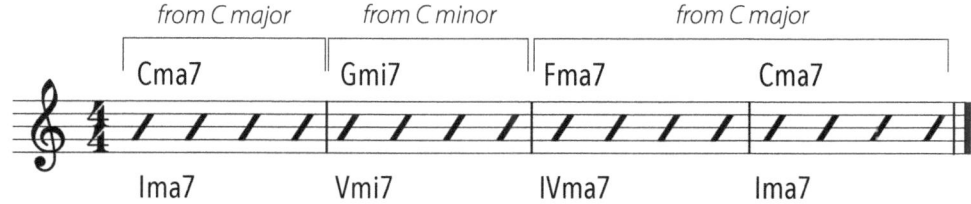

In this progression A♭ma7 is labeled ♭VIma7. The diatonic VI chord is Ami7.

Progression in C Major

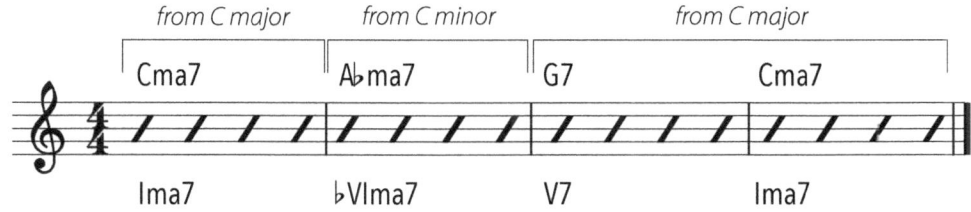

In this progression B♭7 is labeled ♭VII7. The diatonic VII chord is Bmi7(♭5).

Progression in C Major

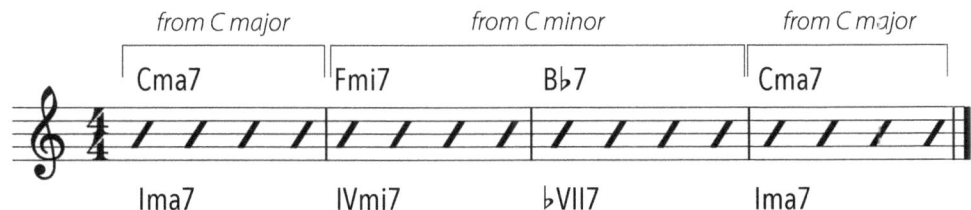

Study the harmonic analysis of these progressions. In the next unit you will analyze more 7th-chord progressions with modal interchange. Know how to recognize modal interchange in a progression and how to label 7th chords borrowed from the parallel minor key. Remember when analyzing ♭IIIma7, ♭VIma7 and ♭VII7 that the "♭" in front of those Roman numerals is important.

FRETBOARD LOGIC

In the last unit you learned to play chords by number using a root map. In this module you will learn the second of four root maps. This is a root map for minor keys, referenced to a Imi7 chord shell voicing on the 6th string.

Root Map 2

This is Root Map 2 and it can be moved to any location and therefore any key on the 6th string.

Root Map 2

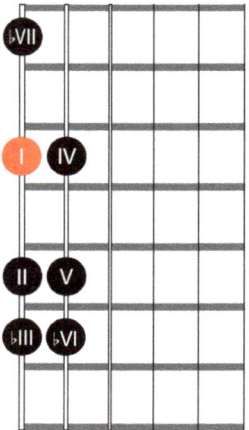

It is essentially the lower part of a Pattern IV minor scale shape with the addition of the ♭7 scale degree on the 6th string, below the tonic. And notice the pattern is written with Roman numerals to correspond to the chords built on each scale degree.

Next, here are the shell voicings that are to be played with each root on the root map.

Root Map 2 Shell Voicings

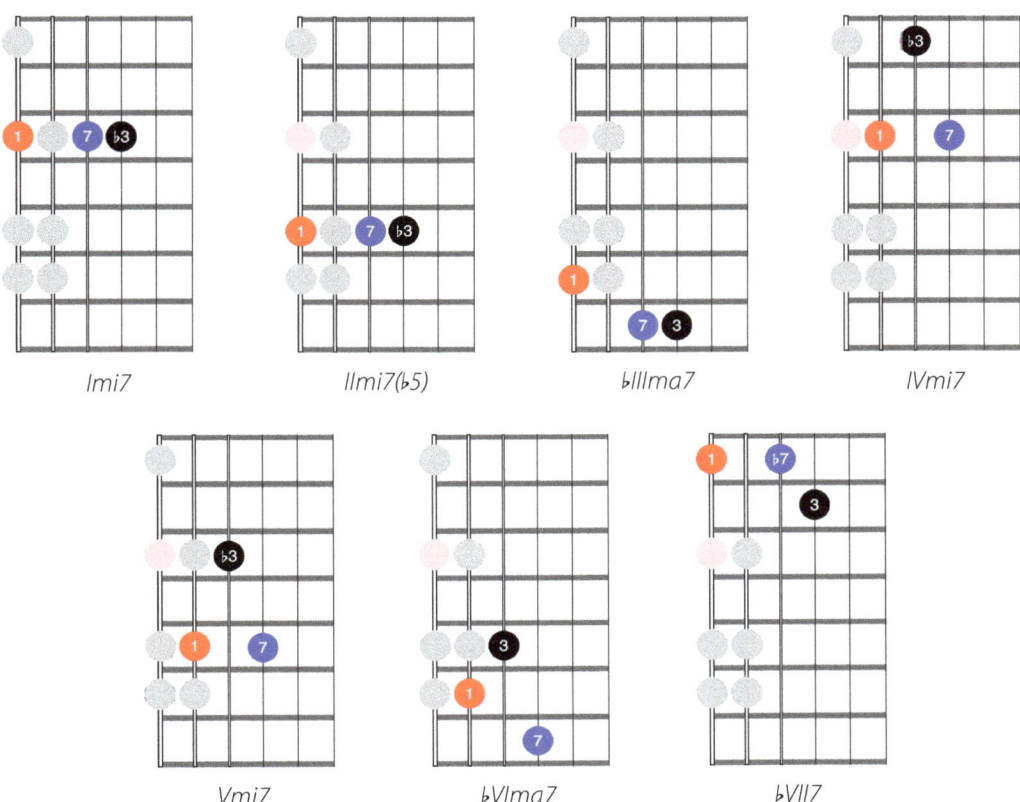

Regardless of the key, the map and associated shell voicings stay the same. The root map can be moved to any key.

Using Root Maps with Barre Chords

Remember that full Pattern IV and II major and minor barre chords can be used with the root maps as well, and that there is no barre chord for VIImi7(b5) in major and IImi7(b5) in minor. This is rarely an issue because these chords are seldom used in triad-based progressions.

Practice this and the first root map and the next two you learn with barre chords as well as the shell voicings.

Root Map Exercise

In the progression exercise below, read the chords that are written in only Roman numerals. You may pick any key, go to that location on the fretboard, and play through the progression. Practice this in several keys and keep the tempo slow. Be sure to use both shell voicings and barre chords, and remember that these for minor keys.

Shell Voicing Practice Progressions - Root Map 2

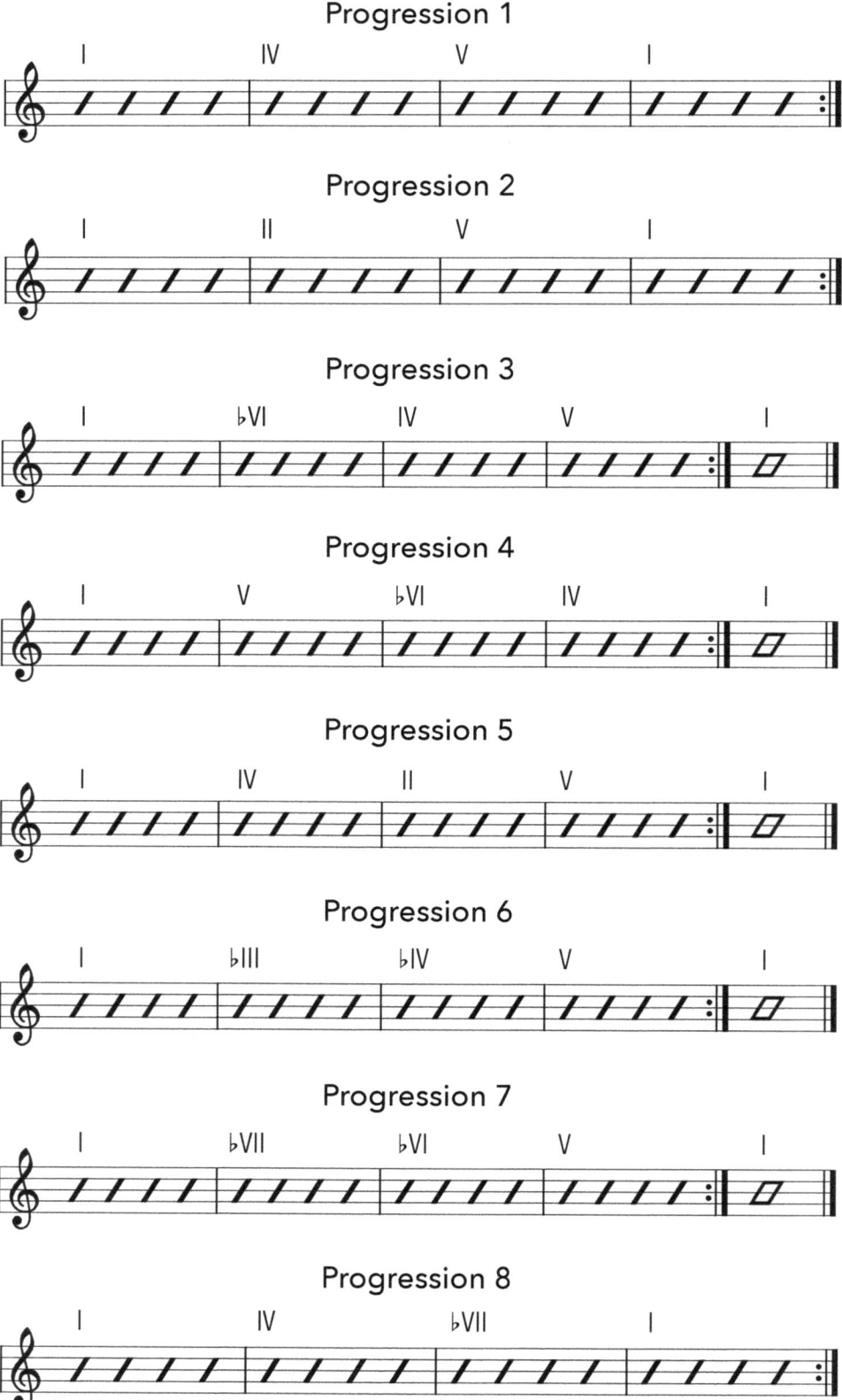

Using Roman numerals I through VII, write your own progressions, too. Pick a key, set your metronome at a slow tempo and play each chord for one measure. The point is to get comfortable with the root map and shell voicings.

Intervals

In the last unit you learned 4th intervals along string sets 1 and 2, 3 and 4, 4 and 5, and 5 and 6. This module looks at the major and minor scales harmonized in 4ths along the 2nd and 3rd strings.

Diatonic 4th Shapes in Major

For demonstration purposes, work in the key of D major. Consider the notes along the 2nd string as the "scale degrees" starting with D at the 3rd fret. Play the D scale along the 2nd string: D, E, F#, G, A, B, C#, D.

D Major Scale on the 2nd String

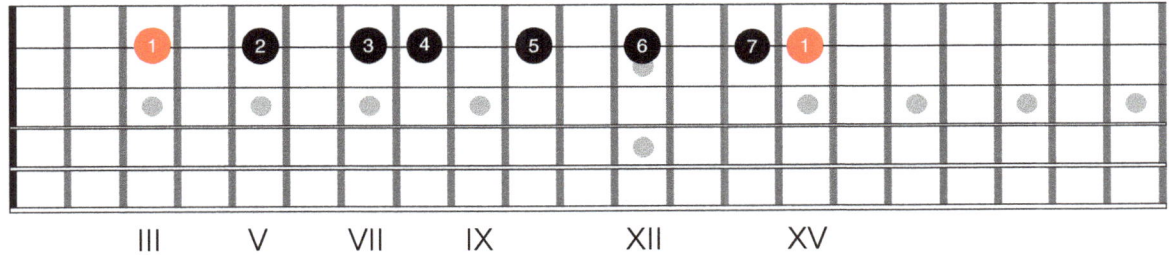

Next, play the note a diatonic 4th lower than each scale degree on the 2nd string. Remember when playing scales in 4ths, think of the higher of the two notes as the melodic guide and remember what you learned about inverted intervals.

Diatonic 4ths on the 2nd and 3rd Strings in Major

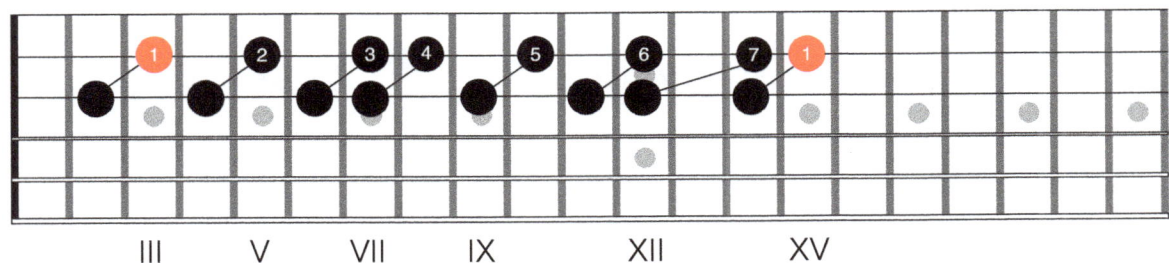

Here is a hint: Think of the quality of the 5th in the chord built on each scale degree to find the correct 4th.

They will all be perfect 5ths, which means a 4th below, except for the 7th scale degree which will be a diminished 5th which is an augmented 4th below. This works for any major key. Track the scale along the 2nd string.

Diatonic 4th Shapes in Minor

Look at the key of D minor. Play the D minor scale along the 2nd string: D, E, F, G, A, B♭, C, and D.

D Minor Scale on the 2nd String

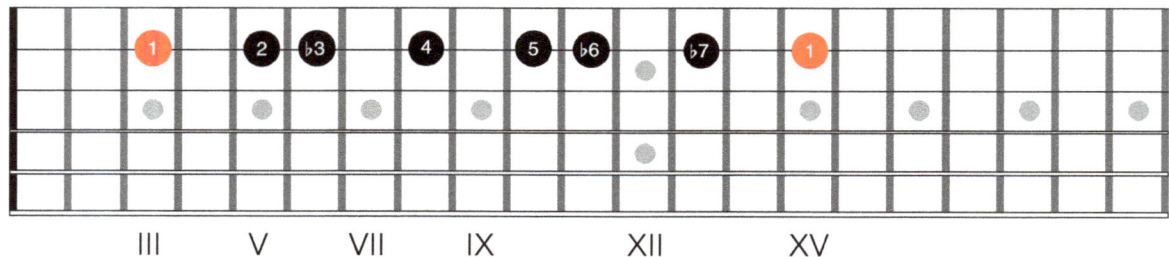

Next, play the note a diatonic 4th lower than each scale degree on the 3rd string. Again, be sure to think of the quality of the 5th in the chord built on each scale degree to find the correct 4th.

Diatonic 4ths on the 2nd and 3rd Strings in Minor

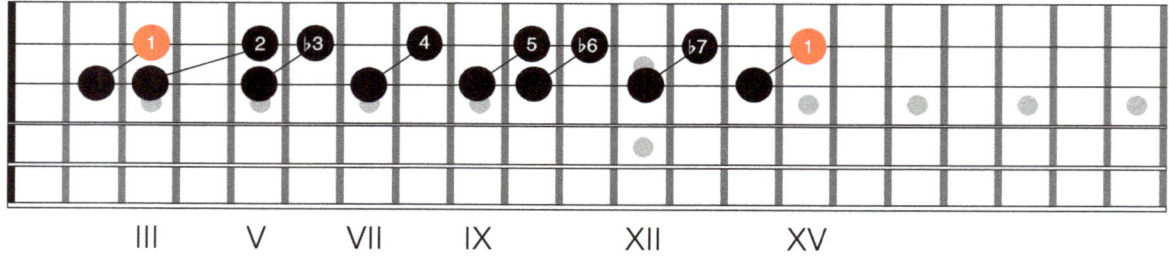

They will all be perfect 5ths, which means a 4th below, except for the 2nd scale degree which will be a diminished 5th which is an augmented 4th below. This works for any minor key. Track the scale along the 2nd string. You will put these intervals to work in the Money Makers modules.

Scales

The Level 4 Improvisation modules provide many opportunities to solo over progressions that shift between parallel major and minor. In the last unit you located both Pattern III major pentatonic and Pattern III minor pentatonic in the same position and key. You identified which notes were in common and which were not.

The goal in this module is similar but instead of pentatonics, use seven-note major and minor scales in position. Identify which notes are common between them and which notes are not. Do this by seeing them side-by-side on the staff and on the fretboard, as well as playing each one, one step at at time.

Here are the two scale patterns side-by-side.

Pattern III Major Scale

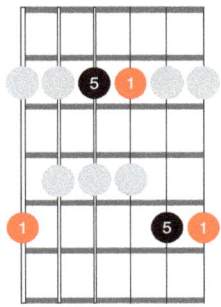

Pattern III Minor Scale

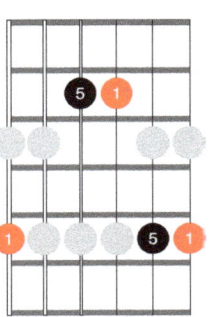

Here is how they look on the staff:

Common Tones in Major and Natural Minor Scales

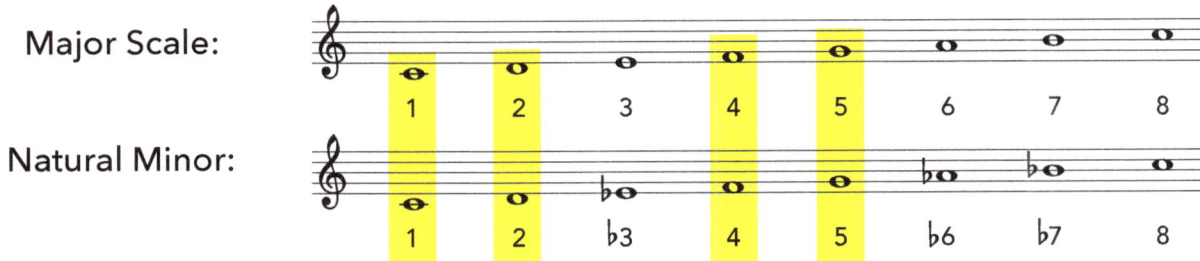

The common notes are 1, 2 ,4, and 5. You can exploit these in soloing as common tones. The notes that are different provide an opportunity to define the change from major to minor when soloing. Study and know them. Use this information in the Improvisation module for this unit.

Before moving on, know Root Map 2, which is a root map for minor keys and based on a 6th-string root pattern similar to Pattern IV minor. Practice playing progressions using this root map in different keys.

RHYTHM GUITAR

Funk Groove #4

In this module you will learn a four-bar rhythm guitar phrase in the key of A Dorian Minor. This part will use the major 6th scale degree of the Dorian mode.

The example has a swung 16th-note subdivision. Follow the rules of pick direction. This four-bar one-chord vamp is played on the top three strings of a Pattern IV A minor chord. It moves from Ami7 to Ami6 to Ami and back to Ami6.

To start, locate the Pattern IV A minor barre chord in 5th position, but play only the top three notes: A, the root, at the 5th fret of the 1st string; E, the 5th, at the 5th fret of the 2nd string; and C, the ♭3rd, at the 5th fret of the 3rd string.

Hold the barre in place throughout the example until the last chord. The movement within the part happens along the 2nd string.

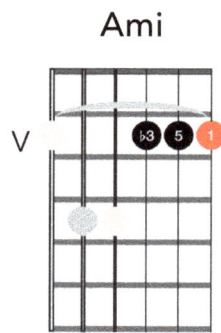

- Start by playing an Ami7 with your 4th finger at the 8th fret of the 2nd string with the 5th fret barre in place.
- Next place your 3rd finger at the 7th fret of the 2nd string. That is F#, the 6th, and it's the major 6th from Dorian. This is an A minor 6 chord.
- To start the second measure, play the three-note Ami chord with the barre only.

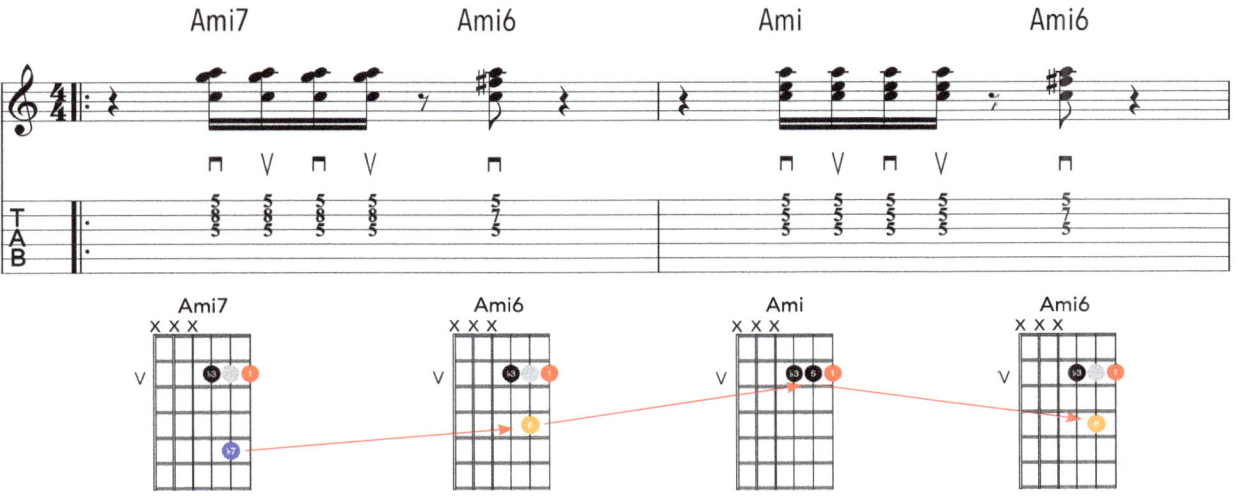

- Next, repeat the Ami 6 chord.
- The third measure is the same as the first measure.

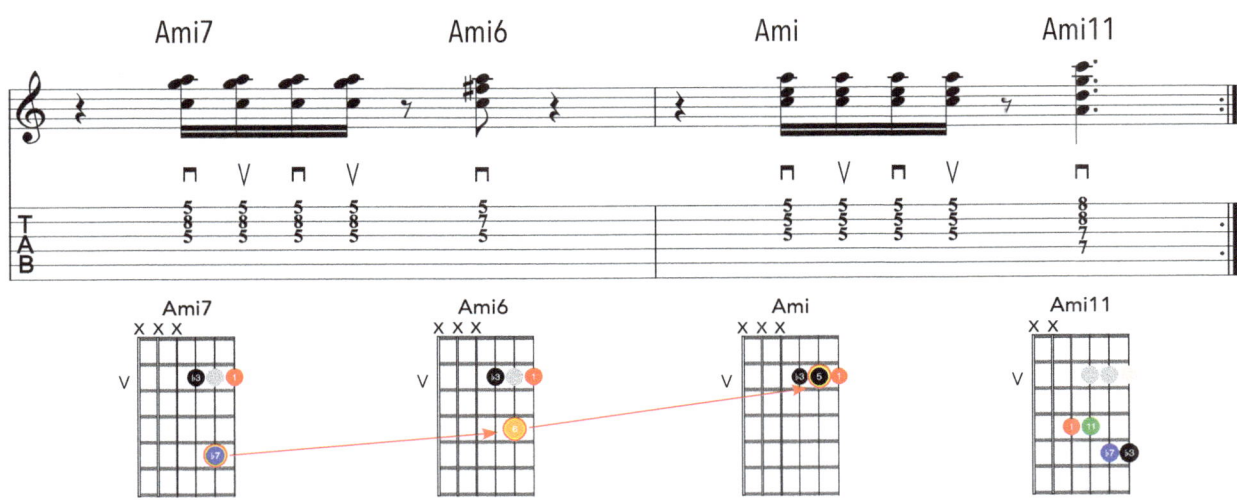

- The fourth measure starts like the second measure but ends with an Ami11.

The Ami11 is a great-sounding chord and easy to play. Reference it to a Pattern IV A minor pentatonic scale. You can finger this a couple of different ways. I suggest you use your 1st finger to play both A on 4th string, 7th fret, and D on the 3rd string, also at the

7th fret. You can use your 2nd, 3rd, or 4th finger to play G on the 2nd string at the 8th fret and C on the 1st string at the 8th fret.

A static A minor chord could be pretty dull but can be made interesting by creating some melodic movement within the voicing. You can easily modify this part by changing the direction of the internal line or using a different rhythm figure. After you learn the written part, I suggest you experiment and find other ways to play it. Keep in mind that repetitive parts are the norm so try to create a repeating pattern that is an actual part. Simple is good!

This a typical Funk part for a minor 7 chord. Log it away for use in other songs in minor keys in the future. On static minor 7 chords, a moving line within the chord voicing can create interest and become a hook for the song.

MONEY MAKERS

In Unit 3 you learned parts that use 4ths from the harmonized major and minor scales. The parts were for strings a 4th apart, and they were written for string set 1 and 2. This unit works with string set 2 and 3. These strings are a 3rd apart. Use the same examples used in Unit 3.

Diatonic 4ths in a Major Key

The first progression is major and is in the key of B♭. This eight-bar progression is very low-key and played at a relatively slow tempo so it's easy to experiment.

Progression in B♭ Major

Review the major scale harmonized in 4ths along the 2nd and 3rd strings you learned in the Fretboard Logic Module.

Diatonic 4ths on the 2nd and 3rd Strings in Major

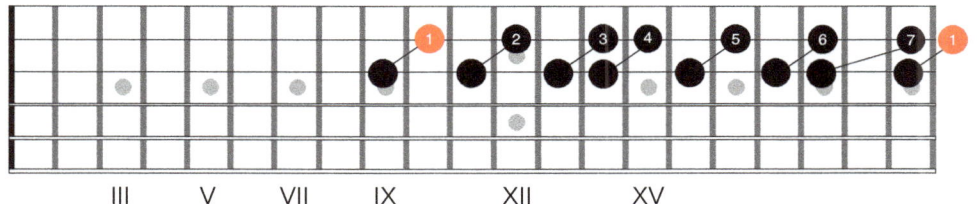

This can be played in any key. Keep in mind that when adjacent strings are harmonized in 4ths, use the higher of the two notes to track the scale.

Here is the part.

Diatonic 4ths in B♭

Again, pay attention to the particular "personality" of 4ths. Test some of your own ideas using these 4ths shapes.

Diatonic 4ths in a Minor Key

Look at the minor progression now. This is the same progression used in the last unit. It is a medium tempo four-bar Rock progression in G minor.

Progression in G Minor

Review the minor scale harmonized in 4ths along the 2nd and 3rd strings you learned in the Fretboard Logic Module.

Diatonic 4ths on the 2nd and 3rd Strings in Minor

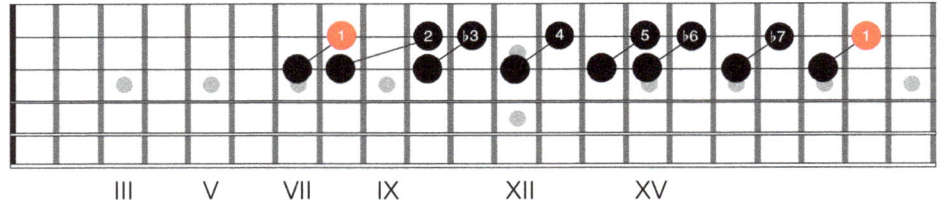

This can be played in any key. Remember, when adjacent strings are harmonized in 4ths, use the higher of the two notes to track the scale.

Here is the part.

Diatonic 4th in G Minor

Again, note the characteristic "personality" of 4ths, now in a minor key. Play around with some of your own ideas using these 4ths shapes. These ideas are transposable to all minor keys!

IMPROVISATION

In the last unit you worked on playing over borrowed chords staying in position. You used pentatonic shells only. In this module you will work on staying in position again but this time expand your note options by using the full seven-note Pattern III major scale and seven-note Pattern III minor scale.

Here is a four-bar chord progression in E major.

Progression in E Major

Analysis of the progression shows that the:

- Ema7 is Ima7.
- Cma7 is ♭VIma7 and borrowed from the parallel E minor scale.
- Ami7 is IVmi7 and borrowed from the parallel E minor scale.
- B7sus is V7 and diatonic in E major.

There are two borrowed chords, but E is still tonic throughout the entire progression. The objective is to stay in position using the Pattern III major and minor scales.

- Over the Ema7 chord, use Pattern III major scale.
- Over the Cma7 and Ami7, stay in position but use the Pattern III minor scale.
- Over the B7sus, go back to the Pattern III E major scale.

Progression in E Major

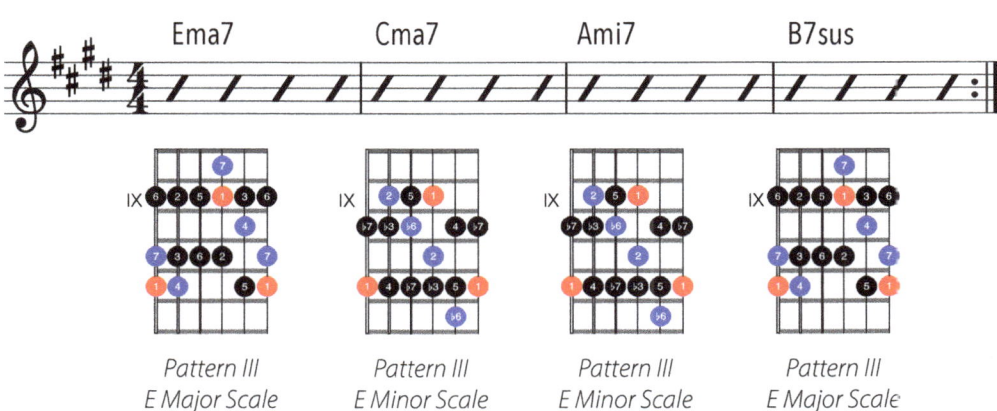

Common Tones

It is always good to know which notes are common to both parallel scales: 1, 2, 4, and 5 are common to both of the parallel seven-note diatonic scales. You can exploit these common tones by playing them on all the chords or use them to pivot in your line.

Common Tones

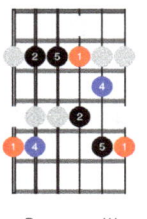
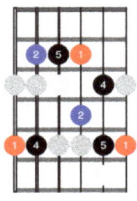

Pattern III *Pattern III*
E Major Scale *E Minor Scale*

Spend a significant amount of time soloing over this using the scales suggested.

Level 4 Unit 4 • Improv Demo

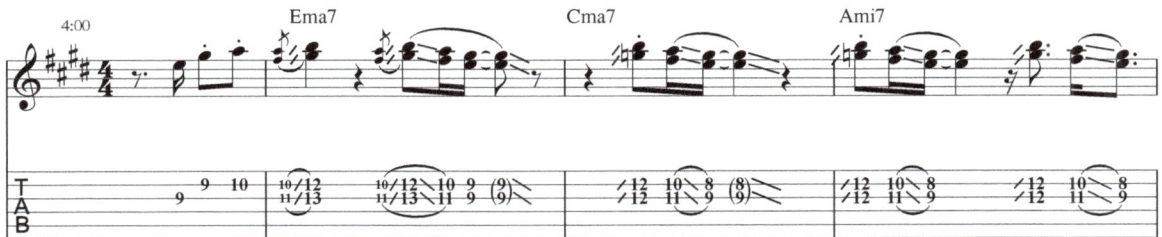

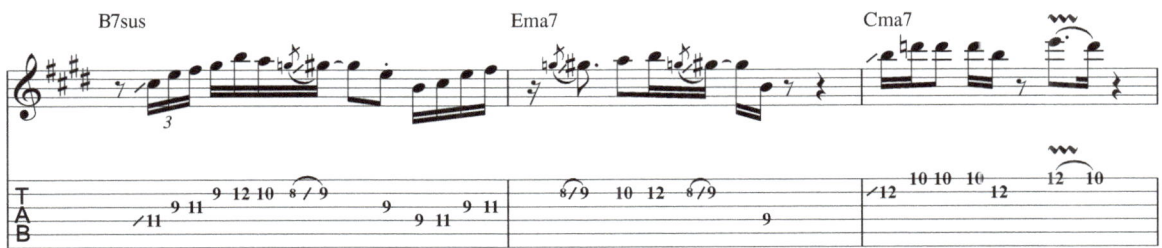

©2021 Fretboard Biology • fretboardbiology.com

PRACTICE

Theory

- ☐ Go to the tabs below the Theory video on the website and complete the quiz.
- ☐ Learn how to analyze chord progressions with 7th chords and modal interchange.

Fretboard Logic

- ☐ Learn Root Map 2 and the associated shell voicings.
- ☐ Learn the major and minor diatonic 4th shapes on string sets that are a 3rd apart.
- ☐ Learn the common tones in the major and minor pentatonic scales.

Rhythm Guitar

- ☐ Practice Funk Groove #4, paying special attention to pick direction.

Money Makers

- ☐ Practice playing major and minor 4th parts over a B♭ major progression.

Improvisation

- ☐ Practice playing solos over an E major progression with modal interchange.

UNIT 5

Learning Modules

> **Theory** - Continue Analyzing 7th Chord Progressions with Modal Interchange

> **Fretboard Logic** - Root Map 3, Root Map 3 Shell Voicings, Root Map Practice Progressions, Major and Minor Scales Harmonized with 5th Shapes, Common Tones in all Major and Minor Pentatonic Scales

> **Rhythm Guitar** - Funk Rhythm Guitar, Funk Groove #5

> **Money Makers** - Money Maker Parts using Diatonic 5th Shapes

> **Improvisation** - Soloing with Modal Interchange

> **Practice** - Continue Practice Routine Development

THEORY

In the last unit you learned how to identify, analyze, and label borrowed 7th chords. Practice your new harmonic analysis skills on a few 7th-chord-based progressions in a few keys. Remember the adjustment to the harmonic analysis process when non-diatonic chords are present. First, analyze and label all the diatonic chords. If there is a non-diatonic chord, look at the parallel minor key to see if it came from there. If so, label it according to the lesson from the last Unit: IImi7(♭5), ♭IIIma7, IVmi7, Vmi7, ♭VIma7 and ♭VII7.

Here are a few progressions to analyze.

Progression in G Major

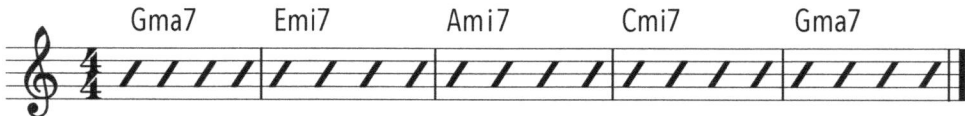

Gma7 is the first and last chord. Assume the progression is in G major and Gma7 is Ima7.

- Emi7 is the diatonic VImi7.
- Ami7 is the diatonic IImi7.
- Cmi7 doesn't belong to G major.
- Check the parallel minor – G minor. Cmi7 is the IVmi7 in G minor.
- Label it IVmi7.

Progression in G Major

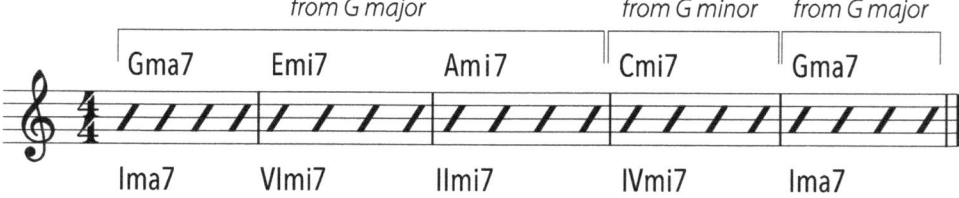

Here is another example:

Progression in E Major

Ema7 is the first and last chord. Assume the progression is in E major and Ema7 is Ima7.
- G#mi7 is the diatonic IIImi7.
- Ama7 is the diatonic IVma7.
- D7 does not belong to E major.
- Check the parallel minor – E minor. D7 is ♭VII7 in E minor. Label it ♭VII7.

Progression in E Major

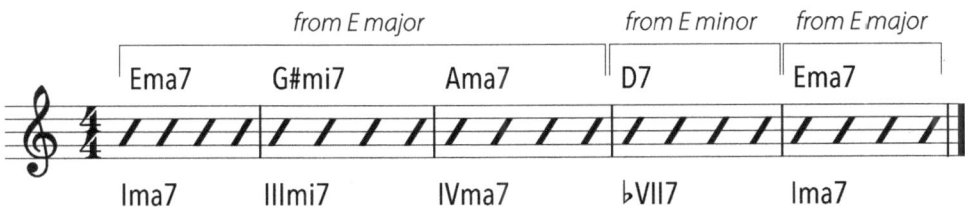

Let's look at another progression.

Progression in D Major

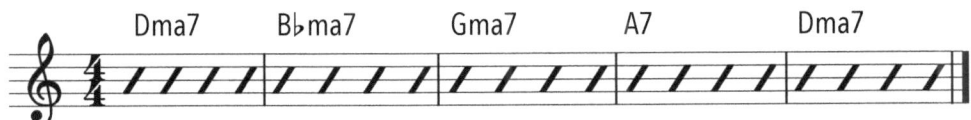

Dma7 is the first and last chord. Assume the progression is in D major and Dma7 is Ima7.
- Skip B♭ma7 – it doesn't fit in D.
- Gma7 is the diatonic IVma7.
- A7 is the diatonic V7.
- Go back to B♭ma7. It doesn't belong to D major.
- Check the parallel minor – D minor. B♭ma7 is ♭VIma7 in D minor. Label it ♭VIma7.

Progression in D Major

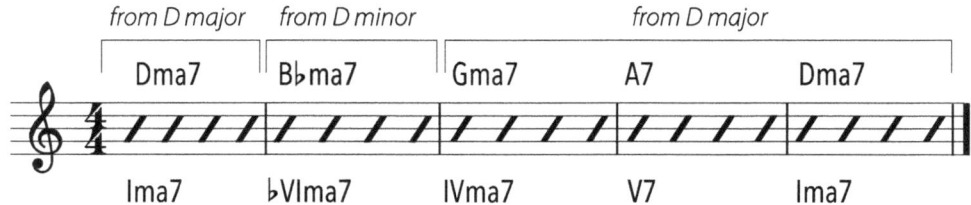

Let's do another.

Progression in C Major

Cma7 is the first and last chord. Assume the progression is in C major and Cma7 is Ima7.

- Ami7 is the diatonic VImi7.
- Fma7 is the diatonic IVma7.
- A♭ma7 doesn't fit. It does not belong to C major.
- Check the parallel minor – C minor. A♭ma7 is ♭VIma7 in C minor. Label it ♭VIma7.
- Gmi7 does not fit. It does not belong to C major.
- Check the parallel minor – C minor. Gmi7 is Vmi7 in C minor. Label it Vmi7.

Progression in C Major

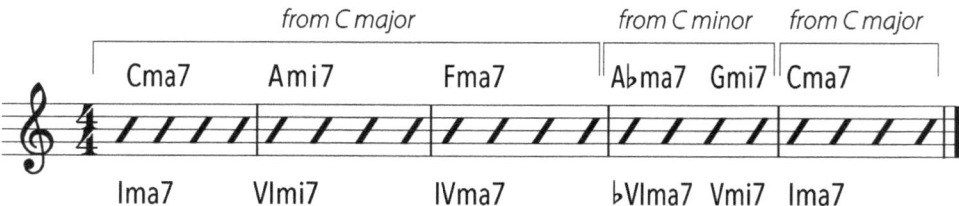

Examine one more progression:

Progression in A Major

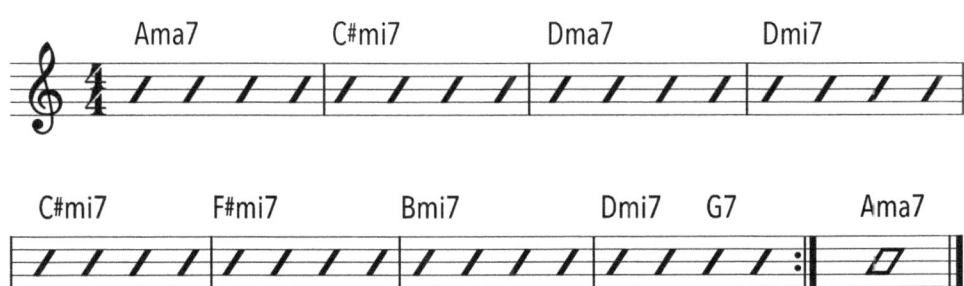

Ama7 is the first and last chord. Assume the progression is in A major and Ama7 is Ima7.

- C#mi7 is the diatonic IIImi7.
- Dma7 is the diatonic IVma7.
- Skip Dmi7 – it does not fit.
- C#mi7 is the diatonic IIImi7 again.
- F#mi7 is the diatonic VImi7 chord.
- Bmi7 is the diatonic IImi7 chord.
- The two Dmi7 chords don't fit. They don't belong to A minor. Check the parallel minor – A minor. Dmi7 is VImi7 in A minor. Label it IVmi7.
- G7 does not fit, either. It does not belong to A major. Check the parallel minor – A minor. G7 is ♭VII7 in A minor. Label it ♭VII7.

Progression in A Major

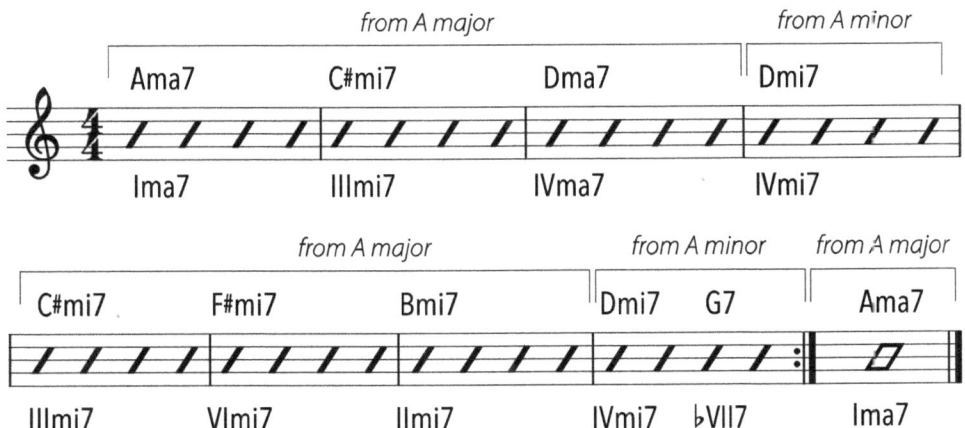

You can now analyze 7th-chord-based progressions with borrowed chords. By understanding modal interchange you've reached another very important point in your study of harmonic analysis.

The major and minor diatonic systems were presented first for a reason. By knowing them well, you can easily recognize chords or notes that don't fit – and therefore you can identify them as non-diatonic. The next step in the process is to learn the various explanations for the non-diatonic notes or chords that appear in songs. The study of modal interchange is the beginning of that gradual process.

You will recall the first exception to diatonic harmony was presented in Level 3. You learned that in a minor key, a Vma or V7 chord can appear in place of the diatonic Vmi or Vmi7. That was one exception to diatonic harmony and now you know another. Modal interchange is probably the most common explanation for non-diatonic chords.

Modal interchange directly affects the notes used when playing solos and the notes used when playing or embellishing chords or writing parts. If a song is in a major key, the note choices come from the major scale of the key.

The next series of Theory modules will discuss inverted chords and how they are notated as slash chords.

FRETBOARD LOGIC

You have learned two root maps that referenced to 6th-string root I chords: One for a major key and one for a minor key. In this module, you will learn the third of four root maps. It's a root map for major keys, referenced to a Ima7 chord shell voicing on the 5th string.

Root Map 3

This is Root Map 3 and it can be moved to any location and therefore, any key on the 5th string.

Root Map 3

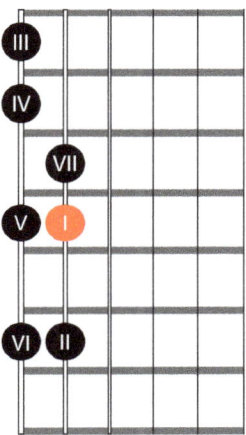

This is essentially the lower part of a Pattern II Major scale shape with the addition of the 3rd and 4th scale degrees on the 6th string below the 5th. Notice the pattern is written with Roman numerals to correspond to the chord built on each scale degree.

Next, here are the shell voicings that are to be played on each root on the root map.

Regardless of the key, the map and associated shell voicing stays the same. It can be moved to the key.

Root Map 3 Shell Voicings

Ima7   *IImi7*   *IIImi7*   *IVma7*

V7   *VImi7*   *VIImi7(♭5)*

Using Root Maps with Barre Chords

Keep in mind that full Pattern IV and II major and minor barre chords can be used with the root maps as well. There is no barre chord for VIImi7(♭5) in major and IImi7(♭5) in minor. This is rarely an issue because these chords are seldom used in triad-based progressions.

Practice this root map and the others with barre chords as well as the shell voicings.

Root Map Exercise

In the progression exercise below, read the chords that are written in only Roman numerals. You may pick any key, go to that location on the fretboard, and play through the progression. Practice this in several keys and keep the tempo slow. Be sure to use both shell voicings and barre chords, and remember that these are for minor keys.

Using Roman numerals I through VII, write your own progressions, too. Pick a key, set your metronome at a slow tempo and play each chord for one measure. The point is to get comfortable with the root map and shell voicings.

Shell Voicing Practice Progressions - Root Map 3

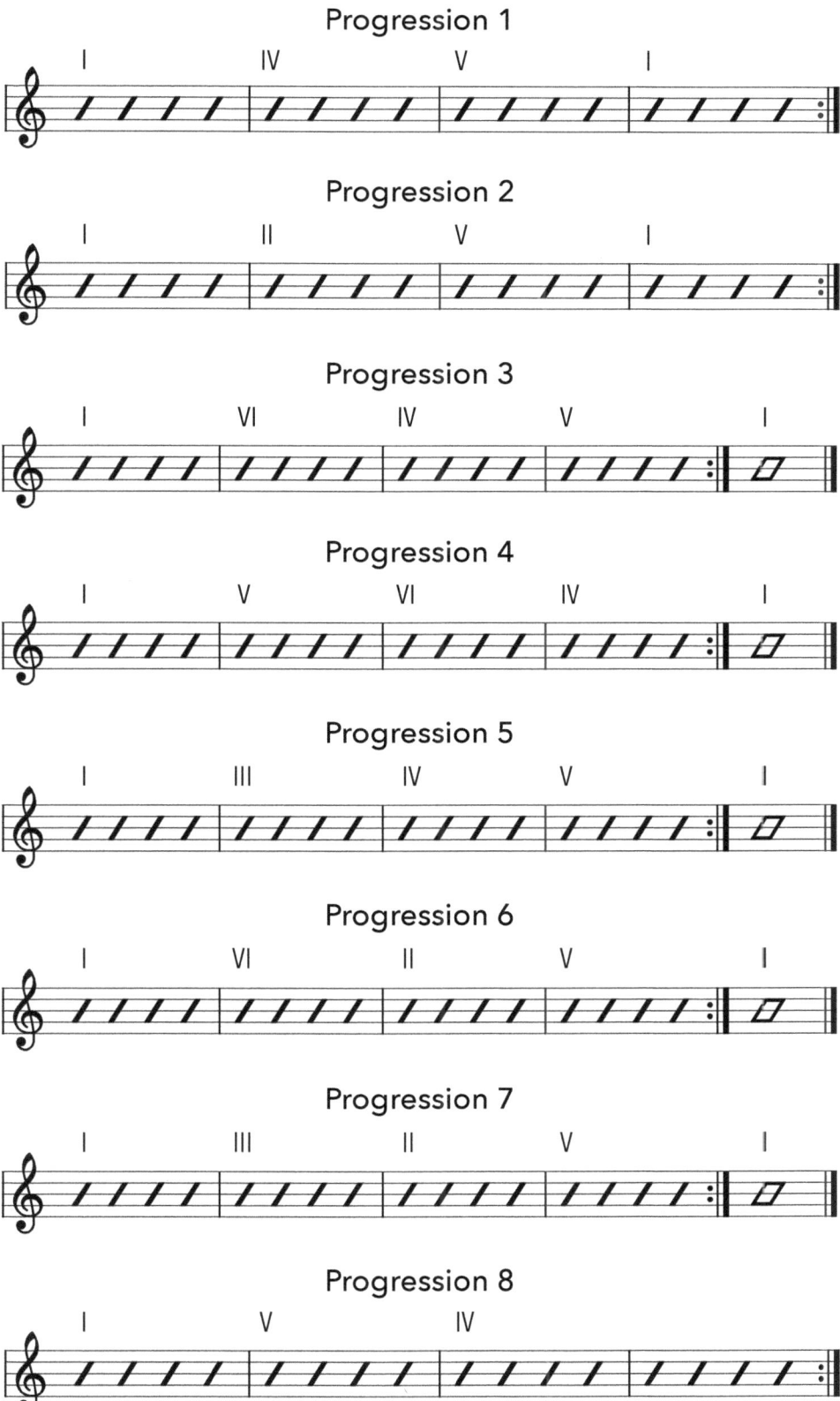

Intervals

You have learned the diatonic 3rd and 4th shapes along adjacent strings as they relate to the diatonic major and minor scales. This module focuses on 5ths.

Diatonic 5th Shapes in Major

For demonstration purposes, start in the key of C major. Consider the notes along the 2nd string as the "scale degrees" starting with C at the 1st fret. Play the C scale along the 2nd string: C, D, E, F, G, A, and B.

C Major Scale on the 2nd String

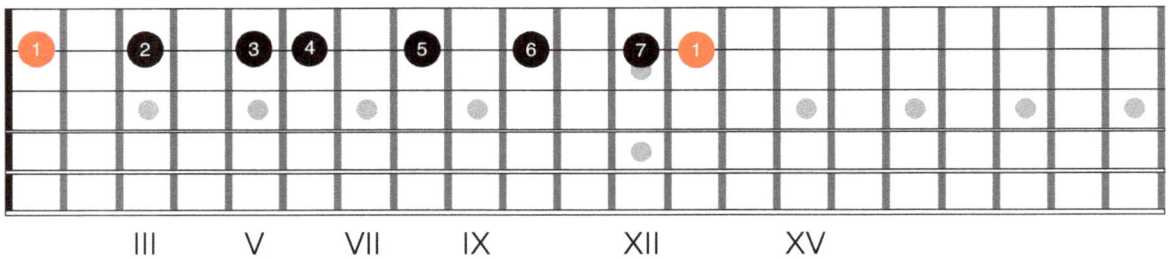

Next, play the note a diatonic 5th higher than each scale degree on the 1st string.

Diatonic 5ths on the 2nd and 1st Strings in Major

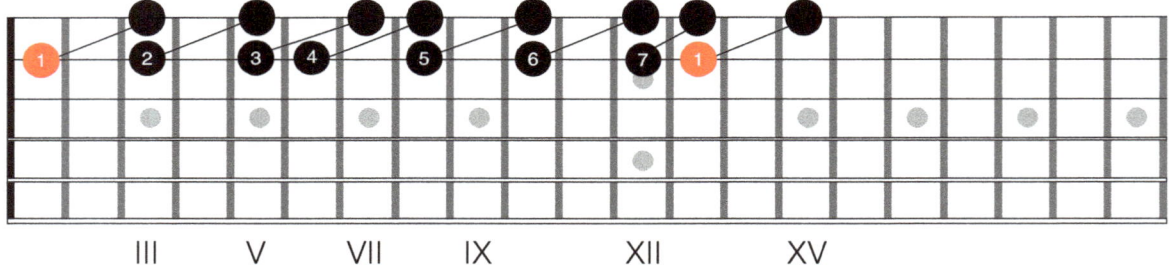

Think of the quality of each chord built on each scale degree to determine whether it should be a perfect or diminished 5th: perfect 5th, perfect 5th, perfect 5th, perfect 5th, perfect 5th, perfect 5th, perfect 5th, and diminished 5th (because the VII is diminished and has a has a diminished 5th). This works for any major key. Track the scale along the 2nd string.

This set of shapes for the major scale works for the strings that are a 4th apart.

- The 2nd and 1st strings.

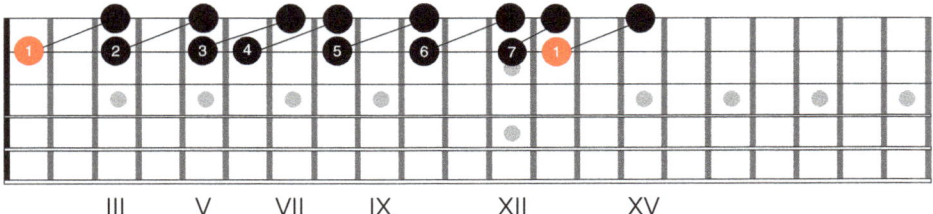

- NOT the 3rd and 2nd strings. They are a 3rd apart.
- The 4th and 3rd strings.

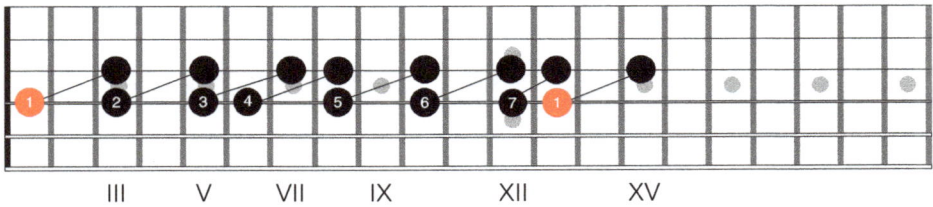

- The 5th and 4th strings.

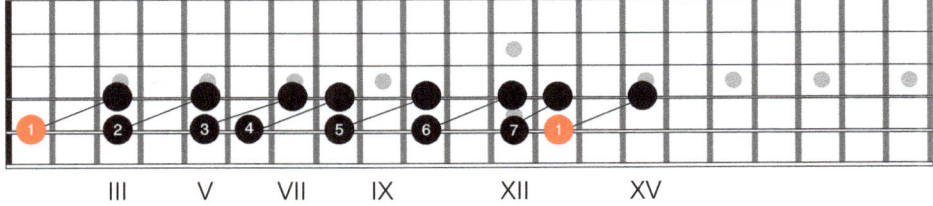

- The 6th and 5th strings.

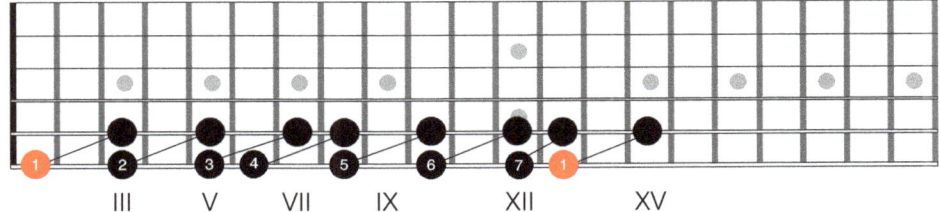

Diatonic 5th Shapes in Minor

Look at the key of C minor. Consider the notes along the 2nd string as the "scale degrees" starting with C at the 1st fret. Play the C minor scale along the 2nd string: C, D, E♭, F, G, A♭, and B♭.

C Minor Scale on the 2nd String

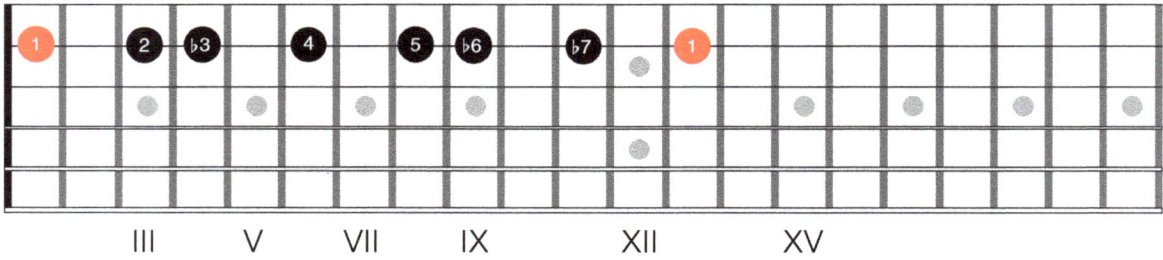

Next, play the note a diatonic 5th higher than each scale degree on the 1st string.

Diatonic 5ths on the 2nd and 1st Strings in Minor

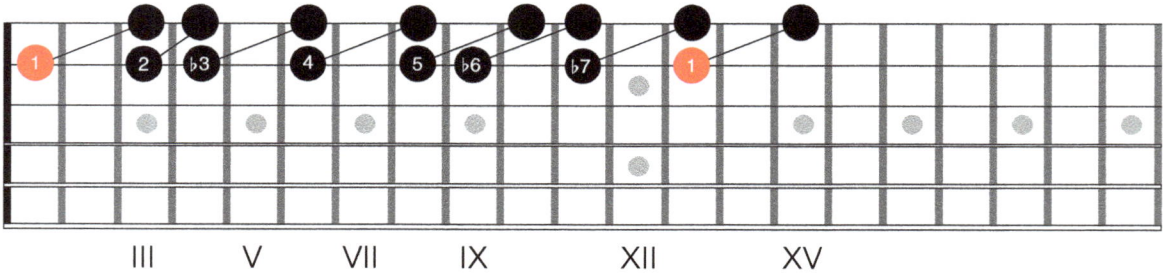

Think of the quality of each chord built on each scale degree to find the correct 5th: perfect 5th, diminished 5th (because the II is diminished and has a diminished 5th), perfect 5th, perfect 5th, perfect 5th, perfect 5th, and perfect 5th. This works for any minor key. Track the scale along the 2nd string.

This set of shapes for the major scale works for the strings that are a 4th apart.

- The 2nd and 1st strings

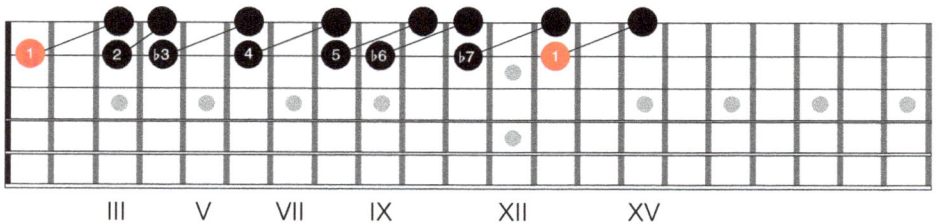

- NOT the 3rd and 2nd strings. They are a 3rd apart.
- The 4th and 3rd strings.

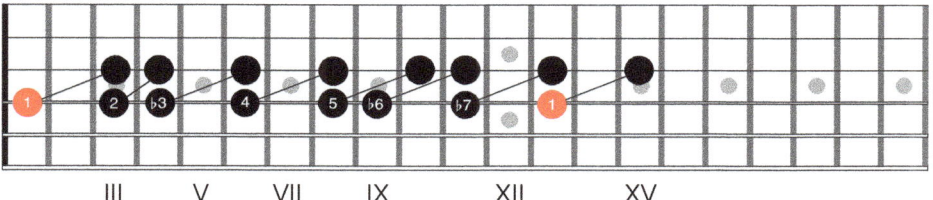

- The 5th and 4th strings.

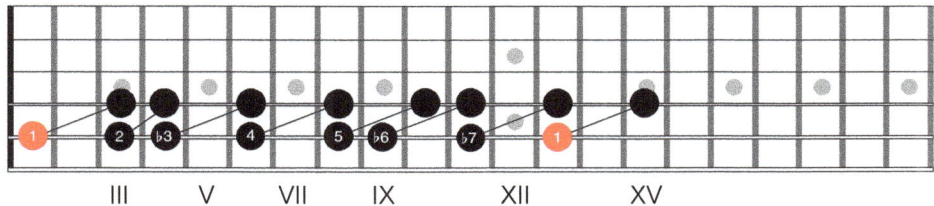

- The 6th and 5th strings

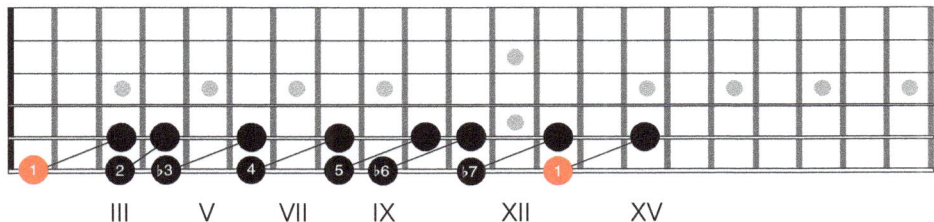

You will put these intervals to work in the Money Maker modules.

Scales

A few modules ago you superimposed Pattern III major pentatonic and Pattern III minor pentatonic. The goal is simple: You need to see the parallel major and minor pentatonic shells in the exact same location; in other words, you need to see them in position. Know the notes that are common to both and which ones are not. The objective in this module is to explore the remaining four octave shapes and how the pentatonic shells for the parallel keys superimpose on each other.

First, review the two side-by-side on the staff again:

Common Tones in Major and Minor Pentatonic Scales

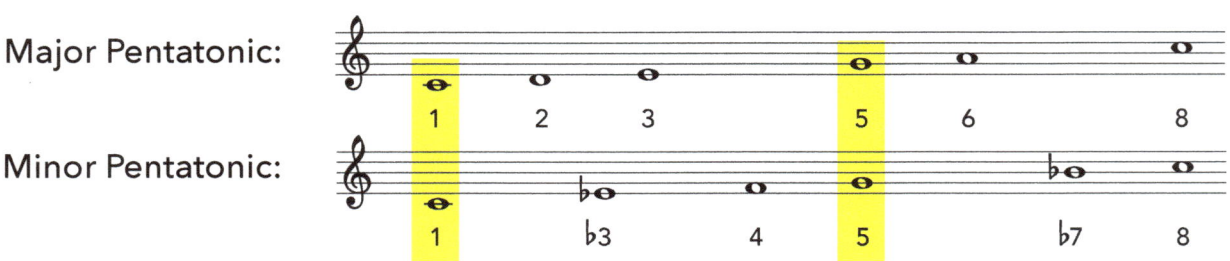

Study the following diagrams that show the parallel pentatonic shells in position, and the common tones.

Pattern I Major Pentatonic

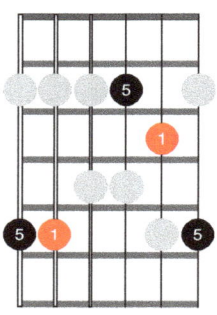

Pattern I Minor Pentatonic

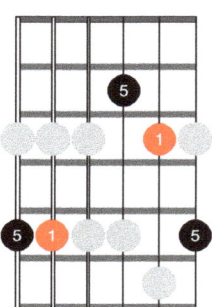

Pattern II Major Pentatonic

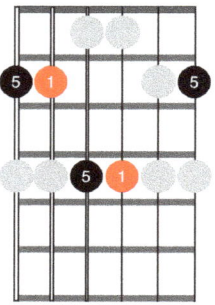

Pattern II Minor Pentatonic

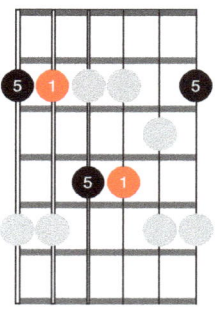

Pattern III Major Pentatonic

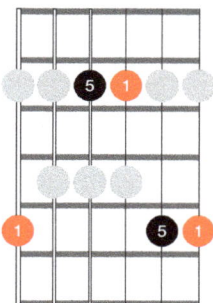

Pattern III Minor Pentatonic

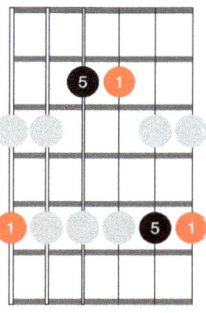

Pattern IV Major Pentatonic

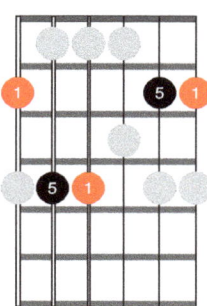

Pattern IV Minor Pentatonic

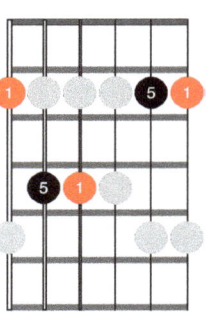

Pattern V Major Pentatonic

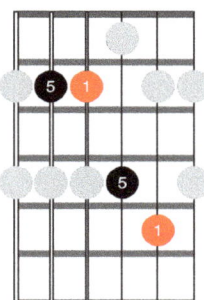

Pattern V Minor Pentatonic

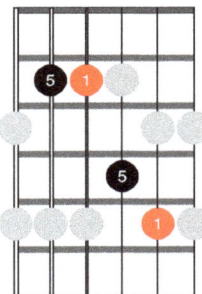

You can exploit the common notes, 1 and 5, of the major and minor pentatonic scales. You can also exploit the notes that are different because they are the notes that define the change from major to minor when soloing.

The best way to learn and retain this information is to use it with backing tracks. You will use this information in the Improvisation module for this unit and in any other progression with modal interchange.

Before you move on, be sure that you know Root Map 3 and practice using it with progressions in different major keys. Know the major and minor scales harmonized in 5ths along string sets 2 and 1, 4 and 3, 5 and 4, and 6 and 5.

RHYTHM GUITAR

Funk Groove #5

The example in this module has two parts. It is a two-bar phrase played over a static D7 chord. The chord part is reminiscent of The Average White Band, and the single note line is reminiscent of LTD. Follow the 16th-note subdivision pick-direction rules.

Part 1

Part 1 starts with a Pattern V D7 shape that is the same as the open D7 you learned earlier in the program.

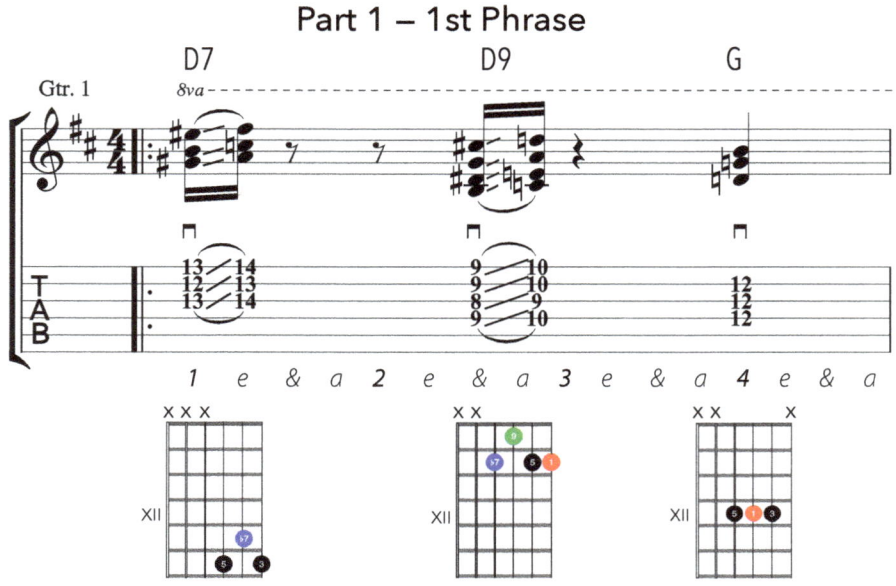

- On beat one, slide from 12th position to 13th position.
- The downbeat of two is a rest, but on the "and" play a D9 voicing you learned back in the Level 1 Blues Rhythm Guitar Modules. It is approached from a half step below with a one-fret slide. Slide from 8th position to 9th position.
- Beat three is a rest.
- On beat four play a G triad barring using either your 3rd or 4th finger.

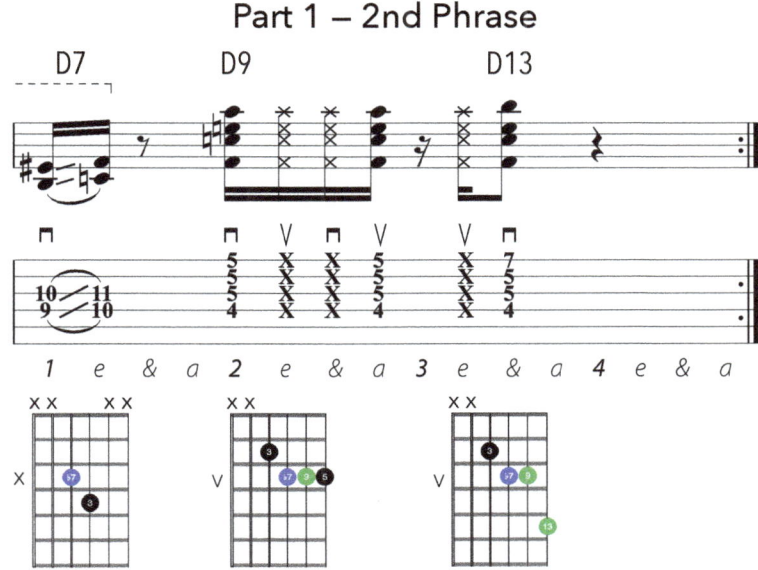

Measure two begins with a classic move.

- On beat one, barre strings 2, 3, and 4 with your 1st finger. Think of this as a Pattern IV Dmi7 chord. Immediately hammer on to the major 3rd, F#, on the 3rd string with your 2nd finger on the second 16th note. The Dmi7 becomes D7.
- On beat two, play D9 on the top four strings in 4th position. Scratch on the second and third 16ths and fret the D9 again on the fourth 16th.
- On beat three, the first 16th is a rest but make the downstroke motion. Scratch on the second 16th and add your 4th finger to the voicing to make it D13 on the "and" of 3.
- Beat four is a rest.

Part 2

Part 2 is popcorn-like but is a more extensive line than most popcorn parts. I suggest you visualize and then play the Pattern II D7 chord or arpeggio to learn this part. The Pattern II D7 chord can clearly be seen in the line.

Part 2 – 1st Phrase

To prepare for beat one, place your 1st finger at the 4th fret of the 4th string on F#. This is the 3rd of D7. To play the part, however, drop your 1st finger one fret to F natural.

- On beat one, play F natural.
- On the second 16th, slide your 1st finger to F#.
- On the third 16th, play the root, D, with your 4th finger at the 7th fret.
- On the fourth 16th, play the ♭7, C natural, with your 2nd finger at the 5th fret of the 3rd string.
- The downbeat of beat two is a rest, but make the downstroke motion.
- On the second 16th, scratch the 6th, B, with your 1st finger at the 4th fret of the 3rd string.
- On the "and" of two, play B, with your 1st finger at the 4th fret of the 3rd string.
- On beat three at the second 16th, play the ♭7, C, with your 2nd finger at the 5th fret of the 3rd string.
- On the "and" of beat three at the fourth 16th, play B, with your 1st finger at the 4th fret of the 3rd string.
- On beat four at the second 16th, play the 5th, A, with your 4th finger at the 7th fret of the fourth string.

Measure two starts like measure one. Beats one and two are the same. The difference is beat three.

Fretboard Biology
Level 4 • Unit 5: Rhythm Guitar
Part 2 – 2nd Phrase

- On beat three, play the 5th, A, with your 4th finger at the 7th fret of the 4th string.
- Beat four is a rest.

A static dominant chord could be pretty dull but it is made interesting by using multiple chord voicings and a more developed popcorn line. You can modify this part by changing or leaving out some of the attacks or changing the direction of the popcorn line.

After you learn this written part, I suggest you experiment with it in other ways. Keep in mind that repetitive parts are the norm so create a repeating pattern that is an actual part. These are typical parts. Log them away for future use in other songs based on dominant chords.

MONEY MAKERS

You learned parts that use 3rds and 4ths from the harmonized major and minor scales. Units 5 and 6 focus on 5ths from both harmonized major and minor keys. This unit addresses the string sets that are a 4th apart and work best on string set 2 and 1. You will learn one example in major and one in minor.

5ths in a Major Key

This is a very mellow and slow track so it's easy to experiment with the shapes. It's an eight-bar progression in the key of E.

Progression in E Major

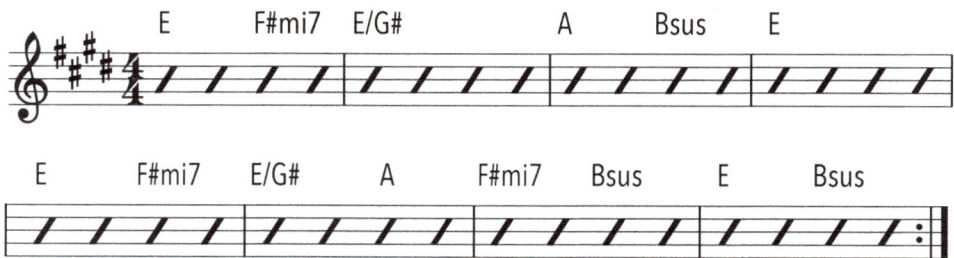

Review the major scale harmonized in 5ths along the 2nd and 1st strings. You just learned this in the Fretboard Logic Module.

Diatonic 5ths on the 2nd and 1st Strings in Major

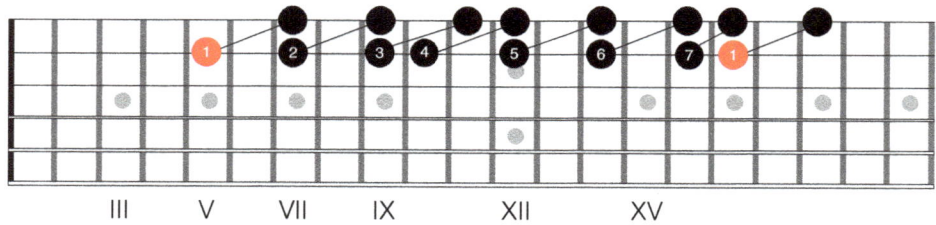

This, like the others, can be played in any key. Remember that when adjacent strings are harmonized in 5ths, use the lower of the two notes to track the scale.

Here is the part.

Diatonic 5ths in E

5ths have a unique "personality". Experiment with some of your own ideas using these 5th shapes, too. This part could be used for string sets 3 and 4, 4 and 5, and 5 and 6, although the lower they are in register, the more unusable they become. Test it for yourself.

5ths in a Minor Key

The next example is in a minor key. This minor progression is an eight-bar Rock shuffle in the key of D minor. Review the minor scale harmonized in 5ths along the 2nd and 1st strings that you learned in the Fretboard Logic Module.

Progression in D Minor

Diatonic 5ths on the 2nd and 1st Strings in Minor

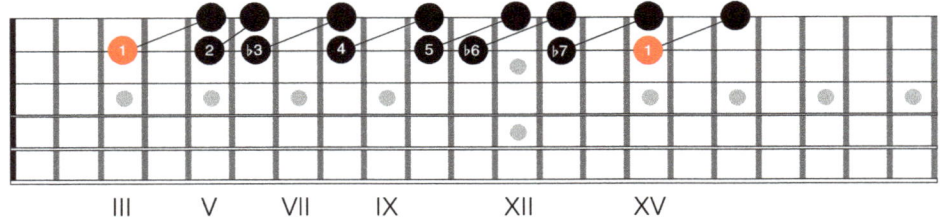

Now here's the part.

Diatonic 5ths in D Minor

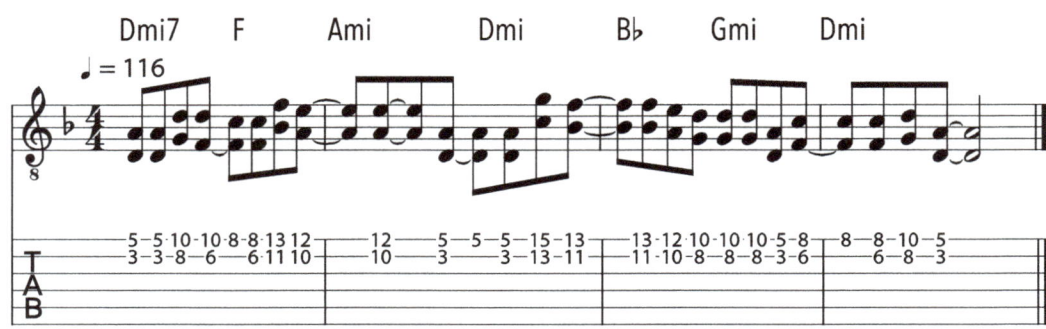

Again, note the "personality" of 5ths in a minor key. Experiment with some of your own ideas using these 5th shapes. This part could also be used for string sets 3 and 4, 4 and 5, and 5 and 6, but as before, the lower they are in register, the more unusable they become.

IMPROVISATION

So far you have been soloing over borrowed chords in the comfort zone of the Pattern III major and Pattern IV minor region on the fretboard. Now it's time to branch out into some other areas of the fretboard that may be a little less familiar.

In the Unit 5 Fretboard Logic Module you explored the other major and parallel minor pentatonic shells in position. Those are Patterns I, II, IV, and V. You learned how they are superimposed on one another. It's really important to know them this way, and to always remember that the notes common to both parallel scales are 1 and 5.

Using what you learned in the Unit 5 Fretboard Logic Module, experiment using all the five major and minor pentatonic shells over this progression.

Here is a four-bar chord progression in C major.

Progression in C Major

Ima   ♭VIIma

The analysis shows that C is the I major chord. B♭ is borrowed from C minor. It's ♭VII. C is the tonic for the entire progression even though the shift is from major to minor.

This goal for this exercise is to work through all five octave shapes, staying in position as you shift from major pentatonic to minor pentatonic. Play a few notes of each scale in each of these octave shapes to start and then improvise a little. Begin in Octave Shape III and then work your way through the others one at a time.

Progression in C Major
(using Pattern III Pentatonic Scales)

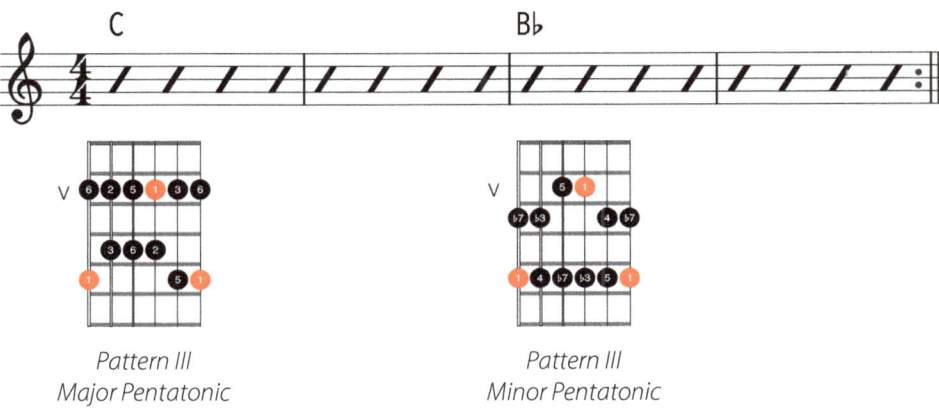

Pattern III   Pattern III
Major Pentatonic   Minor Pentatonic

Progression in C Major
(using Pattern IV Pentatonic Scales)

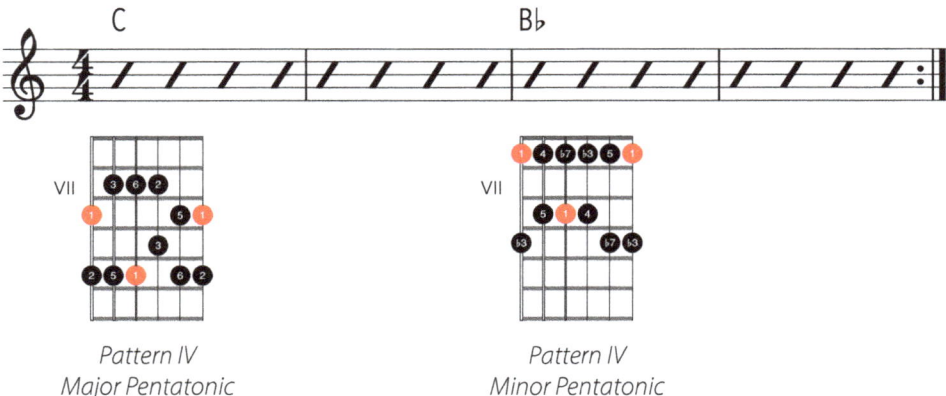

Pattern IV Major Pentatonic • Pattern IV Minor Pentatonic

Progression in C Major
(using Pattern V Pentatonic Scales)

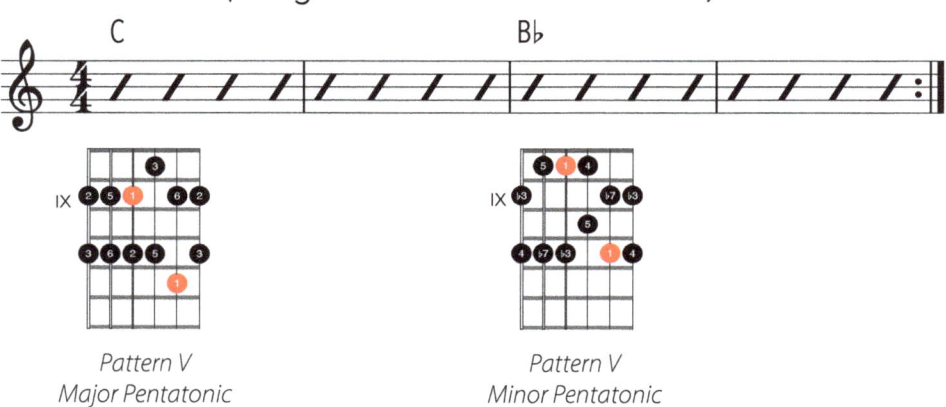

Pattern V Major Pentatonic • Pattern V Minor Pentatonic

Progression in C Major
(using Pattern I Pentatonic Scales)

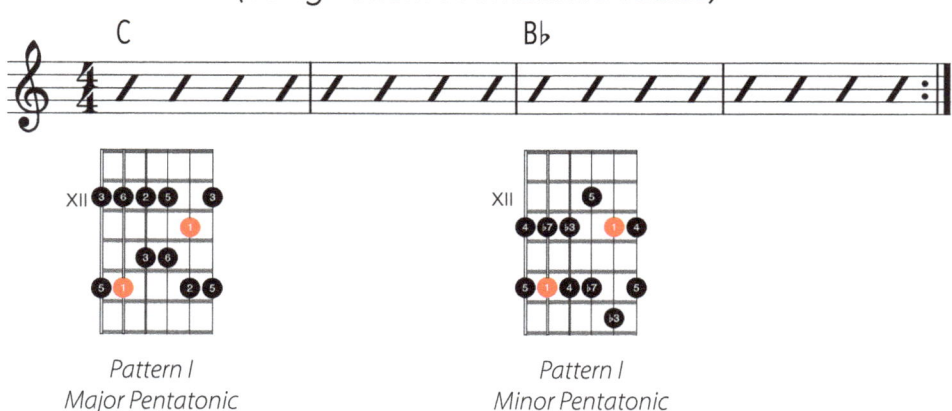

Pattern I Major Pentatonic • Pattern I Minor Pentatonic

Fretboard Biology — Level 4 • Unit 5: Improvisation

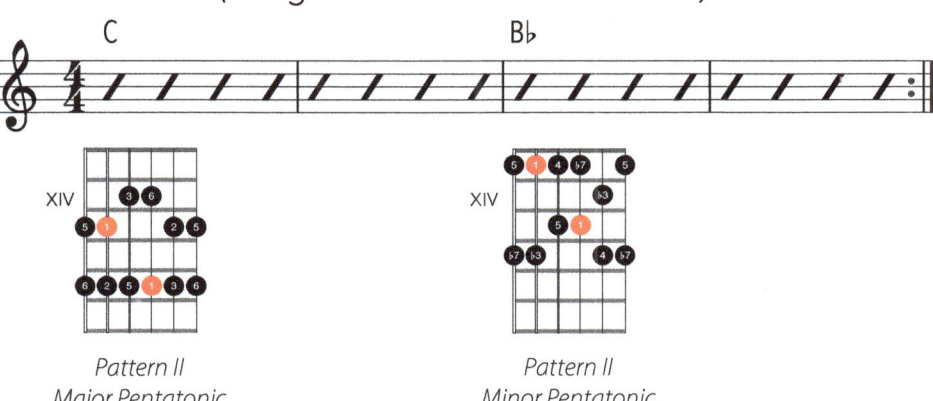

Progression in C Major
(using Pattern II Pentatonic Scales)

Pattern II Major Pentatonic

Pattern II Minor Pentatonic

When you practice this progression, I suggest starting in 5th position in Octave Shape II and shift between Pattern III major pentatonic and Pattern III minor pentatonic. Next move to Pattern IV and repeat the process. Then move to Pattern V, then to Pattern I, and then to Pattern II. When you start feeling comfortable, move through a l of them freely.

Level 4 Unit 5 • Improv Demo

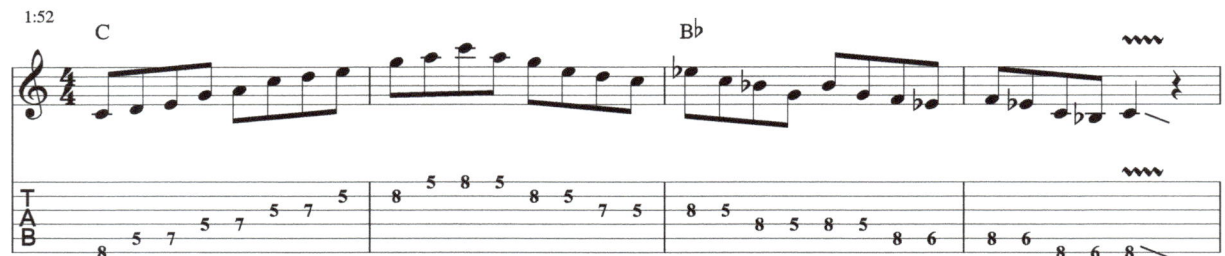

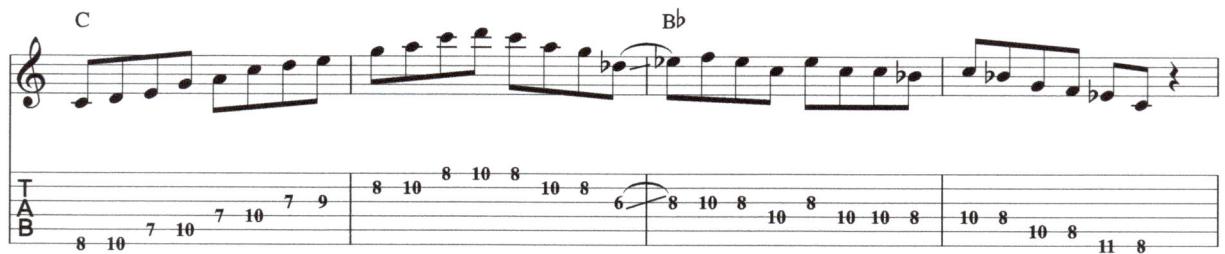

Fretboard Biology
Level 4 • Unit 5: Improvisation
127

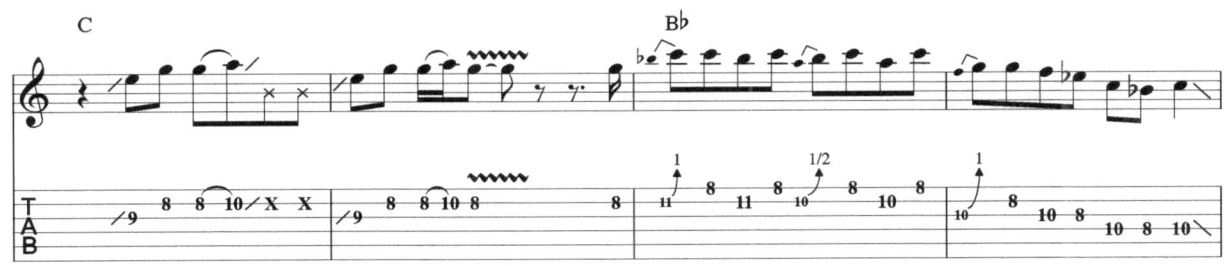

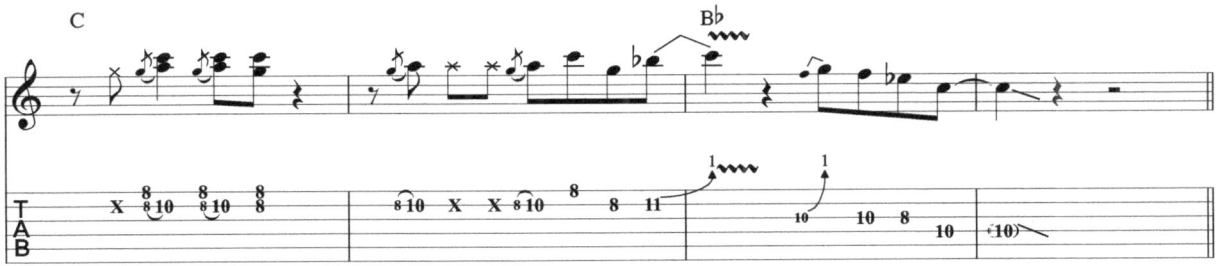

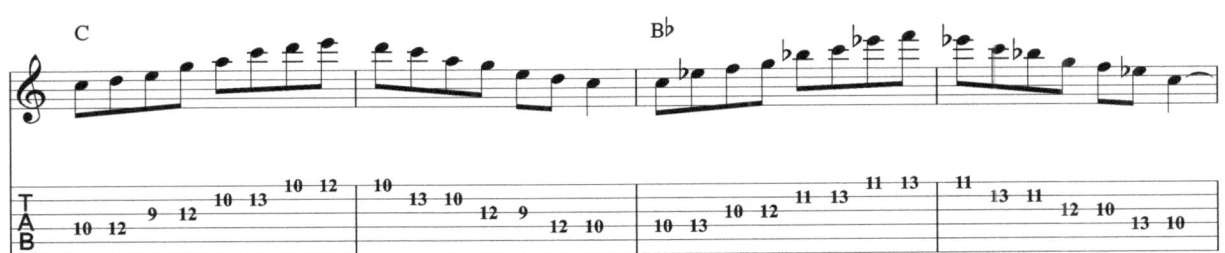

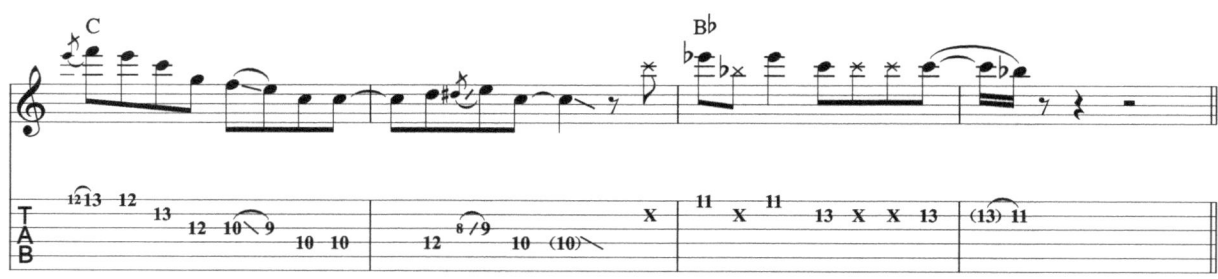
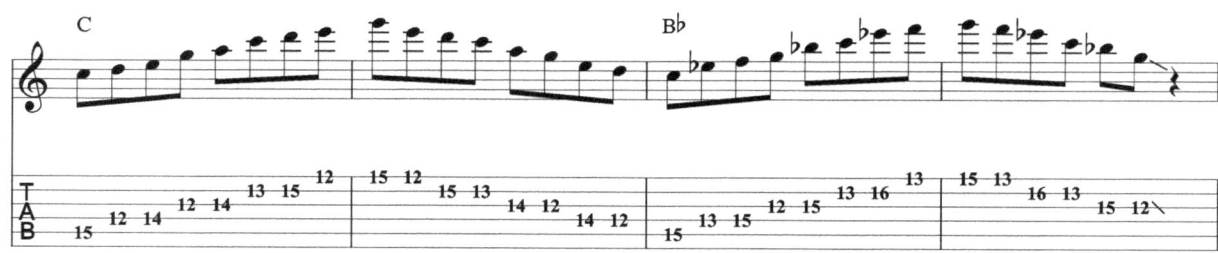
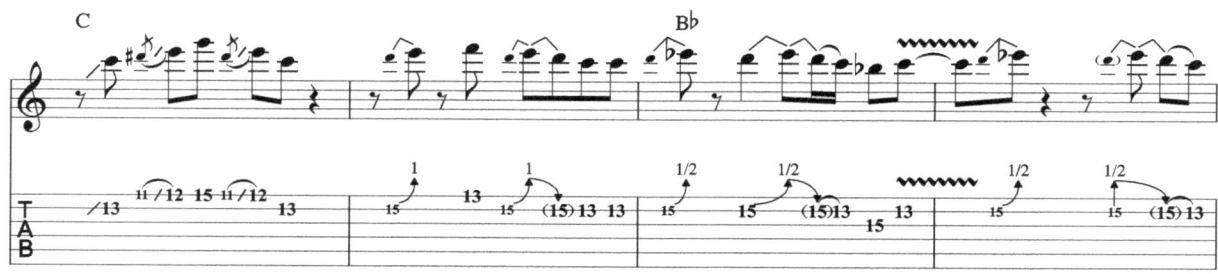
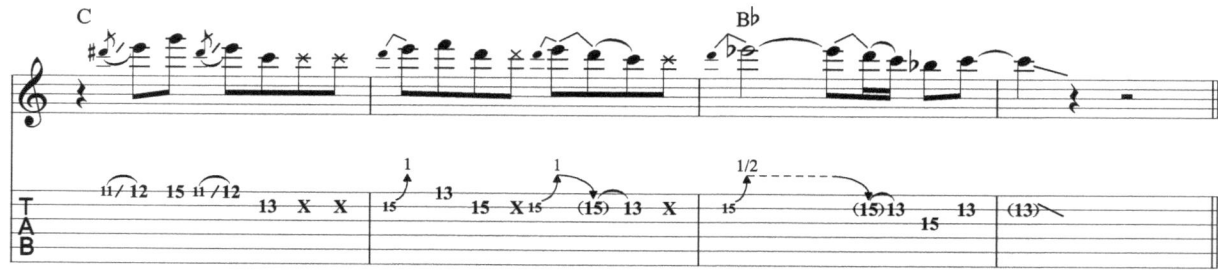

Fretboard Biology
Level 4 • Unit 5: Improvisation
129

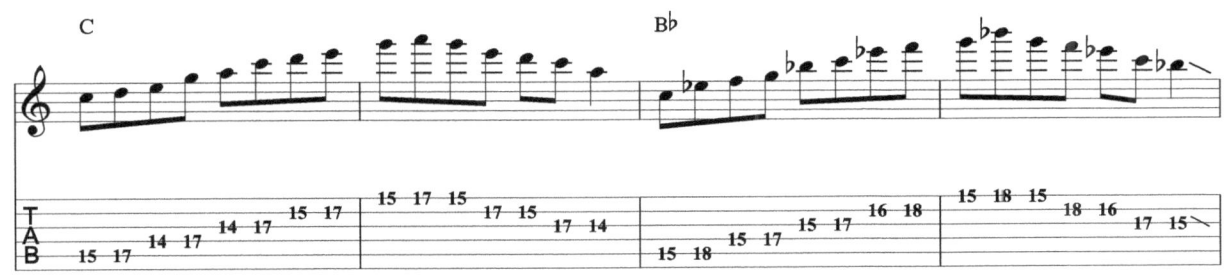
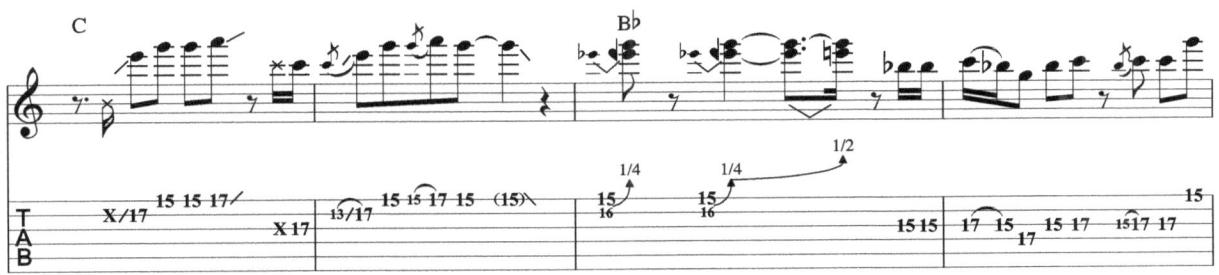
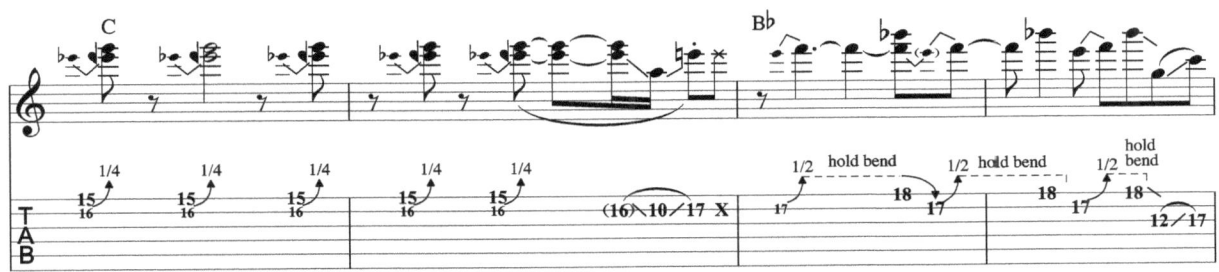
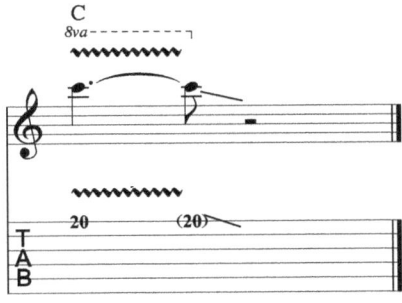

PRACTICE

Theory

- ❏ Go to the tabs below the Theory video on the website and complete the quiz.
- ❏ Practice analyzing chord progressions with 7th chords and modal interchange.

Fretboard Logic

- ❏ Learn Root Map 3 and the associated shell voicings.
- ❏ Learn the major and minor diatonic 5th shapes on string sets that are a 4th apart.
- ❏ Learn the common tones in the major and minor pentatonic scales.

Rhythm Guitar

- ❏ Practice Funk Groove #5, paying special attention to pick direction.

Money Makers

- ❏ Practice playing major and minor 5th parts over major and minor progressions.

Improvisation

- ❏ Practice playing solos over a C major progression with modal interchange.

UNIT 6

Learning Modules

> **Theory** - Inversions, Voicings, Inverted Triads, Open and Closed Voicing, Ensemble chords

> **Fretboard Logic** - Root Map 4, Root Map 4 Shell Voicings, Root Map Practice Progressions, Major and Minor Scales harmonized with 5th Shapes, Common Tones in all Major and Natural Minor Scales

> **Rhythm Guitar** - Classic R&B

> **Money Makers** - Money Maker Parts using Diatonic 5th Shapes

> **Improvisation** - Soloing with Modal Interchange

> **Practice** - Continue Practice Routine Development

THEORY

This unit is about inversions. Triads are built by placing a 3rd and 5th above a root. 7th chords are built by placing 3rd, 5th, and 7th above a root. There are occasions where the lowest note played in a chord is a chord tone that is not the root. When this happens, the chord is said to be inverted and these chords are called "inversions".

Before beginning the discussion, let's review a few important definitions:

Voicing

The exact placement of the notes of a chord on the staff and fretboard.

Closed Voicing

The notes of a chord arranged close together, usually in 3rds stacked above the root, in (musical) alphabetical order. The C triad in closed voicing is voiced C, E, G (which is R-3rd-5th).

Open Voicing

The notes of a chord arranged in any order that is NOT closed voicing. The C triad in open voicing might be voiced C, G, E (which is R-5th-3rd). This requires spreading the chord tones out wider than an octave.

Root Position

A chord voiced with the root as the lowest note.

Inversion

A chord voiced with a note other than the root as the lowest note.

First Inversion

A chord voiced with the 3rd as the lowest note.

Second Inversion

A chord voiced with the 5th as the lowest note.

Third Inversion

A chord voiced with the 7th as the lowest note.

Fingering

The way fingers are arranged on the fretboard to play a chord, scale, or arpeggio.

Let's look deeper into a few of these definitions.

Root Position

When you learn to build chords, you place a 3rd, a 5th, and sometimes a 7th above the root. If the notes of a triad are arranged in order, it's voiced 1-3-5.

The chord tones of the common Pattern IV barre chord are voiced root, 5th, root, 3rd, 5th, root. The root is the lowest note of the voicing. The other chord tones are arranged (or voiced) 1-5-1-3-5-1. A Pattern IV barre chord is in root position because the root is the lowest note but it is not closed voiced because the chord tones are not voiced in order (root, 3rd, 5th). Instead, it is open voiced. Some of the chord tones are played in more than one octave.

You first learn to build chords with the root as the lowest note. This is effective for learning how to build triads and for expanding them to 7th, 9th, 11th, and 13th chords. In practice, most chords are played with the root voiced as the lowest note, if not by the guitar, at least somewhere in the band. Generally, the bass player plays the root, at least on the first beat of each chord. When the root is voiced as the lowest note, the chord is said to be in root position. Here are some root position chords.

Root Position Triads

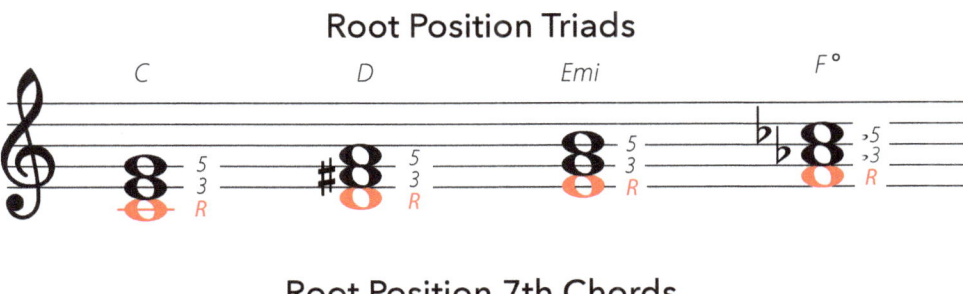

Root Position 7th Chords

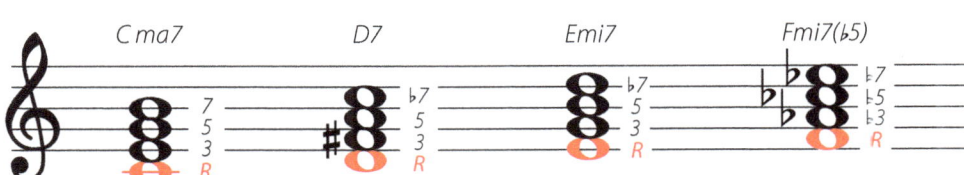

Inversion

When the 3rd, 5th, or 7th is voiced as the lowest note, the chord is said to be inverted or in an inversion.

First Inversion

When a chord has the 3rd voiced as the lowest note it is in "first inversion".

First Inversion Triads

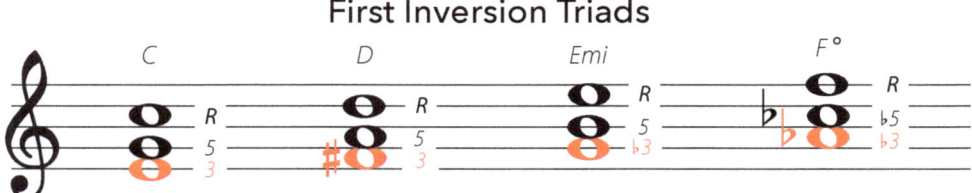

First Inversion 7th Chords

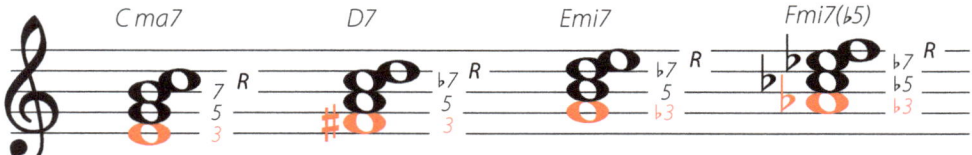

Second Inversion

When a chord has the 5th voiced as the lowest note it is in "second inversion".

Second Inversion Triads

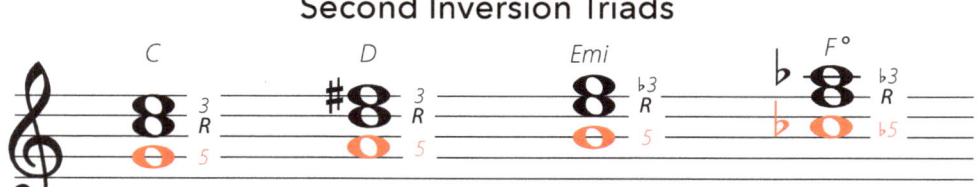

Second Inversion 7th Chords

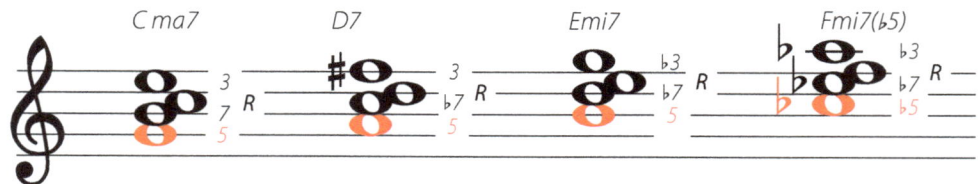

Third Inversion

When a chord has the 7th voiced as the lowest note it is in "third inversion".

Third Inversion 7th Chords

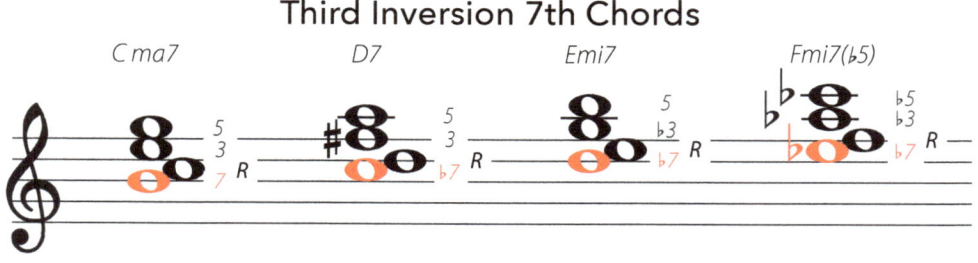

Let's take a look at these inversions side-by-side so you can see how the inversions relate to each other.

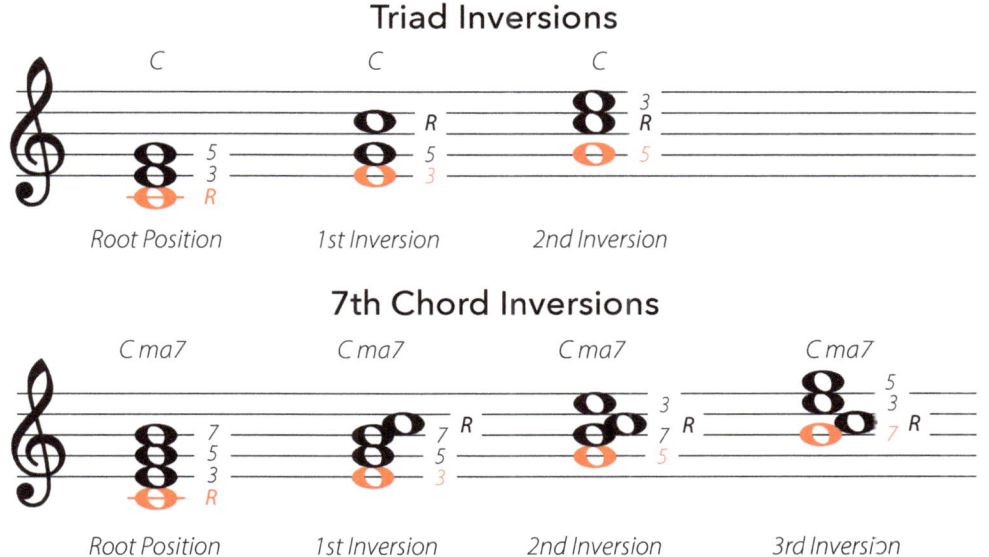

Closed Voicing

As stated earlier, when you first learn to build chords, you arrange the chord tones in 3rds and in alphabetical order above the root, as in A-C-E, B-D-F, C-E-G, etc. When the notes are voiced as close together as possible it is called a closed voicing. As shown in the example, both root-position chords and inversions can be in closed voicing.

Open Voicing

When the notes are not in closed position, meaning they are spread out, as in 1-5-3 or 1-5-7-3, it is called open voicing. Like with closed voicing, open voicings can be in root position or inverted. Notice that even though notes are moved into a different order in open voicings compared to closed voicings, the chord itself remains in either root position, first inversion, second inversion, or third inversion. This is because the lowest note of a chord voicing determines whether the chord is in root position or in an inversion.

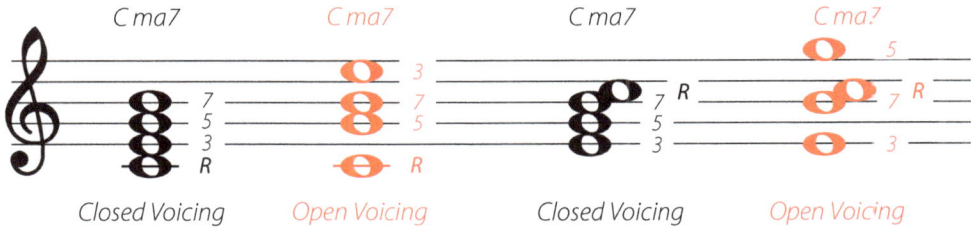

There are several reasons for using inverted chords in a progression. The most common is to facilitate a smoother, more step-wise bass line. That topic was touched on in Level 2 and will be examined further in upcoming modules.

Ensemble Chords

Here is an important point to consider. A listener hears the totality of the harmony when listening to an arrangement. The combination of all the instruments make up the chord. In an orchestra, for example, the string bass section may play the root and the other chord tones are played by the cellos, violins, and other instruments. No single instrument is playing the entire chord but the listener hears a complete chord. The various chord tones are played by different parts of the ensemble.

In a band the same thing often happens. For example, it is common for the bass player to play the root but for the guitar or keyboard the play an inversion on their instrument. The listener still hears the root as the lowest note played in the band because the bass is playing it. In some genres, it's a good idea for chording instruments to avoid the root as the lowest note. This keeps the lower register of the overall sound uncluttered. In some instances, where the bass plays the root, voicing the root again higher in a guitar or keyboard part is avoided because it's considered undesirable. There is no rule for this. It's a matter of taste and stylistic judgment.

It is possible for the guitar or keyboard to voice a chord in an inversion while the bass player plays the root. In this case, the ensemble is root position while some individual instruments are voiced in an inversion. The opposite can happen, too. Often, for the sake of creating a smooth and step-wise bass line, the bass may play a chord tone other than the root while the instruments above, guitar and/or keyboard, play in root position. In these cases, it is normal for the higher instruments to avoid voicing a root within a 5th of the bass note. This keeps the lower register uncluttered because when two or more notes are played together in a low register, the sound is pretty muddy. No matter whether the chord voicings played by individual instruments are in root position or an inversion, the bass determines whether the ensemble is in root position or in an inversion.

The fact that a chord is inverted does not affect the note choices when soloing. If an inversion is made up of all diatonic notes, the source of notes for soling over it is still the key. If an inversion is from a borrowed chord, the source of notes for soling over it is the parallel key scale. There will be much more on topic this as you move through the program.

FRETBOARD LOGIC

You have learned three root maps so far. In this module you will learn the fourth: a root map for minor keys, referenced to a IImi7 chord shell voicing on the 5th string.

Root Map 4

This is Root Map 4 and it can be moved to any location and therefore any key on the 5th string.

Root Map 4

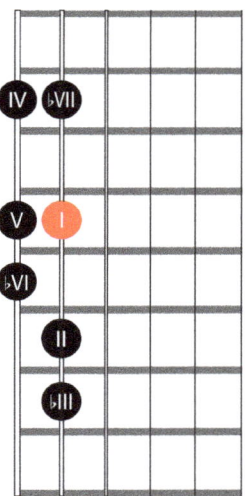

This is basically the lower part of a Pattern II Minor scale shape with the addition of the ♭7 and 4th scale degrees on the 6th and 5th strings. Like the other root maps, the pattern is written with Roman numerals to correspond to the chords built on each scale degree.

Next, here are the shell voicings that are to be played with each root on the root map.

Root Map 4 Shell Voicings

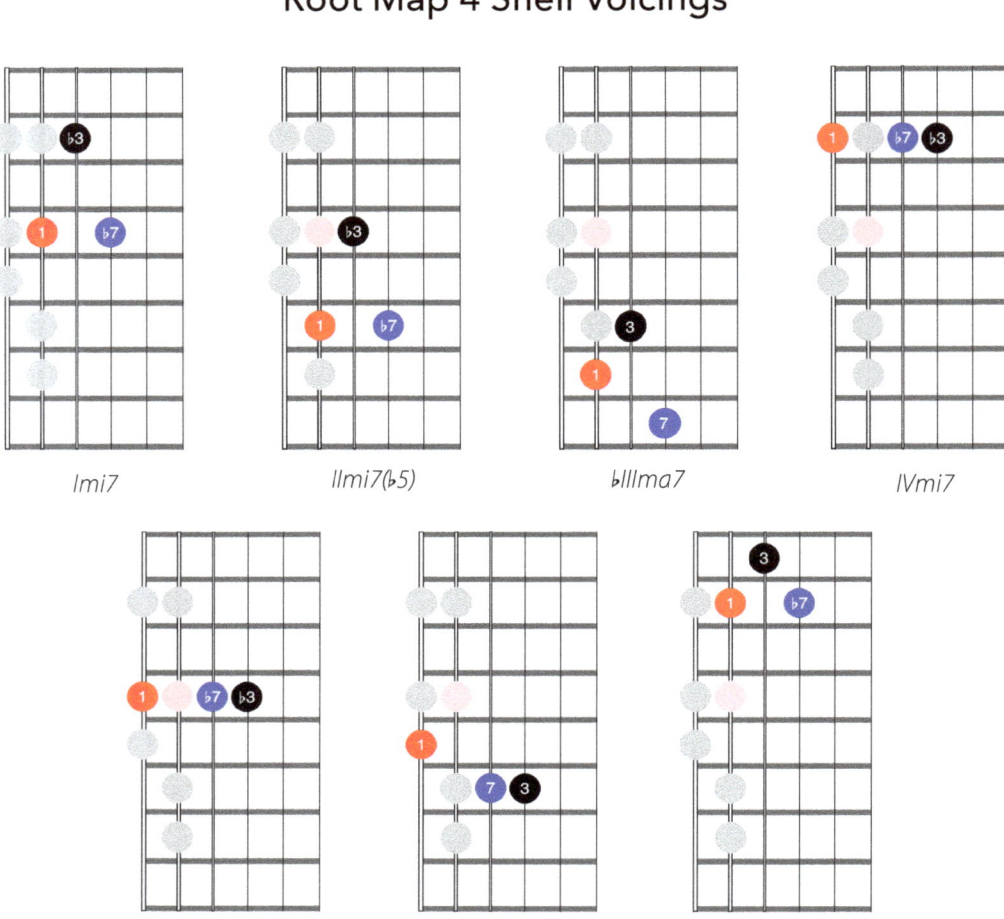

Regardless of the key, the map and associated shell voicings stay the same. Just move it to the key where you want to play.

Root Map Exercise

In the progression exercise below, read the chords that are written in Roman numerals only. You can pick any key, go to that location on the fretboard, and play through the progression. Practice this in several keys and keep the tempo slow. Be sure to use both shell voicings and barre chords, and remember that these are in a minor key.

Shell Voicing Practice Progressions - Root Map 4

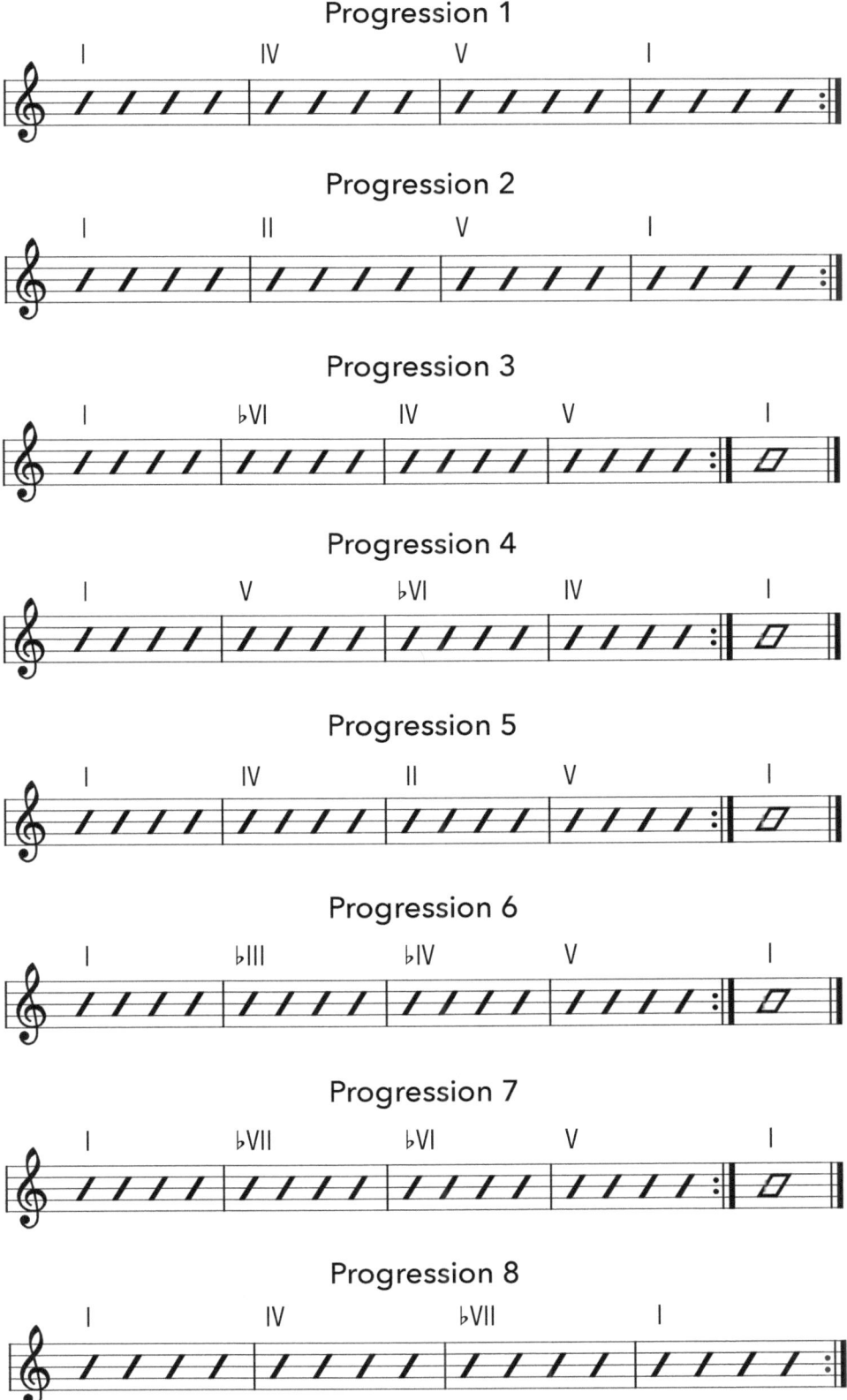

Using Roman numerals I through VII, write your own progressions, too. Pick a key, set your metronome at a slow tempo and play each chord for one measure. The point is to get comfortable with the root map and shell voicings.

Intervals

In the last unit you learned the major and minor scales harmonized in 5ths along string sets 2 and 1, 4 and 3, 5 and 4, and 6 and 5. In this module you will learn the major and minor scales harmonized in 5ths along the 3rd and 2nd strings.

Diatonic 5th Shapes in Major

For demonstration purposes, start in the key of A major. Consider the notes along the 3rd string as the "scale degrees" starting with A at the 2nd fret. Play the A scale along the 3rd string: A, B, C#, D, E, F#, G#, and A.

A Major Scale on the 3rd String

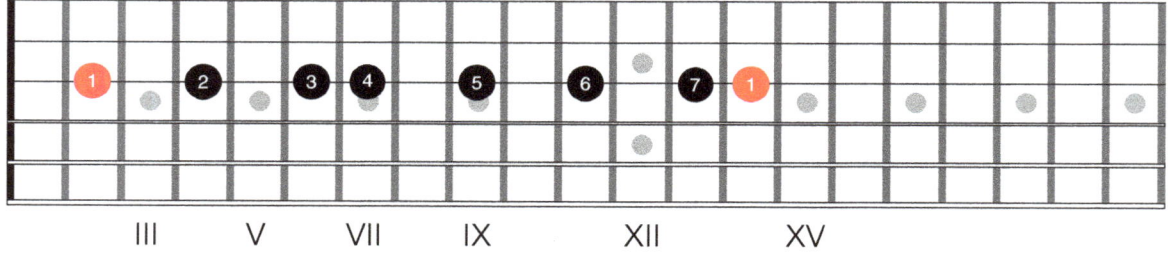

Next, add the note a diatonic 5th higher than each scale degree on the 2nd string.

Diatonic 5ths on the 3rd and 2nd Strings in Major

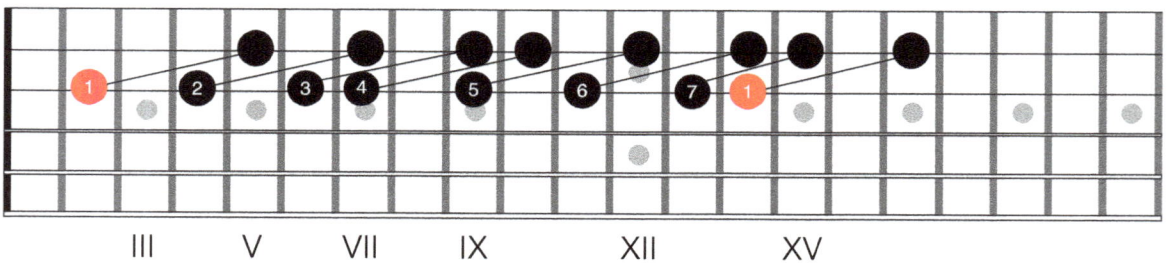

Think of the quality of each chord built on each scale degree to determine whether it's a perfect or diminished 5th: perfect 5th, perfect 5th, perfect 5th, perfect 5th, perfect 5th, perfect 5th, perfect 5th, diminished 5th (because the VII is diminished and has a diminished 5th). This works for any major key. Track the scale along the 3rd string.

Diatonic 5th Shapes in Minor

Consider the notes along the 3rd string as the "scale degrees" starting with A at the 2nd fret. Play the A minor scale along the 3rd string: A, B, C, D, E, F, G, A.

A Minor Scale on the 3rd String

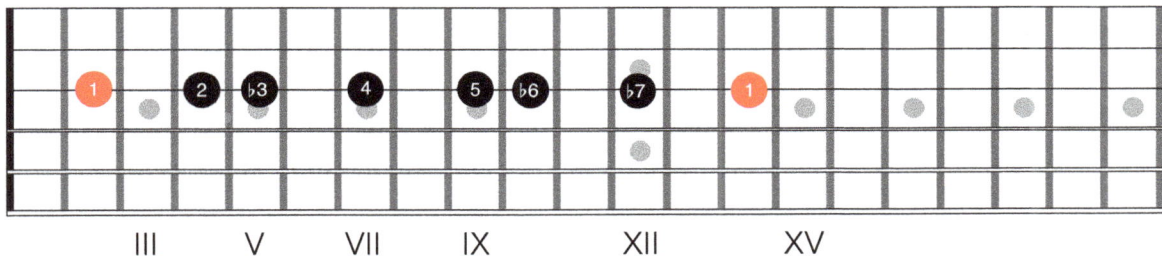

Next, play the note a diatonic 5th higher than each scale degree on the 2nd string.

Diatonic 5ths on the 3rd and 2nd Strings in Minor

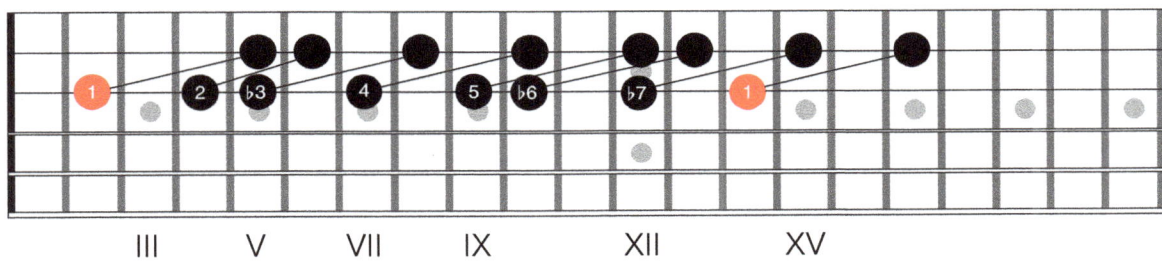

Think of the quality of each chord built on each scale degree to find the correct 5th: perfect 5th, diminished 5th (because the II is diminished and has a diminished 5th), perfect 5th, perfect 5th, perfect 5th, perfect 5th, and perfect 5th. This works for any minor key. Track the scale along the 3rd string.

These interval shapes will be used in the Money Maker modules.

Scales

You soloed over progressions that shift between parallel major and minor. A few modules ago you superimposed Pattern III major and minor scales and the goal was simple – you need to see the parallel major and minor scales in the exact same location.

First, let's review them side-by-side again on the staff.

Common Tones in Major and Natural Minor Scales

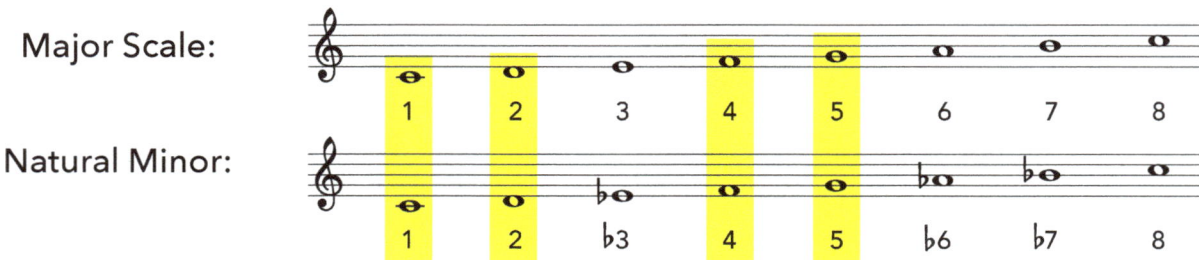

The common notes are 1, 2, 4, and 5. You can exploit these as common tones. The notes that are different are your opportunity to define the change from major to minor when soloing. Study them and know them. Use this information in the Improvisation module for this unit.

Study the following diagrams that show how parallel major and minor scales superimpose on each other.

Pattern I Major Scale

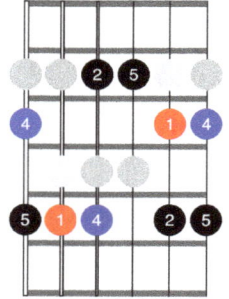

Pattern I Minor Scale

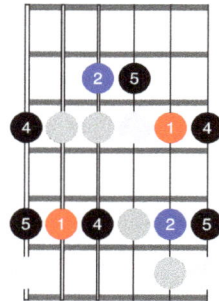

Pattern II Major Scale

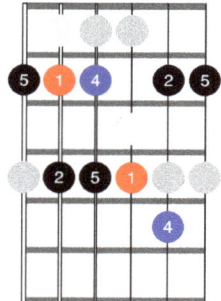

Pattern II Minor Scale

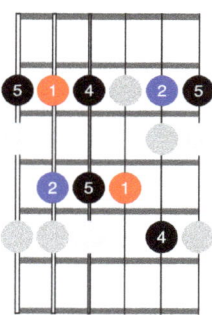

Fretboard Biology
Level 4 • Unit 6: Fretboard Logic

Pattern III Major Scale
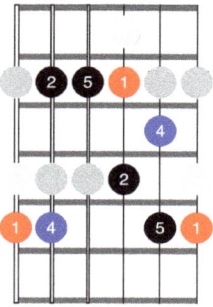

Pattern III Minor Scale
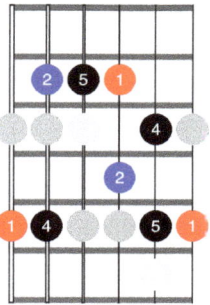

Pattern IV Major Scale
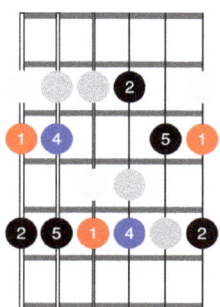

Pattern IV Minor Scale
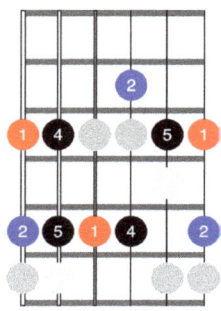

Pattern V Major Scale
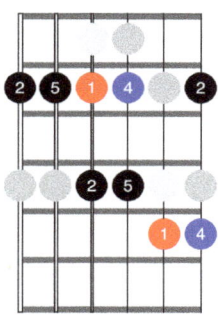

Pattern V Minor Scale
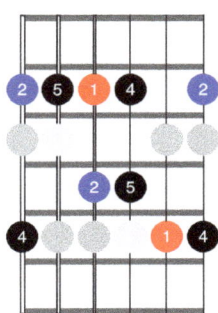

The best way to learn and retain this information is to use it with backing tracks. Use this information in the Improvisation module for this unit and in any other progression with modal interchange.

Before moving on, be sure you know Root Map 4 and practice using it with progressions in different major keys. Also, know the major and minor scales harmonized in 5ths along string set 3 and 2.

RHYTHM GUITAR

Classic R&B

The next series of units will discuss Classic R&B rhythm guitar. R&B stands for Rhythm and Blues, and from the 1940s up to today the style has evolved, as has the sound. The label "R&B" is defined in several ways depending on the range of genres and eras you wish to include. The term R&B has been used as a catch-all term for a variety of styles developed by African Americans and has been applied to Blues, Electric Blues, Rock & Roll, Soul, Gospel, and Funk. In this unit we will remove Blues, Rock & Roll, Funk, and what is sometimes called "Contemporary R&B", and focus on the "Classic R&B" guitar parts that might be played in the music of James Brown, Wilson Picket, and Sam & Dave, and by guitarists such as Steve Cropper.

The focus will be on the guitar parts that were typical in the 1960s and '70s. You will notice there are bits and pieces of chord and interval information in Classic R&B that also appear in Blues and Country. That is because Blues is at the heart of most American Pop styles from Jazz to Rock to Country to R&B to Funk. Like Blues, Jazz, and Rock & Roll, R&B was developed by African Americans but quickly gained popularity across racial lines.

Remember that all of these Rhythm Guitar modules are intended to introduce you to the basic rhythm parts in a particular genre. We are not starting with complicated parts. There are a lot of flashy rhythm guitar parts out there that you will want to learn, but those will be easier once you have a solid understanding of fundamental rhythm guitar in each style.

The rhythm sections on the classic recordings were very strong and the drum and bass parts defined the grooves. Generally, piano and/or Hammond B3 organ established the harmonic pad and the guitars played repetitive percussion-like and/or moving chordal parts. The harmony was often triad-based, but dominant 7th or dominant 9th chords were also prevalent. Sometimes 6th chords were used in certain contexts. The parts presented in this unit are reasonable facsimiles from some standard classic R&B songs.

Chip Parts

In this module you will learn to play what we will call "chips". These are a simple kind of part where the guitar plays on beats two and four. The guitar is used in a percussive way to double and reinforce the snare drum on the back beat. The goal is to lock with the snare drum making your guitar and the snare sound like one crisp snap. There are a variety of ways to embellish the 2 & 4 chip but first, focus on playing the basic part cleanly and in time.

When playing chips, your sound needs to be crisp but not painful to the listener, so make your pickup selection and amp sound accordingly. The part will naturally cut because the chip is played in the top three or four strings with a sharp and short attack. The chip can be played with either downstrokes or upstrokes. Experiment with both techniques. Upstrokes will generally make the higher strings more pronounced because you are striking them first. It is also important to experiment with the size of the "footprint" of each attack, ranging from very short to a full 8th-note value. A small footprint would be very short and sharp. There will be some new chord voicings in these examples to add to your chord vocabulary. The focus in each of these examples is on the top three or four strings. The 5th and 6th strings don't lend themselves to the crisp sharp sound you need.

Example 1

The first example is a common vamp moving from I7 to IV7 in the key of E. For I7, use an E9 chord. Because of the time that elapses between attacks, it is very easy to rush (or drag) and play out of sync with the snare. To avoid that, I often subdivide with quarter notes or 8th notes by bouncing or moving my picking hand on the "in between" quarter or 8th notes to make it easier to stay locked. Of course, don't make any contact with the strings with these extra movements. Often you can key on the hi-hat which might be playing 8th notes.

Progression in E Major

Example 2

The next example is in C minor moving from Imi7 to ♭VI7. Use a Cmi7 for Imi7 and an A♭9 for ♭VI7. And remember the same thing on this one – try subdividing with some picking-hand movement without striking the strings.

Progression in C Minor

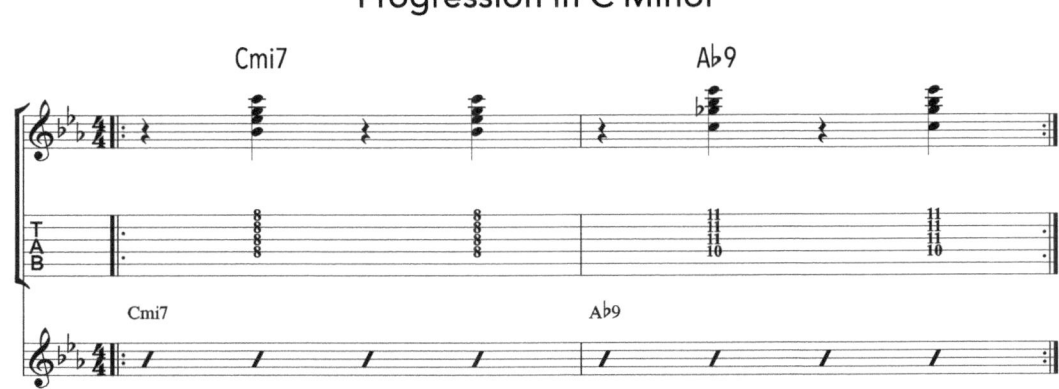

Example 3

The next example is in G and moves from Ima to IIIma to IVma to IIma. Use the top four strings of a Pattern IV major triad for all four chords. And remember the same thing on this one: Try subdividing with some picking-hand movement without striking the strings.

Progression in G Major

12/8 Time

Many R&B ballads are felt (and sometimes written) in 12/8 time. 12/8 feel can be written in 4/4 but subdivided by 8th-note triplets or written in 12/8 with a strong pulse on beats one, four, seven, and ten. Nobody thinks of it in terms of one, four, seven, and ten, though. "1-2-3-4" is the normal count-off regardless of whether it is written in 12/8 or 4/4. The chips are played on two and four if written in 4/4. Subdividing with some picking-hand movement without striking the strings helps keep you in time.

Keep what you have learned in this module as part of your permanent vocabulary. Remember that R&B guitar parts are generally repetitive and are an important part of the total rhythm section sound. Chips are a guitar part normally played on beats two and four and should lock with the snare drum back beat. Chips are usually played on the top three or four strings and can be played with a downstroke or upstroke.

MONEY MAKERS

In Unit 5 you learned parts that use 5ths from the harmonized major and minor scales. This unit works with string set 2 and 3 and uses the same examples as Unit 5. These strings are a 3rd apart.

Diatonic 5ths in a Major Key

The first progression is in the key of E major, and is a slow and mellow track so it's easy to experiment with the shapes.

Progression in E Major

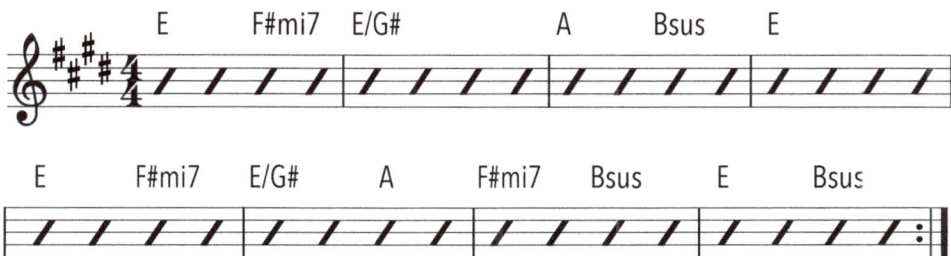

Review the major scale harmonized in 5ths along the 3rd and 2nd strings that you recently learned in the Fretboard Logic Module. It was demonstrated in the key of A. Keep in mind that when using 5ths, think of the lower of the two notes as the melodic guide.

Diatonic 5ths on the 3rd and 2nd Strings in Major

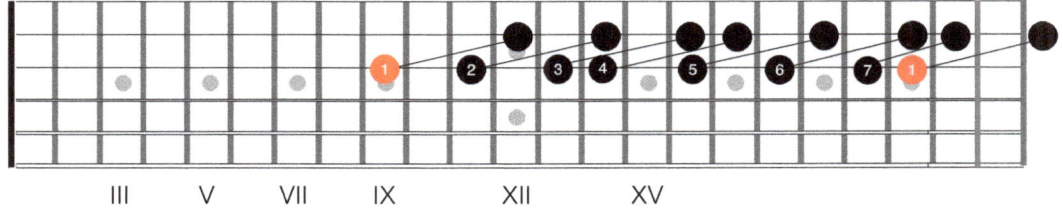

As with all the other harmonized scales, this can be played in any key – but keep in mind that when adjacent strings are harmonized in 5ths, use the lower of the two notes to track the scale.

Here is the part.

Diatonic 5ths in E

Experiment with some of your own ideas using these 5th shapes.

Diatonic 5ths in a Minor Key

The minor progression is the same one we used in the last unit. It's an eight-bar Rock shuffle in the key of D minor.

Progression in D Minor

Diatonic 5ths on the 3rd and 2nd Strings in Minor

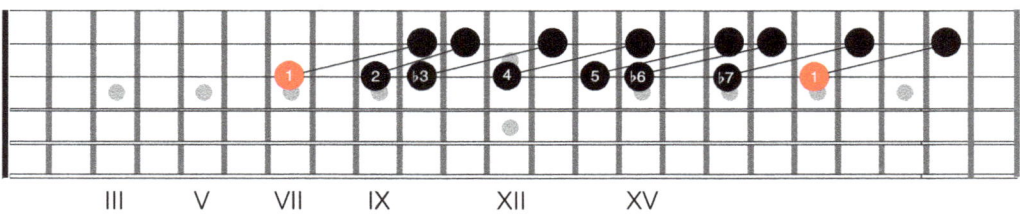

Review the minor scale harmonized in 5ths along the 3rd and 2nd strings that you just learned in the Fretboard Logic Module. It was demonstrated in the key of A minor.

Here is the part.

Diatonic 5ths in D Minor

As in the previous unit, note the "personality" of 5ths in a minor key. Experiment with some of your own ideas using these 5th shapes. Remember that these ideas are transposable to all minor keys!

IMPROVISATION

In the last unit you experimented playing over borrowed chords using pentatonic shells in all five octave shapes. In this module you will play over borrowed chords using the seven-note major and minor scales in all five octave shapes. The goal is similar to that of the last unit. You need to expand beyond the comfortable Patterns III and IV octave shapes and explore all of the others.

Use what you learned about superimposing minor patterns on top of major patterns in the Fretboard Logic Module to solo over this progression.

Here is a four-bar chord progression in D major.

Progression in D Major

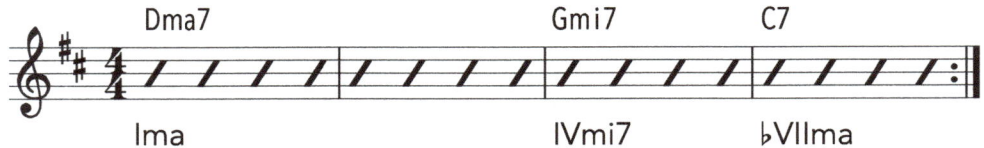

Analysis of this progression shows Dma7 as Ima7. Gmi7 is borrowed from the parallel minor, D minor, and is labeled IVmi7. C7 is borrowed from the parallel minor, D minor, and is labeled bVII7. D is the tonic for all chords in the progression.

Work through all five octave shapes staying in position as you shift from major to minor. Start with Pattern I and work through each octave shape. Play through the scales first to get acquainted and then improvise using the scales as your menu of notes.

Progression in D Major
(using Pattern I Major and Minor Scales)

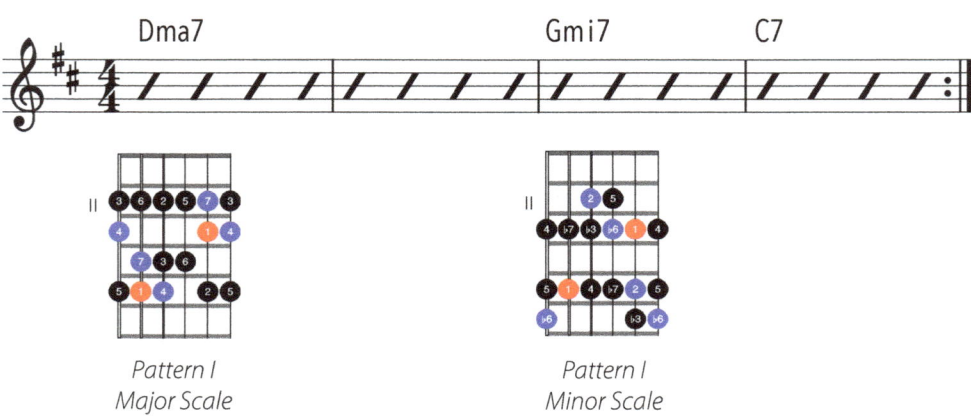

Pattern I Major Scale

Pattern I Minor Scale

Progression in D Major
(using Pattern II Major and Minor Scales)

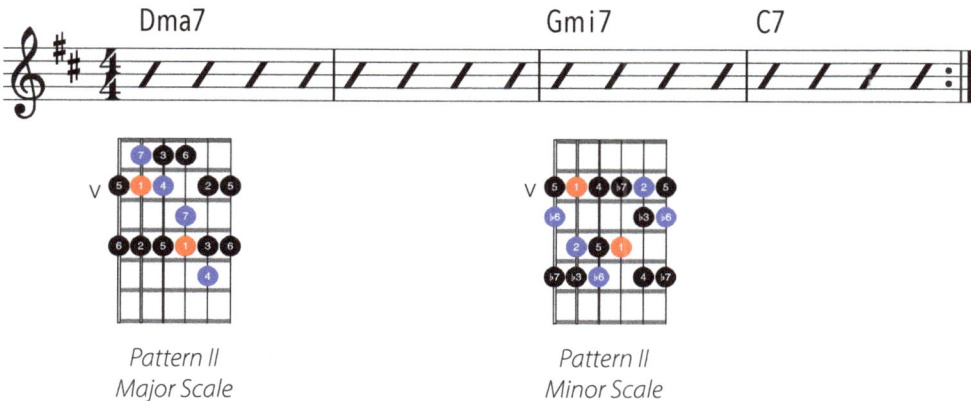

Pattern II Major Scale

Pattern II Minor Scale

Progression in D Major
(using Pattern III Major and Minor Scales)

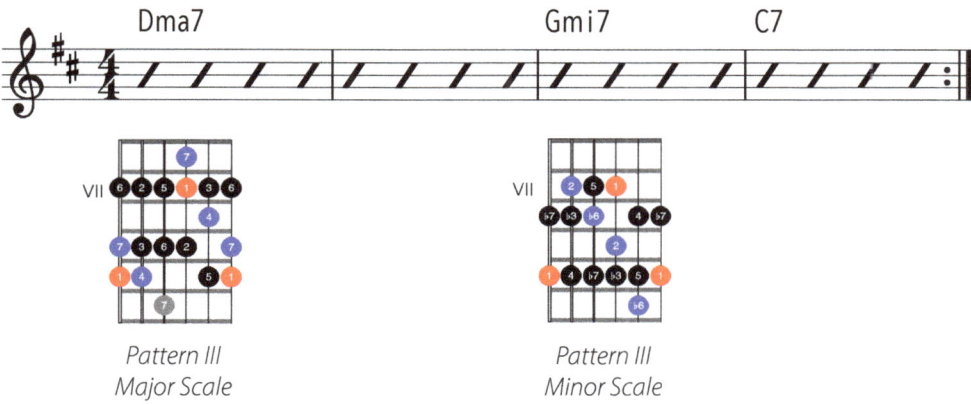

Pattern III Major Scale

Pattern III Minor Scale

Progression in D Major
(using Pattern IV Major and Minor Scales)

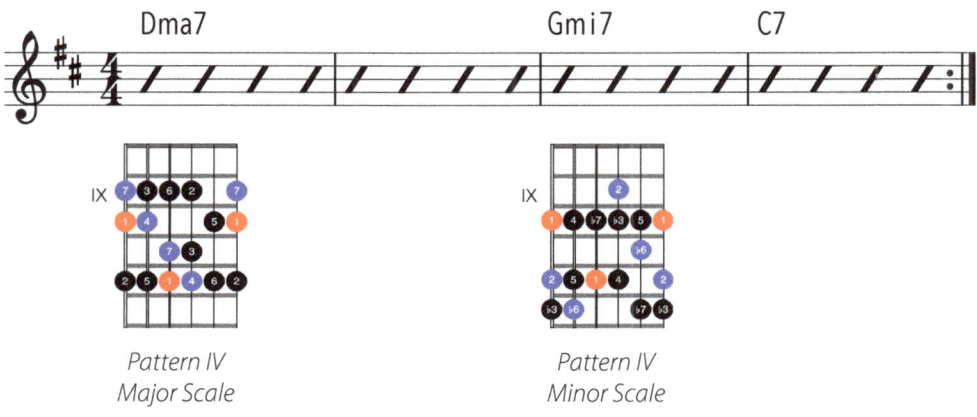

Pattern IV Major Scale

Pattern IV Minor Scale

Progression in D Major
(using Pattern V Major and Minor Scales)

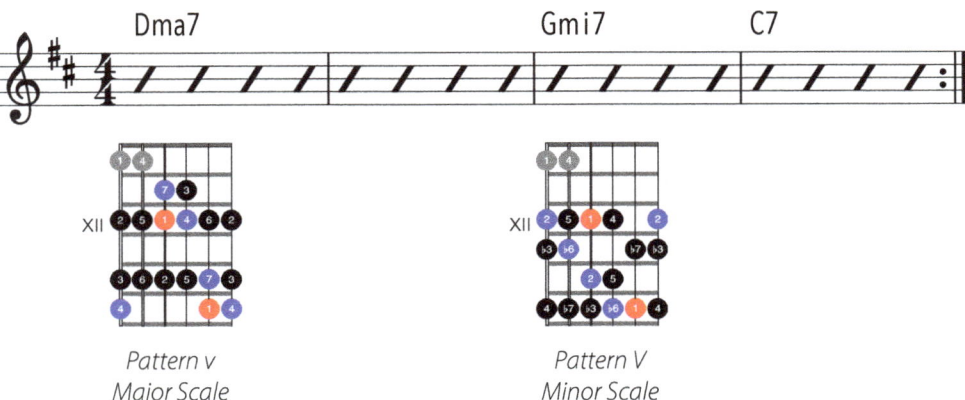

To practice this example, I suggest starting in Pattern I, and shift between the Pattern I major and Pattern I minor scales. Next move to Pattern II and repeat the exercise. Then move to Pattern III, then to Pattern V, and then to Pattern V. When you start feeling comfortable, move through all of them randomly.

Level 4 Unit 6 • Improv Demo

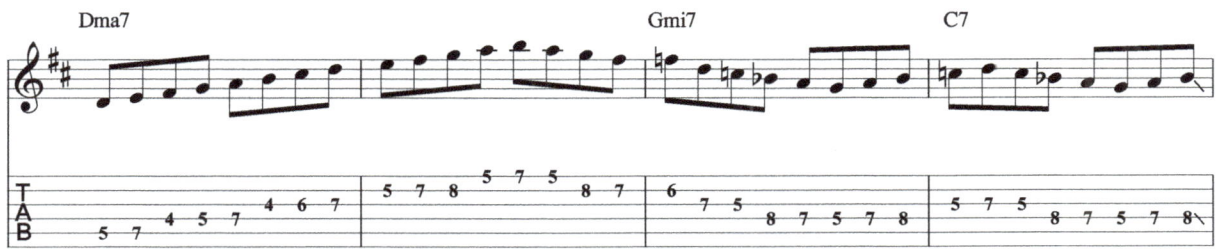

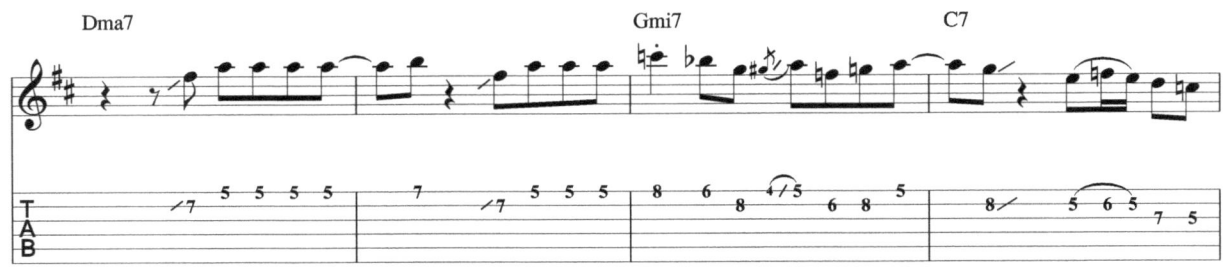
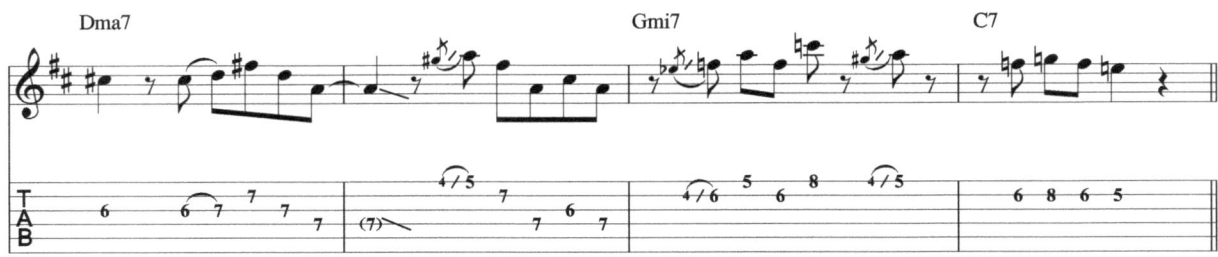
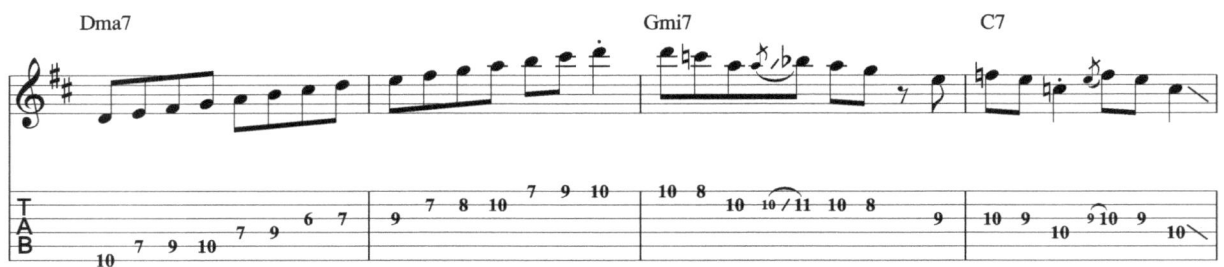
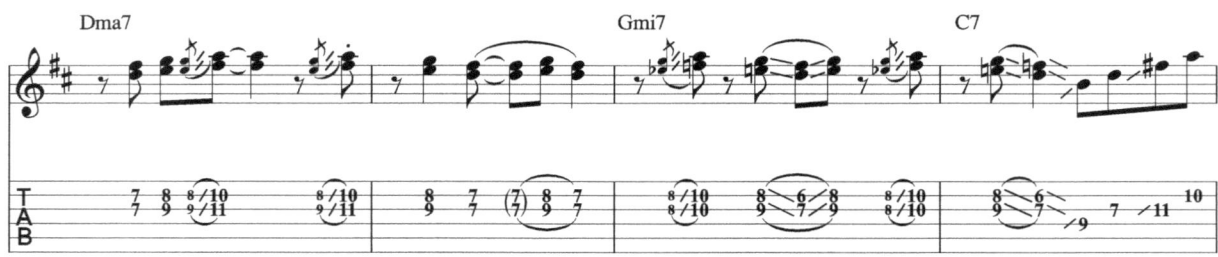

Fretboard Biology
Level 4 • Unit 6: Improvisation

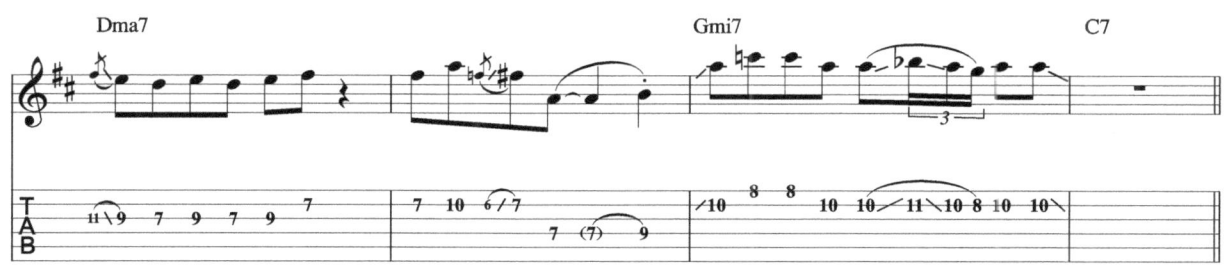

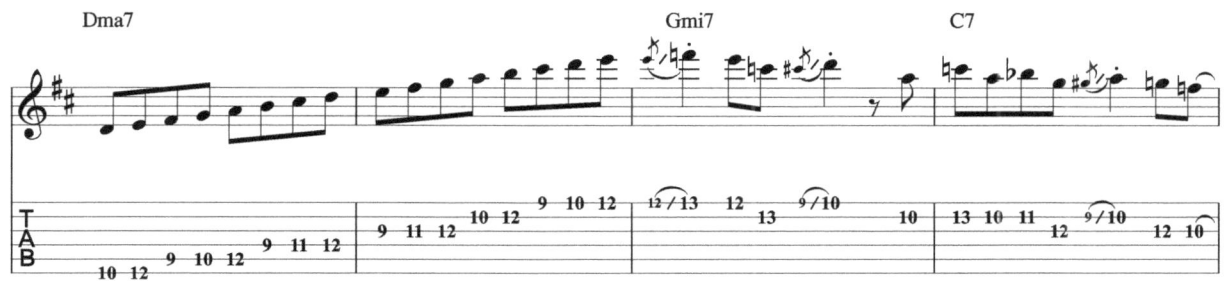

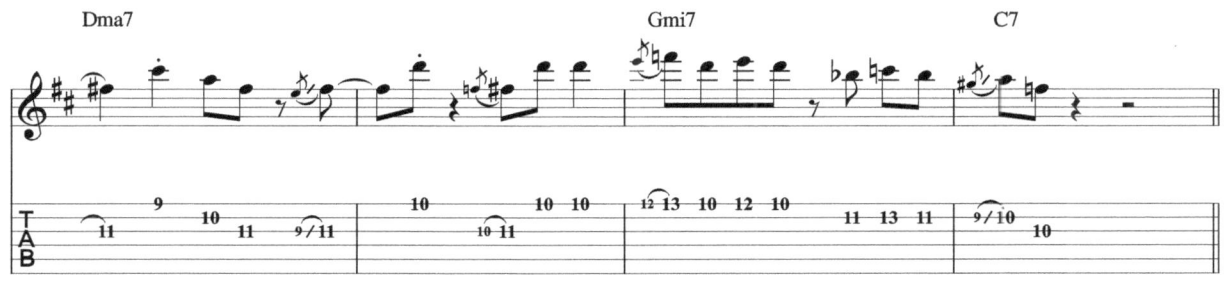

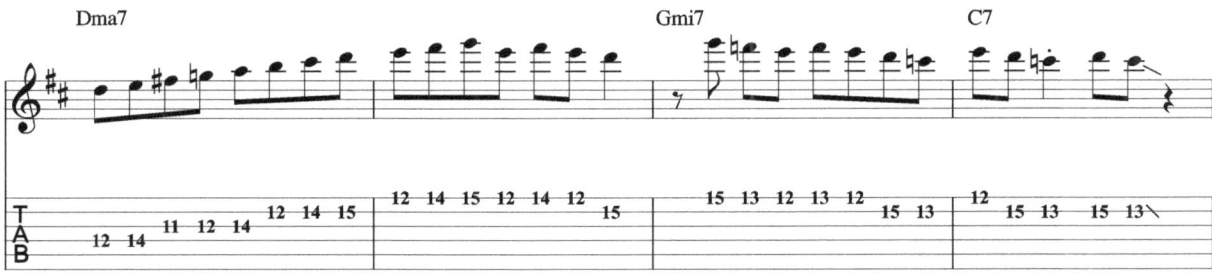

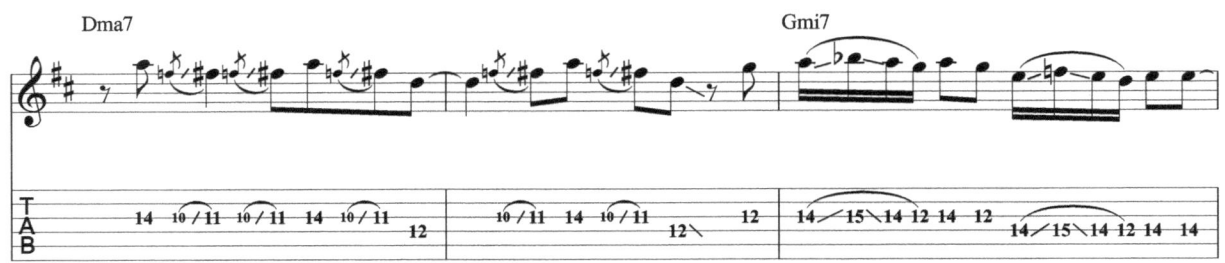
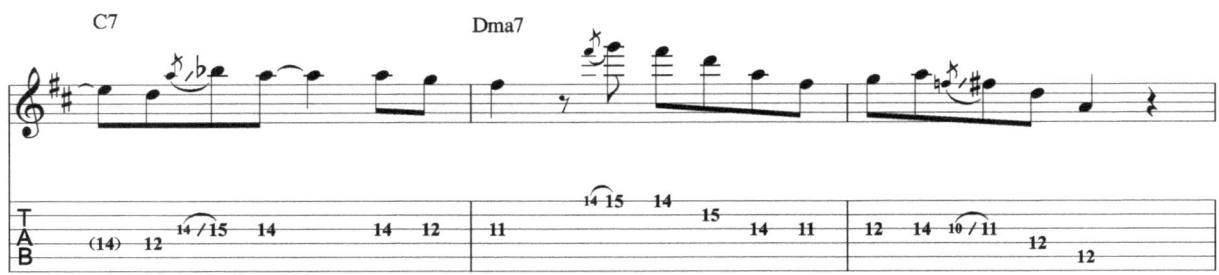
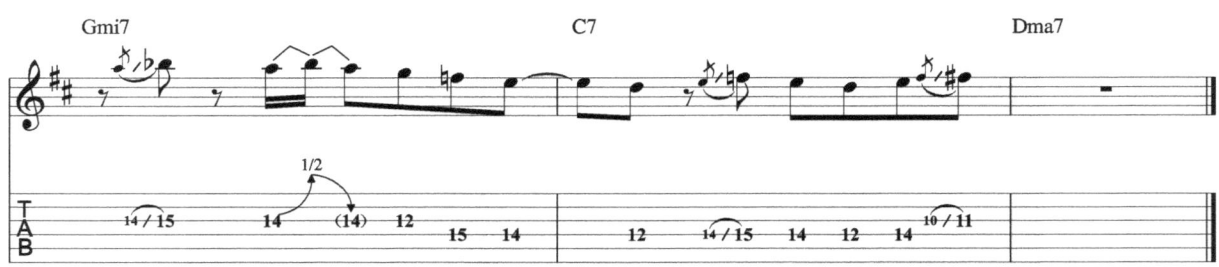

PRACTICE

Theory

- ☐ Go to the tabs below the Theory video on the website and complete the quiz.
- ☐ Learn the common terms associated with inversions and voicings.

Fretboard Logic

- ☐ Learn Root Map 4 and the associated shell voicings.
- ☐ Learn the major and minor diatonic 5th shapes on string sets that are a 3rd apart.
- ☐ Learn the common tones in the major and Natural Minor scales.

Rhythm Guitar

- ☐ Practice playing chip parts in R&B progressions.

Money Makers

- ☐ Practice playing major and minor 5th parts over major and minor progressions.

Improvisation

- ☐ Practice playing solos over an D major progression with modal interchange.

UNIT 7

Learning Modules

> **Theory** - Triad and 7th Chord Inversions, Writing Inversions on the Staff, Recognizing Inversions on the Staff

> **Fretboard Logic** - Inverted Open Chords, Major and Minor Scales harmonized with 6th Shapes, Modal Interchange with Arpeggios

> **Rhythm Guitar** - Classic R&B Parts

> **Money Makers** - Money Maker Parts using Diatonic 6th Shapes

> **Improvisation** - Soloing with Modal Interchange

> **Practice** - Continue Practice Routine Development

THEORY

This module provides more detail about inversions. There are several reasons for using inverted chords in a progression. In most cases, inversions facilitate a smoother, more step-wise bass line. How inversions are used in progressions will be covered in an upcoming module.

Even when a chord is inverted, the actual root is still the root, even though it is not voiced at the bottom of the chord. In an inverted chord, the lowest note is NOT the root.

Here is a review of the root-position triads and 7th chords that were presented in the last unit.

C Major Triad

- Root position C major triad has the root as the lowest note (bass note)
- First inversion C major triad has the 3rd as the lowest note (bass note)
- Second inversion C major triad has the 5th as the lowest note (bass note)

C Major Triad Inversions

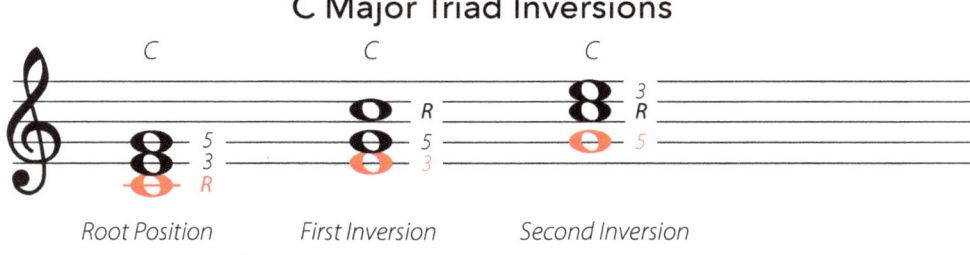

Root Position   First Inversion   Second Inversion

C Minor Triad

- Root position C minor triad has the root as the lowest note (bass note)
- First inversion C minor triad has the ♭3rd as the lowest note (bass note)
- Second inversion C minor triad has the 5th as the lowest note (bass note)

C Minor Triad Inversions

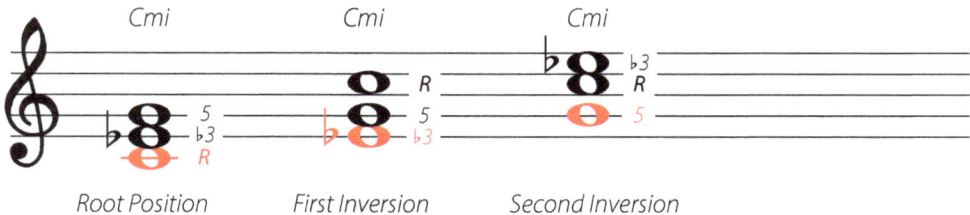

Root Position   First Inversion   Second Inversion

Now let's look at 7th chords. This may be redundant but it's important to be thorough.

C Major 7 Chord

- Root position Cma7 chord has the root as the lowest note (bass note)
- First inversion Cma7 chord has the 3rd as the lowest note (bass note)
- Second inversion Cma7 chord has the 5th as the lowest note (bass note)
- Third inversion Cma7 chord has the 7th as the lowest note (bass note)

CMa7 Chord Inversions

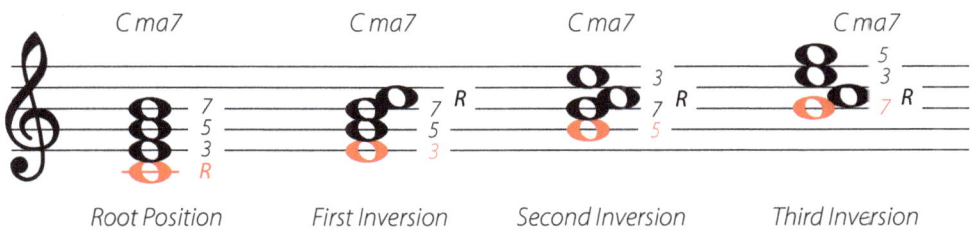

C Dominant 7 Chord

- Root position C7 chord has the root as the lowest note (bass note)
- First inversion C7 chord has the 3rd as the lowest note (bass note)
- Second inversion C7 chord has the 5th as the lowest note (bass note)
- Third inversion C7 chord has the ♭7th as the lowest note (bass note)

C7 Chord Inversions

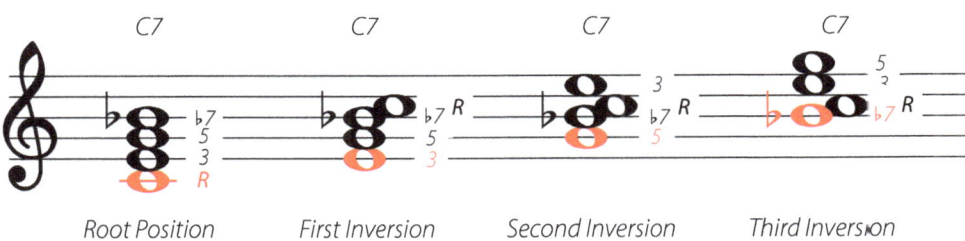

C Minor 7 Chord

- Root position Cmi7 chord has the root as the lowest note (bass note)
- First inversion Cmi7 chord has the ♭3rd as the lowest note (bass note)
- Second inversion Cmi7 chord has the 5th as the lowest note (bass note)
- Third inversion Cmi7 chord has the ♭7th as the lowest note (bass note)

Cmi7 Chord Inversions

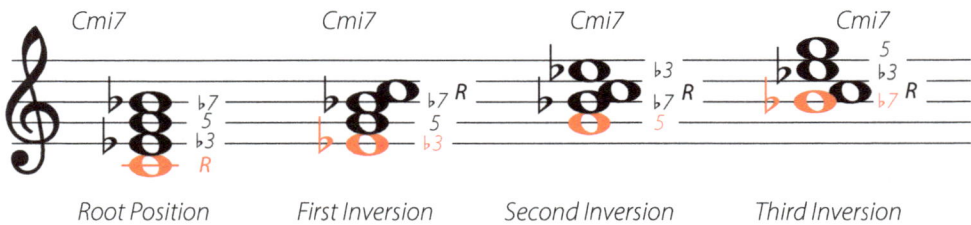

C Minor 7(♭5) Chord

- Root position Cmi7(♭5) chord has the root as the lowest note (bass note)
- First inversion Cmi7(♭5) chord has the ♭3rd as the lowest note (bass note)
- Second inversion Cmi7(♭5) chord has the ♭5th as the lowest note (bass note)
- Third inversion Cmi7(♭5) chord has the ♭7th as the lowest note (bass note)

Cmi7(♭5) Chord Inversions

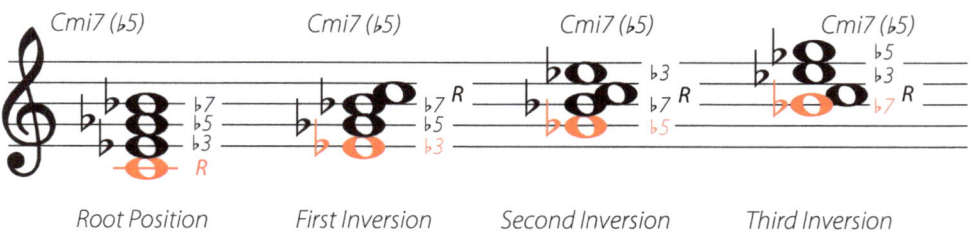

Writing Inversions on the Staff

To write an inversion on the staff or to spell it verbally to another musician, I suggest these simple and easy steps:

- Step 1: Think of the chord in root position and spell it from lowest to highest notes.
- Step 2: Identify the chord tone (3rd, 5th, or 7th) that is voiced in the bass for the inversion you want to spell.
- Step 3: Spell the chord tones in the appropriate order from lowest to highest.

Writing the First Inversion of Ama7

If asked to spell a *first inversion* Ama7 chord:

- Step 1: Spell out the chord in root position: A-C#-E-G#
- Step 2: Write the 3rd of the Ama7 chord as the lowest (or bass) note: C#
- Step 3: Spell the Ama7 from the bottom up starting on C#: C#-E-G#-A
  (chord tones can be arranged in any order as long as C# is the lowest note)

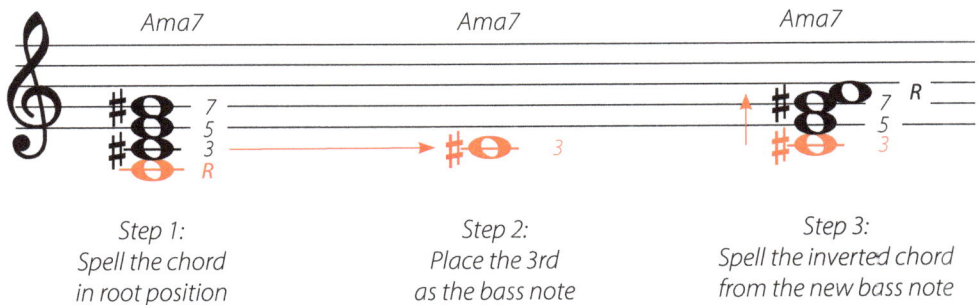

Step 1:
Spell the chord
in root position

Step 2:
Place the 3rd
as the bass note

Step 3:
Spell the inverted chord
from the new bass note

Writing the Second Inversion of Emi7

If asked to spell a *second inversion* Emi7 chord:

- Step 1: Spell it in root position: E-G-B-D
- Step 2: Write the 5th of the Emi7 chord as the bass note: B
- Step 3: Spell the Emi7 from the bottom up starting on B: B-D-E-G
  (chord tones can be arranged in any order as long as B is the lowest note)

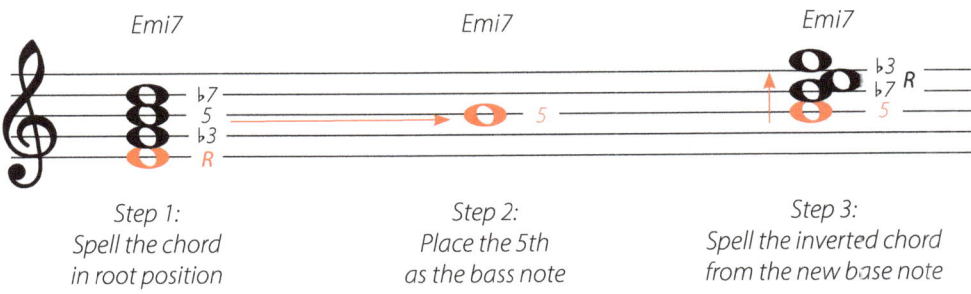

Step 1:
Spell the chord
in root position

Step 2:
Place the 5th
as the bass note

Step 3:
Spell the inverted chord
from the new base note

Writing the Third Inversion of C7

If asked to spell a *third inversion* C7 chord:

- Step 1: Spell it in root position: C-E-G-B♭
- Step 2: Write the 7th of the C7 chord as the bass note: B♭
- Step 3: Spell the C7 from the bottom up starting on B♭: B♭-C-E-G
  (chord tones can be arranged in any order as long as B♭ is the lowest note)

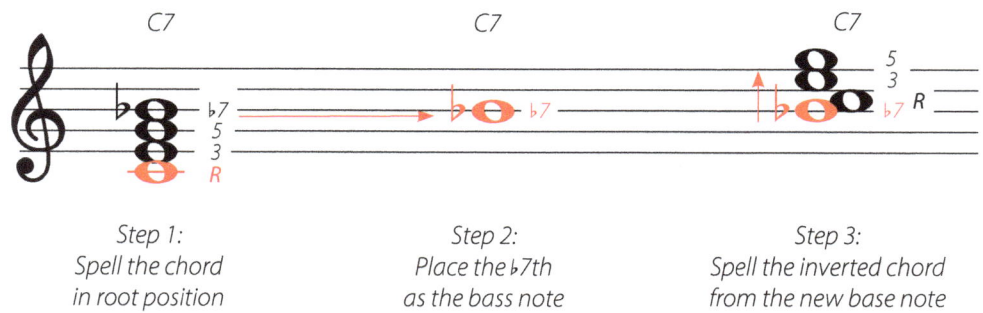

Step 1:
Spell the chord
in root position

Step 2:
Place the ♭7th
as the bass note

Step 3:
Spell the inverted chord
from the new base note

Writing the First Inversion of Bmi7(♭5)

If asked to spell a *first inversion* Bmi7(♭5) chord:

- Step 1: First spell it in root position: B-D-F-A
- Step 2: Write the ♭3rd of the Bmi7(♭5) chord as the bass note: D
- Step 3: Spell the Bmi7(♭5) from the bottom up starting on D: D-F-A-B
  (These can be arranged in any order as long as D is the lowest note)

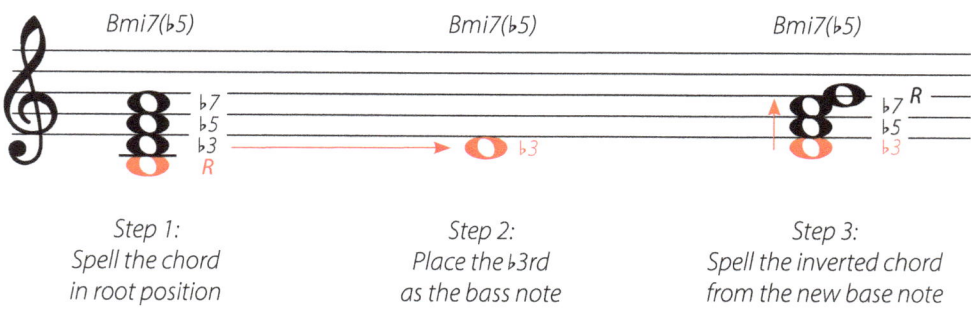

Step 1:
Spell the chord
in root position

Step 2:
Place the ♭3rd
as the bass note

Step 3:
Spell the inverted chord
from the new base note

Recognizing Inversions on the Staff

To recognize an inversion written on the staff or to communicate verbally to another musician, I suggest these simple and easy steps:

- Step 1: Collect all the letter names.
- Step 2: Rearrange them in thirds – that is, put them in every-other-letter order.
- Step 3: Determine how the chord is spelled when the notes are arranged in thirds.
- Step 4: Determine which note would be the lowest if in root position.

Try a few. Imagine you are looking at your guitar and you have come up with a chord but you don't know how to name it. Or perhaps another musician tells you the notes they are playing but they can't articulate what the chord is.

What Chord Inversion is this? F#, A, D

Your fingers are playing these notes from the bottom up: F#, A, D. They are not all arranged in 3rds. F# to A is a minor 3rd but A to D is a perfect 4th. Follow the steps above to find the chord inversion:

- Step 1: Collect all the notes: F#, A, D
- Step 2: Rearrange the note into 3rds: D, F#, A.
  - D to F# is a 3rd
  - F# to A is a 3rd
- Step 3: Determine the name of the chord spelled D-F#-A: This is a D triad.
- Step 4: What inversion is a D triad with F# voiced in the bass? First inversion. The conclusion is that you are playing a first inversion D major triad.

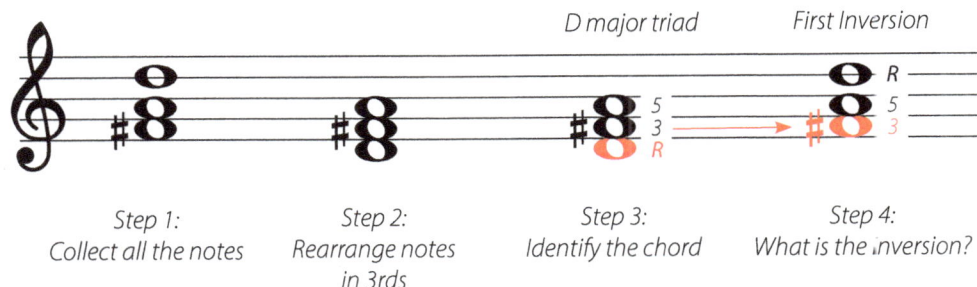

Step 1:
Collect all the notes

Step 2:
Rearrange notes in 3rds

Step 3:
Identify the chord

Step 4:
What is the inversion?

What Chord Inversion is this? D, G, B

Your fingers are playing these notes from the bottom up: D, G, B. They're not all arranged in 3rds. D to G is a perfect 4th and G to B is a minor 3rd. Follow the steps to find the chord inversion:

- Step 1: Collect all the notes: D, G, B
- Step 2: Rearrange them in 3rds: G, B, D
  - G to B is a 3rd
  - B to D is a 3rd
- Step 3: Determine the name of the chord spelled G-B-D: It is a G triad.
- Step 4: What inversion is a G triad with D voiced in the bass? Second inversion. The conclusion is that you are playing a second inversion G major triad.

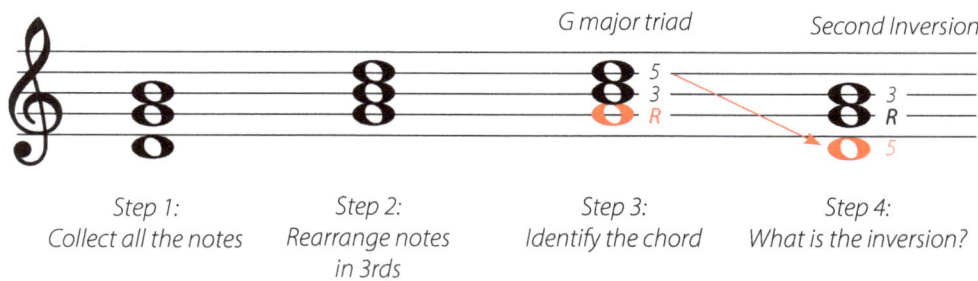

What Chord Inversion is this? C, E, A

Your fingers are playing these notes from the bottom up: C, E, A. They're not all arranged in 3rds. C to E is a 3rd but E to A is a perfect 4th. Follow the steps to find the chord inversion:

- Step 1: Collect all the notes: C, E, A
- Step 2: Rearrange them in 3rds: A, C, E
  - A to C is a 3rd
  - C to E is a 3rd
- Step 3: Determine the name of the chord spelled A-C-E: It is an A minor triad.
- Step 4: What inversion is an A minor triad with C voiced in the bass? First inversion. The conclusion is that you are playing a first inversion A minor triad.

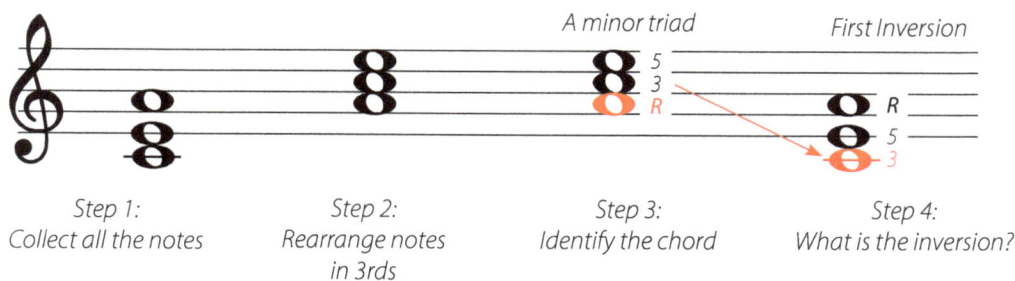

Fretboard Biology — Level 4 • Unit 7: Theory

What Chord Inversion is this? E♭, G, B♭, C

Your fingers are playing these notes from the bottom up: E♭, G, B♭, C. They're not all arranged in 3rds. E♭ to G is a 3rd, G to B♭ is a 3rd, B♭ to C is a 2nd. Follow the steps to find the chord inversion:

- Step 1: Collect all the notes: E♭, G, B♭, C
- Step 2: Rearrange them in 3rds: C, E♭, G, B♭
    - C to E♭ is a 3rd
    - E♭ to G is a 3rd
    - G to B♭ is a 3rd
- Step 3: Determine the name of the chord spelled C-E♭-G-B♭: It is a C minor 7 chord.
- Step 4: What inversion is a C minor 7 chord with E♭ voiced in the bass? First inversion. The conclusion is that you are playing a first inversion C minor 7.

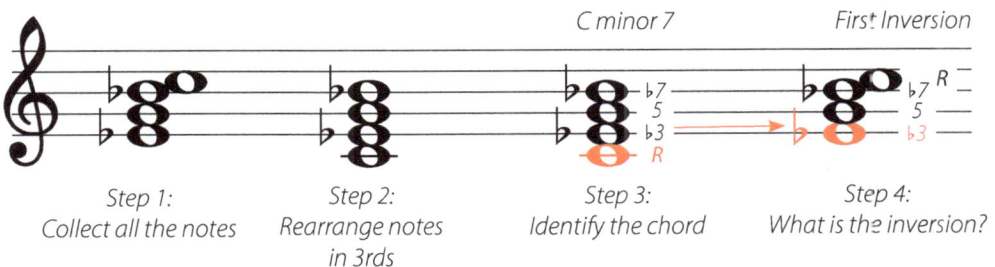

Step 1: Collect all the notes
Step 2: Rearrange notes in 3rds
Step 3: Identify the chord
Step 4: What is the inversion?

FRETBOARD LOGIC

Inverted Chords

You've learned about inverted chords from a theory standpoint. Now you will learn to play inversions for open string chords. The voicings are shown here but you can figure them out on your own if you know the chord tones of the open chords.

It's not complicated. To figure them out, I suggest that you start with the open chord in root position. To play a first inversion chord, find the lowest 3rd available and play the rest of the notes of the chord that are higher. If you want to play a second inversion chord, find the lowest 5th and play the rest of the notes that are higher. If you want to play a third inversion chord, find the lowest 7th and play rest of the notes that are higher.

Look at these examples:

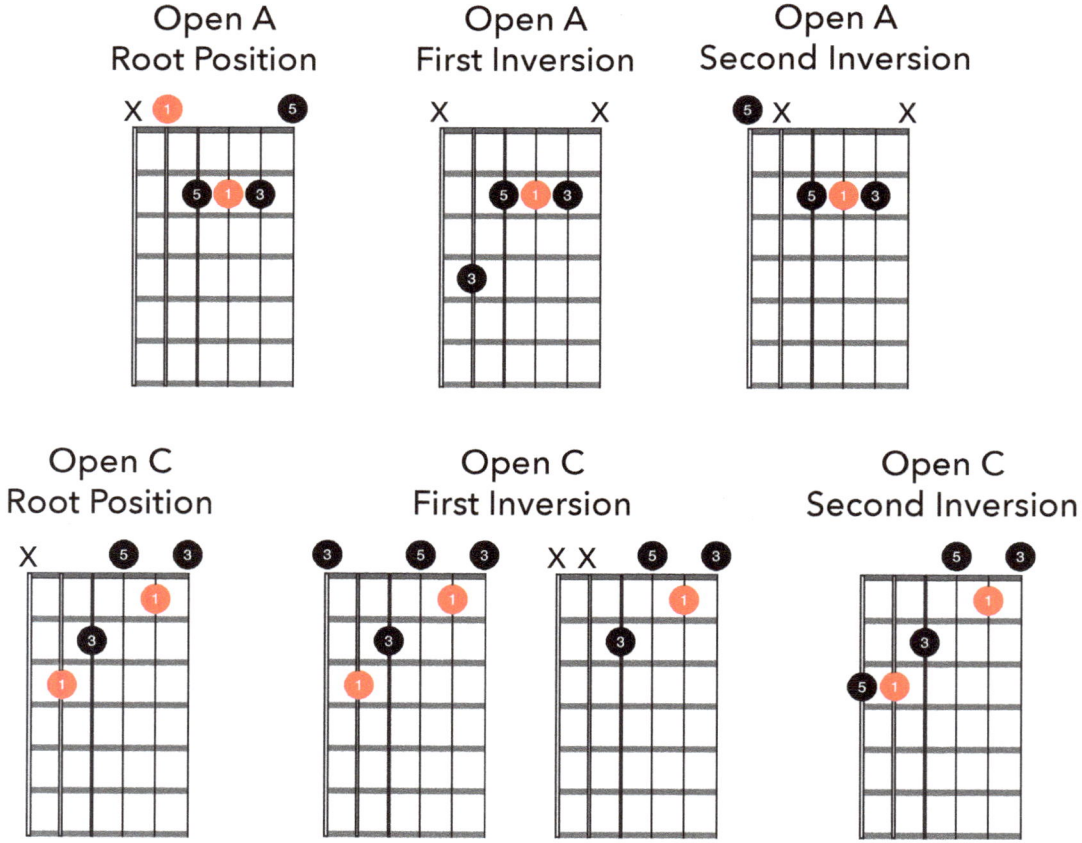

Open D Root Position	Open D First Inversion	Open D Second Inversion
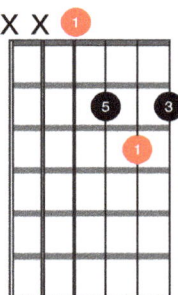	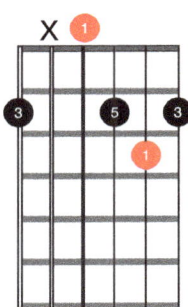	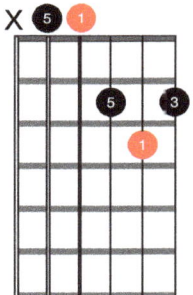

Open E Root Position	Open E First Inversion	Open E Second Inversion
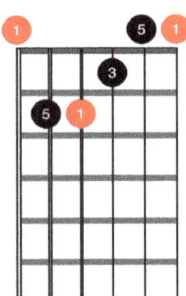	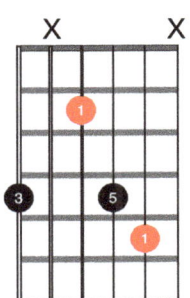	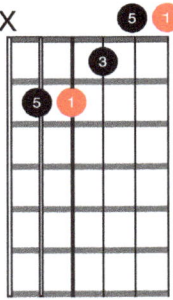

Open G Root Position	Open G First Inversion	Open G Second Inversion
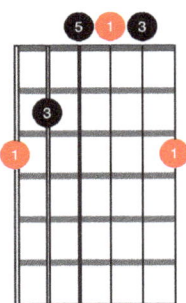	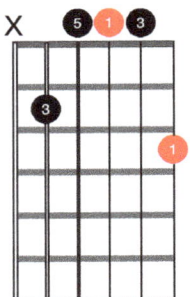	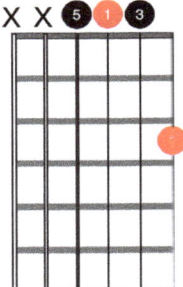

Open Ami Root Position	Open Ami First Inversion	Open Ami Second Inversion
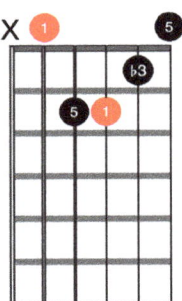	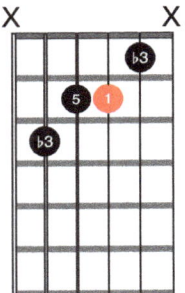	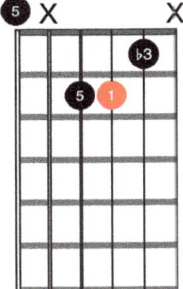

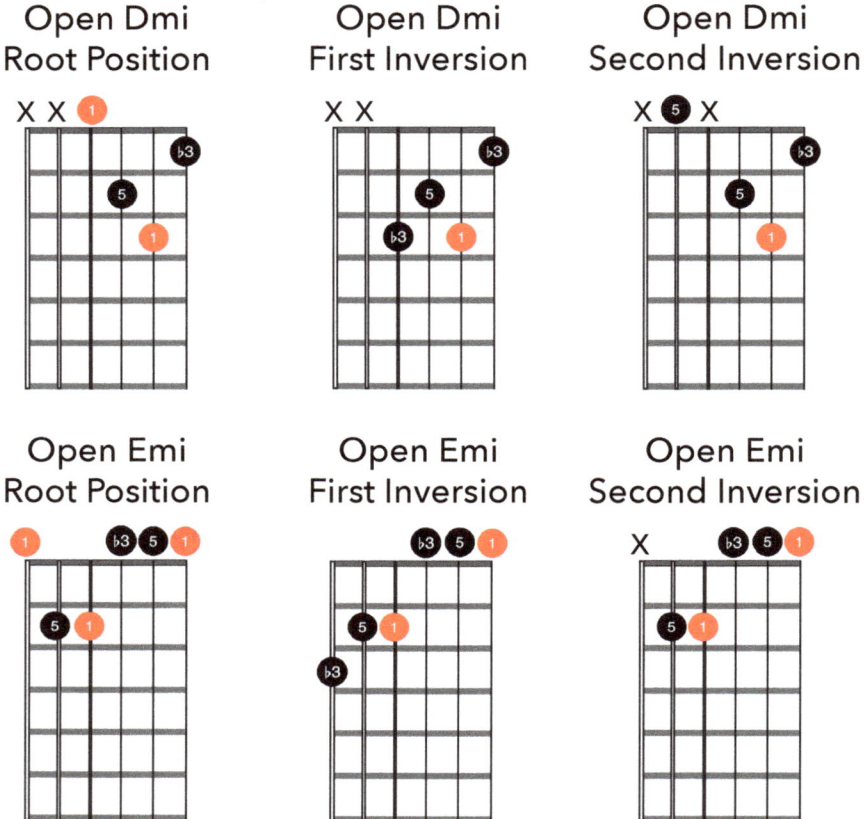

Voicings for inversions can be derived from barre chords, too. You may not be aware that you learned inversions with Super Shapes in Level 2. Review them and examine each of the three-string triad shapes to see what chord tone is voiced in the bass.

It's good to memorize all of the voicings in this module but it's much more important to be able to figure them out for yourself. Focus more attention on that than memorizing every shape. You will undoubtedly develop your "go-to" shapes to use when you are sight reading a chart. When you have time to work out your fretting-hand movements, you may work out other ideas.

Intervals

You have learned the diatonic 3rd, 4th, and 5th shapes along adjacent strings as they relate to the diatonic major and minor scales. With 3rds and 5ths, use the bottom note of the pair as the melodic guide. In other words, the lower of the two notes plays the scale and the note a 3rd or 5th higher is harmonized from the scale.

With 4ths, think of the higher of the two notes as the melodic guide. The lower note, which is a 4th below, is the same as a note a 5th above the note on the 1st string.

In this module you will learn about 6ths. The top note is the melodic guide. If you think in terms of inverted intervals, the bottom note of a 6th shape played an octave higher is the 3rd of the guide note.

Diatonic 6th Shapes in Major

For demonstration purposes, start in the key of G major. Consider the notes along the 1st string as the "scale degrees" starting with G at the 3rd fret. Play the G scale along the 1st string: G, A, B, C, D, E, F#, G.

G Major Scale on the 1st String

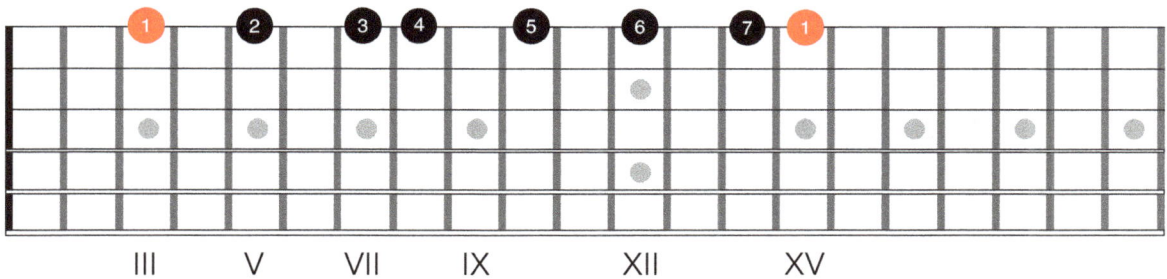

Next, play the note a diatonic 6th lower than each scale degree on the 3rd string.

Diatonic 6ths on the 1st and 3rd Strings in Major

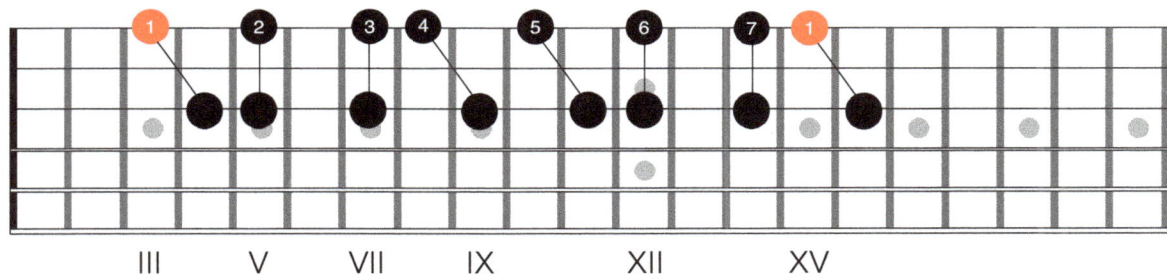

This works for any major key. Track the scale along the 1st string. This set of shapes for the major scale works for these string sets:

- The 1st and 3rd strings

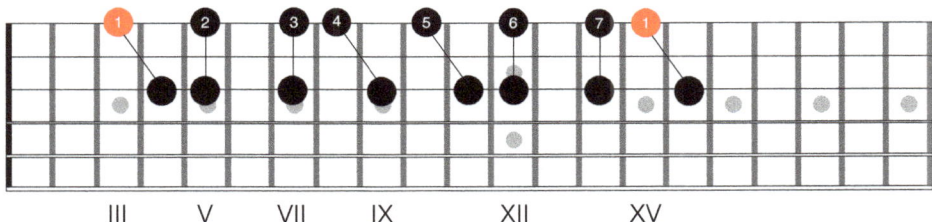

- The 2nd and 4th strings

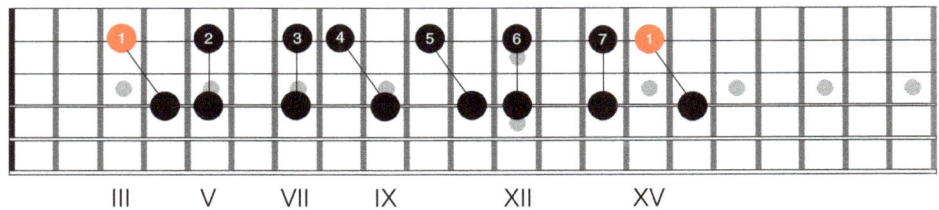

These shapes (using string set 1 and 3 and string set 2 and 4) cross the B/G line. The shapes that do not cross the B/G line (string set 3 and 5 and string set 4 and 6) have a different shape. Let's examine those now.

Start in the key of A major. Consider the notes along the 3rd string as the "scale degrees" starting with A at the 2nd fret. Play the A scale along the 3rd string: A, B, C#, D, E, F#, G#.

A Major Scale on the 3rd String

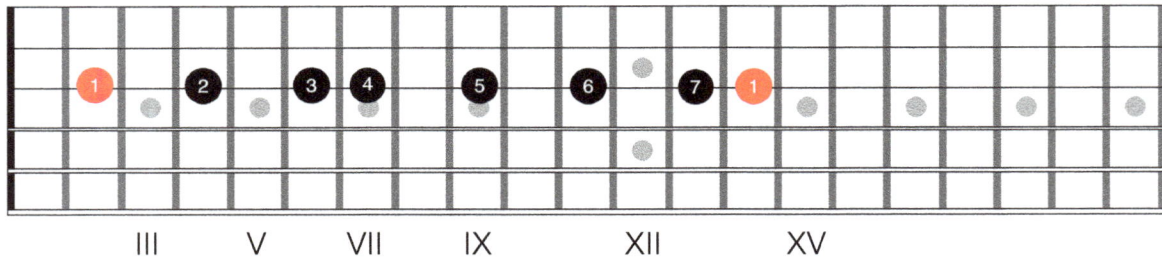

Next, play the note a diatonic 6th lower than each scale degree on the 3rd string.

Diatonic 6ths on the 3rd and 5th Strings in Major

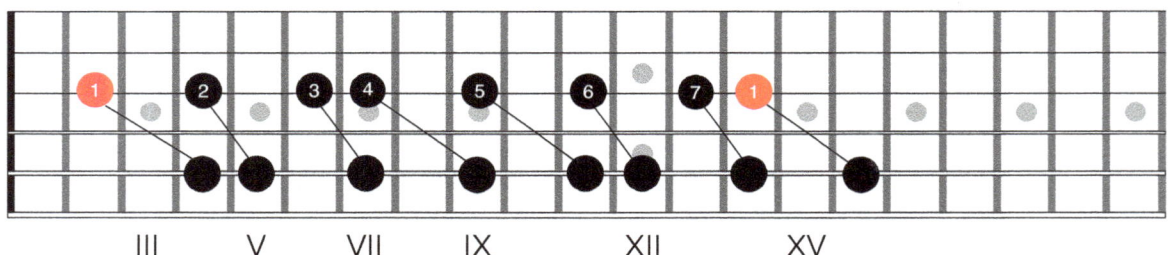

This works for any major key. Track the scale along the 3rd string. This set of shapes for the major scale works for these string sets:

- The 3rd and 5th strings

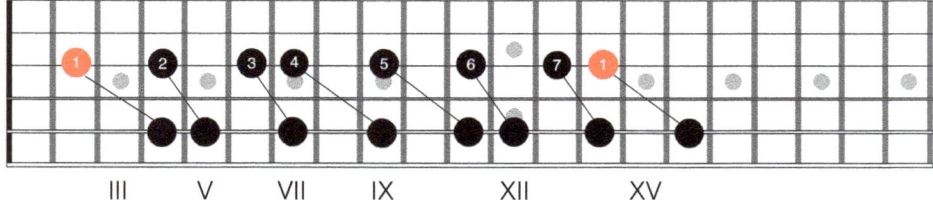

- The 4th and 6th strings.

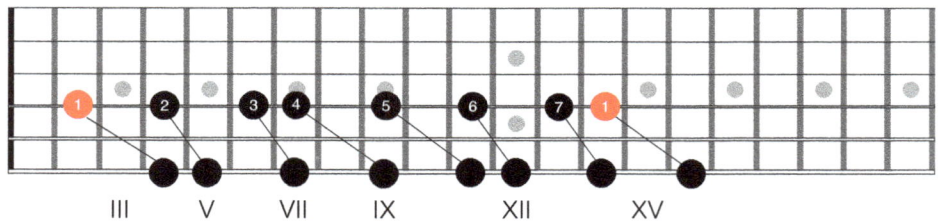

Diatonic 6th Shapes in Minor

Now look at minor. Consider the notes along the 1st string as the "scale degrees" starting with G at the 3rd fret. Play the G minor scale along the 1st string: G, A, B♭, C, D, E♭, F, G.

G Minor Scale on the 1st String

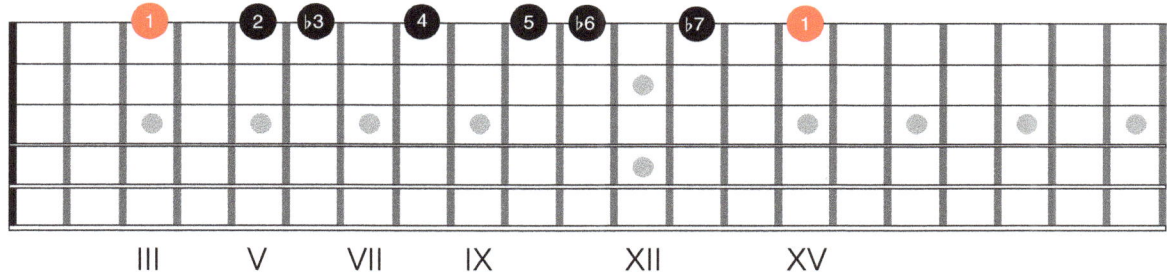

Next, play the note a diatonic 6th lower than each scale degree on the 3rd string.

Diatonic 6ths on the 1st and 3rd Strings in Minor

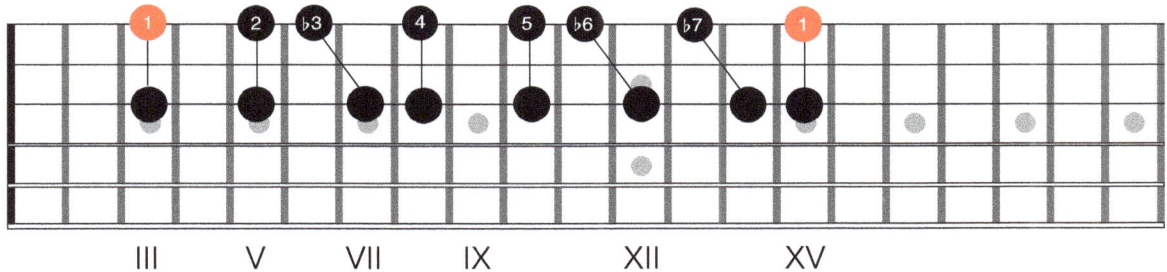

This works for any minor key. Track the scale along the 1st string. This set of shapes for the minor scale works for these string sets:

- The 1st and 3rd strings

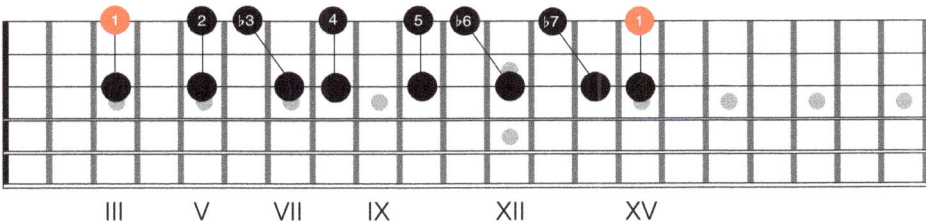

- The 2nd and 4th strings

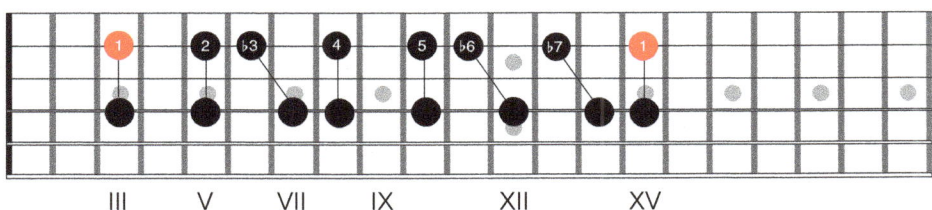

These shapes cross the B/G line. The shapes that do not cross the B/G line have a different shape. Let's examine those now.

Start in the key of A minor. Consider the notes along the 3rd string as the "scale degrees" starting with A at the 2nd fret. Play the A minor scale along the 3rd string: A, B, C, D, E, F, G.

A Minor Scale on the 3rd String

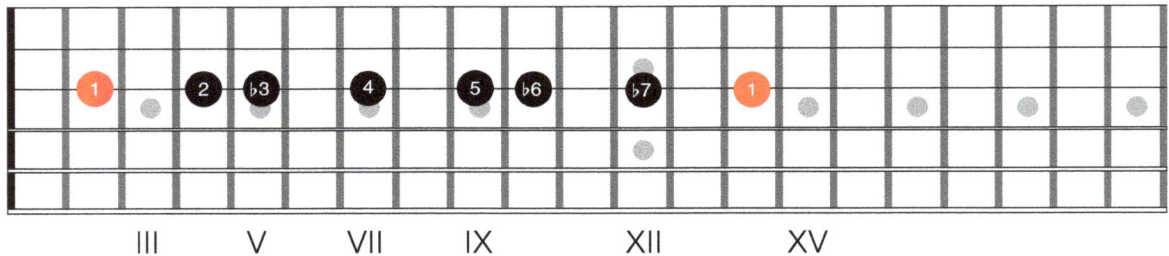

Next, play the note a diatonic 6th lower than each scale degree on the 3rd string.

Diatonic 6ths on the 3rd and 5th Strings in Minor

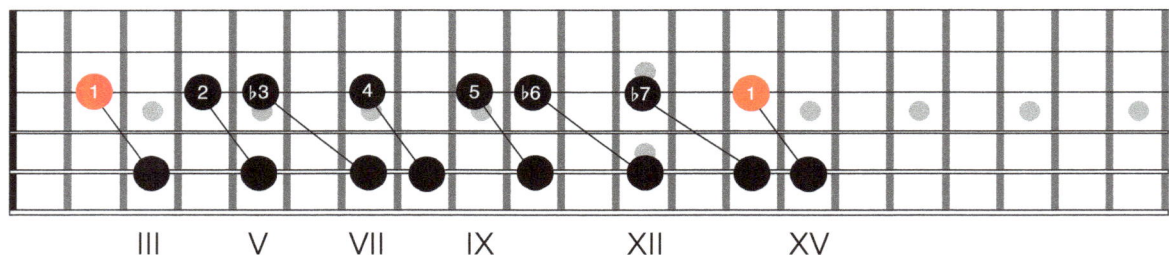

This works for any minor key. Track the scale along the 3rd string. This set of shapes for the minor scale works for these string sets:

- The 3rd and 5th strings

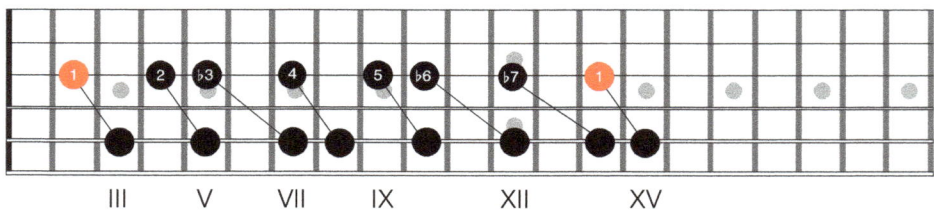

- The 4th and 6th strings

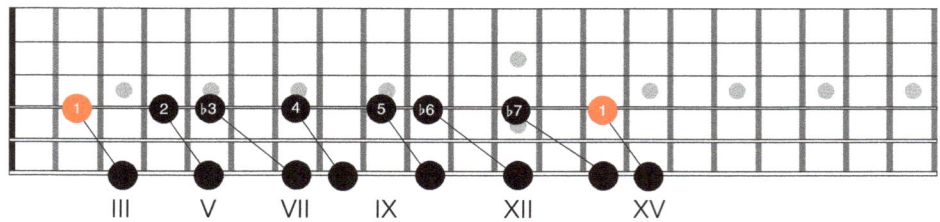

Arpeggios

There has been a lot of focus on modal interchange in Level 4. You have soloed over progressions that shifted between parallel major and minor keys using scales and the key-center approach. Through all this you have learned how parallel major and minor scales superimpose on each other. Now that you have some experience shifting between parallel keys with scales, look at this a little differently and think about chord tones.

You organize diatonic arpeggios in position to help integrate chord tones into your solos. The in-position arpeggio idea works well for soloing over progressions with modal interchange, too. It just requires expanding the number of arpeggios you see within an octave shape to include those of both parallel major and minor.

The goal in this module is to see both the major and minor scales harmonized with triads in the same octave shape. First compare the harmonized scales on the staff:

Harmonized Major and Natural Minor Scales

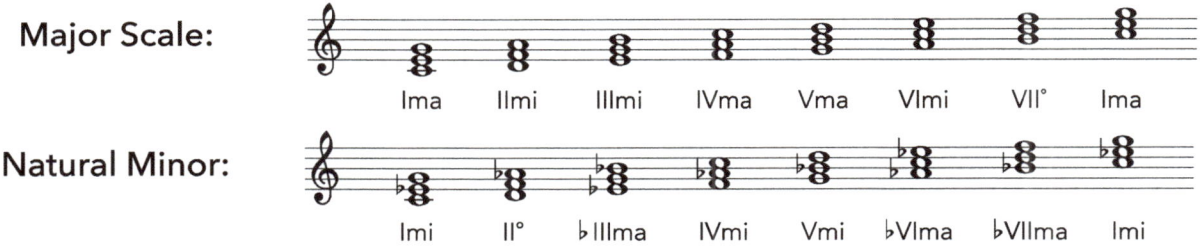

Next, look at the triad arpeggios of the harmonized major and minor scales in Octave Shape IV shown side-by-side, the major scale on the left and the minor scale on the right. Focus on how they all fit within the octave shape so you can access them quickly when soloing.

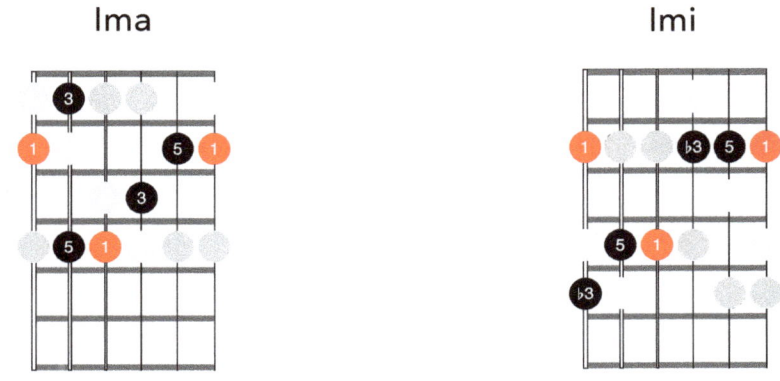

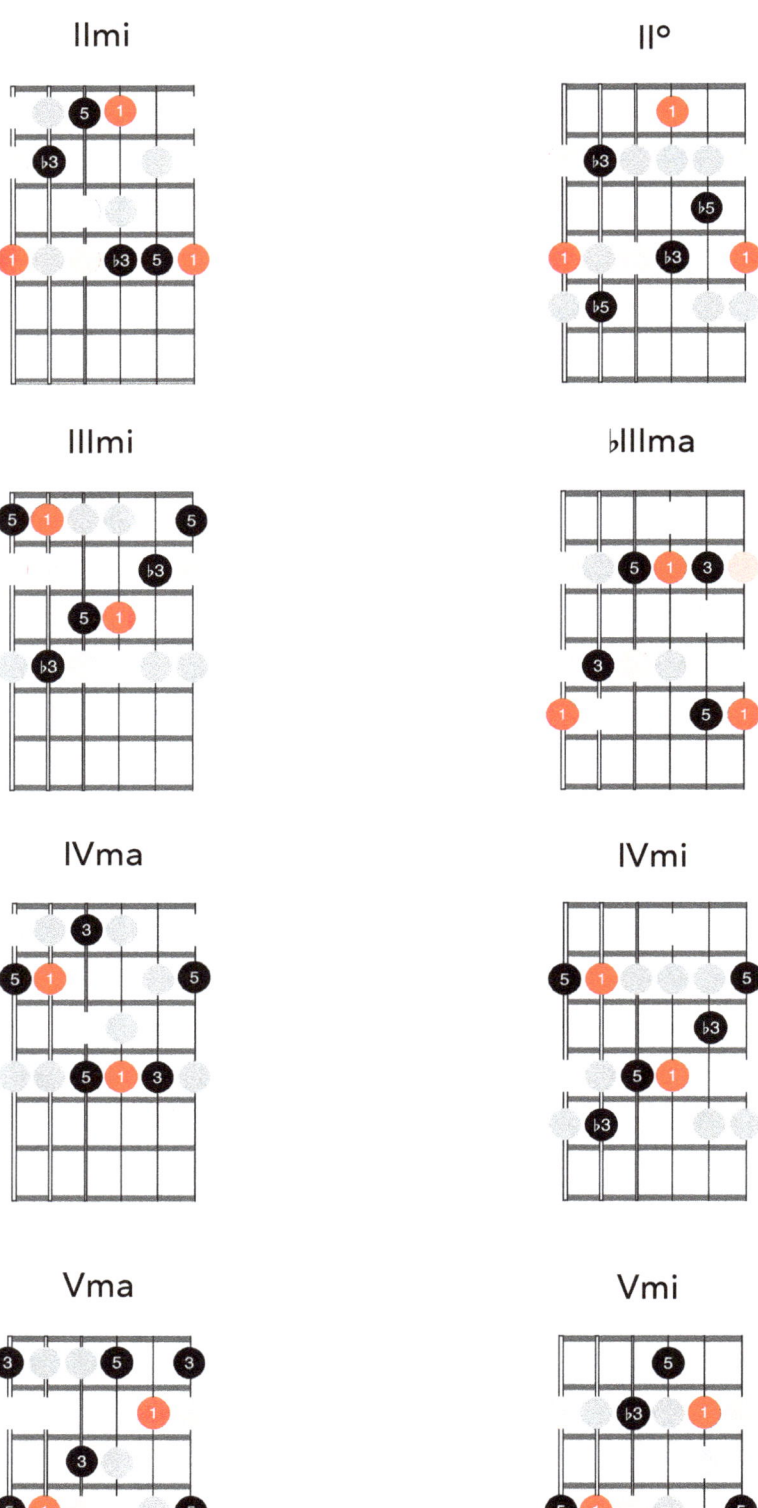

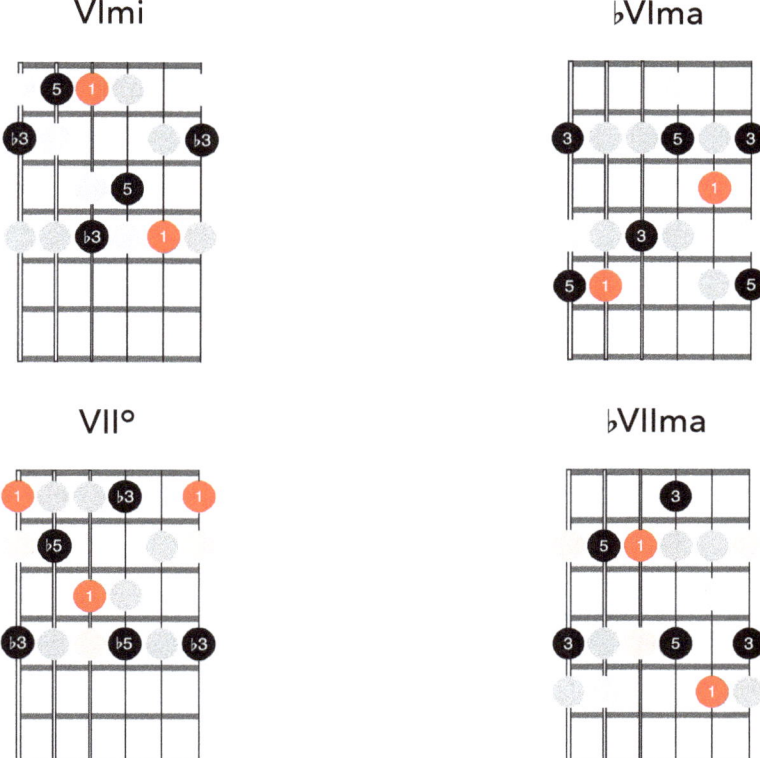

You have already worked on in-position arpeggios using 7th chords, so this should be familiar concept. Keep in mind that the diminished-triad arpeggios are sort of impractical to play because they have such a large gap between the ♭5 and the octave of the root. You have several options for practicing the triad arpeggios of the harmonized parallel major and minor scales. Depending on your time and goals, pick one or all of the ideas below.

- Practice the progression in the Improvisation module using these arpeggios. It requires you to transition between arpeggios. Practice on other progressions, too.
- Study and visualize, but don't play them. Here's why: It's more important to know where the chord tones are than to be able to run up and down the entire shapes. Remember, one of the primary ways to use chord tones is to target them as the first note of a new chord when soloing, rather than playing them in their entirety.
- Play through the arpeggios I through VII, switching back and forth between the arpeggio from the major scale to the arpeggio from the parallel minor. You could also go through all the arpeggios from major and then those from minor.

I recommend that more than anything else you internalize the process of finding the shapes so that even if you don't memorize or remember all the arpeggio shapes, you remember how to locate and build them.

RHYTHM GUITAR

This module has more examples of Classic R&B rhythm guitar parts. The parts presented in all these units are modeled after some standard classic R&B songs.

In this module you will learn a part that has moving chord parts. You will notice that you have already used these moves in the Level 1 Blues Rhythm Guitar Module. Since the "B" in R&B stands for Blues, this should not be a surprise.

Part 1

The first example is a common vamp moving from I7 to IV7 in the key of E.

Progression in E Major

For E7, we'll base the part loosely on an E9 voicing. E9 is a derivative of E7.

For IV7, which is an A7, we'll base the part on an A9 voicing. And again, for now, just understand that A9 is an embellished A7 chord.

Begin with the I chord – the Pattern II E7. Here are the chord tones: R, 5, ♭7, 3, 5.

Pattern II - E7 Barre Chord

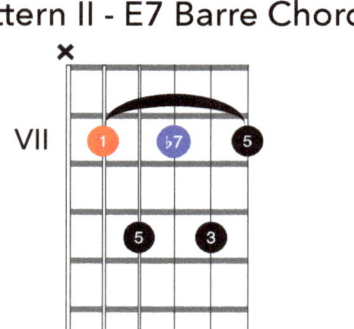

For this part, focus on the top three strings: R, 3, 5. Keep the "ghost" of the Pattern I barre chord in mind at all times.

Pattern II - E Major

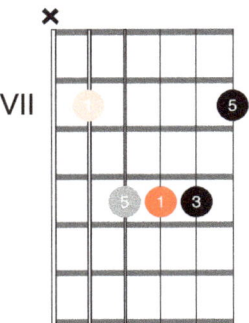

Next find the 6th located a whole step above the 5th on the E string. Barre just strings 1, 2, and 3 with your 1st finger at the 9th fret. You are playing a three-note shape: R, 3rd, 6th. I recommend you use either your 1st or 4th finger for this part.

E6

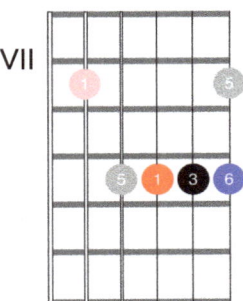

Keep that picture in your mind as you slide this three-note shape down a whole step to the ♭7th, 9th, and 5th. Continue to use either your 1st or 4th finger.

E9

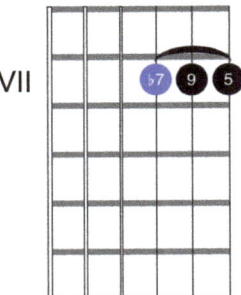

The essence of the move in this part is to move the shape back and forth between these two spots.

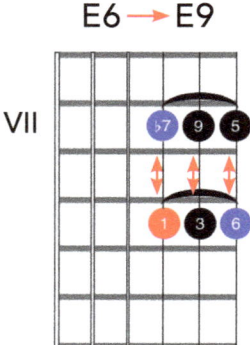

To play the example, start with the lower position and quickly slide up to the higher position and then back down.

The smallest subdivision for this part is an 8th note, so you can use all downstrokes or use alternate picking. That means all attacks on beats two and three are downstrokes. The chord on the "and" of beat three is not picked. It is articulated as a slide from the chord you played on beat three. If you pick it, it will sound rough and clunky.

Next, move to the A7. This part is a derivative of a Pattern IV A barre chord in 5th position. Remember the chord tones are R, 5, R, 3, 5, R. For this part, focus on the top four strings: R, 3, 5, R.

Pattern IV - A Major

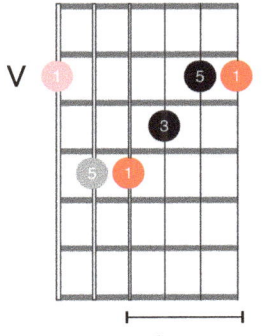

Top four strings

Next find the 6th, which is a whole step above the 5th on the B string.

Pattern IV - A6

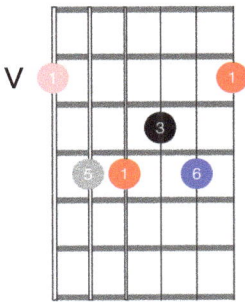

Next, temporarily omit the note played by your 1st finger on the 1st string. That leaves the R, 3rd, and 6th; just a three-note shape. I recommend you use your 2nd, 3rd and 4th fingers for this part.

Pattern IV - A6

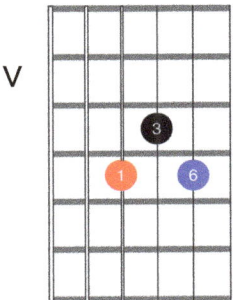

As you play the move on this chord, visualize the Pattern IV barre chord this was derived from.

Keep the image in your mind as you slide this three-note shape down a whole step. When you slide the shape down a whole step the chord tones are ♭7th, 9th, and 5th. Still use your 2nd, 3rd, and 4th fingers. The 9th is like a 2nd; we'll explain that in a later Theory module. The essence of the first move in this part is to move this shape back and forth between these two spots.

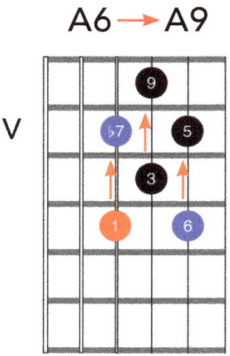

Slide down one step

Now, let's add the final piece. When you have the shape at the 6th and 7th frets, add your 1st finger on the 1st string at the 5th fret. That is the root.

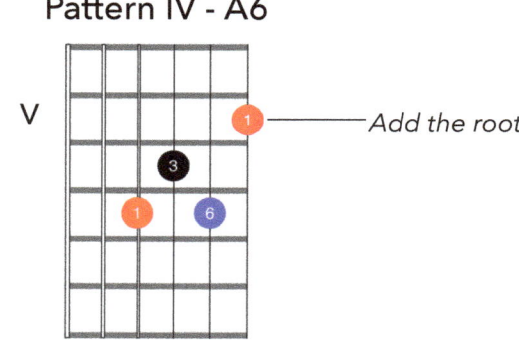

Here is the part.

Because the smallest subdivision for this part is an 8th note, you can use alternate picking. It makes playing the A on the 1st string easier.

Part 2

Next, learn a complimentary popcorn part for the same track. The popcorn part is the single line and muted guitar part you learned about in the Reggae and Funk Rhythm Guitar Modules. This kind of part is generally based on the pentatonic shell. In this example, the part lives inside the Pattern III E major pentatonic shell in 9th position.

Pattern III E Major Pentatonic

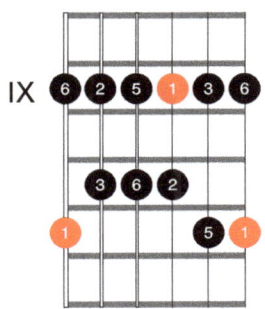

Mute the strings either with the palm of your picking hand or by reducing the pressure in your fretting hand (or both). Don't vary the part very much. Relentless repetitiveness is the key to making these parts all fit together.

Popcorn Part

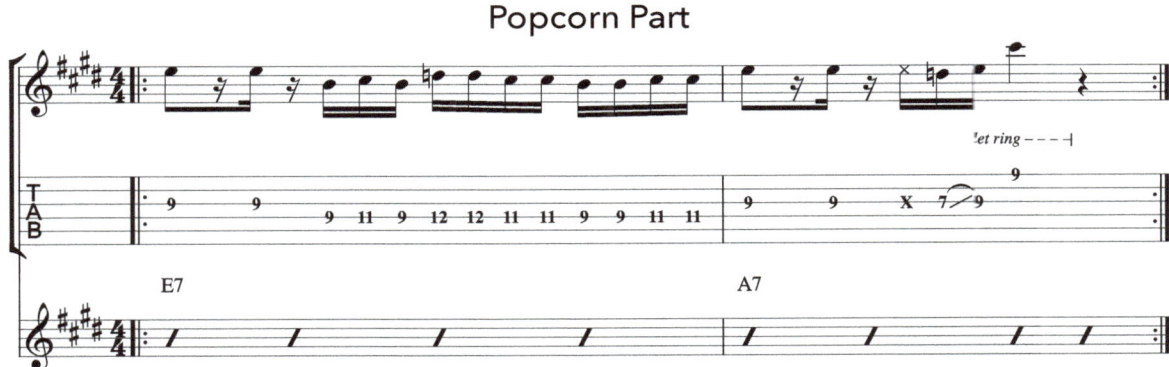

In the first measure, the notes all fit neatly on the 3rd and 4th strings. In the second measure the popcorn continues until the final three notes. They are part of a 6th interval shape embellishment.

I suggest a dryer and brighter tone for this part. On a Strat pickup configuration, the middle/bridge pickup combo works well. Keep these parts in your vocabulary. They can be used in many songs based on dominant 7 chords.

MONEY MAKERS

You learned parts that use 3rds, 4ths, and 5ths from the harmonized major and minor scales. Unit 7 focuses on 6ths from both harmonized major and minor keys. This unit focuses on the two-string sets that cross the B/G line. You will learn one example in major and one in minor.

Diatonic 6ths in a Major Key

The first progression is in the key of G major.

Progression in G Major

Review the major scale harmonized in 6ths along the 1st and 3rd strings you recently learned in the Fretboard Logic Module. Use the higher of the two notes to track the scale.

Diatonic 6ths on the 1st and 3rd Strings in Major

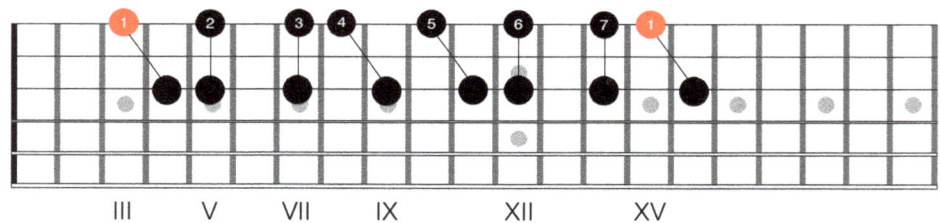

Diatonic 6ths in G

Next, do the same part on string set 2 and 4. Again, use the higher of the two notes to track the scale.

Diatonic 6ths on the 2nd and 4th Strings in Major

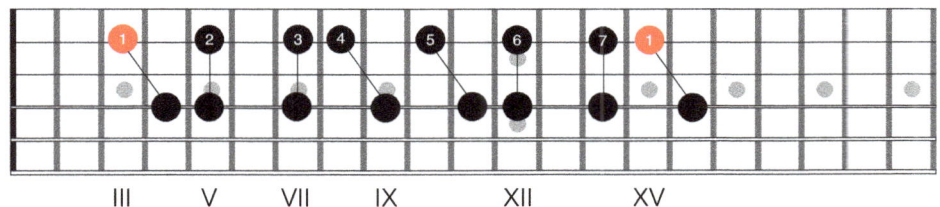

Diatonic 6ths in G

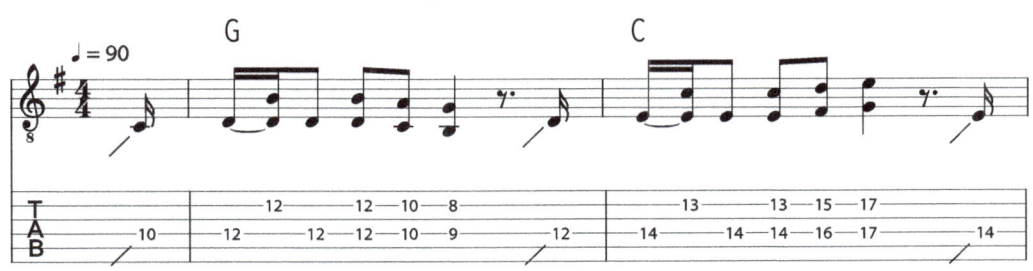

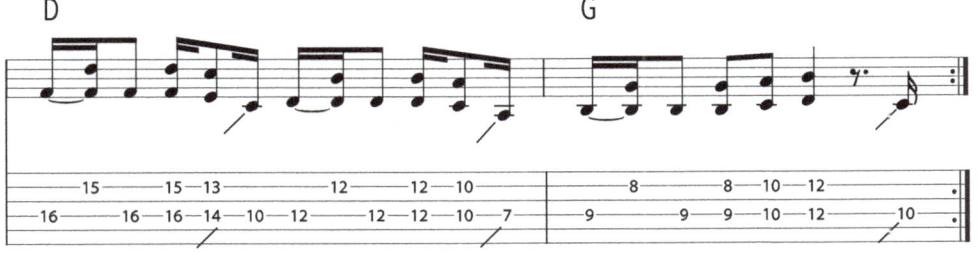

Note the "personality" of 6ths. Experiment with some of your own ideas using these 6th shapes.

Diatonic 6ths in a Minor Key

Here is an example in a minor key. This is a slow, four-bar Rock ballad progression. The part plays out over two times through the progression, in other words, eight bars.

Progression in F Minor

Review the minor scale harmonized in 6ths along the 1st and 3rd strings you recently learned in the Fretboard Logic Module. Use the higher of the two notes to track the scale.

Diatonic 6ths on the 1st and 3rd Strings in Minor

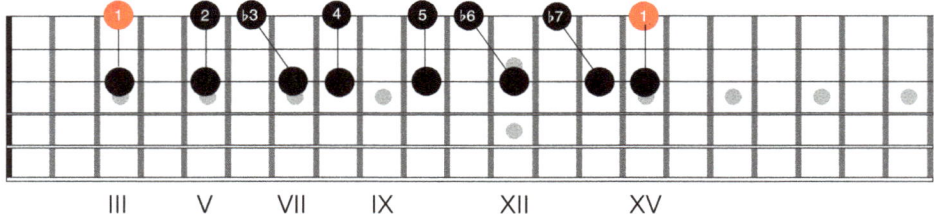

Here is the part.

Diatonic 6ths in F Minor

Next, do the same part on string set 2 and 4. Again, use the higher of the two notes to track the scale.

Diatonic 6ths on the 2nd and 4th Strings in Minor

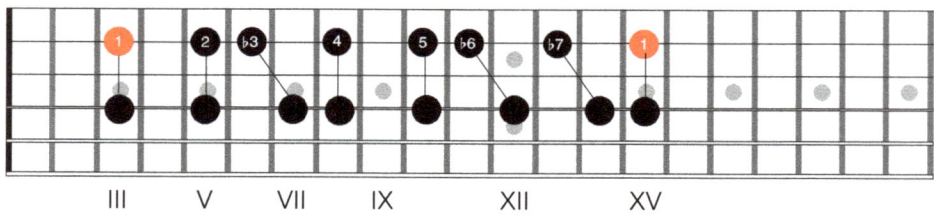

Diatonic 6ths in F Minor

As with the other intervals, note the characteristic "personality" of 6ths in a minor key. Experiment with some of your own ideas using these 6th shapes. Remember that these ideas are transposable to all minor keys!

IMPROVISATION

Our goal will evolve a bit in this module. The focus is still on modal interchange and what notes to play over borrowed chords, but rather than just thinking about parallel scales, it is time to think about chord tones and targeting specific chord tones of a borrowed chord. This will make your lines clearly delineate where modal interchange occurs.

We'll ease into this idea with a simple two-chord progression at a slow tempo. This progression is in C and moves from C major to its relative minor, C minor.

Progression in C Major

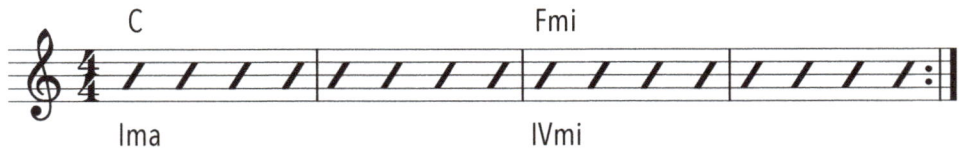

Cma is Ima and Fmi is IVmi, borrowed from C minor. C is the tonic through both chords. For now, work within the Pattern IV octave shape for both C major and C minor. The chord-tone approach works in any octave shape, provided you know the right scale and arpeggio shapes. The objective is to clearly mark the shift from major to the parallel minor by targeting chord tones.

In the Pattern IV C octave shape, here is the C major scale and the Ima arpeggio, as well as the C minor scale and IVmi arpeggio.

Pattern IV C Major Scale   Pattern IV Cma Triad Arpeggio

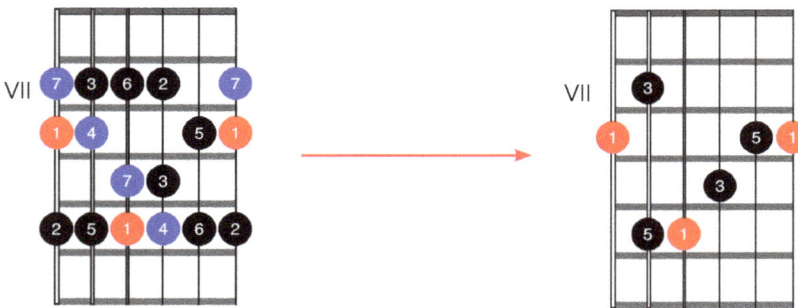

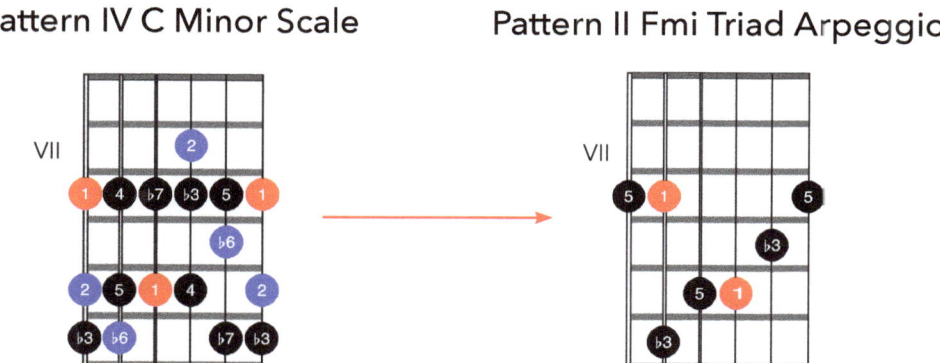

These scales and arpeggios will be the source of notes for this exercise. One note of Fmi in particular will make this change very clear. Target A♭ on the F minor and there will be no doubt about the shift.

A♭ is effective because it is a chord tone of Fmi and it is not in the C major scale. It is part of the C minor scale so it clearly marks the change. Remember, effective use of chord tones doesn't require you to play only chord tones. It is fine to use scale tones to connect chord tones. But it is a good idea to target a chord tone as the first note you play on a new chord.

Use these ideas over the chord progression:

- Over the C major, the chord tones are C, E, and G, and the C major scale is appropriate. The Pattern IV Cma arpeggio is already familiar to you.
- Over the Fmi, the chord tones are F, A♭, and C, and the C minor scale is appropriate. When transitioning to the Fmi chord, try to target A♭ as the first note some of the time.

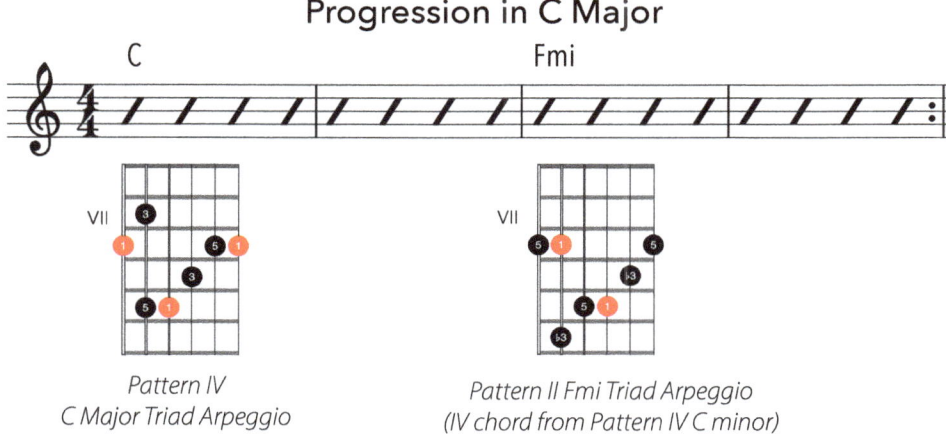

The next Improvisation module will expand on this concept to include 7th chord arpeggios. This requires a lot of practice so don't rush through this.

Level 4 Unit 7 • Improv Demo

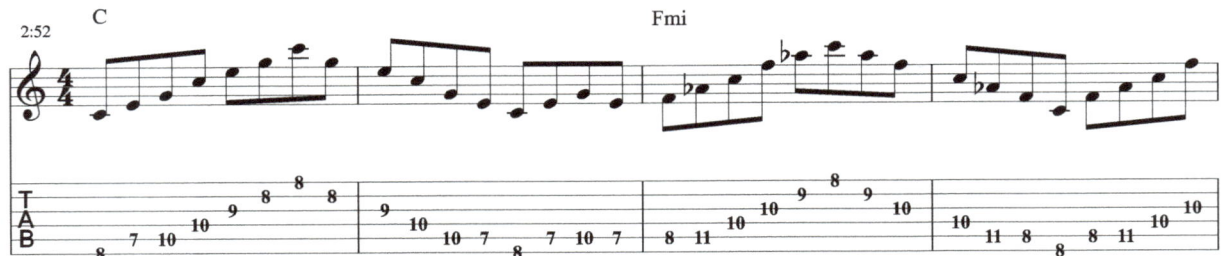

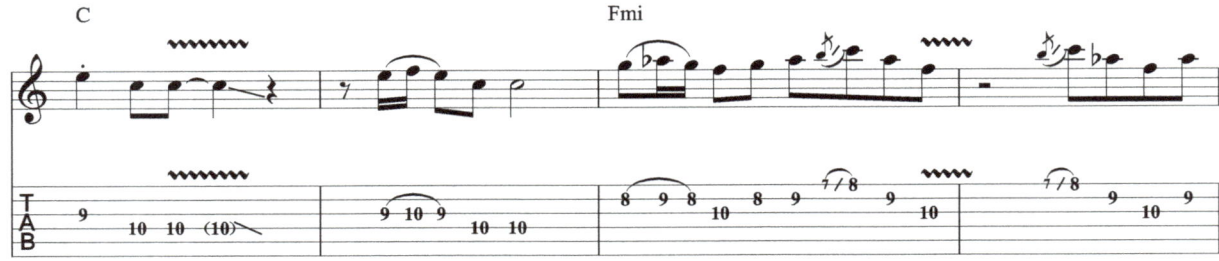

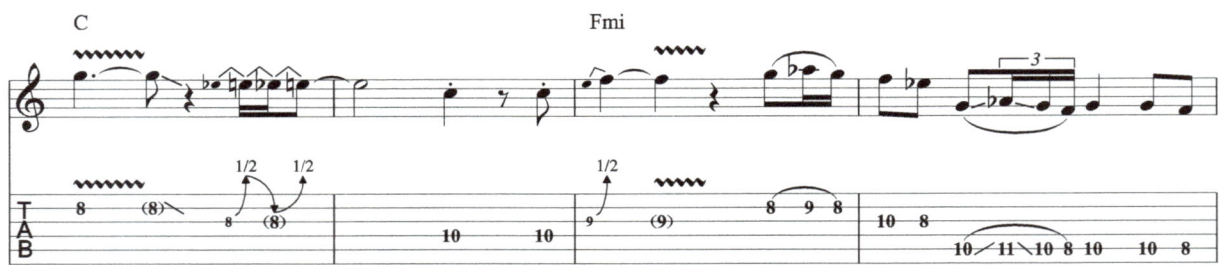

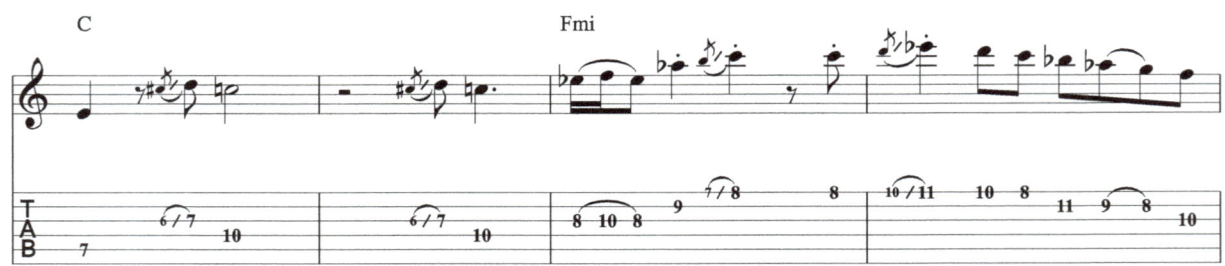

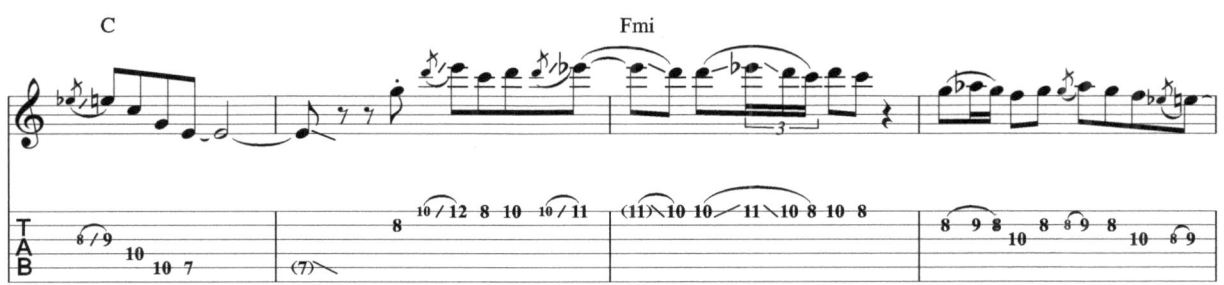
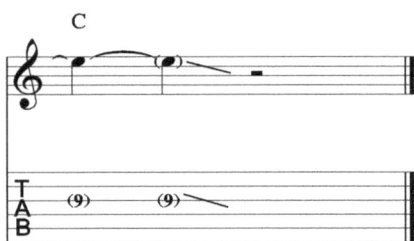

PRACTICE

Theory

- ❏ Go to the tabs below the Theory video on the website and complete the quiz.
- ❏ Learn the triad and 7th chord inversions.
- ❏ Learn how to write and recognize inversions on the staff.

Fretboard Logic

- ❏ Learn the inverted open chord voicings.
- ❏ Learn the diatonic 6th shapes.
- ❏ Practice using modal interchange with triad arpeggios.

Rhythm Guitar

- ❏ Practice the classic R&B parts, paying special attention to pick direction.

Money Makers

- ❏ Practice playing major and minor diatonic 6th parts over major and minor progressions.

Improvisation

- ❏ Practice playing solos over an C major progression with modal interchange.

UNIT 8

Learning Modules

> **Theory** - Slash Chord Symbols, Using Inversions in Progressions

> **Fretboard Logic** - Chord Inversions in Progressions, Major and Minor Scales harmonized with 7th Shapes, Using 7th Chord Arpeggios with Modal Interchange

> **Rhythm Guitar** - Classic R&B

> **Money Makers** - Money Maker Parts using Diatonic 7th Shapes

> **Improvisation** - Soloing with Modal Interchange

> **Practice** - Continue Practice Routine Development

THEORY

There are several reasons for using inverted chords in a progression. In most cases, inversions facilitate a smoother, more step-wise bass line. This module examines common ways inversions are used in chord progressions. This provides context for all that's been presented about inversions. This module also goes deeper into why inverted chords are used. First you need to learn how to write inversions as chord symbols.

Slash Chord Symbols

In popular music, chord symbols provide an alternative to reading the notes of a chord spelled on the staff. You learned that "C" means a C major triad, Cma7 means a C major 7th chord, and so on. There are chord symbols to represent inversions as well. You may have seen what is called a "slash chord". Slash chords can be used to notate inverted chords. Here is how they work.

A slash chord symbol has three parts:

1. A chord symbol slightly elevated and/or to the left. This tells the musician what chord to play.
2. A forward-facing slash.
3. A single letter on the right and/or sometimes slightly lower than the chord symbol on the left. This tells the musician what note is to be voiced at the bottom of the chord – in other words, in the bass.

In this example the musician is to play a C triad with E voiced as the lowest note.

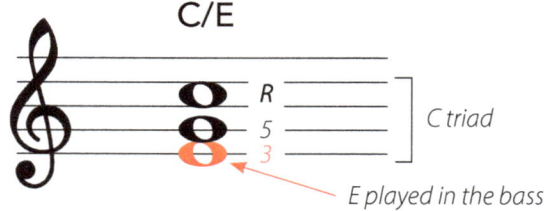

In this example the musician is to play a G triad with D voiced as the lowest note.

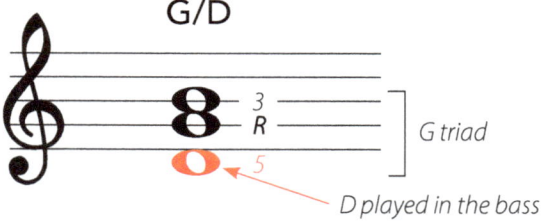

In this example the musician is to play a Bmi7 chord with A voiced as the lowest note.

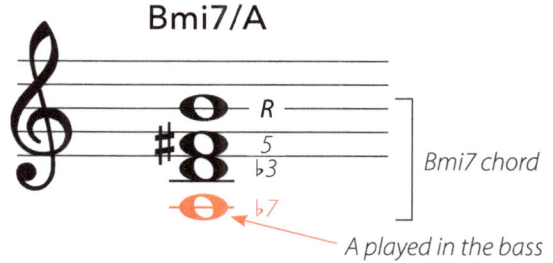

You can already appreciate how well slash chords work for notating inversions. For example, the C/E shown earlier means a C triad with E in the bass. That is a first inversion C major triad. The bass note is E, the 3rd. If the 3rd is voiced in the bass, the chord is in first inversion. The root is still C. Don't assume the bass note is always the root and don't assume the root of a chord is always voiced in the bass.

The G/D shown earlier means a G triad with D in the bass. That is a second inversion G major triad. The root is still G. The bass note is D, the 5th. If the 5th is voiced in the bass, the chord is in second inversion.

The Bmi7/A shown earlier means a Bmi7 chord with A in the bass. That's a third inversion B minor 7 chord. The root is still B. The bass note is A, the 7th. If the 7th is voiced in the bass, the chord is in third inversion.

Here are more examples of inversions written as slash chords:

Inversions Written as Slash Chords

SLASH CHORD	INVERSION
Dmi/F	First inversion Dmi
F/C	Second inversion F
C°/G♭	Second inversion C°
A+/C#	First inversion A+
Cmi/G	Second inversion Cmi
A♭/C	First inversion A♭
B♭ma7/F	Second Inversion B♭ma7
F#mi7/A	First inversion F#mi7

There is sometimes confusion with some slash chords. Compare the two symbols below:

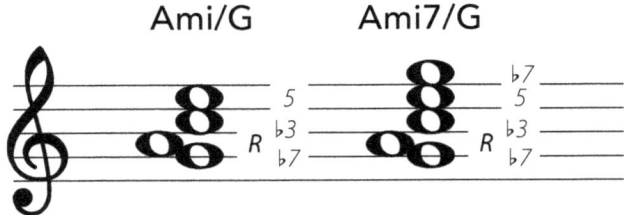

The first symbol is clearly an A minor triad with G in the bass. But what is G to an A minor chord? It is the ♭7. If the 7th is voiced in the bass, the chord is said to be in third inversion. That makes this a third inversion Ami7.

The second symbol is just what it says. It is Ami7 with G in the bass. Like the other chord, if the 7th is voiced in the bass, the chord is said to be in third inversion. That makes this a third inversion Ami7, too.

So what is the difference? It's really a matter of interpretation and how you voice the chord tones above the bass note. The Ami7/G could imply a full Ami7 (A, C, E, and G) played and then a G in the bass, or it could imply what you think of with the Ami/G – just a triad with a ♭7th in the bass.

Voicing the ♭7th (G) twice, once in the bass and again in the chord above, is not always desirable. Because it is played twice in the voicing, G will sort of dominate the sound of the chord. Make your decision on a case-by-case basis and perhaps ask the person who wrote the chart or is leading the band how they want the chord voiced.

Using Inversions in Progressions

Look at the common ways inversions are used in progressions. The two most common uses of inversions are:

- To create a smooth and step-wise bass line in a progression where, if the bass played the roots, the line would be angular because of the wide intervals.
- To "pedal" on a single note while the chords above are changing.

Creating Smoother Bass Lines

First, let's look at how inversions can facilitate a smoother bass line. Take a look at this short chord progression in the key of C. If all the chords are played in root position, the bass line is somewhat angular. Follow the red line.

Progression in C Major

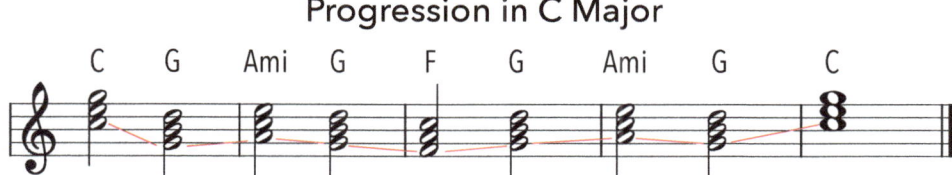

If you use a first inversion G in a couple of places (G/B), the bass line is considerably smoother. Compare the contour of the bass line in the two versions. Follow the red line.

Progression in C Major with Inversions

Here is a progression in the key of A. If all the chords are played in root position, the bass line is angular.

Progression in A Major

If inversions are used in a couple of places, the bass line is considerably smoother.

Progression in A Major with Inversions

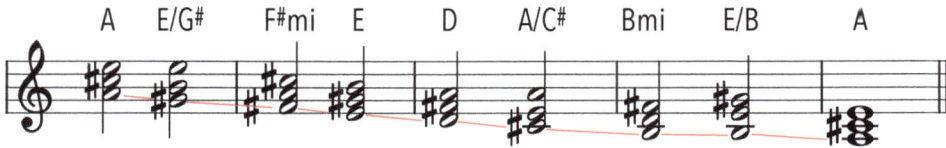

Examine this chord progression in the key of A minor. If all the chords are played in root position the bass line is angular.

Progression in A Minor

| Ami | Ami7 | D | Dmi | Ami | E | Ami | E |

If inversions are used in a couple of places, the bass line is considerably smoother.

Progression in A Minor with Inversions

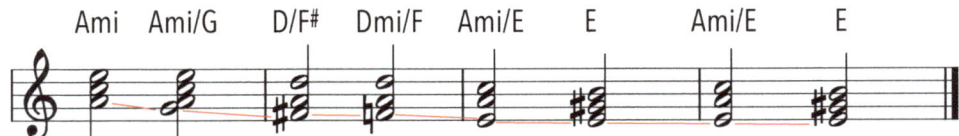

| Ami | Ami/G | D/F# | Dmi/F | Ami/E | E | Ami/E | E |

You will play all of these examples in the Fretboard Logic Module. This all makes more sense when you actually play and hear the inversions in context.

It should be noted again that depending on the arrangement and context, sometimes only the bass player is playing the notes that make the "ensemble chord" inverted. Remember, we'll call it the ensemble chord because that's the totality of what the audience hears.

Sometimes some or all instruments are playing the inversion. It all depends on what the arranger or leader wants to hear. If only the bass player is playing a bass note that is not the root, avoid playing a root in your voicing within a 5th of the bass player's note. This will prevent the dissonance that results from playing two or more low notes close together.

Creating a Pedal

Next, look at how inversions are used to play what is called a "pedal" through a series of chords. A pedal is a note that is common to several successive chords and is usually in the bass. Take a look at this two-chord progression in the key of A.

If the chords are played in root position the bass line is angular.

Progression in A Major

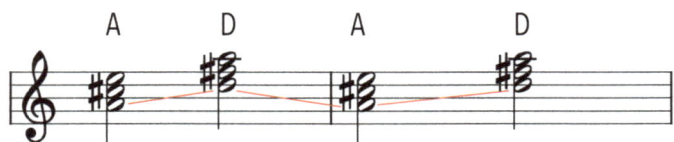

| A | D | A | D |

However, A can be played as a pedal under both chords like this:

Progression in A Major with a Pedal on A

Here's another example:

Progression in C Minor

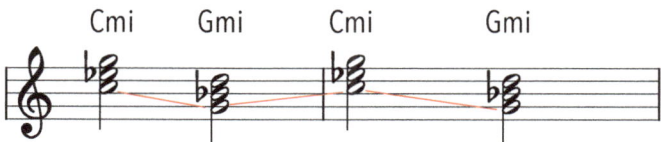

And now with a G pedal:

Progression in C Minor with a Pedal on G

FRETBOARD LOGIC

Chord Inversions

In the Theory Module you learned how slash chords are used in progressions. The two most common uses of inversions are:

- To create a smooth and step-wise bass line in a progression where the wide intervals would make the line angular if the bass played the roots.
- To "pedal" on a single note while the chords above move.

Creating Smoother Bass Lines

First, look at how inversions can facilitate a smoother bass line. Play this short chord progression in C that you studied in the Theory Module using a combination of root position open and barre chords. Because the chords are played in root position, the bass line is angular. (Note that the notes on the staff don't reflect the exact voicings in the chord diagrams.)

Progression in C Major

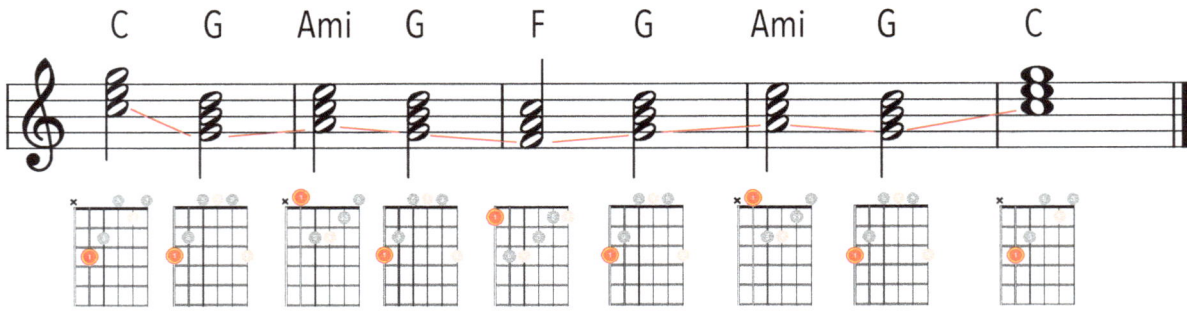

Next, use a first inversion G in a couple of places (that's G/B). This makes the bass line much smoother and by-step. (Notes on the staff don't reflect the voicings in the diagrams.)

Progression in C Major with Inversions

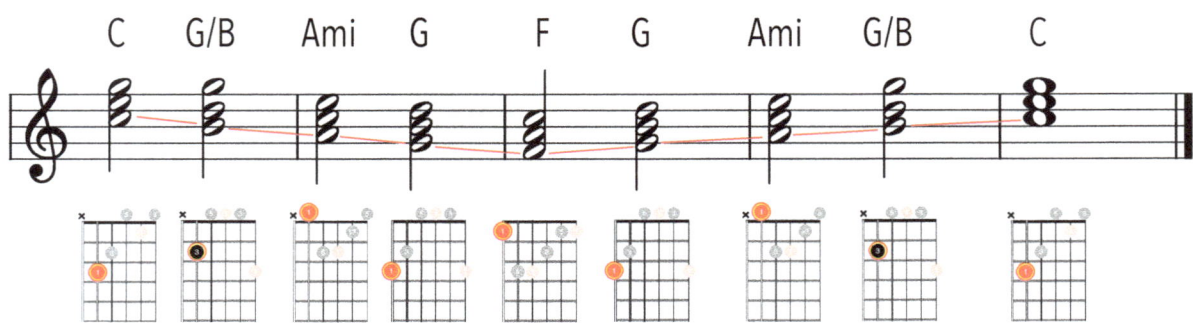

Next, play this progression in the key of A that you studied in the Theory Module using root position chords. Notice in this example that the bass line is angular.

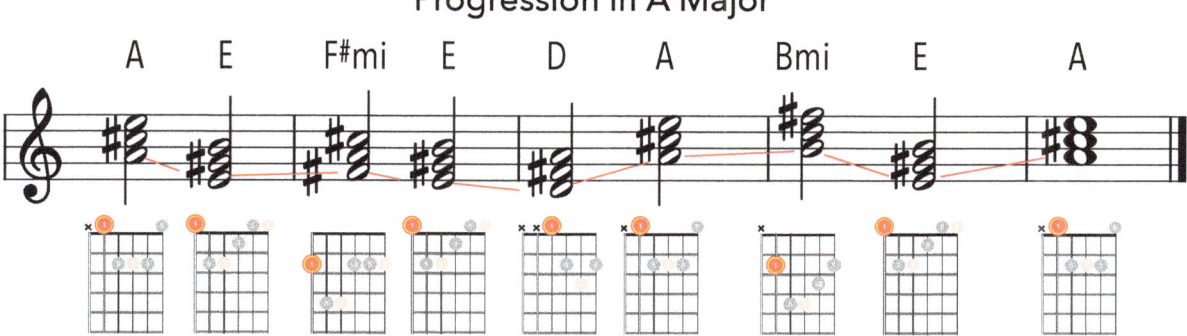

Now use inversions in a couple of places: E/G# and A/C#. This makes the bass line much smoother.

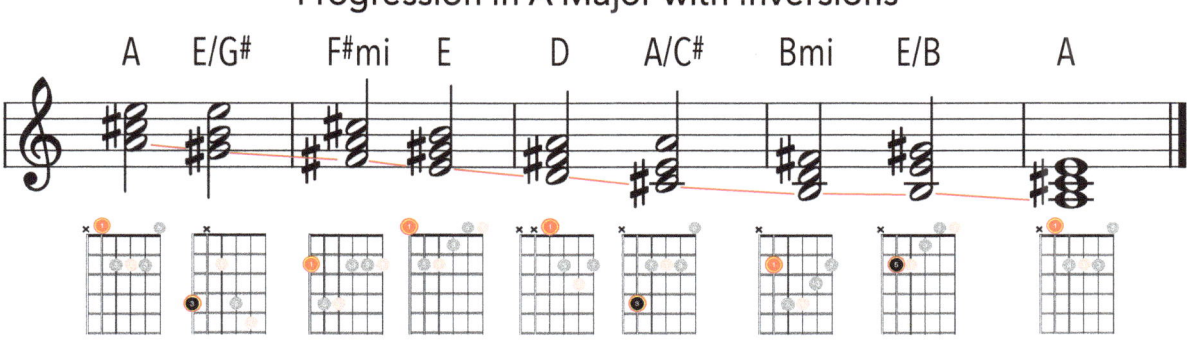

Next, play this progression in the key of A minor that you studied in the Theory Module using root position chords. Again, the bass line is angular.

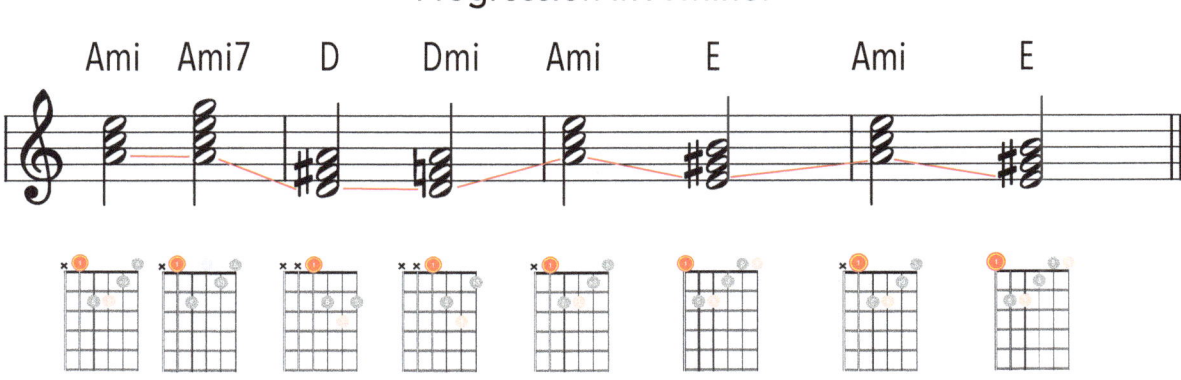

Now, use inversions in a couple of places and the bass line is much smoother.

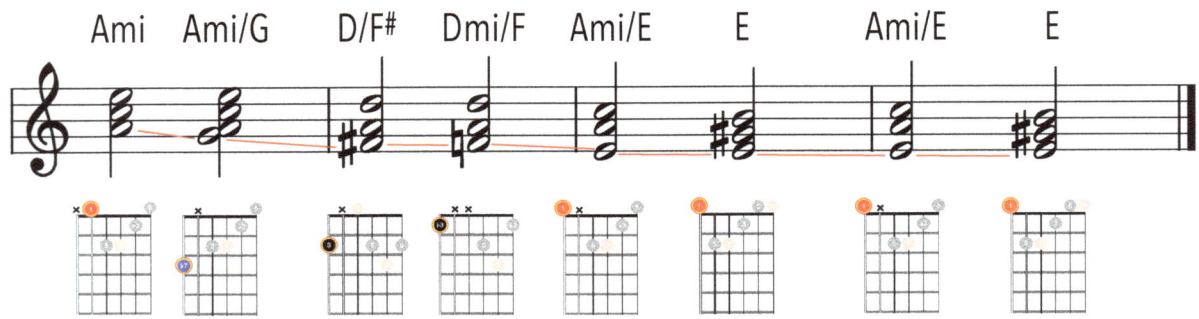

Creating a Pedal

You learned in the Theory Module that there are instances where, for dramatic effect, a single bass note will be held as a pedal through a series of chords. The bass note is common to each chord in the series.

Play this two-chord progression in the key of A.

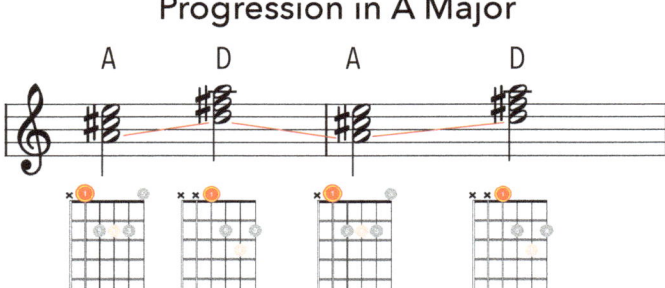

Next play it with the A pedal.

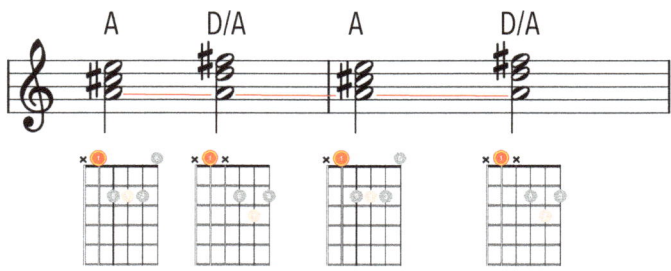

Here is another example.

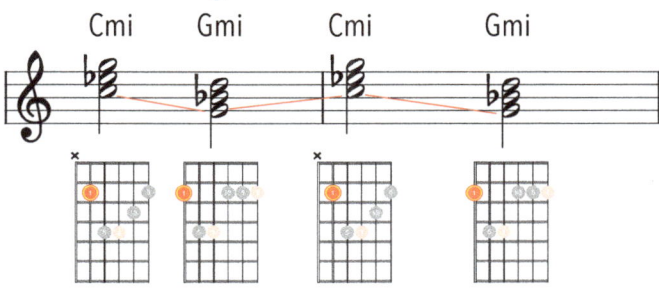

With a G pedal.

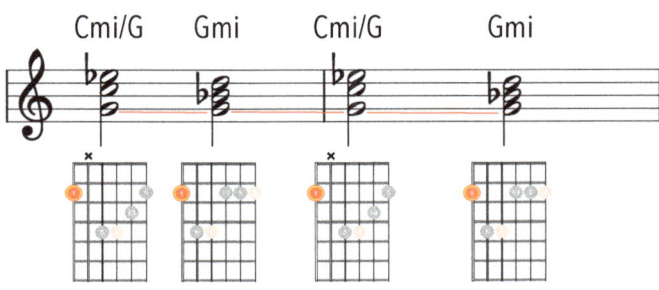

Intervals

You have learned the diatonic 3rd, 4th, 5th, and 6th shapes along adjacent and some non-adjacent strings as they relate to the diatonic major and minor scales. With 3rds and 5ths you use the bottom note of the pair as the guide. With 4ths and 6ths you think of the higher of the two notes as the melodic guide.

In this module you learn about 7ths. With 7ths, the bottom note is the melodic guide. Start with string set 3 and 1 and string set 4 and 2 because they cross the B/G line.

Diatonic 7th Shapes in Major

For demonstration purposes, start in the key of A major. Consider the notes along the 3rd string as the "scale degrees" starting with A at the 2nd fret. Play the A scale along the 3rd string: A, B, C#, D, E, F#, G#

A Major Scale on the 3rd String

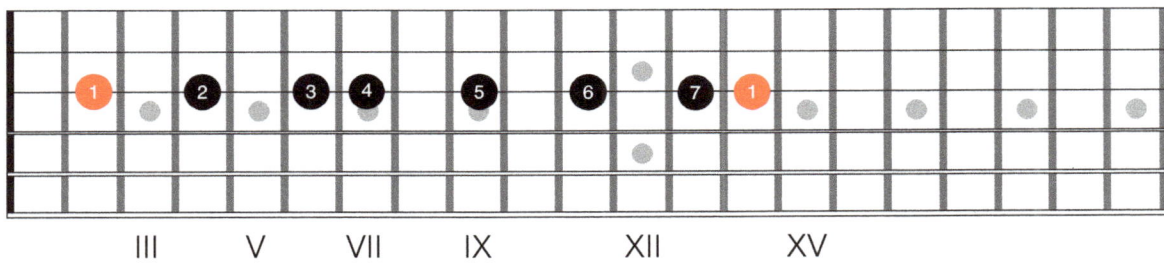

Next, play the note a diatonic 7th higher than each scale degree on the 1st string.

Diatonic 7ths on the 3rd and 1st Strings in Major

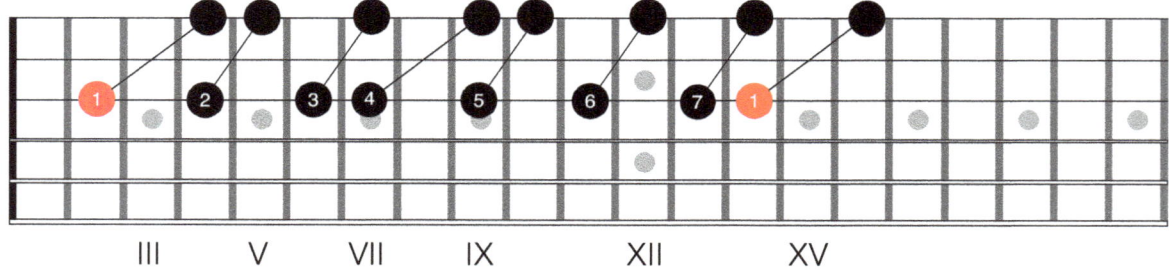

This works for any major key. Track the scale along the 3rd string. This set of shapes for the major scale works for these string sets:

- The 3rd and 1st strings

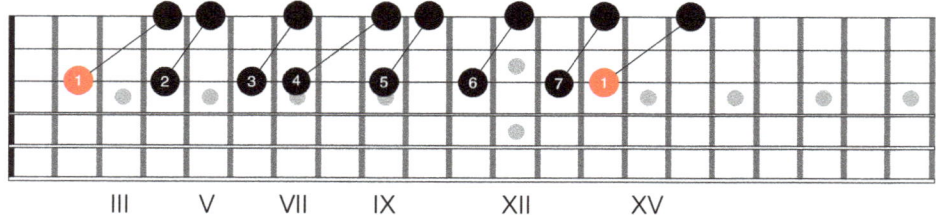

- The 4th and 2nd strings

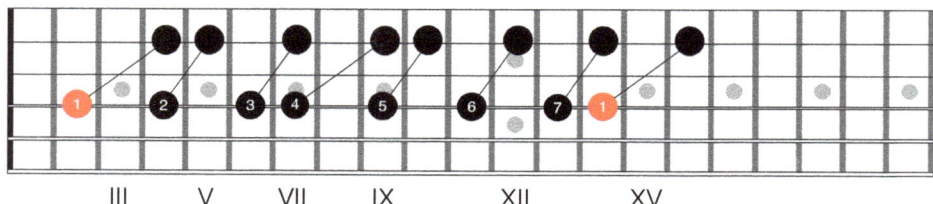

Let's look at string set 5 and 3 and string set 6 and 4 because they do not cross the B/G line.

For demonstration purposes, start in the key of C major. Consider the notes along the 5th string as the "scale degrees" starting with C at the 3rd fret. Play the C scale along the 5th string: C, D, E, F, G, A, and B.

C Major Scale on the 5th String

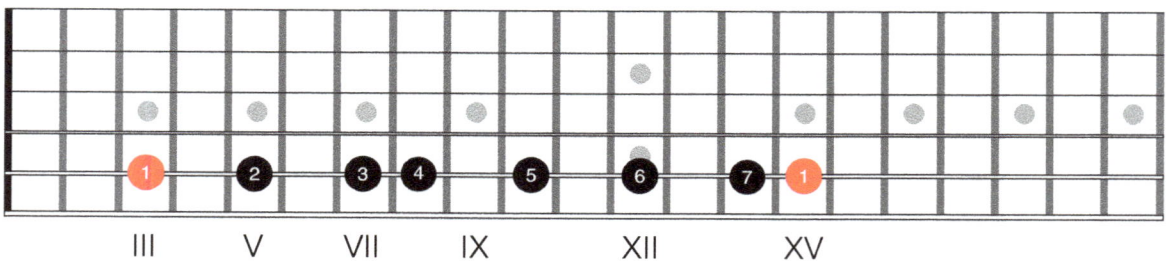

Next, play the note a diatonic 7th higher than each scale degree on the 3rd string.

Diatonic 7ths on the 5th and 3rd Strings in Major

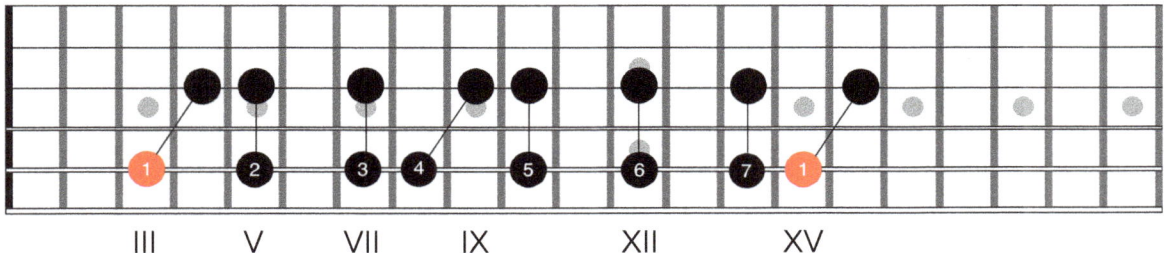

This works for any major key. Track the scale along the 5th string. This set of shapes for the major scale works for these string sets:

- The 5th and 3rd strings

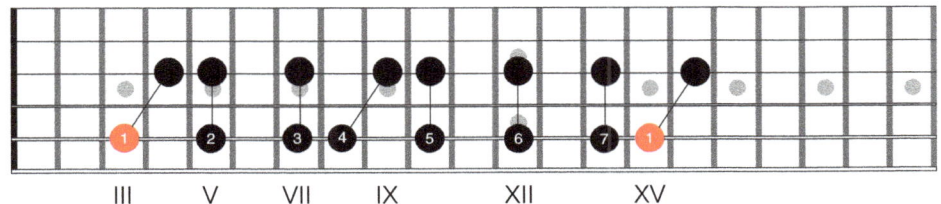

- The 6th and 4th strings.

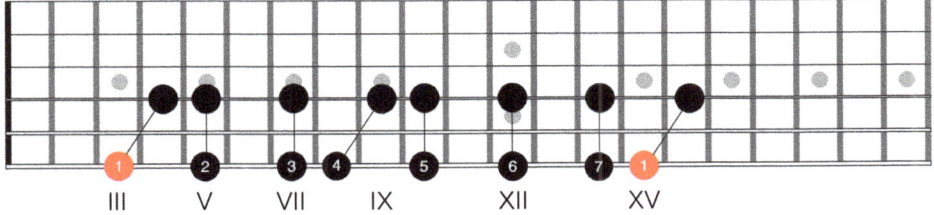

Diatonic 7th Shapes in Minor

Look at the key of A minor. Consider the notes along the 3rd string as the "scale degrees" starting with A at the 2nd fret. Play the A minor scale along the 3rd string: A, B, C, D, E, F, G.

A Minor Scale on the 3rd String

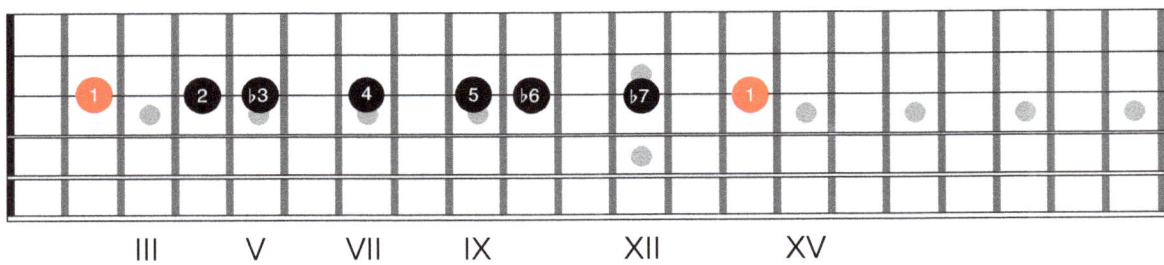

Next, play the note a diatonic 7th higher than each scale degree on the 1st string.

Diatonic 7ths on the 3rd and 1st Strings in Minor

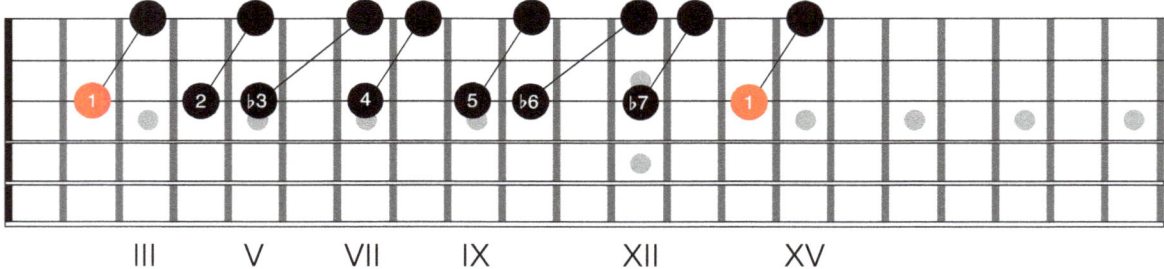

This works for any minor key. Track the scale along the 3rd string. This set of shapes for the major scale works for these string sets:

- The 3rd and 1st strings

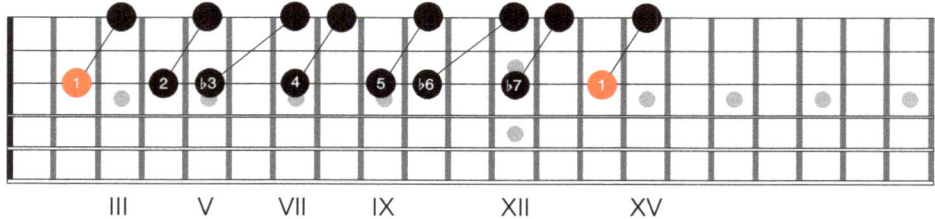

- The 4th and 2nd strings

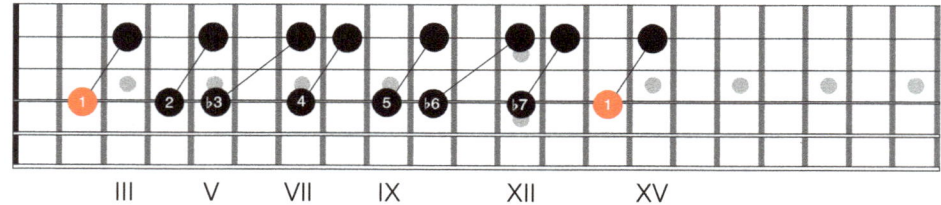

Look at string set 5 and 3 and string set 6 and 4 because they do not cross the B/G line.

For demonstration purposes, start in the key of C minor. Consider the notes along the 5th string as the "scale degrees" starting with C at the 3rd fret. Play the C minor scale along the 5th string: C, D, E♭, F, G, A♭, B♭.

C Minor Scale on the 5th String

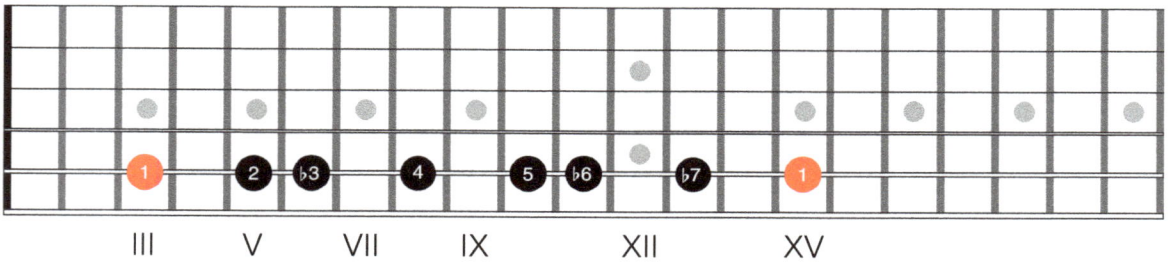

Next, play the note a diatonic 7th higher than each scale degree on the 3rd string.

Diatonic 7ths on the 5th and 3rd Strings in Minor

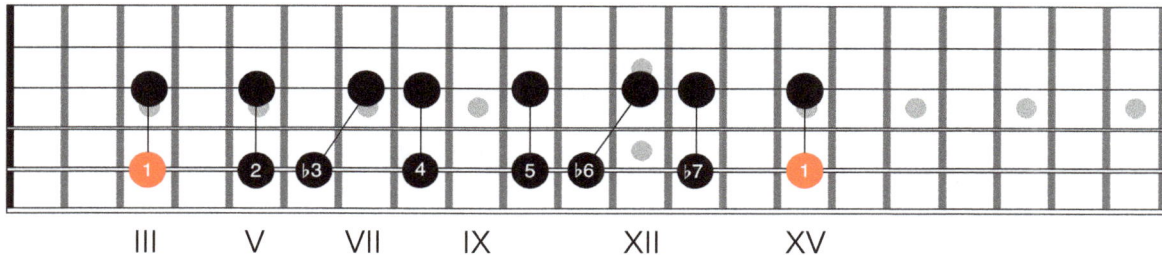

This works for any minor key. Track the scale along the 5th string. This set of shapes for the major scale works for these string sets:

- The 5th and 3rd strings

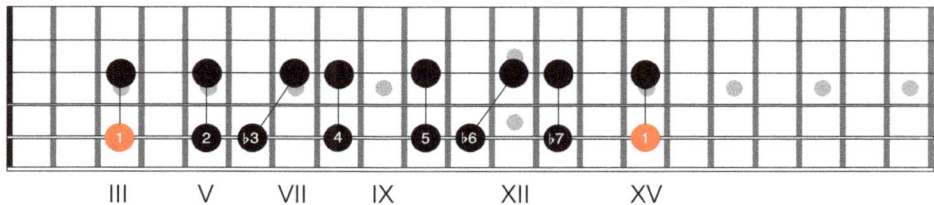

- The 6th and 4th strings

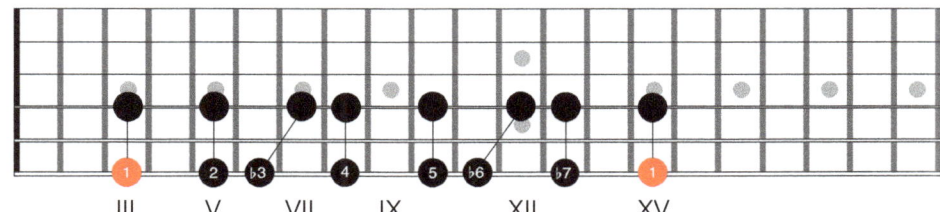

You will work with these diatonic 7th shapes in the Money Maker modules.

Arpeggios

Continue the focus on using chord tones in progressions with modal interchange. The last unit compared the triad arpeggios of harmonized parallel scales. Remember that the in-position arpeggio idea works well for soloing over progressions with modal interchange, too. It requires expanding the number of arpeggios you visualize within an octave shape to include those of both parallel major and minor.

Here are the parallel scales harmonized with 7th chords:

Harmonized Major and Natural Minor Scales with 7th Chords

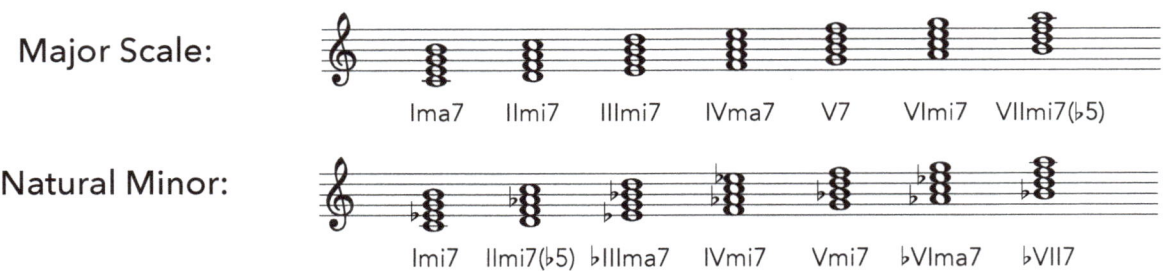

Next, here are the 7th chord arpeggios of the harmonized major and minor scales in Octave Shape II shown side-by-side. The idea is for you to understand how they all fit within the octave shape and then be able to access them quickly when soloing. You have already worked on in-position arpeggios so this should be very familiar to you.

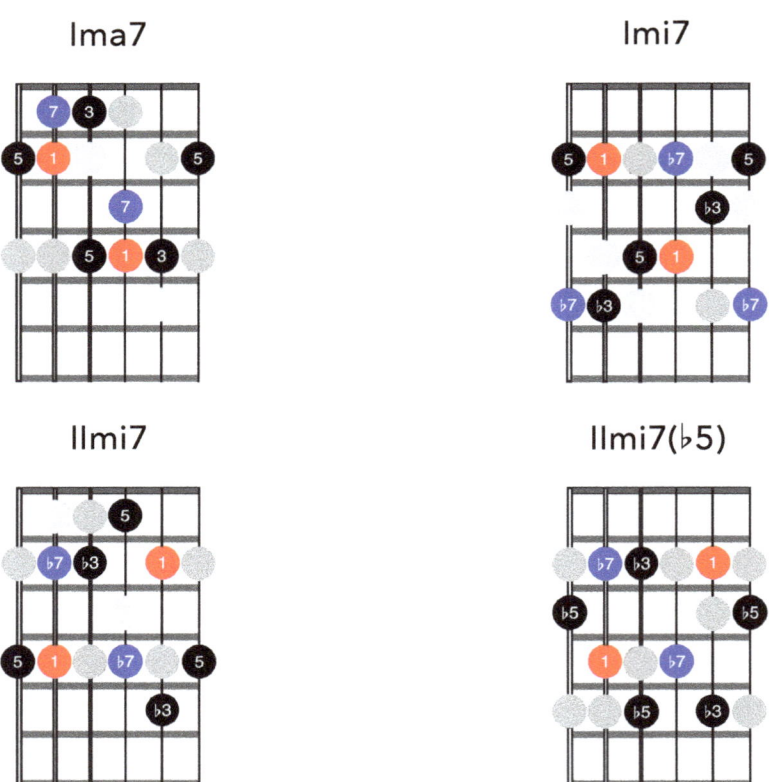

Fretboard Biology — Level 4 • Unit 8: Fretboard Logic

IIImi7
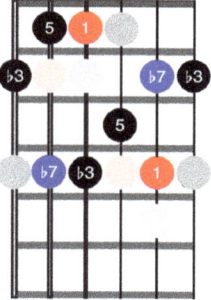

bIIIma7
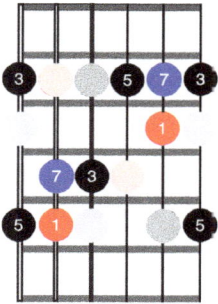

IVma7
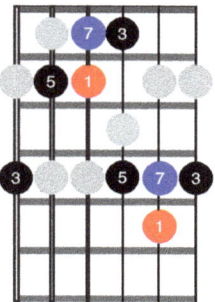

IVmi7
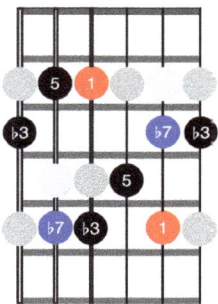

V7
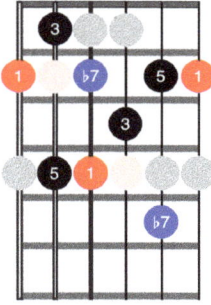

Vmi7
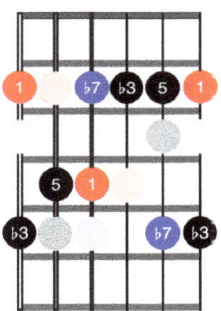

VImi7
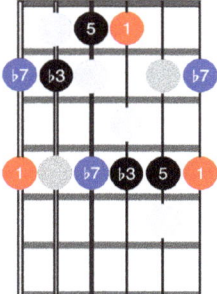

bVIma7
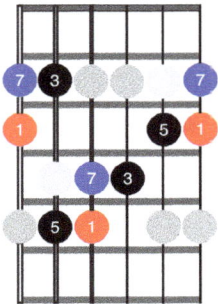

 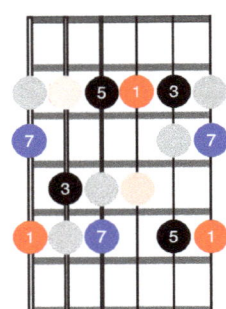

None of this material is new to you. The difference here is that the arpeggios of parallel keys are organized side-by-side. Your goal is to understand how the arpeggios of harmonized parallel scales fit within each octave shape and then be able to access them when soloing. This isn't learned quickly so just incorporate this into your practice routine as part of how you work through your arpeggios.

As your practice routine evolves, it is important to have consistency but it is also important to have variety. You can create variety with material you already know by changing the way you practice it. Now you have another way to practice arps: in position with parallel keys.

In the Practice modules I have also suggested having two or even three rotating practice routines. That idea could be applied here. For example, perhaps Monday, Wednesday, and Friday you could practice in-position arpeggios in major and minor keys separately. On Tuesday, Thursday, and Saturday you could practice in-position arpeggios as they are presented here, in parallel keys.

Ultimately the most important way to practice this material is with the progressions in the Improvisation modules. This material can be practiced on all of the other Level 4 Improv progressions because they all are examples of modal interchange.

RHYTHM GUITAR

In this module of Classic R&B rhythm guitar parts you will learn to use a combination of 3rds and 6th interval shapes. The example in this module is in the spirit of guitarist Steve Cropper.

The progression for this example is four bars in length, in the key of G, and it contains a borrowed chord (modal interchange).

An analysis of this progression shows that:

- G is Ima
- B♭ is ♭IIIma (borrowed from the parallel minor)
- C is IVma

I suggest mainly downstrokes for this example with an exception on the B♭ and C chords which I will explain shortly. It will make your attacks sound more consistent throughout the example.

For the I chord, G, play the part in the vicinity of a Pattern IV barre chord. Look at the chord tones for reference: R, 5, R, 3, 5, R.

Pattern IV G Major Barre Chord

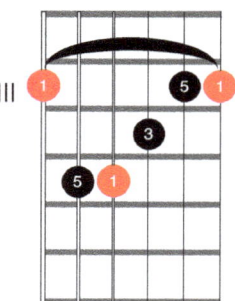

The first three points of this will be on the 2nd and 3rd strings. For the first point, play the ♭7 on the 2nd string at the 6th fret with your 2nd finger. It's three frets higher than the 5th at the 6th fret. That is a minor 3rd higher. Then play the 5th on the 3rd string at the 7th fret using your 3rd finger. Be sure to see the "ghost" of the Pattern IV barre chord as you locate these notes.

Ima First Point

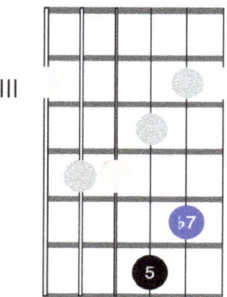

For the second point, locate the 6th one fret below the ♭7 on the 2nd string at the 5th fret. Locate the 4th at the 5th fret of the 3rd string. This double stop can be played with either your 3rd or 4th finger by barring. Don't use your 1st finger because you'll need it for the next move. Be sure to see the "ghost" of the Pattern IV barre chord as you locate these notes.

Ima Second Point

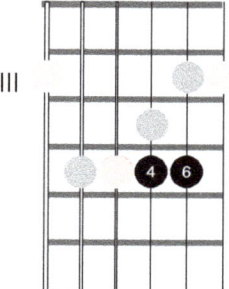

For the third point, play both the 2nd and 3rd strings at the 3rd fret with your 1st finger. The note on 3rd string is B♭, the minor 3rd, and the note on the 2nd string is D, the 5th. Immediately hammer on the 3rd string at the 4th fret with your 2nd finger. You are hammering from the B♭ (minor 3rd) to B natural (major 3rd). Again, be sure to see the "ghost" of the Pattern IV barre chord as you locate these notes.

Ima Third Point

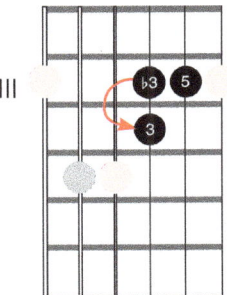

For the fourth point, play the root at the 5th fret of the 4th string with your 3rd finger.

Ima Fourth Point

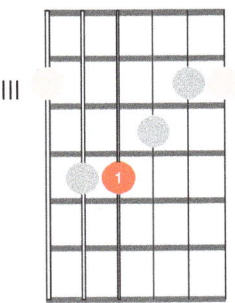

For the last point of this first part, look at the 1st and 3rd strings in a Pattern IV barre chord: The root on the 1st string and the 3rd on the 3rd string. Slide into the major 3rd at the 4th fret of the 3rd string with your 2nd finger and add the root at the 3rd fret on the 1st string with your 1st finger.

Ima Fifth Point

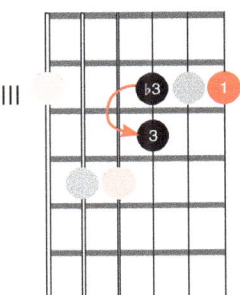

With your picking hand, play the 3rd string with your pick and the 1st string with your 3rd finger. This is an easy reach and gives you a nice bit of dynamic control.

For the ♭IIIma chord, there is a two-point move. As with the G, look at the 1st and 3rd strings in a Pattern IV B♭ barre chord: The root on the 1st string and the 3rd on the 3rd string.

For the first point, visualize the Pattern IV B♭ barre chord in 6th position. Slide into the major 3rd at the 7th fret of the 3rd string with your 2nd finger picking with a downstroke. Add the root at the 6th fret on the 1st string with your 1st finger. In your picking hand, play the note on the 1st string with your 3rd finger.

♭IIIma First Point

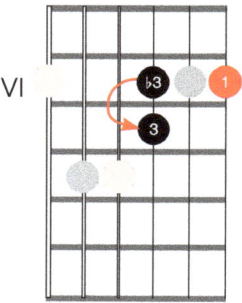

For the second point, with your 1st and 3rd fingers still in place where you started, place your 3rd finger at the 8th fret of the 3rd string and your 4th finger at the 8th fret of the 1st string. Use your pick and a downstroke on the 3rd string and your picking hand 3rd finger for the 1st string. Then slide that shape up to the next location at the 10th fret.

♭IIIma Second Point

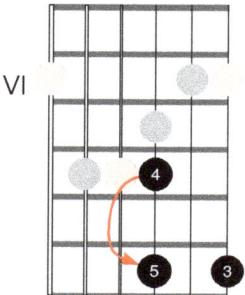

It should be noted that the two notes at the end of this move are also chord tones of the B♭. The D at the 10th fret of the 1st string is the major 3rd of a B♭, and the F at the 10th fret of the 3rd string is the 5th of the B♭.

For the IVma chord, you will repeat what we did on the B♭ chord, except you will reference the Pattern IV C barre chord.

IVma First Point

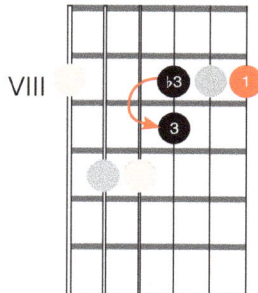

IVma Second Point

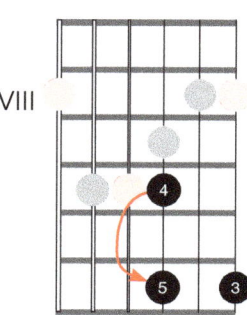

The last part returns to G and is similar to the opening line. For the first point, play the ♭7 on the 2nd string at the 6th fret with your 2nd finger and the 5th on the 3rd string at the 7th fret with your 3rd finger.

Ima First Point

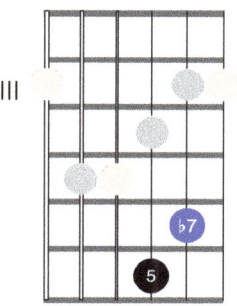

For the second point, play the 5th on the 2nd string at the 3rd fret and the ♭3rd also at the 3rd fret of the 3rd string.

Ima Second Point

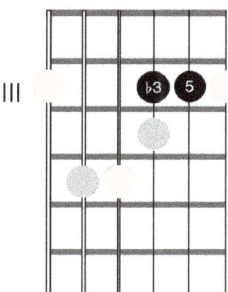

For the third point, play the 6th on the 2nd string at the 5th fret and the 4th at the 5th fret of the 3rd string.

Ima Third Point

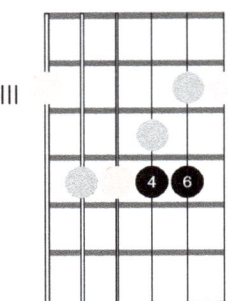

For the final notes, play the root on the 4th string at the 5th fret, then the ♭3 at the 3rd fret of the 3rd string, then the major 3rd at the 4th fret of the 3rd string and finish on the root on the 4th string at the 5th fret.

Ima Fourth Point

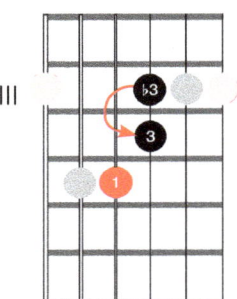

This kind of part sounds great on a Telecaster-style guitar. The pickup switch setting depends on the pickup configuration. You want a bright tone but not painful to the listener. With other guitars, experiment with pickup settings that mimic that classic Tele sound. For reference, listen to some classic R&B recordings of artists like Sam & Dave.

Make these figures part of your permanent vocabulary. They are appropriate for R&B, Blues, Country, and Rock.

MONEY MAKERS

So far, you have learned parts that use 3rds, 4ths, 5ths, and 6ths from the harmonized major and minor scales. In this unit you will learn to use 7ths from both harmonized major and minor keys. The 7th shapes for these examples are on string sets that cross the B/G line: string set 3 and 1 and string set 4 and 2. You will learn one example in major and one in minor.

Diatonic 7ths in a Major Key

The first progression is in the key of E major.

Progression in E Major

Review the major scale harmonized in 7ths along the 3rd and 1st strings that you recently learned in the Fretboard Logic Module. You recall that when harmonizing a scale in 7ths, use the lower of the two notes to track the scale.

Diatonic 7ths on the 3rd and 1st strings in Major

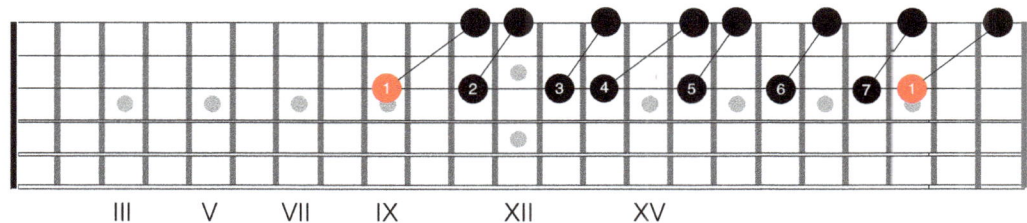

Here is the part.

Diatonic 7ths in E

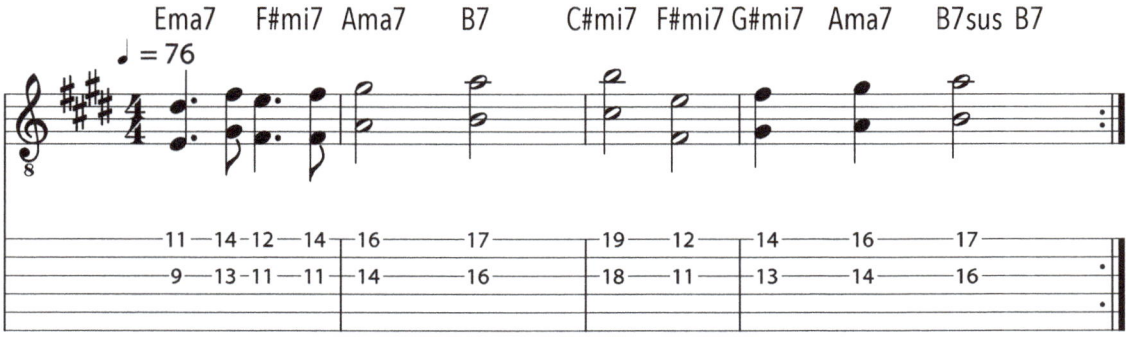

Do the same thing on string set 2 and 4. Again, use the lower of the two notes to track the scale.

Diatonic 7ths in E

Note the "personality" of the sound of 7ths.

Diatonic 7ths in a Minor Key

The minor progression is a four-bar Rock progression in the key of C minor.

Progression in C Minor

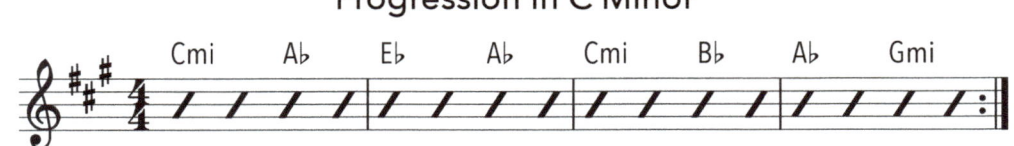

Next play the minor scale on string set 1 and 3 harmonized in 7ths.

Diatonic 7ths on the 3rd and 1st strings in Minor

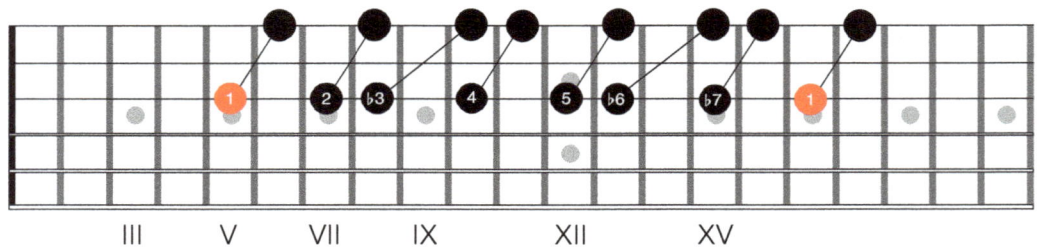

Here is the part.

Do the same thing on string set 2 and 4. Again, use the lower of the two notes to track the scale.

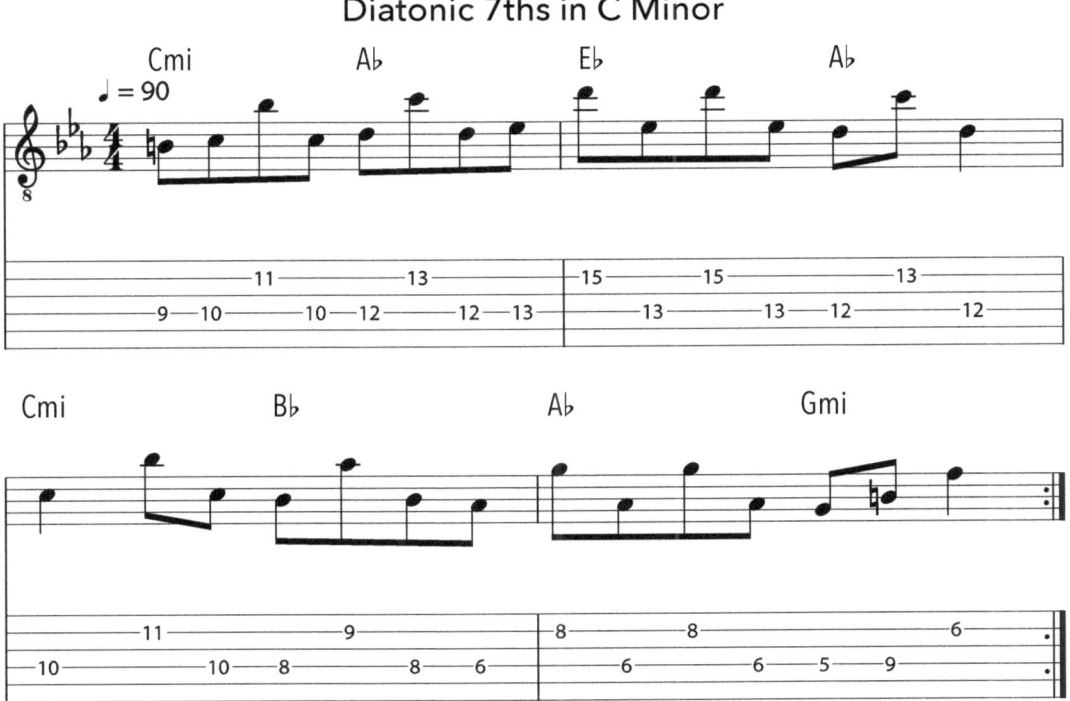

Again, note the "personality" of 7ths in a minor key. Experiment with some of your own ideas using these 7th shapes.

IMPROVISATION

This module keeps the focus on using chord tones to target specific notes in a borrowed chord. This helps your lines clearly delineate where modal interchange occurs. The difference in this module is that you will use 7th chord arpeggios. You know the five parallel major and minor scale patterns harmonized with 7th chords from the Fretboard Logic Module. You will use that information in this module in a two-chord progression.

This progression is in D and moves from D major to its relative minor, D minor.

Progression in D Major

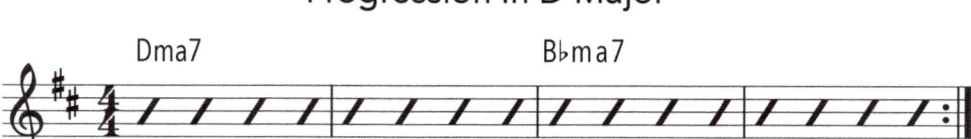

Dma7 is the Imaj7 chord and B♭ma7 is the ♭VIma7, borrowed from D minor, the parallel minor scale. D is the tonic through all four bars. In the last unit you worked in Pattern IV. Here, you will work in Pattern II for both D major and D minor, but of course this will work in any octave shape if you use the right scale and arpeggio shapes.

It's important to work through this material at a really slow tempo so you have time to react and find the next note. There are plenty of tracks from other levels and modules you can use to practice this idea when you're ready for longer progressions and faster tempos. The objective is to clearly mark the shift from major to the parallel minor by targeting chord tones.

In the Pattern II D octave shape, here is the major scale and the Ima7 arpeggio.

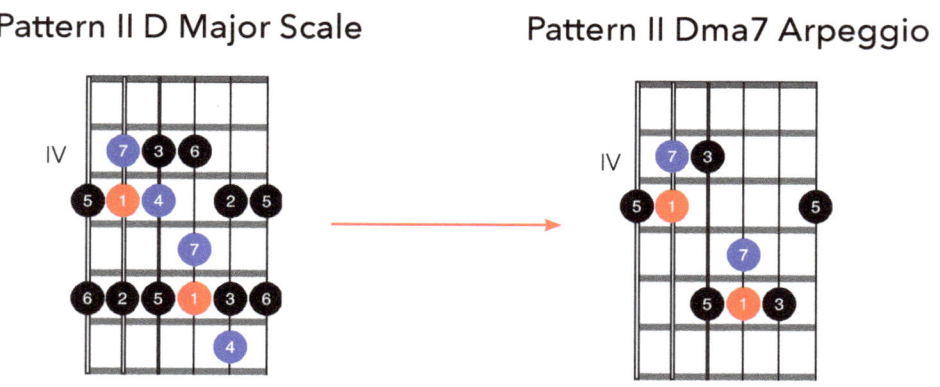

In the Pattern II D octave shape, here is the D minor scale and the ♭VIma7 arpeggio.

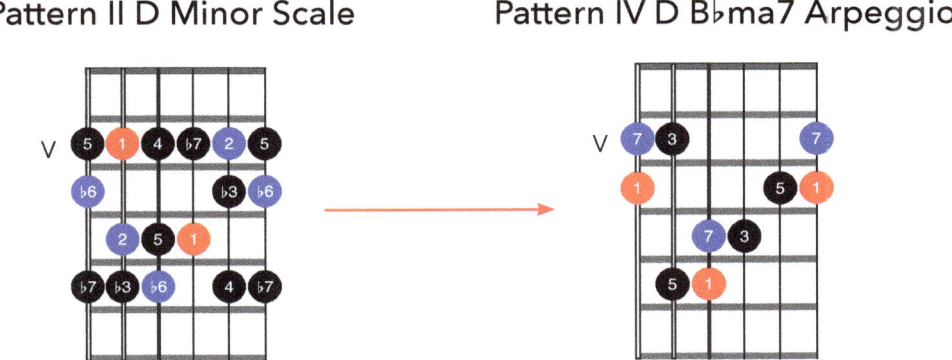

These scales and arpeggios will be the source of notes for this exercise. There are two notes of the B♭ma7 will make this change clear. Target B♭ and F on the B♭ma7 and there will be no doubt about the shift. Why these notes? First, they're both chord tones of B♭ma7. Second, they are not in the D major scale. They are part of the D minor scale so they clearly mark the change. Remember that using chord tones doesn't mean you play only chord tones. But it's a good idea to target a chord tone as the first note you play on a new chord.

Try these ideas over the chord progression. Over the Dma7, the chord tones are D, F#, A, C# and of course the D major scale is appropriate. When you transition to B♭ma7, try to target B♭ or F as the first note.

For each octave shape, outline each arpeggio first. Next, blend the Dma7 arpeggio and D major scale over Dma7 and the B♭ma7 arpeggio and D minor scale over B♭ma7.

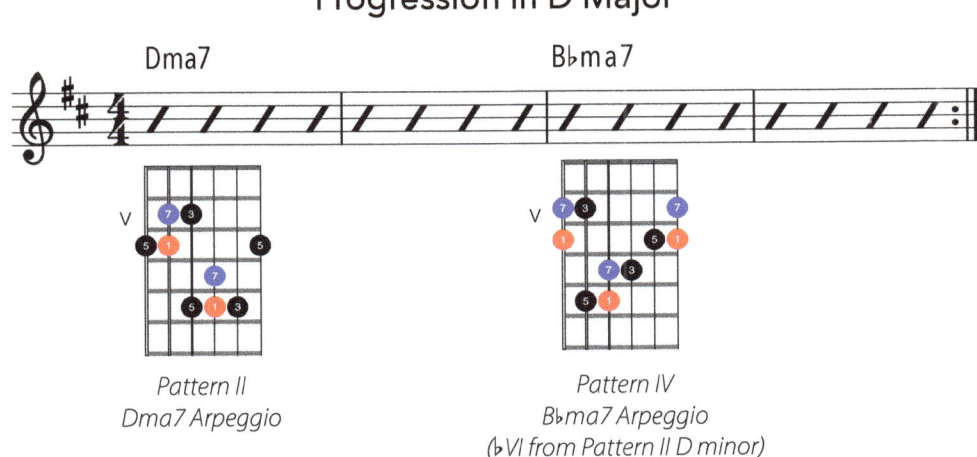

At some point I encourage you to go back and work through the progressions in Units 1 through 6 again, this time using the chord tone approach. You'll recall that some of those progressions are triad-based and some are 7th chord-based. And some have four chords, so there is a real challenge.

Level 4 Unit 8 • Improv Demo

©2021 Fretboard Biology • fretboardbiology.com

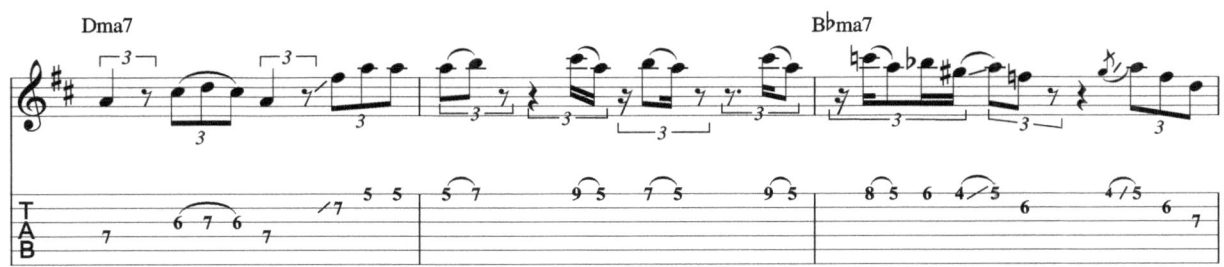
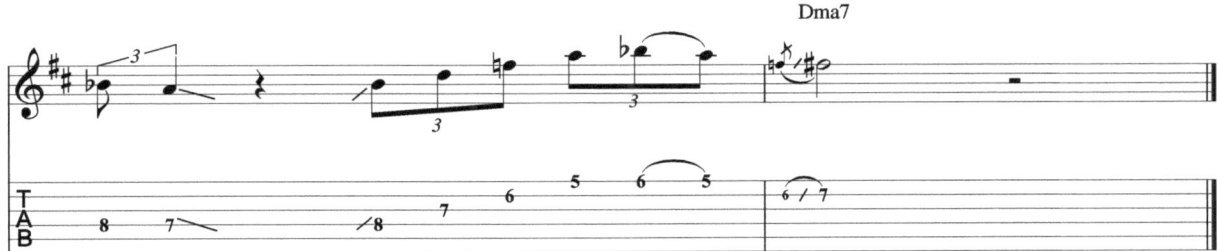

PRACTICE

Theory

- ❑ Go to the tabs below the Theory video on the website and complete the quiz.
- ❑ Learn how slash chords are notated and used to represent inversions.

Fretboard Logic

- ❑ Learn how inversions are used in chord progressions.
- ❑ Learn the diatonic 7th shapes.
- ❑ Practice using modal interchange with 7th-chord arpeggios.

Rhythm Guitar

- ❑ Practice thee R&B Groove in G, paying special attention to pick direction.

Money Makers

- ❑ Practice playing major and minor 7th parts over major and minor progressions.

Improvisation

- ❑ Practice playing solos over a D major progression with modal interchange.

UNIT 9

Learning Modules

> **Theory** - Analyzing Progressions with Inversions

> **Fretboard Logic** - Ensemble Chords, Octave Interval Shapes in Major, Patterns I-V Major and Minor In-Position Triad Arpeggios

> **Rhythm Guitar** - Classic R&B Groove in E

> **Money Makers** - Money Maker parts using Octave Shapes, In-Position Octave Shapes in Major

> **Improvisation** - Soloing with Modal Interchange

> **Practice** - Continue Practice Routine Development

THEORY

This module teaches how to determine the function of inversions when analyzing a chord progression. The following explanation is painfully detailed but the concept is quite simple: Slash chords that are inversions are named by their root, not their bass note.

The fact that a chord is inverted does not affect your note choice when soloing. If an inverted chord is made up of all diatonic notes, the source of notes for soling over it is still the notes in the key. If an inverted chord is a borrowed chord, the source of notes for soling over it is the scale of the parallel key.

Analyze a few of the progressions from Unit 8.

Progression in C Major

I suggest you first analyze the root position chords. This allows you to get the easy chords out of the way. Next, examine each slash chord, which in this unit are all inversions.

Step One: Analyze the root position chords.

Progression in C Major

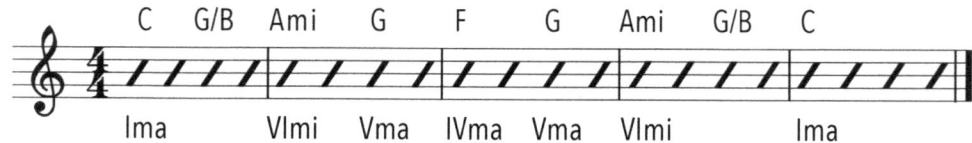

Step Two: Analyze the slash chords. To analyze G/B, ask these questions:
- Which part of the symbol is the chord? G
- Which letter is the bass note? B
- Is the bass note, B, part of a G chord? Yes
- What chord tone of a G chord is B? The 3rd
- If the 3rd is in the bass, what inversion is it? First inversion
- What is the root of G/B? G
  (G is still the root even though B is voiced in the bass. This is simply a G chord.)
- What is a G chord in the key of C? Vma

A good way to notate a slash chord's function and inversion is to write the Roman numeral to the left of the slash and the number of the chord tone voiced in the bass on the right like this: Vma/3. G/B is Vma/3. "Vma" in this symbol indicates the chord function, and "3" in this symbol indicates the chord tone voiced in the bass. The complete analysis is:

Progression in C Major

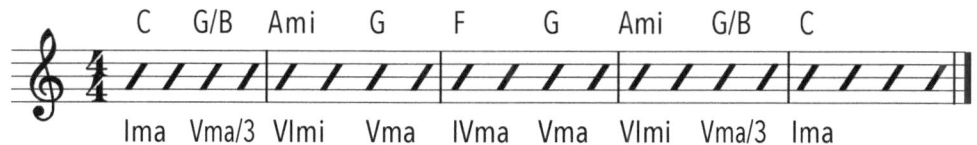

Here's another.

Progression in A Major

The last chord indicates this progression is probably in A. Again, I suggest you first analyze the root position chords and then examine each slash chord.

Step One: Analyze the root position chords first and pass over the slash chords.

Progression in A Major

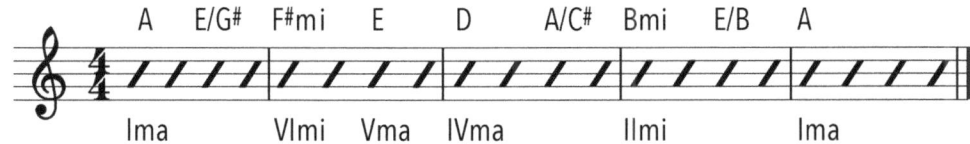

Step Two: Analyze the slash chords. To analyze E/G#, ask these questions:
- Which part of the symbol is the chord? E
- Which letter is the bass note? G#
- Is the bass note, G#, part of the E chord? Yes
- What chord tone of an E chord is G#? The 3rd
- If the 3rd is in the bass, what inversion is it? First inversion
- What is the root of E/G#? E
  (E is still the root even though G# is voiced in the bass. This is simply an E chord.)
- What is an E chord in the key of A? Vma

Your analysis for E/G# is Vma/3. Vma in this symbol indicates the chord function, and 3 indicates the chord tone voiced in the bass.

Next, to analyze A/C#, ask these questions:
- Which part of the symbol is the chord? A
- Which letter is the bass note? C#
- Is the bass note, C#, part of the A chord? Yes
- What chord tone of an A chord is C#? The 3rd
- If the 3rd is in the bass, what inversion is it? First inversion
- What is the root of A/C#? A
  (A is still the root even though C# is voiced in the bass. This is simply an A chord.)
- What is an A chord in the key of A? Ima

Your analysis for A/C# is Ima/3. Ima in this symbol indicates the chord function, and 3 indicates the chord tone voiced in the bass.

Next, to analyze E/B, ask these questions:
- Which part of the symbol is the chord? E
- Which letter is the bass note? B
- Is the bass note, B, part of the E chord? Yes
- What chord tone of an E chord is B? The 5th
- If the 5th is in the bass, what inversion is it? Second inversion
- What is the root of E/B? E
  (E is still the root even though B is voiced in the bass. This is simply an E chord.)
- What is an E chord in the key of A? Vma

Your analysis for E/B is Vma/5. Vma in this symbol indicates the chord function, and 5 indicates the chord tone voiced in the bass.

So the complete analysis is:

Progression in A Major

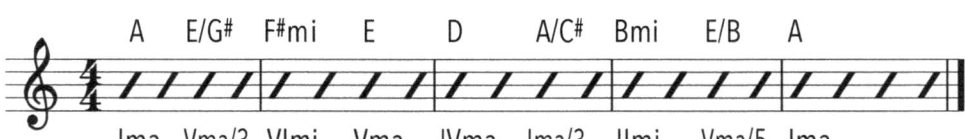

Here is another.

Progression in A Minor

The last chord indicates this progression is probably in A minor. Analyze the root position chords first and then examine each slash chord.

Step One: Analyze the root position chords.

Progression in A Minor

Step Two: Analyze the slash chords. To analyze Ami/G, ask these questions:
- Which part of the symbol is the chord? Ami
- Which letter is the bass note? G
- Is the bass note, G, part of the Ami chord? Yes
- What chord tone of an Ami chord is G? The ♭7
- If the ♭7 is in the bass, what inversion is it? Third inversion
- What is the root of Ami/G? A
  (A is still the root even though G is voiced in the bass. This is simply an Ami7 chord.)
- What is an Ami7 chord in the key of Ami? Imi7

Your analysis for Ami/G is Imi/♭7. Imi in this symbol indicates the chord function, and ♭7 indicates the chord tone voiced in the bass.

Next, to analyze D/F#, ask these questions:
- Which part of the symbol is the chord? D
- Which letter is the bass note? F#
- Is the bass note, F#, part of the D chord? Yes
- What chord tone of a D chord is F#? The 3rd
- If the 3rd is in the bass, what inversion is it? First inversion

- What is the root of D/F#? D
  (A is still the root even though F# is voiced in the bass. This is simply a D chord.)
- What is an D chord in the key of Ami? IVma

Your analysis for D/F# is IVma/3. IVma in this symbol indicates the chord function, and 3 indicates the chord tone voiced in the bass.

Next, to analyze the Dmi/F, ask these questions:
- Which part of the symbol is the chord? Dmi
- Which letter is the bass note? F
- Is the bass note, F, part of the Dmi chord? Yes
- What chord tone of a Dmi chord is F? The ♭3rd
- If the ♭3rd is in the bass, what inversion is it? First inversion
- What is the root of Dmi/F? D
  (D is still the root even though F is voiced in the bass. This is simply an Dmi chord.)
- What is an E chord in the key of A? Vma

Your analysis for Dmi/F is IVmi/♭3. IVmi in this symbol indicates the chord function, and ♭3 indicates the chord tone voiced in the bass.

Next, to analyze the Ami/E, ask these questions:
- Which part of the symbol is the chord? Ami
- Which letter is the bass note? E
- Is the bass note, E, part of the Ami chord? Yes
- What chord tone of an Ami chord is E? The 5th
- If the 5th is in the bass, what inversion is it? Second inversion
- What is the root of Ami/E? A
  (A is still the root even though E is voiced in the bass. This is simply an Ami chord.)
- What is an Ami chord in the key of Ami? Imi

Your analysis for Ami/E is Imi/5. Imi in this symbol indicates the chord function, and 5 indicates the chord tone voiced in the bass.

So the complete analysis is:

Progression in A Minor

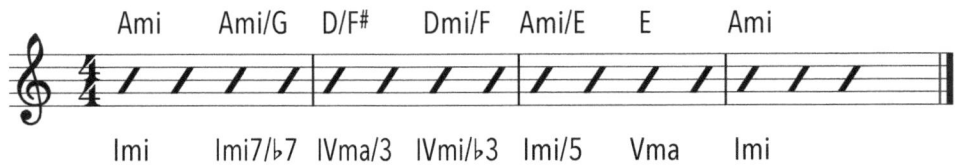

Remember that an inverted chord is analyzed according to its root, not its bass note. The function of a chord doesn't change just because a note other than the root is voiced in the bass. This looks harder than it is!

FRETBOARD LOGIC

Ensemble Chords

Think about an orchestra where each instrument plays single note lines. An entire chord can be represented because different chord tones are played by individual instruments throughout the ensemble. The listener perceives the sound of a chord based on the totality of the sound coming from the ensemble.

It is exactly the same with small or large bands: The listener hears the combination of the bass, guitar, keyboard, horns, and vocals as one big instrument. With that as a starting point, sometimes only the bass player plays the note that make the "ensemble chord" either in root position or inverted. For now, we'll use the term "ensemble chord" because it's a descriptive term for the totality of the chord that the audience hears.

Depending on the style, arrangement, and context, instruments that play the chords, like guitar and keyboard, may be playing inverted voicings. But because the listener hears the bass playing the root, the band sounds like it is in root position. The ensemble chord is in root position because the lowest note played (by the bass) is the root. And likewise, if the listener hears the bass playing the 3rd, 5th, or 7th, the band sounds like it is playing an inversion. The ensemble chord is inverted because the bass is playing the 3rd, 5th, or 7th.

There are instances where the chording instruments are playing the inversion and the bass player is also playing the 3rd, 5th, or 7th. It all depends on what the arranger or leader wants to hear. Remember, the low E string on bass guitar is only one octave below the low E on guitar. The E played at the 7th fret of the A string on bass is in the same octave as the low E on guitar.

KEY POINT: If only the bass is making the ensemble chord an inversion by playing the 3rd, 5th, or 7th, be careful to not play roots of your voicings within a 5th above the bass note and, of course, never below it. If you voice the root within a 5th of the bass player, your note and the bass' note will sound uncomfortable and muddy, and maybe even dissonant.

If guitar is the only instrument and there is no band, play the full chord as written, whether in root position or inverted. But when a bass player is present, you have to be careful not to voice your chords too close to the notes played on bass.

Here's an example progression with slash chords.

Because the bassist plays the lower note of several slash chords, which are inversions,

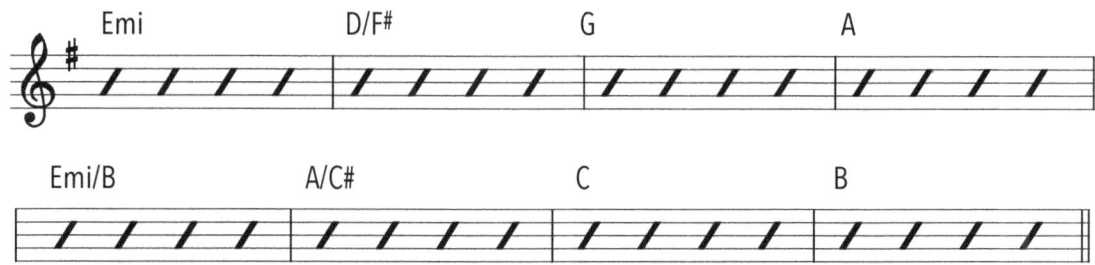

the ensemble chord for those chords will be perceived by the audience as inverted, regardless of the note the guitar or keyboard player voices in the bass on their instrument.

The guitar and keyboard players should be careful to NOT voice the lowest note of their voicing too close to the bass player's note. Usually a 5th away is the lower-register limit, and even that is often too close. Remember, the reason to not voice within a 5th is because the density of notes in the lower register can have a muddy or even dissonant effect on the overall sound of the band.

There are many decisions to be made when playing a chord progression. One important decision is about what note to voice at the bottom of your chord. Sometimes an arrangement calls for the bass to be doubled an octave above. Every situation is different and there are several factors that should influence your decision about whether to play the bass notes or not. As you gain experience playing many styles in many settings, you will build an awareness about what is appropriate.

Being familiar with the style you're playing is a key factor. The more experience you have, the easier the decisions are because you know what is common in various styles. Often times it's good to find out the musical director, band leader, or producer wants. If it's your song, experiment both ways to see what fits your needs.

It's important to know that when sight reading a chord chart with a bass player, it's usually better to just play the chord part of the slash chord until you get a sense of what is needed. If the bass is playing the part correctly, it will sound fine and nothing will be missing.

Intervals

So far, you have learned all of the diatonic interval shapes along two-string sets as they relate to both harmonized major and minor scales.

This module focuses on octaves. It is important to learn how to play major and minor scales using octave shapes on a several sets of strings.

Octave Shapes in Major

First, play the G major scale on string set 6 and 4. For this string set, use an octave interval shape that looks like Pattern IV. Here is the G major scale using the 6th string as the guide. Keep the octave interval shape the same along the entire scale using this string set.

Octave Shapes on the 6th and 4th Strings (Pattern IV)

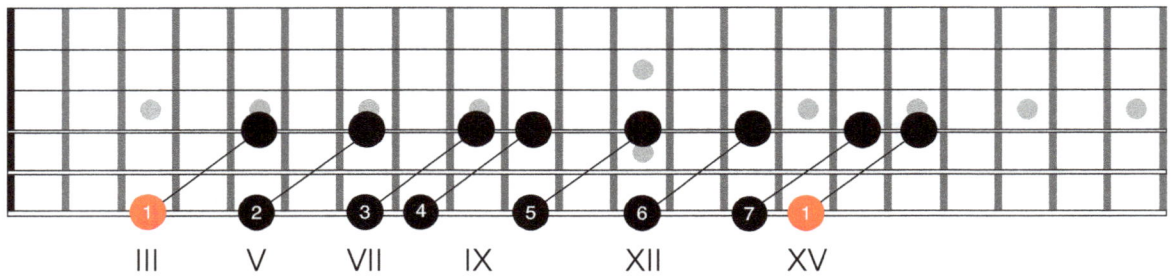

Next, play the C major scale on string set 5 and 3. For this string set, use an octave interval shape that looks like Pattern II. Here is the C major scale using the 5th string as the guide. Keep the octave interval shape the same along the entire scale using this string set.

Octave Shapes on the 5th and 3rd Strings (Pattern II)

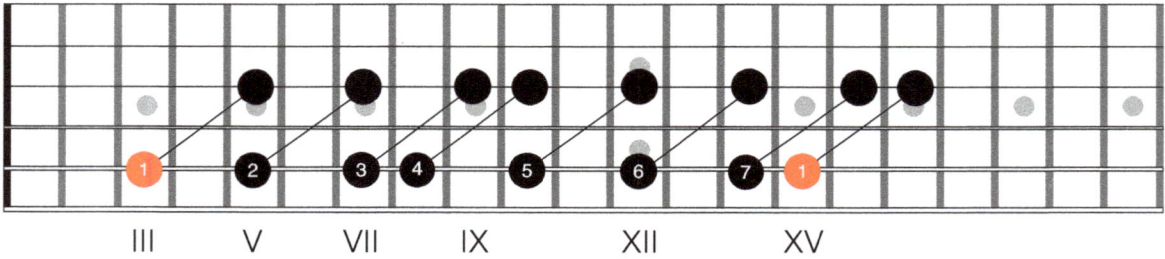

Next, play the E major scale on string set 4 and 2. For this string set, use an octave interval shape that looks like Pattern V. Here is the E major scale using the 4th string as the guide. Keep the octave interval shape the same along the entire scale using this string set.

Octave Shapes on the 4th and 2nd Strings (Pattern V)

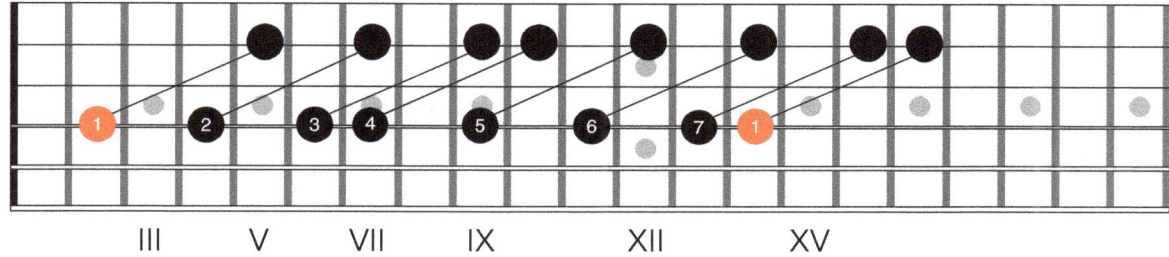

Next, play the A major scale on string set 3 and 1. For this string set, use an octave interval shape that looks like Pattern III. Here is the A major scale using the 3rd string as the guide. Keep the octave interval shape the same along the entire scale using this string set.

Octave Shapes on the 3rd and 1st Strings (Pattern III)

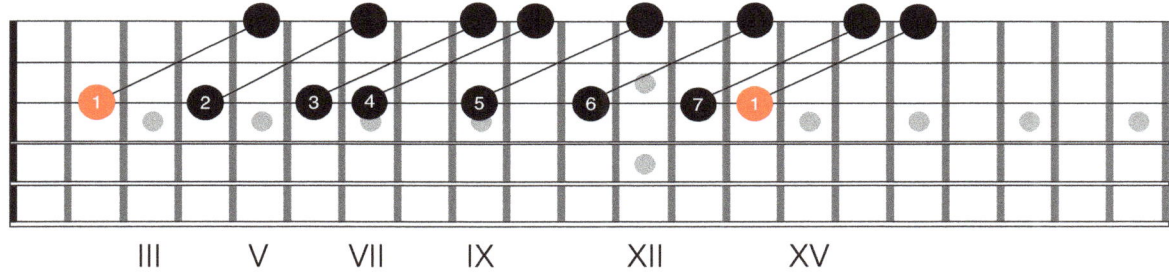

Now play the C major scale on string set 5 and 2. For this string set, use an octave interval shape that looks like Pattern I. Keep the octave interval shape the same along the entire scale using this string set.

Octave Shapes on the 5th and 2nd Strings (Pattern I)

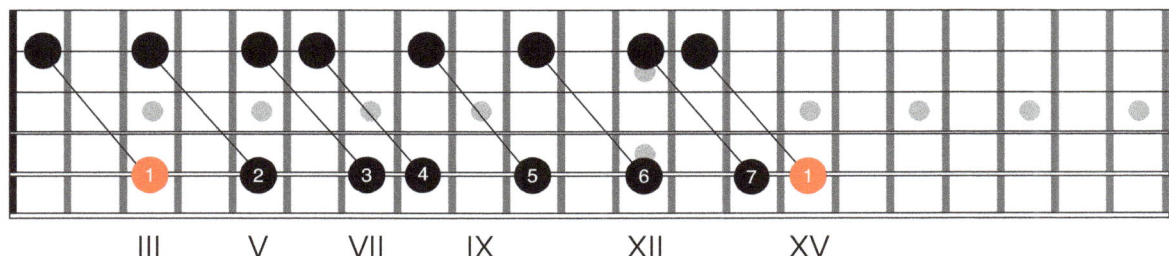

Next play the G major scale on string set 4 and 1. For this string set, use an octave interval shape that looks like the upper part of Pattern IV. Keep the octave interval shape the same along the entire scale using this string set.

Octave Shapes on the 4rth and 1st Strings (Pattern IV)

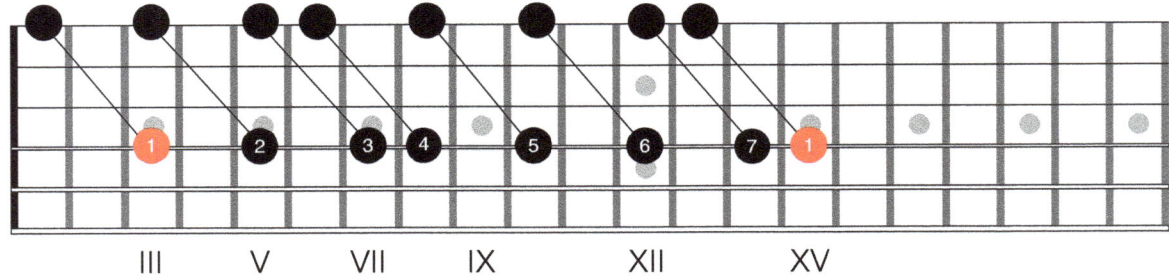

You can play scales with octaves in position, too. This is a bit more challenging because the shapes change as your transition from low to high or vice versa. You will learn the in-position octaves when playing through examples in the Money Makers modules.

Arpeggios

Continue to focus on modal interchange using chord tones. Unit 7 compared the in-position triad arpeggios of parallel keys in Pattern IV. Now let's look at all five octave shapes so you have the complete picture.

Pattern I Major and Minor In-Position Triad Arpeggios

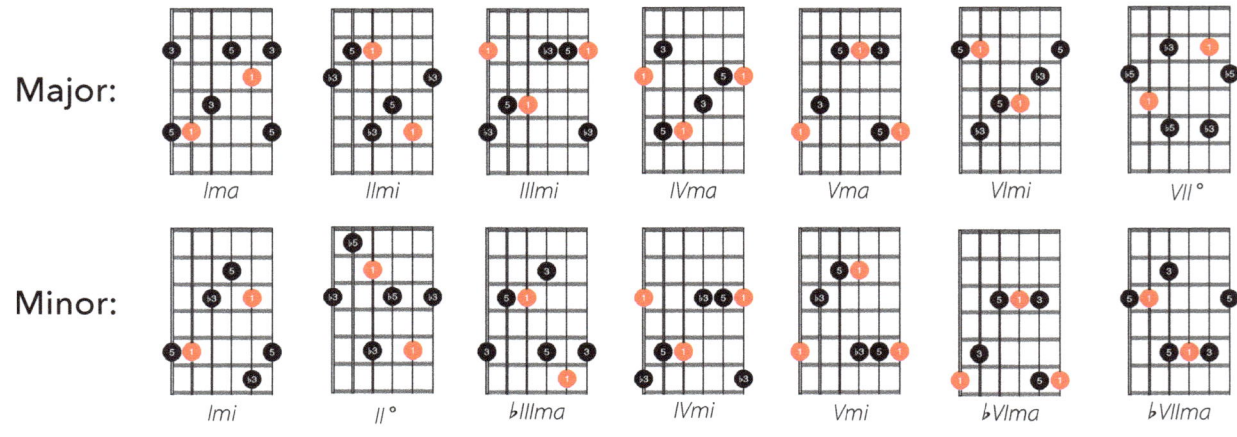

Pattern II Major and Minor In-Position Triad Arpeggios

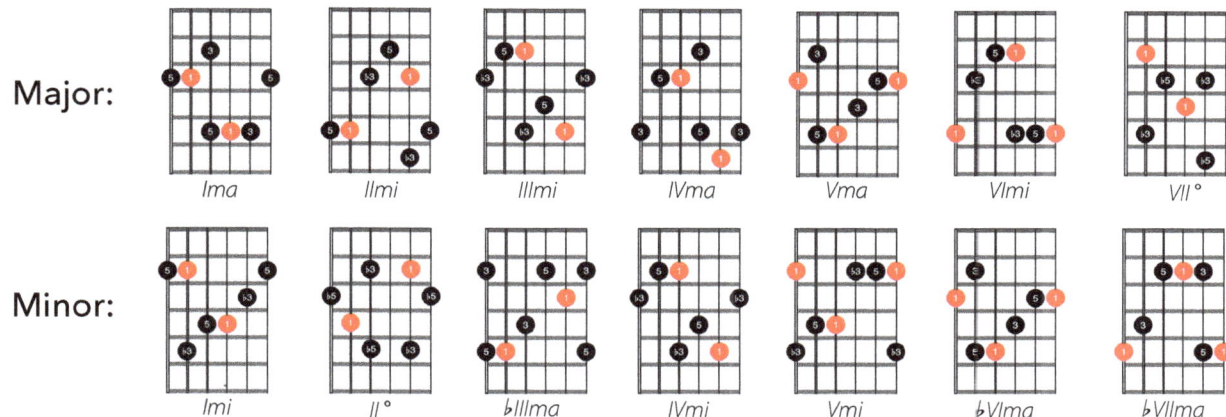

Pattern III Major and Minor In-Position Triad Arpeggios

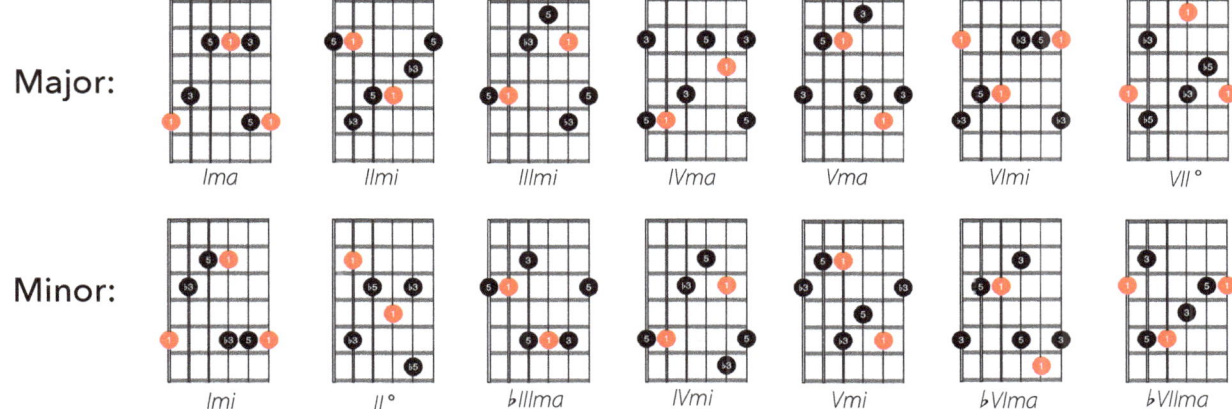

Pattern IV Major and Minor In-Position Triad Arpeggios

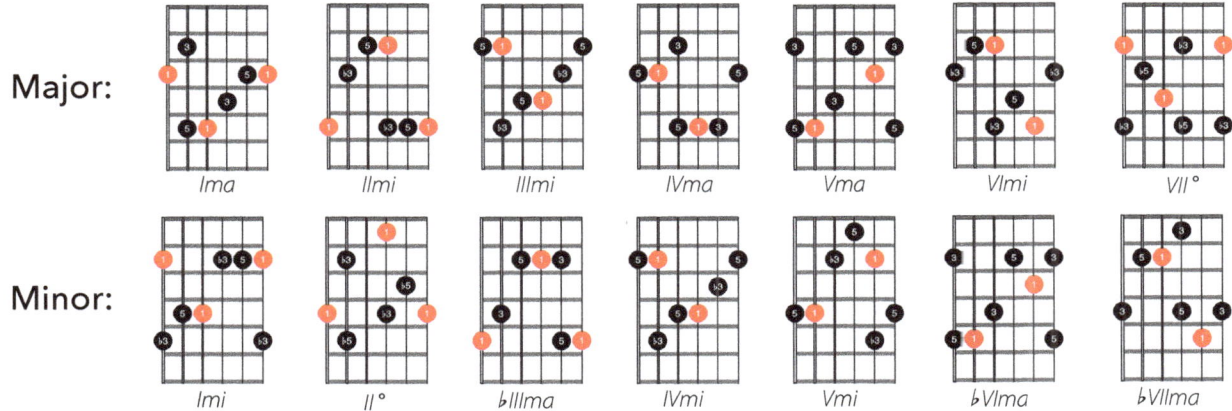

Pattern V Major and Minor In-Position Triad Arpeggios

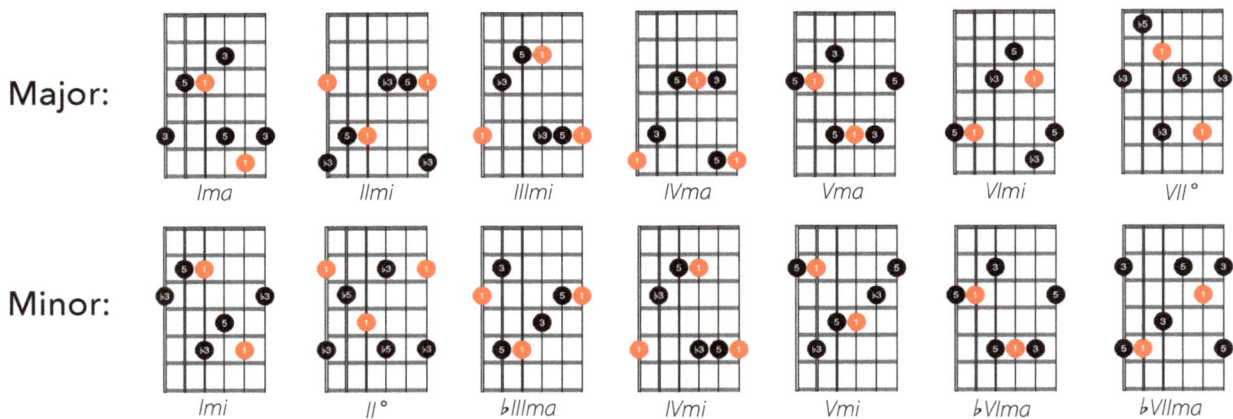

None of this material is new to you. The difference here is that the arpeggios of parallel keys are organized next to each other.

RHYTHM GUITAR

In this module of Classic R&B rhythm guitar parts you will use 6th interval shapes that move over dominant 7th chords. The shapes will be familiar to you and are great for re-purposing in other songs in a variety of genres. The part explained here, like so many, is referenced to a Pattern IV barre chord shape so keep that in mind as you visualize it.

This example is written for a two-chord progression in E.

R&B Groove in E

The four-point moving part will essentially be the same for both chords, just adjusted for the specific location of E7 and A7. Go to 12th position. Here is a Pattern IV E barre chord with the chord tones labeled: R, 5, R, 3, 5, R.

Pattern IV E Major Barre Chord

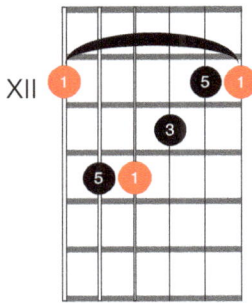

As in a previous example, first just look at the 1st and 3rd strings. The root on the 1st string and the 3rd on the 3rd string.

For the first point, play the root on the 1st string with your 1st finger and the 3rd on the 3rd string with your 2nd finger.

Point 1

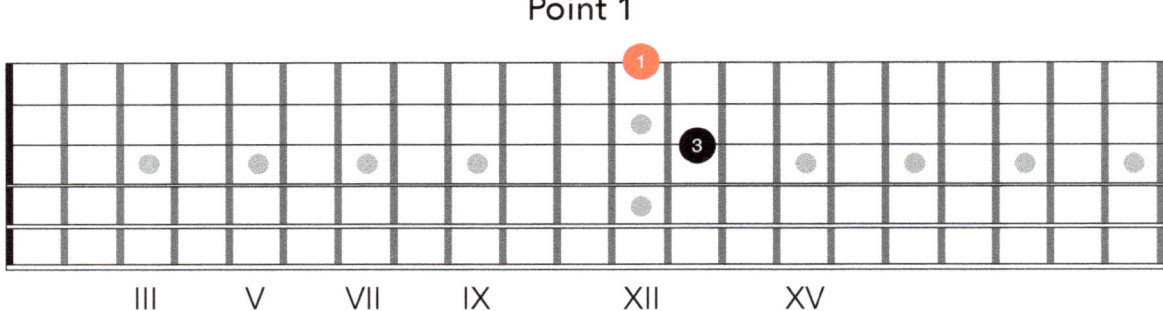

For the second point, keep the same formation with your 1st and 3rd fingers, and slide them down together one fret (or a whole step), so that your 1st finger is now at the 10th fret playing D, the b7, and your 2nd finger is now at the 11th fret playing F#, the 9th.

Point 2

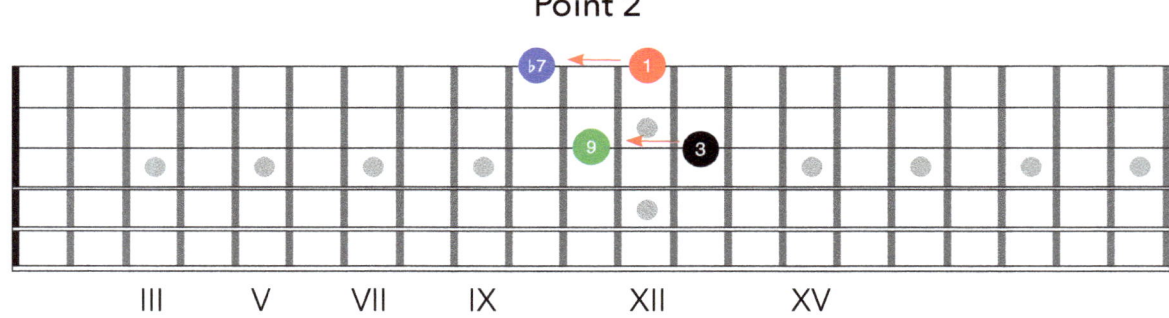

Last, place your 3rd finger at the 12th fret of the 4th string and your 4th finger at the 12th fret of the 2nd string. Slide that shape up to the 14th fret and then back to the 12th fret. It should be noted that the two notes at the end of this move are also chord tones of E7: B at the 12th fret of the 2nd string is the 5th of E, and D at the 12th fret of the 4th string is the b7 of E.

Point 3

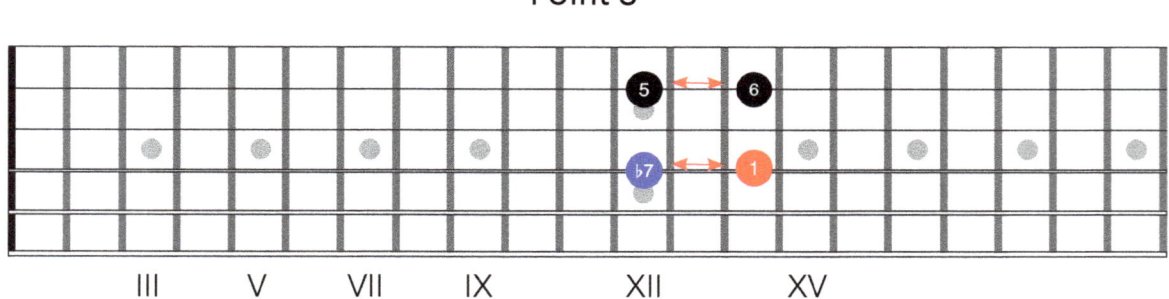

Next move on to the IV7 chord, which is A7. We will reference a Pattern IV A barre chord shape. You will replicate the same move you used for E7 for the A7.

Start with your 1st finger on A, the root, at the 5th fret of the 1st string and your 2nd finger on C#, the 3rd, at the 6th fret of the 3rd string. Keep the same formation with your 1st and 3rd fingers and slide them down together one fret (or a whole step). Your 1st finger is at the 3rd fret playing G, the ♭7. Your 2nd finger is at the 4th fret playing B, the 9th.

Place your 3rd finger at the 5th fret of the 4th string and your 4th finger at the 5th fret of the 2nd string. Next, slide that shape up to the 7th fret and then back to the 5th fret. It should be noted that the two notes at the end of this move are also chord tones of A7: E at the 5th fret of the 2nd string is the 5th of A, and G at the 5th fret of the 4th string is the ♭7 of the A.

You know from your study of chord tones that you are playing the root and major 3rd of a major triad. You know from your study of interval shapes that this is a minor 6th. And you also know from your study of inverted intervals in theory that a minor 6th interval is an inverted major 3rd and vice versa. Play this as a double stop, or you can separate the two notes.

Picking-Hand Technique

As we discussed earlier, you can play these with your picking hand in a few different ways:

- The first way is to use the standard alternate-picking rules if you're playing single notes. Then, for double stops, strum across strings 1, 2, and 3 and mute the 2nd string since it isn't included in the part.
- Another way is to use the flat pick playing a downstroke on the 3rd string and the 3rd finger on your picking hand to pick the 1st string.
- And still another way is to use the thumb on the 3rd string and the 3rd finger on your picking hand to pick the 1st string.

As you experiment with these shapes on the fretboard, practice all of these picking-hand techniques. They are not hard and there are occasions when each is the right choice.

These parts can be moved to any Pattern IV major chord shape. This part works great for almost all dominant 7th chords in R&B and straight ahead Blues or Funk. Log this away as part of your vocabulary. A chip part on beats two and four will work with this part, too. Both parts are compatible with each other if two guitarists are in the band.

MONEY MAKERS

So far, you have learned parts that use 3rds, 4ths, 5ths, 6ths, and 7ths from the harmonized major and minor scales. This unit focuses on octaves. With octave shapes there is nothing to harmonize, since it is the same note played in two different octaves. The sound of octaves played on guitar is really unique and can be heard in a wide range of styles.

Review the octave interval shapes used to play melodic lines that were presented in the Fretboard Logic Module.

- The 2nd interval shape applies to octaves played on string set 6 and 4 and string set 5 and 3.

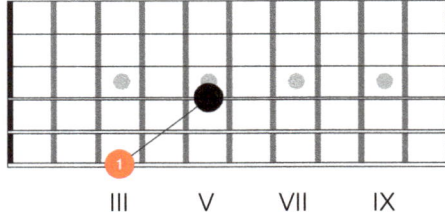 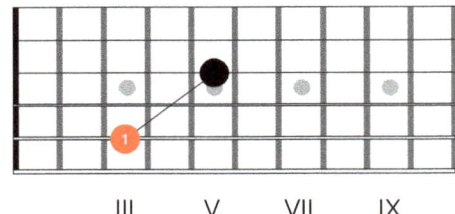

- The 2nd interval shape applies to octaves played on string set 4 and 2 and string set 3 and 1.

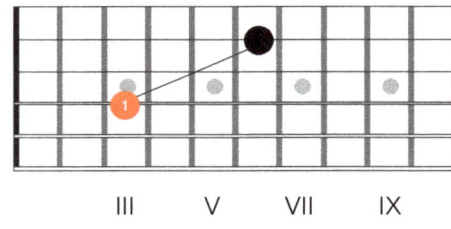 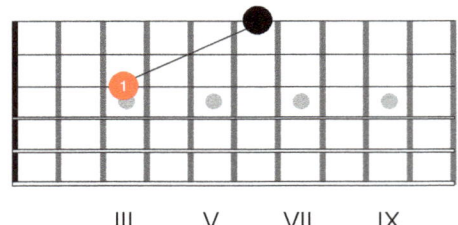

- The third octave interval shape applies to octaves played on string set 5 and 2 and string set 4 and 1.

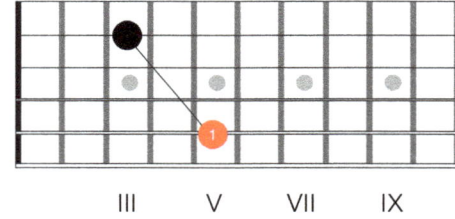 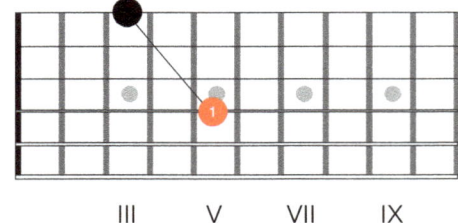

Pick a major scale and experiment playing linearly up each of these string sets. Track the scale on either the upper or lower note. That is up to you. For now, with your picking hand, use your thumb to play the lower note and your 3rd finger for the upper note. Details about picking-hand techniques for playing octaves will be discussed a little later in this module.

You learned how to play scales linearly along the same string sets using these octave shapes, but now let's look at how to play these in position. Let's explore how to play the major scale with octaves. This is where it gets interesting because it will require using a combination of shapes to cross the B/G line. It is a bit overwhelming but worth a few minutes of exploration to see where the challenges are.

Look at the Pattern IV A major scale:

Pattern IV A Major Scale

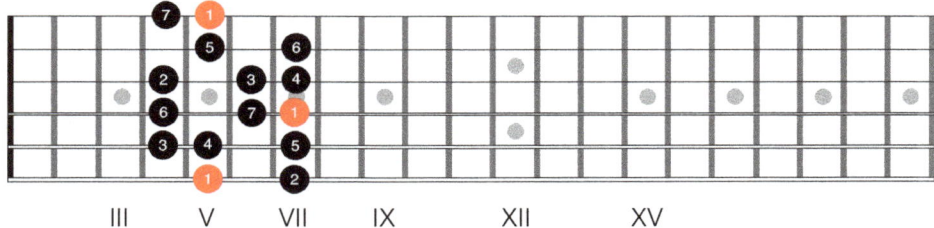

- To play it with octaves, start with the string set 6 and 4 combination for scale degrees 1 and 2.

Pattern IV A Major Scale Played in Octaves

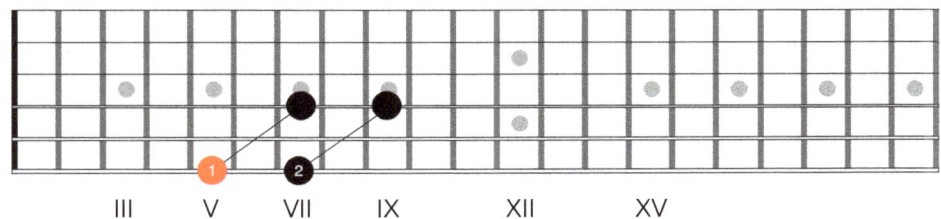

- For scale degrees 3, 4, and 5, move to string set 5 and 3.

Pattern IV A Major Scale Played in Octaves

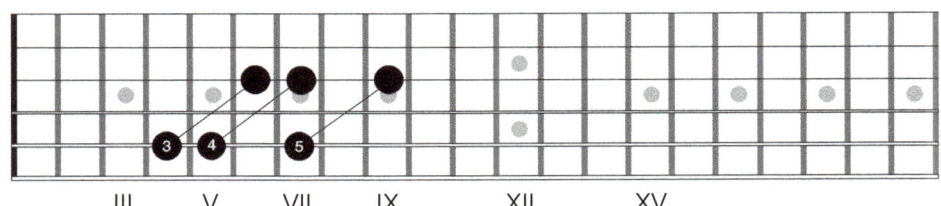

- For scale degree 6 move to string set 4 and 2. This is a different shape.

Pattern IV A Major Scale Played in Octaves

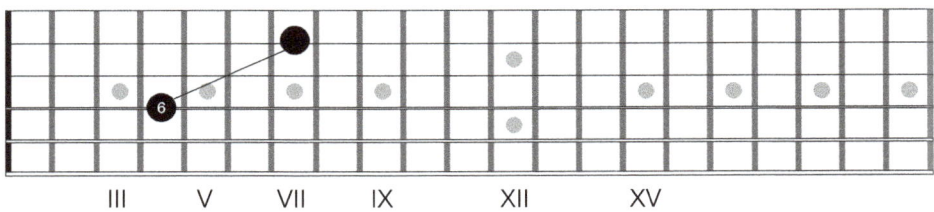

- Finish with the 7th scale degree and the tonic on string set 4 and 1.

Pattern IV A Major Scale Played in Octaves

This only one of many options for how to play the notes of a scale or arpeggio sort of in position. There is really no right or wrong way to do it. I suggest you find what works for you and gradually venture out. Like all things on the fretboard, it is about referencing a shape to something you feel secure about, and that could be different for everyone.

Picking-Hand Technique

There are a few different picking-hand techniques for playing octaves.

- Earlier in this module I suggested you use your thumb and 3rd finger. Be sure to mute the string or strings between the two strings being fretted. That can be accomplished by slightly slanting the 1st finger to make contact with the string that is not to ring.
- Another technique is to use the pick and 3rd finger. This requires muting of the string or strings in between those being fretted as well.
- Another technique is to use the thumb only and sort of strum across the string set in use. This, too, requires muting of the string or strings in between.
- Another technique is to use a pick and sort of strum across the string set in use. This, too, requires muting of the string or strings in between.

Spend some time with each technique to see what feels comfortable for you. You may eventually use all of them for different situations. The fleshy sound of thumb and 3rd finger or thumb only has a full but mellower sound. The techniques that use the pick have a crisper sound.

Spend some time playing octaves both linearly and in position in all five scale patterns. I suggest just you start by playing over an Ama7 vamp. Octaves used in solo lines have a distinct "personality". Experiment with some of your own ideas.

IMPROVISATION

In this and the next modules you will be challenged to play longer progressions with multiple shifts between the major key and its parallel minor. This is very common and deserves a lot of practice.

The progression in this module is more challenging than some of the previous ones because it is twice as long and also requires you to move in and out of modal interchange several times within the eight-bar loop.

The challenges, after establishing the major sound on the opening chord, is to know where the modal shift occurs, to play the appropriate notes on the borrowed chords and then to get back to the major sound. Then do that again within a couple of measures.

This Classic Rock-sounding track is in the key of A. The modal interchange occurs in two places. Look closely at the analysis:

Progression in A Major

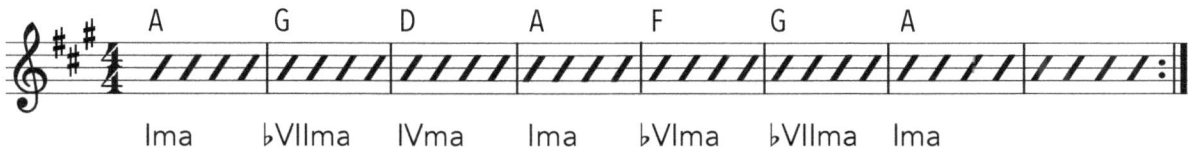

The key center throughout the entire progression is A, but examine each chord and determine where the major sound is appropriate or its parallel minor.

- The A and D chords are from the A major scale, so the A major sound is appropriate for them on the first, third, fourth, seventh, and eighth measures.
- The G and F chords are from A minor scale, so the A minor sound is appropriate for them on the second, fifth, and sixth measures.

I suggest pentatonic scales for this, at least to start. The primary objective is to meet the logistical challenge of playing the right sound at the right time. For this progression, make the pattern choices as easy as possible. As you ease into playing the longer progressions you should limit the amount of information you try to manage on the fly. Go back to what you used in Unit 1 where you took a very simple approach of moving the same "generic pentatonic shape" between two spots. That works here, too.

For the A major sounds use the Pattern III major pentatonic and mix in some major money makers. For the A minor sounds, use Pattern IV minor pentatonic and mix in some minor money makers. As in Unit 1, just move from 2nd position to 5th position.

Pattern III Major Pentatonic

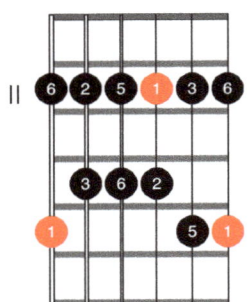

Pattern IV Minor Pentatonic

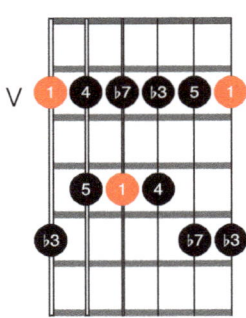

As you go through this progression, focus on playing the A major pentatonic over the chords that are diatonic to the major key, and A minor pentatonic over the chords that are borrowed from the parallel minor. They're marked in the example below.

Progression in A Major

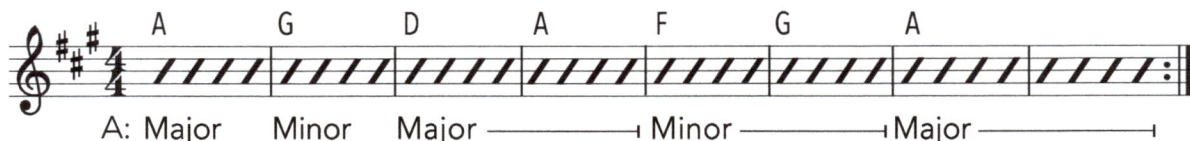

It is a very realistic scenario to see a progression like this, so it's important to get used to moving freely between parallel keys when soloing.

Level 4 Unit 9 • Improv Demo

PRACTICE

Theory

- ❑ Go to the tabs below the Theory video on the website and complete the quiz.
- ❑ Learn how to analyze progressions with inversions.

Fretboard Logic

- ❑ Learn how the bass and other instruments interact to create an ensemble chord.
- ❑ Learn the diatonic octave interval shapes in major.
- ❑ Practice Patterns I-V major and minor in-position triad arpeggios.

Rhythm Guitar

- ❑ Practice the R&B Groove in E, paying special attention to pick direction.

Money Makers

- ❑ Practice playing octave shape parts over major progressions.
- ❑ Practice playing in-position octave interval shapes.

Improvisation

- ❑ Practice playing solos over an A major progression with modal interchange.

UNIT 10

Learning Modules

> **Theory** - Level 4 Summary

> **Fretboard Logic** - Octave Interval Shapes in Minor, Patterns I-V Major and Minor In-Position 7th Chord Arpeggios

> **Rhythm Guitar** - Classic R&B Groove in B♭

> **Money Makers** - Money Maker Parts using Diatonic Octave Shapes, In-Position Octave Shapes in Minor

> **Improvisation** - Soloing with Modal Interchange

> **Practice** - Continue Practice Routine Development

THEORY

Level 4 Theory has covered some very important topics. The focus has been on harmonic analysis for progressions with modal interchange and inversions. It's time to review these topics.

Modal Interchange

When a progression borrows melody notes and chords from its parallel key, that is modal interchange. It is common for a major key to borrow from its parallel minor. The emotional effect on the listener is a shift from happy to sad or, as some might characterize it, to Bluesy or melancholy.

Modal interchange directly affects the notes you use when playing melodies or solos, and when playing or embellishing chords or write other parts. If a song is in a major key, your note choices come from the major scale of the key. If a song in a major key borrows chords from the parallel minor key, your note choices come from the parallel minor scale for the duration of those borrowed chords. Modal interchange is very common. As you gain more experience analyzing progressions, you will recognize it sooner and sooner. It will become automatic.

Inversions

When a note other than the root is voiced in the bass, a chord is said to be an inversion or, more simply, inverted. Make sure you know these terms:

- Voicing
- Closed voicing
- Open Voicing
- Fingering
- Root position
- Inversion
- First inversion
- Second inversion
- Third inversion

Know how to spell inverted chords and know the components of every chord, whether they are in root position or inverted. For example, a Cma7 is made up of C, E ,G, and B. Cma7/G is also made up of C, E ,G, and B. The difference is that G is voiced in the bass.

Inversions can be notated with a chord symbol called a slash chord. In a slash chord, the chord symbol to the left and/or slightly elevated tells the musician what chord to play. The single letter on the right and/or slightly lower tells the musician what single note is to be voiced at the bottom of the chord.

The two most common ways inversions are used in progressions are:

- to smooth out the bass line
- to create a pedal in the bass

An inverted chord is analyzed according to its root, not according to the bass note. In other words, the function of a chord doesn't change just because a note other than the root is voiced in the bass.

The fact that a chord is inverted does not affect your note choices when soloing. If an inversion is made up of all diatonic notes, the source of notes for soling over it is still the key. If an inversion is a borrowed chord, the source of notes for soling over it is the parallel key scale.

FRETBOARD LOGIC

Intervals

Unit 10 completes your study of scales played with interval shapes. Here, you will learn the minor scale played in octaves.

Octave Shapes in Minor

First, examine the G minor scale played in octaves on string set 6 and 4. For this string set, use an octave interval shape that looks like Pattern IV. Here is the G minor scale using the 6th string as the guide. Keep the octave interval shape the same along the entire scale using this string set.

Octave Shapes on the 6th and 4th Strings (Pattern IV)

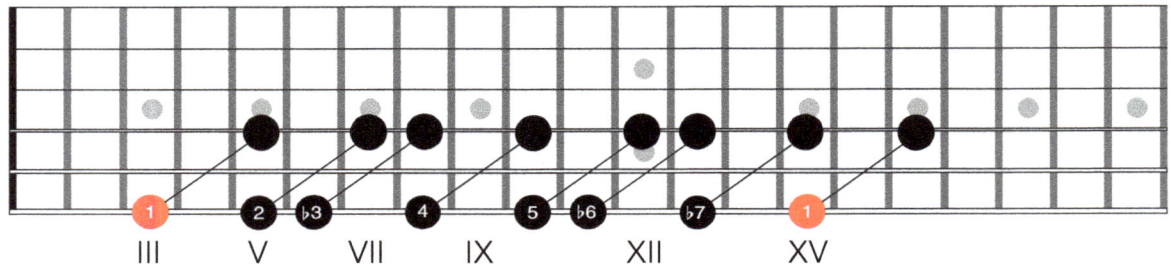

Next, examine the C minor scale played in octaves on string set 5 and 3. For this string set, use an octave interval shape that looks like Pattern II. Here is the C minor scale using the 5th string as the guide. Keep the octave interval shape the same along the entire scale using this string set.

Octave Shapes on the 5th and 3rd Strings (Pattern II)

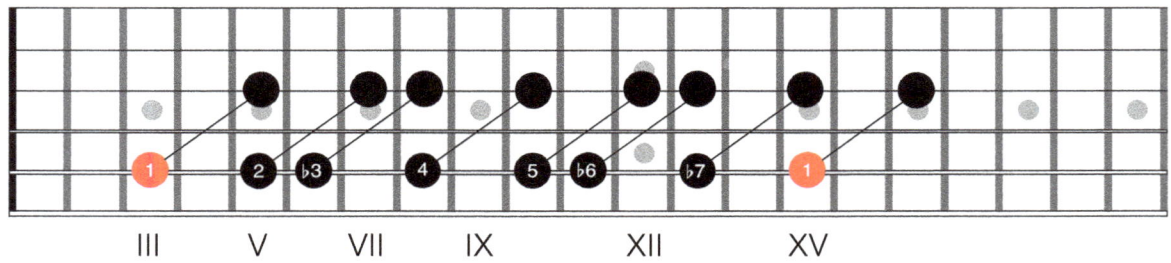

Next, examine the E minor scale played in octaves on string set 4 and 2. For this string set, use an octave interval shape that looks like Pattern V. Here is the E minor scale using the 4th string as the guide. Keep the octave interval shape the same along the entire scale using this string set.

Octave Shapes on the 4th and 2nd Strings (Pattern V)

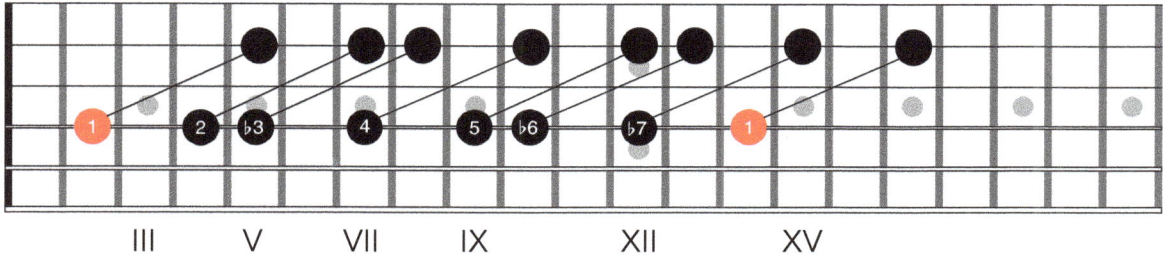

Next, examine the A minor scale played in octaves on string set 3 and 1. For this string set, use an octave interval shape that looks like Pattern III. Here is the A minor scale using the 3rd string as the guide. Keep the octave interval shape the same along the entire scale using this string set.

Octave Shapes on the 3rd and 1st Strings (Pattern III)

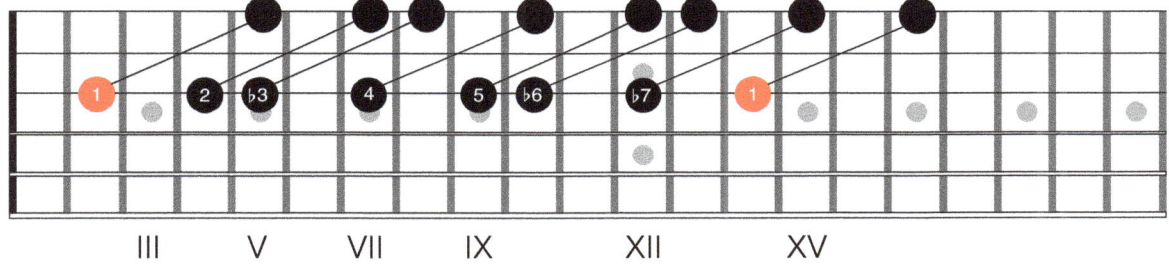

Next, examine the C minor scale played in octaves on string set 5 and 2. For this string set, use an octave interval shape that looks like Pattern I when played on string set 5 and 2. Keep the octave interval shape the same along the entire scale using this string set.

Octave Shapes on the 5th and 2nd Strings (Pattern I)

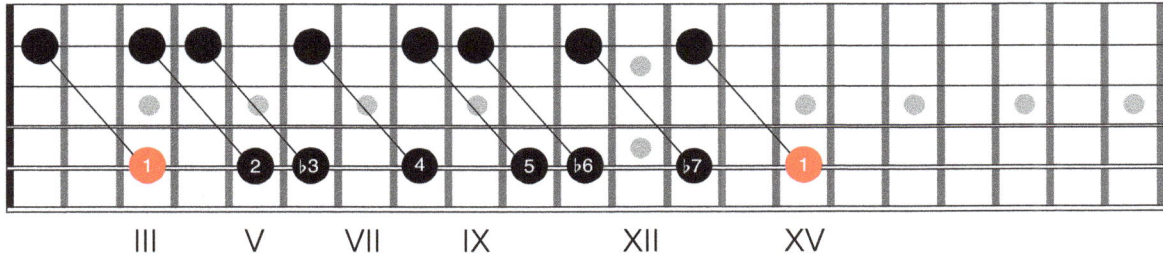

Finally, examine the G minor scale played in octaves on string set 4 and 1. For this string set, use an octave interval shape that looks like the upper part of Pattern IV when played on string set 4 and 1. Keep the octave interval shape the same along the entire scale using this string set.

Octave Shapes on the 4th and 1nd Strings (Pattern IV)

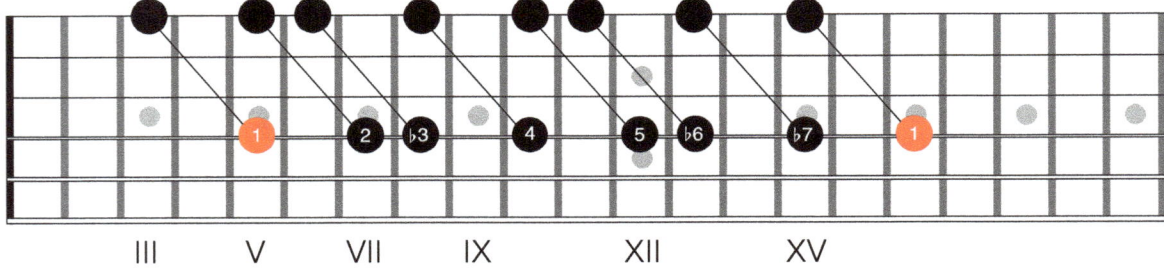

You can also work on playing scales with octaves in position. This is quite a bit more challenging because the shapes change as your transition from low to high or vice versa. You will have a chance to use these octave shapes in the Money Makers modules.

Arpeggios

Continue to focus on modal interchange using chord tones. Unit 8 compared the 7th chord arpeggios of parallel keys in Pattern II. Now look at all five octave shapes so you have the complete picture.

Pattern I Major and Minor In-Position 7th Chord Arpeggios

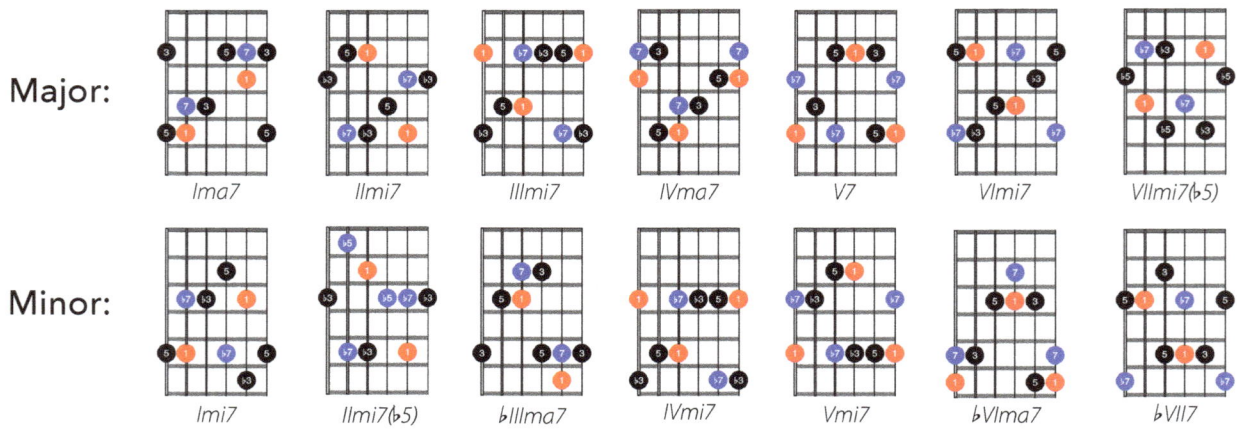

Pattern II Major and Minor In-Position 7th Chord Arpeggios

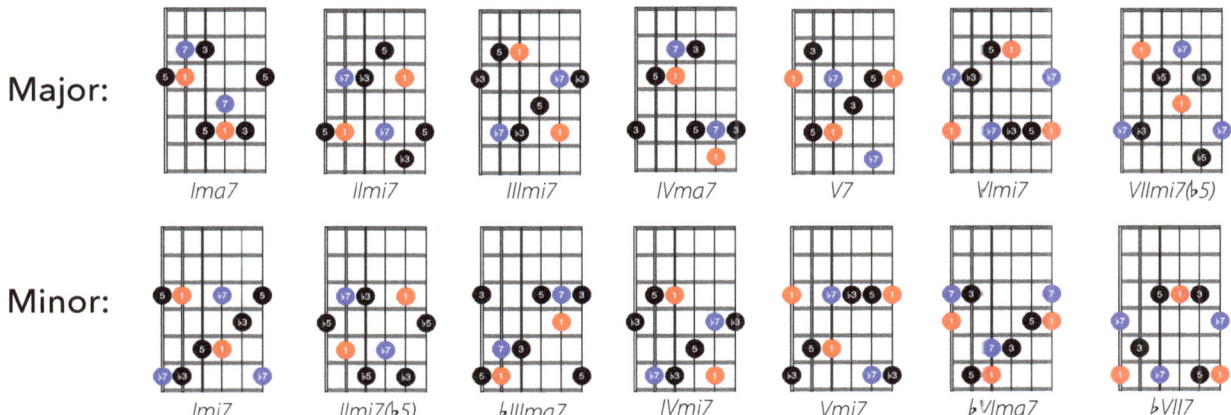

Pattern III Major and Minor In-Position 7th Chord Arpeggios

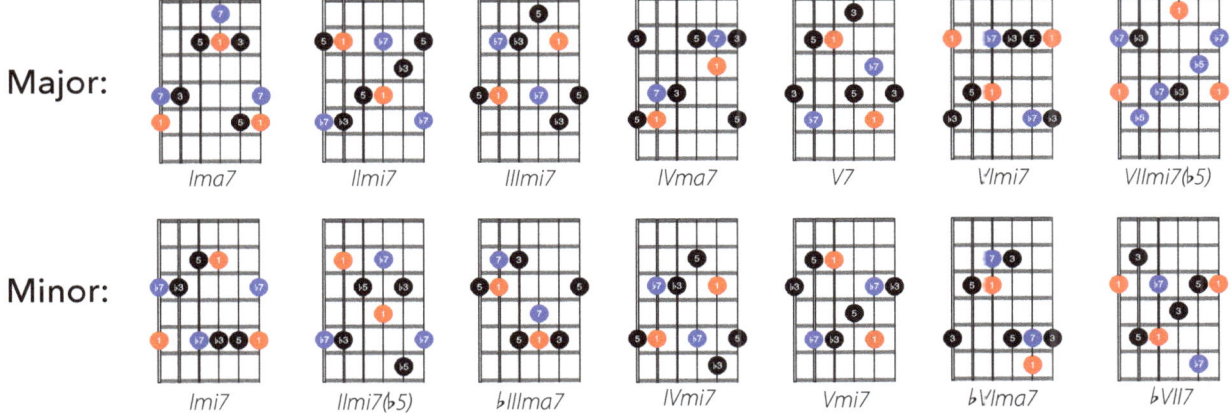

Pattern IV Major and Minor In-Position 7th Chord Arpeggios

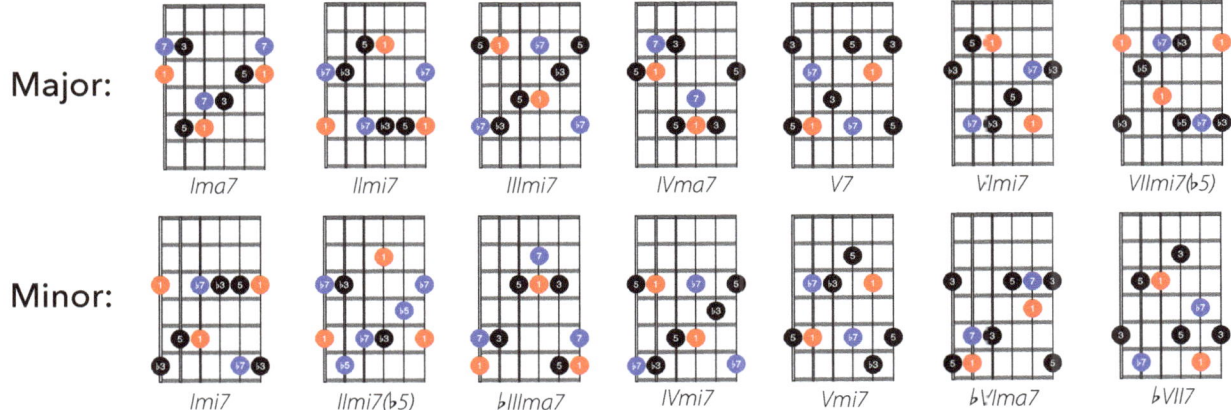

Pattern V Major and Minor In-Position 7th Chord Arpeggios

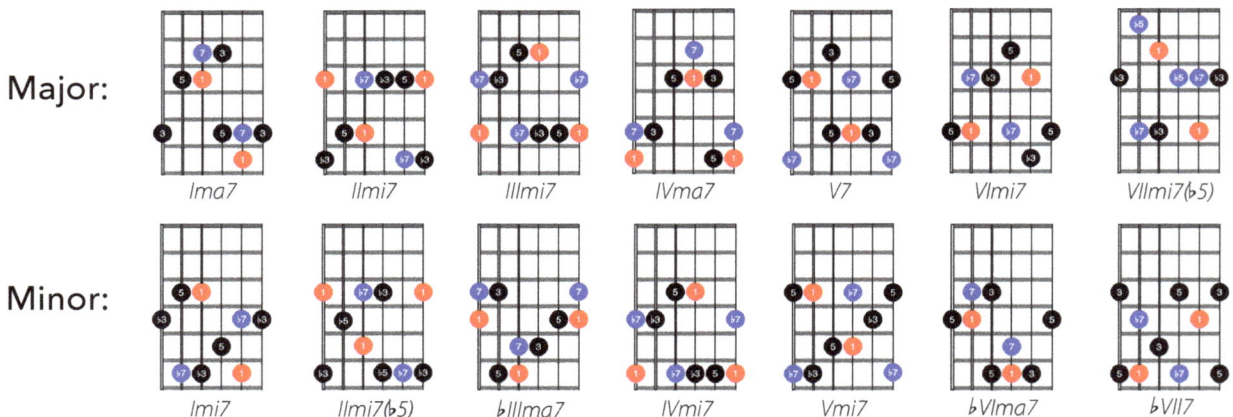

None of this material is new to you. The difference here is that the arpeggios of parallel keys are organized side-by-side. Your goal is to understand how they all fit within the octave shape and then be able to access them quickly when soloing. Remember, you can organize your practice into two or even three rotating practice routines to cover all the material on a regular basis.

Wrap Up

You learned essential information about chords in Level 4. Let's review a few important points:

- Even though 7th chords are built with four notes – Root, 3rd, 5th, and 7th – only three of them are considered essential chord tones. Essential chord tones are the notes required for a chord to represent its quality. Essential chord tones are the root, 3rd and 7th. The 5th is not essential.

- Shell voicings consist of only the essential chord tones. They are one of the keys to efficiency when comping and they make playing extended chords possible. Be sure you are understand the eight shell voicings you learned. It is also important to know that that in all shell voicings, the 3rd and 7th are on the middle two strings.

- A root map concept is a pragmatic way to navigate through chord changes while comping. It facilitates playing chords by number instead of by chord name, making transposition much easier. Playing by root map is also really helpful when sight reading a chord chart. Imagine the challenge for your eyes and brain trying to go back and forth looking at the music, then your hand, then the music, back and forth over and over. If you have the root maps memorized, you can focus on keeping your place in the music.

- You learned a lot about inversions:
  - the common ways they appear in songs
  - how they are notated on the page
  - how to play them

- Understand what notes to play when you see a slash chord. If you are playing with a bass player, your priority is the chord and not the bass note. Be sure to keep at least a 5th between your lowest note and the bass player's note. If no bass player is present, the bass note should be played by you.

- The interval work you did will pay off as you integrate the information from the Fretboard Logic and Money Maker modules into your solos. Solos don't have to be all monophonic, meaning one note at a time. Varying the texture in your solos by using double stops is worth exploring, but it's made much easier by knowing the scales harmonized in 3rds, 4ths, 5ths, 6ths, and 7ths that you learned in Level 4.

- Modal interchange is so common that it almost goes unnoticed. Other than the shift in the mood from happy to sad and then back again, the listener never feels a tonal-center change. Because it is so common, it is even more important for you to be in control of your note choices when it appears in a song. There was a lot of parallel scale and harmonized scale information presented in Level 4; more than is reasonable to learn in a short period of time. Make this an ongoing area of study.

RHYTHM GUITAR

In this last module of Classic R&B rhythm guitar parts you will learn to use double stop 3rd and 4th interval shapes as well as a standard Pattern IV chord lick.

This is an eight-bar example in the key of B♭.

R&B Groove in B♭

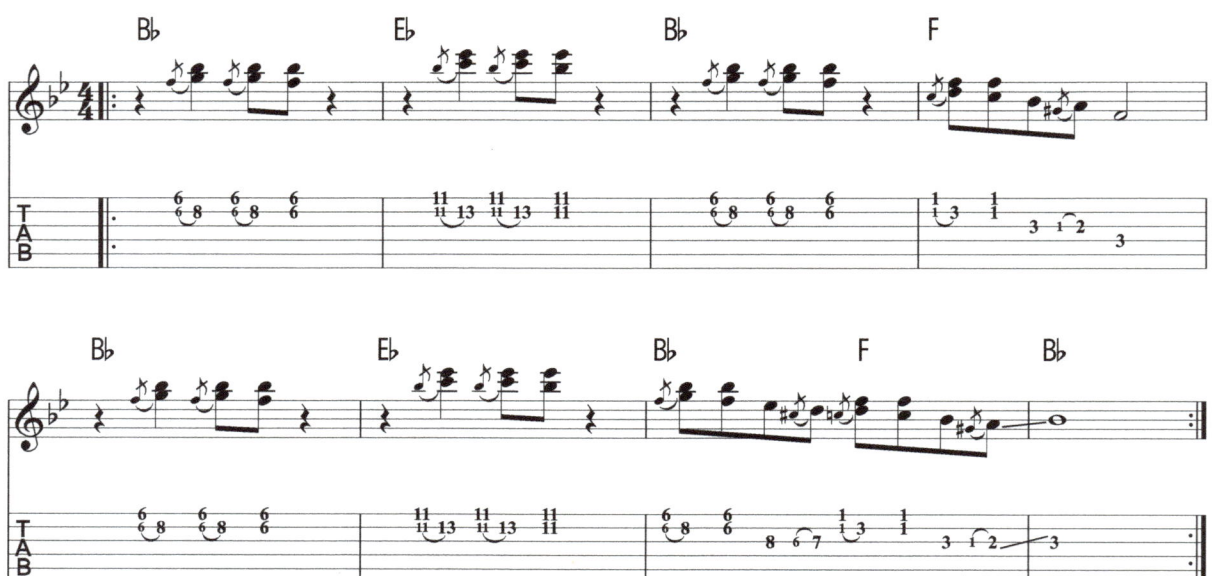

The same moving part will be used on all three chords, just adjusted for the specific locations of B♭, E♭, and F. And before we get too far into the fretting hand material, know that you will use all downstrokes for this part to keep the sound of the attacks consistent. The tempo is slow enough where this is not an issue.

In the first measure, go to 6th position. Here is a Pattern IV B♭ barre chord with the chord tones labeled: R, 5, R, 3, 5, and R.

Pattern IV B♭ Major Barre Chord

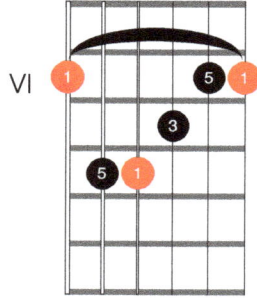

Focus on the 1st and 2nd strings. The root, B♭, is on the 1st string and the 5th, F, is on the 2nd string. Play both notes by barring with your 1st finger. Then, hammer on the 2nd string only at the 8th fret. That note is G, the 6th of the chord. Hammer this twice. This is the main figure of this whole example.

Measure 1: B♭

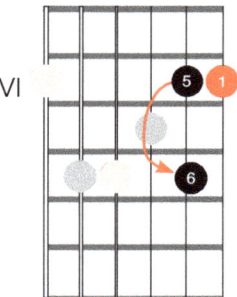

In the second measure, go to 11th position. Here is a Pattern IV E♭ barre chord. Again, just play the 1st and 2nd strings. The root, E♭, is on the 1st string and the 5th, B♭, is on the 2nd string. Play both notes by barring with your 1st finger. Just like you did with the B♭ chord in bar one, hammer on the 2nd string only at the 13th fret. That note is C, the 6th of the chord.

Measure 2: E♭

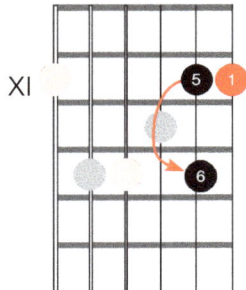

In the third measure, repeat what you played in the first measure.

In the fourth measure for the F chord, the part is varied slightly. Start the same way as the other measures. Go to 1st position. Here is a Pattern IV F barre chord with the chord tones labeled: R, 5, R, 3, 5, and R. Start with the first two strings. The root, F, is on the 1st string and the 5th, C, is on the 2nd string. Play both notes by barring with your 1st finger.

Next, hammer on the 2nd string only at the 3rd fret. That note is D, the 6th of the chord. Hammer this once, then play the first two strings again by barring with your 1st finger at the 1st fret.

Measure 4: F

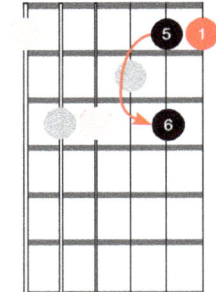

Next, use your 3rd or 4th finger (your choice) to play both the 2nd and 3rd strings at the 3rd fret. That's D on the 2nd string and B♭ on the 3rd string.

Measure 4: F

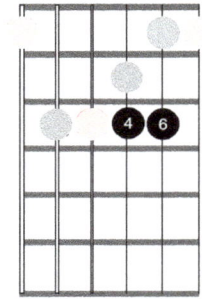

Next, use your 1st finger to play both the 2nd and 3rd strings at the 1st fret. That is C, the 5th, on the 2nd string, and A♭, the minor 3rd, on the 3rd string. Immediately hammer on the 3rd string with your 2nd finger at the 2nd fret. That is A, the major 3rd of the F chord.

Measure 4: F

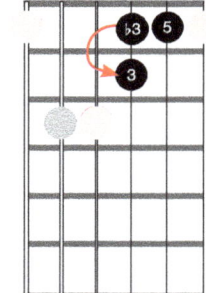

Finish the figure by playing F, the root, with your 3rd finger at the 3rd fret of the 4th string. You can see the F barre chord is outlined with this lick.

Meaure 4: F

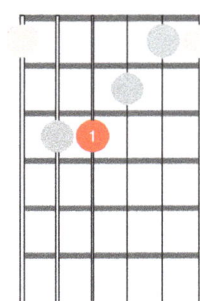

In the fifth measure, B♭, play the same thing you played in the first measure.

In the sixth measure, E♭, play the same thing you played in the second measure.

The seventh measure is the most challenging. It borrows from the f gure of the fourth measure. Go to B♭ at the 6th position. You will be using the top four strings in this figure. Start with the first two strings. The root, B♭, is on the 1st string and the 5th, F, is on the 2nd string. Play both notes by barring with your 1st finger.

Next, hammer on the 2nd string only at the 8th fret. Hammer this once then play the first two strings again by barring with your 1st finger at the 6th fret.

Measure 7: B♭

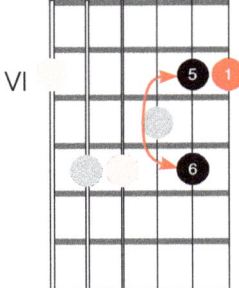

Next, use your 3rd or 4th finger (your choice) to play both the 2nd and 3rd strings at the 8th fret. That's G on the 2nd string and E♭ on the 3rd string.

Measure 7: B♭

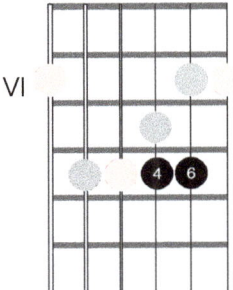

Next, use your 1st finger to play both the 2nd and 3rd strings at the 6th fret. That is F, the 5th, on the 2nd string and D♭, the minor 3rd, on the 3rd string. Immediately hammer on the 3rd string with your 2nd finger at the 7th fret. That's D, the major 3rd of the B♭ chord.

Measure 7: B♭

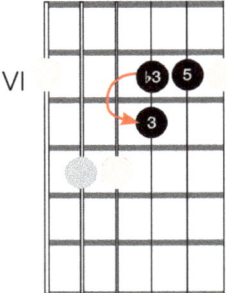

Immediately go to F at 1st position and play the same figure you just played on the B♭.

Play the first two strings by barring with your 1st finger. Then hammer on the 2nd string only at the 3rd fret. Hammer this once, then play the first two strings again.

Measure 7: F

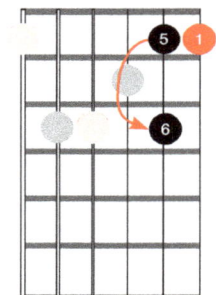

Next, use your 3rd or 4th finger to play both the 2nd and 3rd strings at the 3rd fret. Then use your 1st finger to play both the 2nd and 3rd strings at the 1st fret.

Measure 7: F

Immediately hammer on the 3rd string with your 2nd finger at the 2nd fret.

Measure 7: F

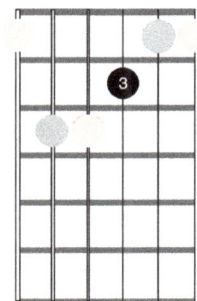

In the eighth measure, finish the figure with a B♭ at the 3rd fret of the 3rd string with your 1st finger followed by the 3rd, D, and root, B♭, in a 6th shape in 6th position.

Measure 8: B♭

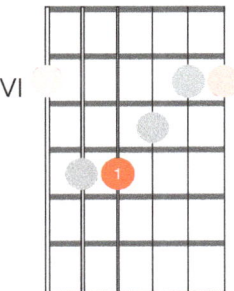

As always, keep these ideas in your vocabulary for use in other songs. By now you can see there are a lot of Classic R&B figures that are based around a Pattern IV barre chord. As you learn other parts from songs, keep that in mind.

MONEY MAKERS

In Unit 9 you learned about using octave shapes in a major context. In this module you will learn about using octaves in a minor context. Again, with octaves there is nothing to harmonize, since the shape is the same note played in two different octaves. The sound of octaves played on guitar is unique and can be heard in a wide range of styles.

Review the octave interval shapes used to play melodic lines that were presented in the Fretboard Logic Module.

- The 1st interval shape applies to octaves played on string set 6 and 4 and string set 5 and 3.

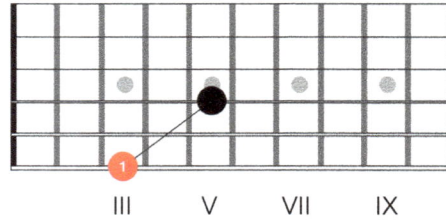 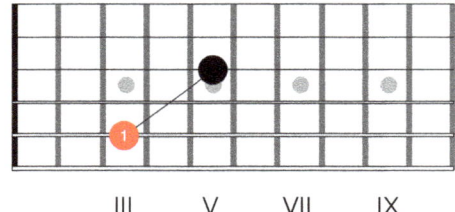

- The 2nd interval shape applies to octaves played on string set 4 and 2 and string set 3 and 1.

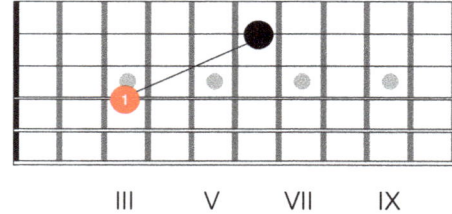 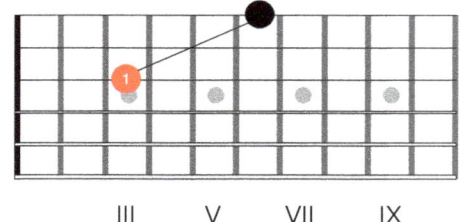

- The 3rd interval shape applies to octaves played on string set 5 and 2 and string set 4 and 1.

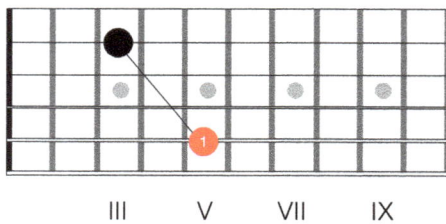 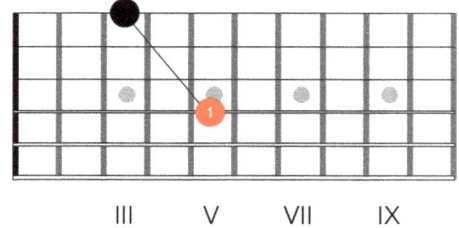

You have learned how to play the minor scale linearly along the same string sets using these octave shapes, but now, let's look at how to play these in position. Let's explore how to play the Natural Minor scale with octaves. This will require using a combination of shapes to cross the B/G line.

For demonstration purposes, let's look at the Pattern IV A minor scale:

Pattern IV A Natural Minor Scale

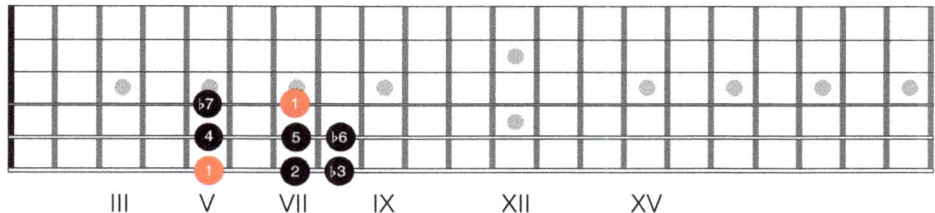

- To play it with octaves, start with the string set 6 and 4 combination for scale degrees 1, 2, and ♭3.

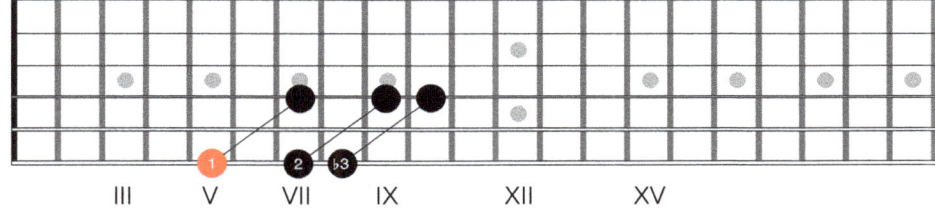

- For scale degrees 4, 5, and ♭6, move to string set 5 and 3.

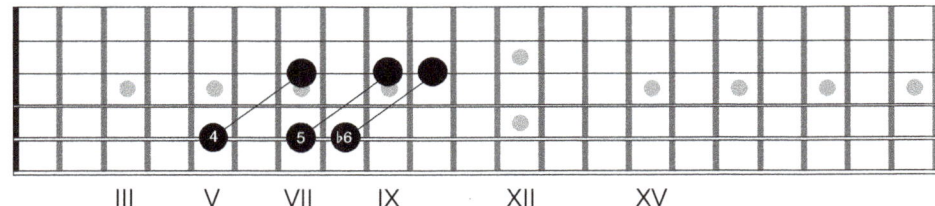

- For scale degrees ♭7 and the octave move to string set 4 and 2.

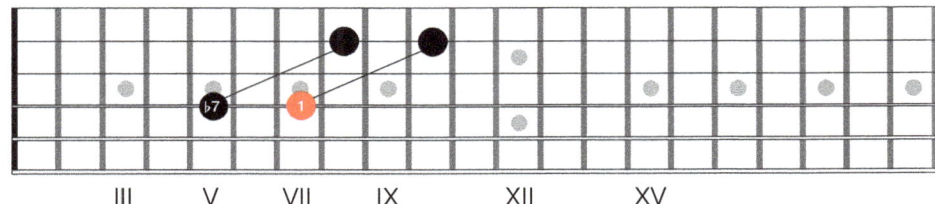

You can continue into the next octave in position in Pattern IV or move linearly up the fretboard on string set 4 and 2.

This is only one option for how to play the notes of a scale or arpeggio in position. There really is no right or wrong way to do it. I suggest you find what works for you and gradually venture out. Like all things on the fretboard, it is about referencing a shape to something you feel secure about, and that could be different for everyone.

You have worked hard at learning the octave shape system and how it works to organize information within the Octave Shape Family Tree. You have also worked hard to connect the octave shapes linearly. There are a variety of ways to visualize the geometry of the fretboard. Over time, they all come together into a clear picture.

Practice using these octaves over a vamp in A minor. Experiment playing the A minor scale linearly up each of the string sets. Track the scale on either the upper or lower note; it's up to you. For now, with your picking hand, strike the string using your thumb for the lower note and your 3rd finger for the upper note. In the last unit you learned other picking-hand techniques for playing octaves.

Note the characteristic "personality" of the sound of octaves in a minor context. Play around with some of your own ideas using octaves.

IMPROVISATION

This is the last module dedicated solely to soloing over borrowed chords and modal interchange. However, this is not the last time you will see borrowed chords. Progressions with modal interchange are as common as those with chords that are all diatonic.

The progression in Unit 9 had two places in the progression where borrowed chords required you to shift from major to minor. The progression in this mocule has the same challenge. It is another eight-bar progression that requires you to move in and out of modal interchange. The logistical challenge is the same: To know where the modal shift occurs, play appropriate notes on the borrowed chords.

Another challenge is that this is a ballad. When soloing on a ballad, your note choices are even more exposed because you spend more time on the notes. The fact that the tempo is slow and the chords are moving by more slowly makes it even more important to make good note choices, particularly for the first note you play on each chord.

This Rock ballad progression is in the key of D. The modal interchange occurs in two places. Look closely at the analysis:

Progression in D Major

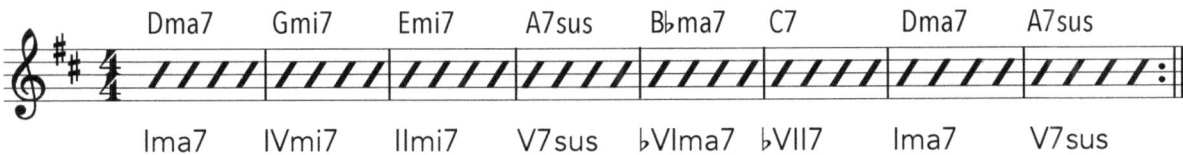

The key center throughout the entire progression is D, but examine each chord and determine whether to play the major or the parallel minor sound.

- The Dma7, Emi7, and A7sus chords are from the D major scale, so the D major sound is appropriate for them on the first, third, fourth, seventh, and eighth measures.
- The Gmi7, B♭ma7, and C7 chords are from the D minor scale, so the D minor sound is appropriate for them on the second, fifth, and sixth measures.

The challenge is to play the right sound at the right time. Playing a chord tone on the first beat of each new chord is always a good idea.

You used a safe approach in the last unit and worked in Pattern III major and Pattern IV minor pentatonic scales. In this module, you can use any approach that you want for soloing through this progression. You can use pentatonic shells, seven-note scales, or arpeggios to target chord tones, or a combination of all three.

Go through this progression and focus on playing the D major scale over the chords that are diatonic to the major key, and D minor scale over the chords that are borrowed from the parallel minor. Under each chord in the progression, it may be useful to note whether it has a major tonality or a minor tonality like the example below.

Progression in D Major

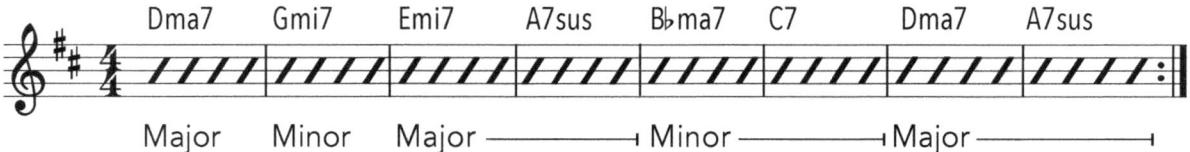

This progression, as with all of them in the Improvisation modules, can be revisited over and over, long after you have moved on to new levels. Each time you come back to a progression you will be more experienced, know the fretboard better and will have new things to play. Have some fun with this one and keep it in your routine for a long time. Use a combination of all three approaches you learned: pentatonic shells, full seven-note scales, and targeted chord tones.

As I said before, this is the last module dedicated specifically to the topic of playing over borrowed chords, but progressions with modal interchange are as common as progression with chords that are all diatonic, so you will continue to see this as you move forward.

The list of chord progressions you have soloed over going back to Level 1 is quite long now. Keep going back and trying your new knowledge over all the progressions you have learned. You will begin to see the same harmonic situations occurring again and again in hundreds and thousands of songs. Harmonic situations are fragments of chord progression or entire progressions. A lick or line that sounds good over a situation in one song will sound good over the same situation in another song. This is vocabulary.

Level 4 Unit 10 • Improv Demo

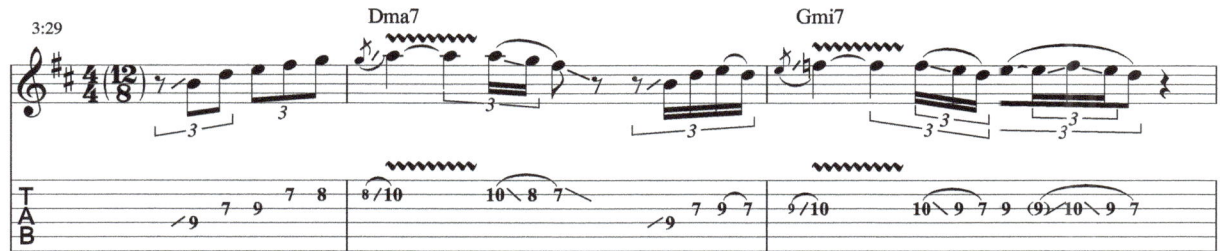
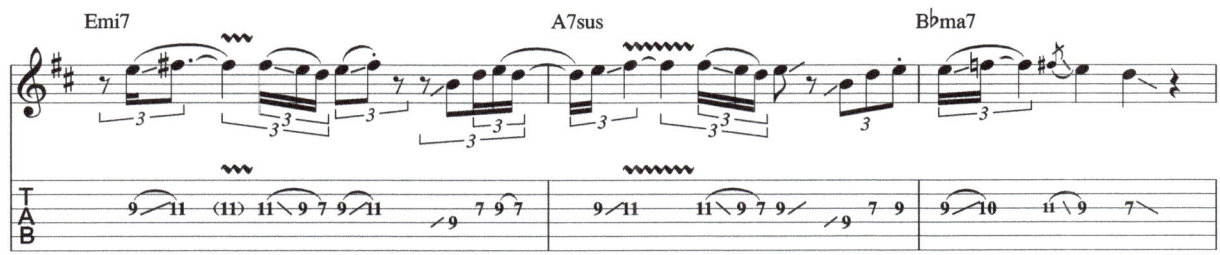
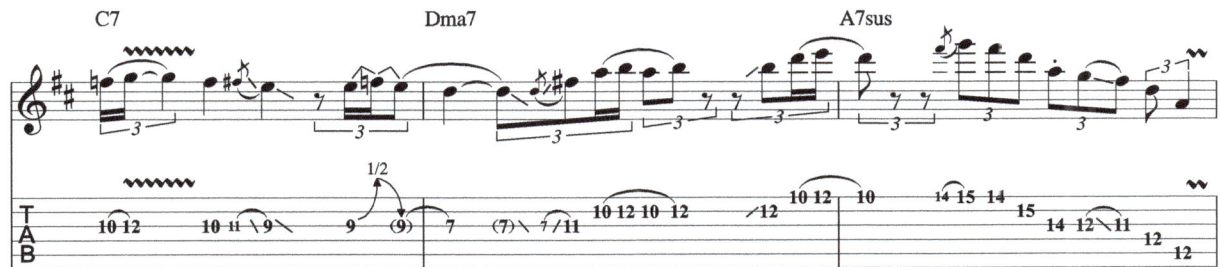

©2021 Fretboard Biology • fretboardbiology.com

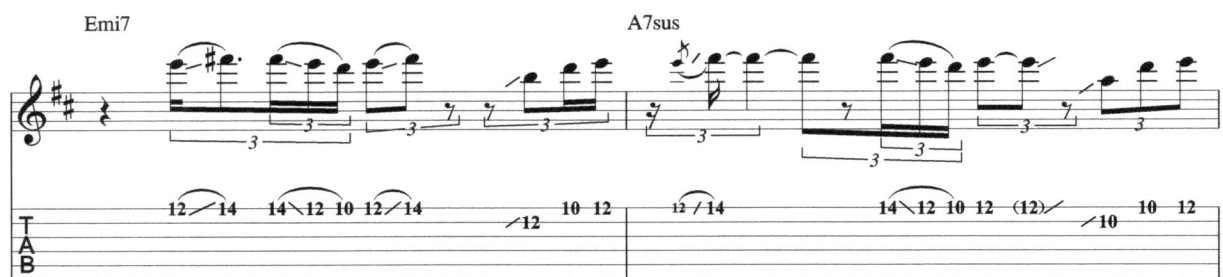
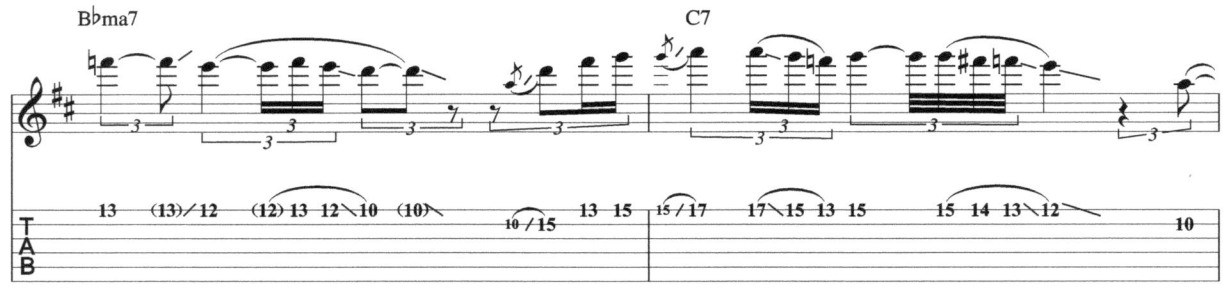
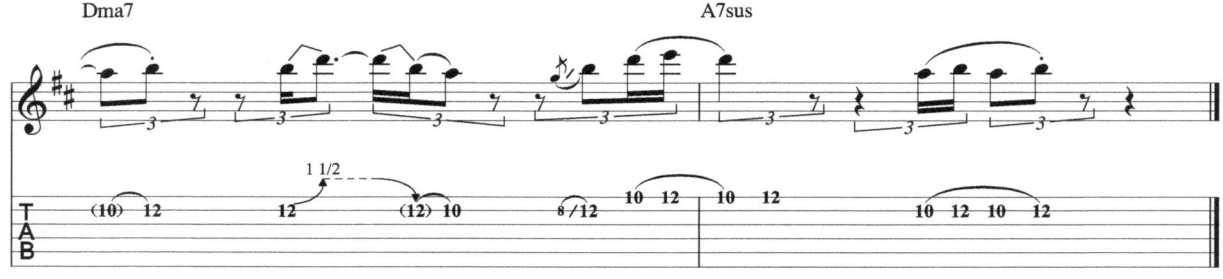

PRACTICE

Theory

- ❏ Go to the tabs below the Theory video on the website and complete the quiz.

Fretboard Logic

- ❏ Learn the diatonic octave interval shapes in minor.
- ❏ Practice Patterns I-V major and minor in-position 7th-chord arpeggios.

Rhythm Guitar

- ❏ Practice the R&B Groove in B♭, paying special attention to pick direction.

Money Makers

- ❏ Practice playing octave shape parts over minor progressions.
- ❏ Practice playing in-position octave interval shapes.

Improvisation

- ❏ Practice playing solos over an D major progression with modal interchange.

Appendices

> **Appendix 1** - Octave Shape Family Trees
> **Appendix 2** - Table of Inverted Intervals
> **Appendix 3** - Shell Voicings
> **Appendix 4** - Root Maps
> **Appendix 5** - Chords

Pattern I Family Tree

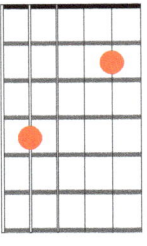

MAJOR

Pentatonic Scale
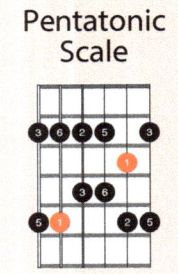

Ionian (Major) Scale
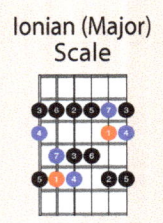

Triad Arpeggio / Augmented Arpeggio
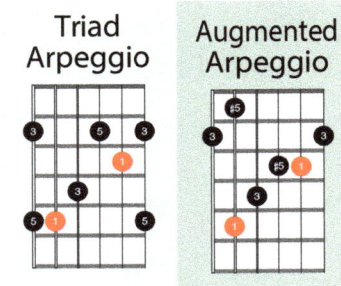

Major 7 Arpeggio / Dominant 7 Arpeggio
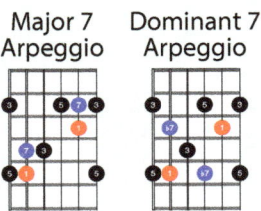

Triad Chord / Augmented Triad
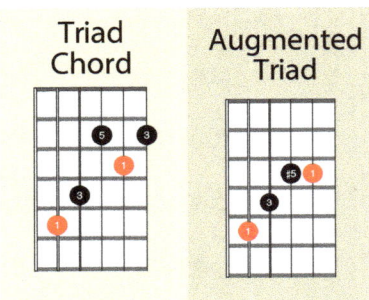

Major 7 Chord / Dominant 7 Chord
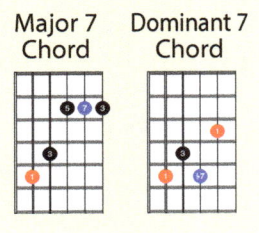

Suspended Chords (Sus 2, Sus 4, 7Sus 4) / Suspended Arpeggios (Sus 2, Sus 4)
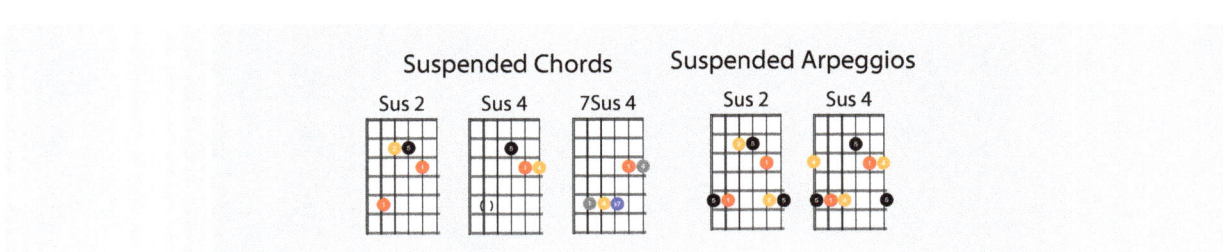

Pattern I Family Tree

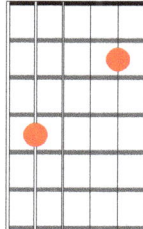

MINOR

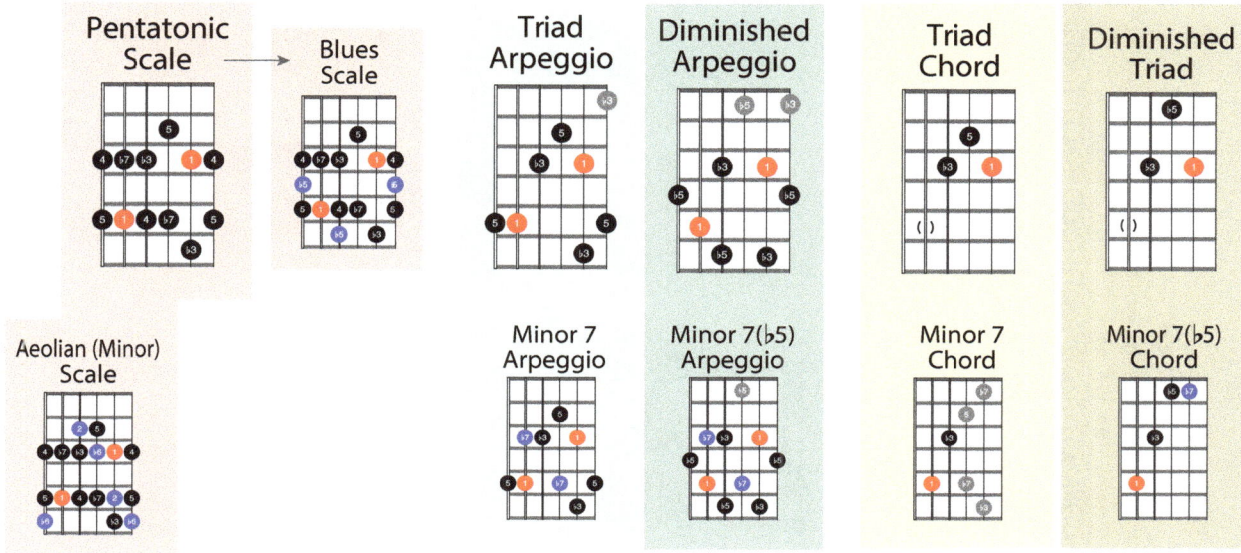

Pattern II Family Tree

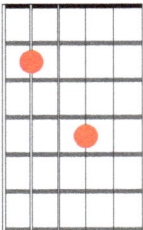

MAJOR

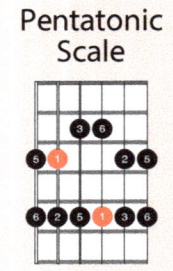
Pentatonic Scale

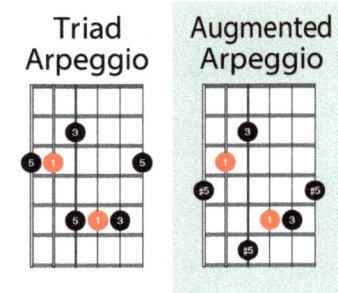
Triad Arpeggio / Augmented Arpeggio

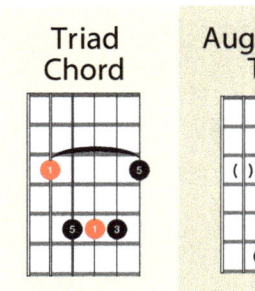
Triad Chord / Augmented Triad

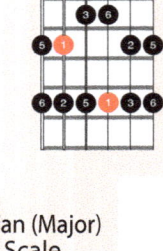
Ionian (Major) Scale

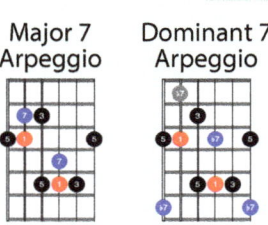
Major 7 Arpeggio / Dominant 7 Arpeggio

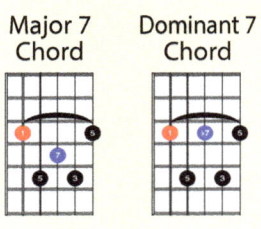
Major 7 Chord / Dominant 7 Chord

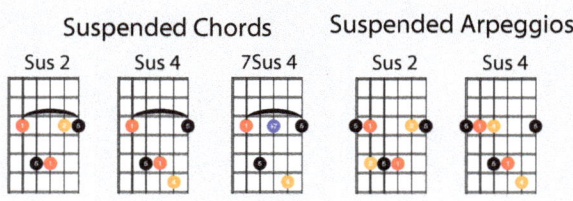
Suspended Chords (Sus 2, Sus 4, 7Sus 4) / Suspended Arpeggios (Sus 2, Sus 4)

Pattern II Family Tree

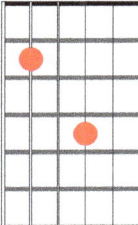

MINOR

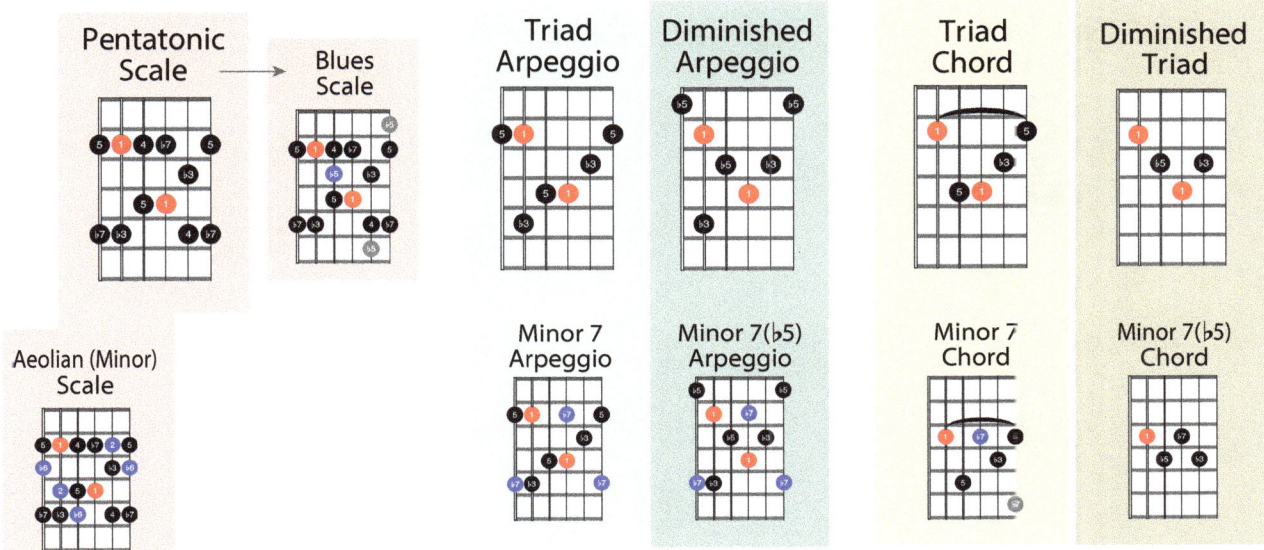

Pattern III Family Tree

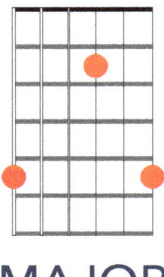

MAJOR

Pentatonic Scale
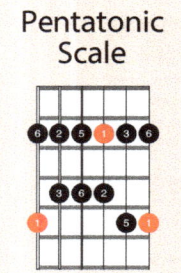

Ionian (Major) Scale
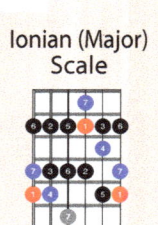

Triad Arpeggio   Augmented Arpeggio
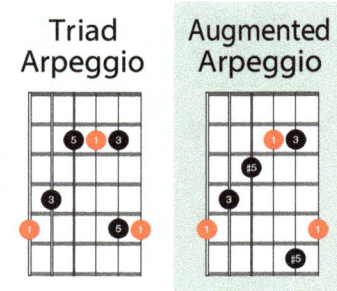

Major 7 Arpeggio   Dominant 7 Arpeggio

Triad Chord   Augmented Triad
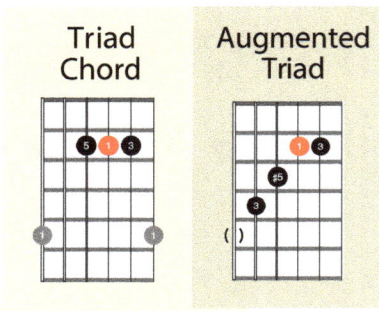

Major 7 Chord   Dominant 7 Chord
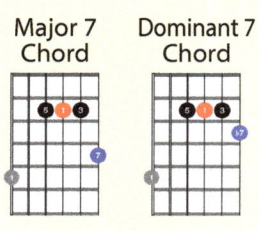

Suspended Chords   Suspended Arpeggios
Sus2   Sus4   Sus6/4   Sus2/4   7Sus4   Sus2   Sus4

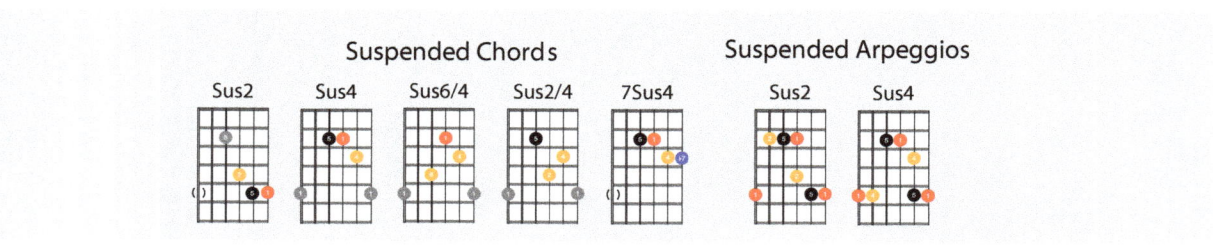

Pattern III Family Tree

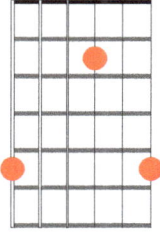

MINOR

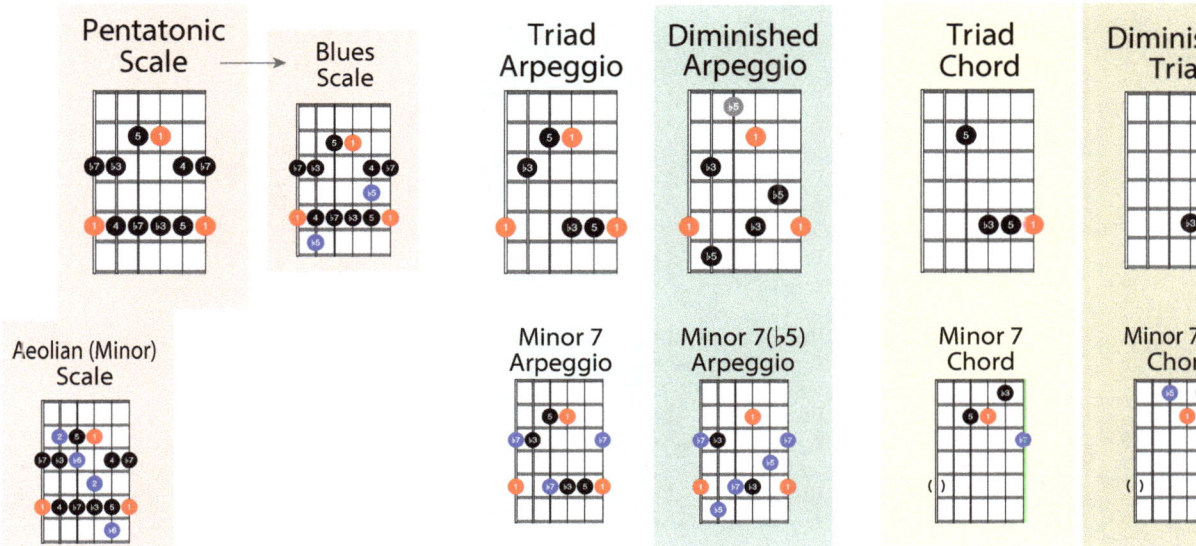

Pattern IV Family Tree

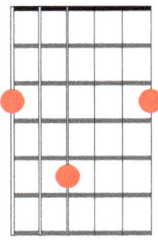

MAJOR

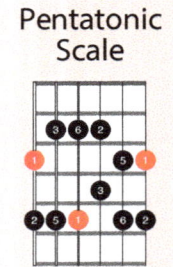

Pentatonic Scale

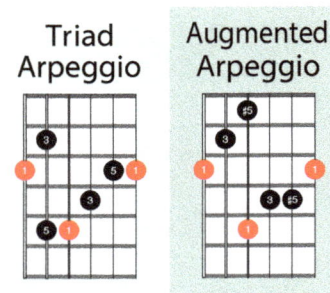

Triad Arpeggio | Augmented Arpeggio

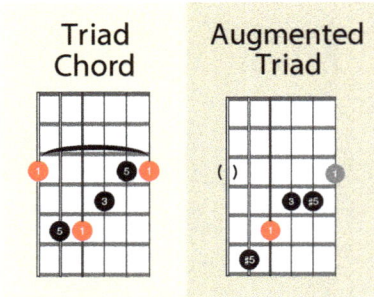

Triad Chord | Augmented Triad

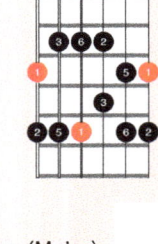

Ionian (Major) Scale

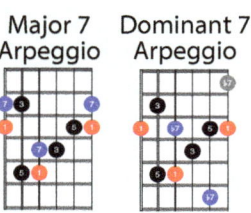

Major 7 Arpeggio | Dominant 7 Arpeggio

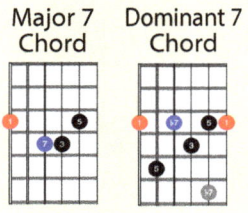

Major 7 Chord | Dominant 7 Chord

Suspended Chords   **Suspended Arpeggios**

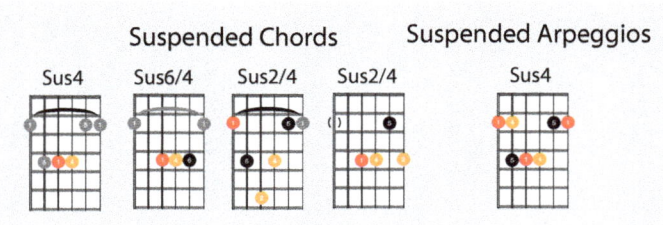

Sus4   Sus6/4   Sus2/4   Sus2/4   Sus4

Pattern IV Family Tree

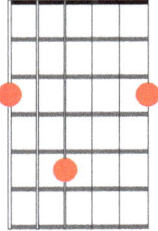

MINOR

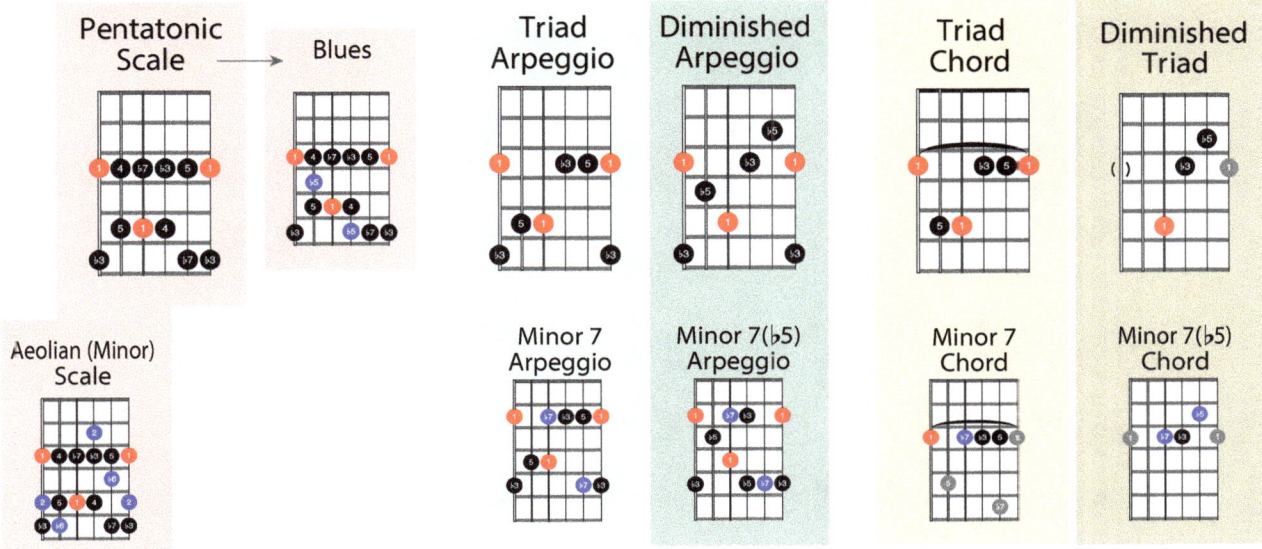

Pattern V Family Tree

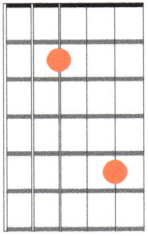

MAJOR

Pentatonic Scale | Triad Arpeggio | Augmented Arpeggio | Triad Chord | Augmented Triad

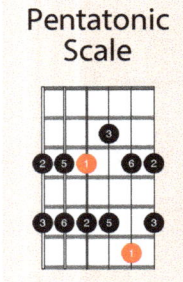
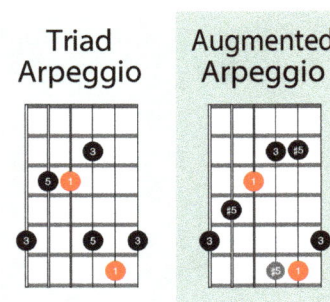
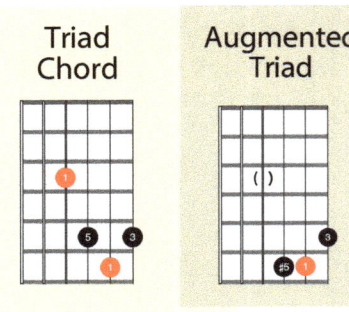

Ionian (Major) Scale | Major 7 Arpeggio | Dominant 7 Arpeggio | Major 7 Chord | Dominant 7 Chord

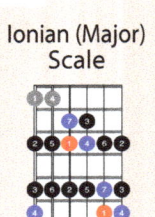

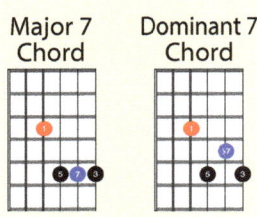

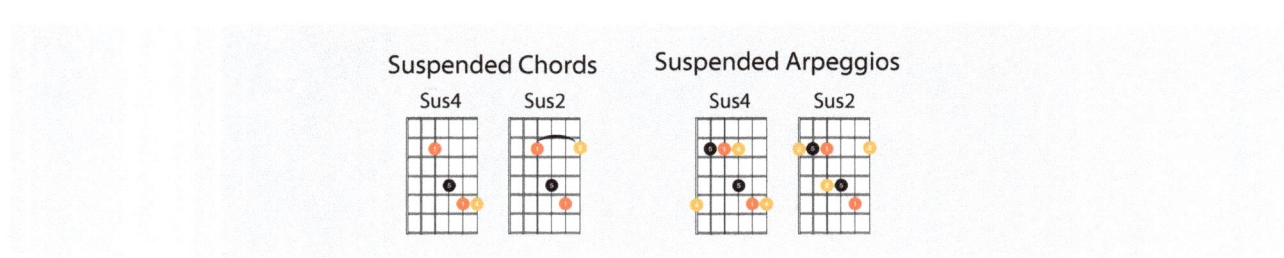

Pattern V Family Tree

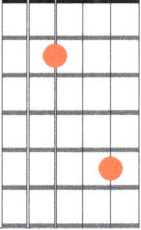

MINOR

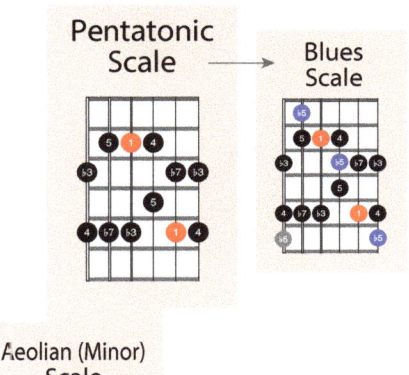

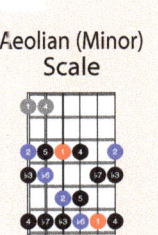

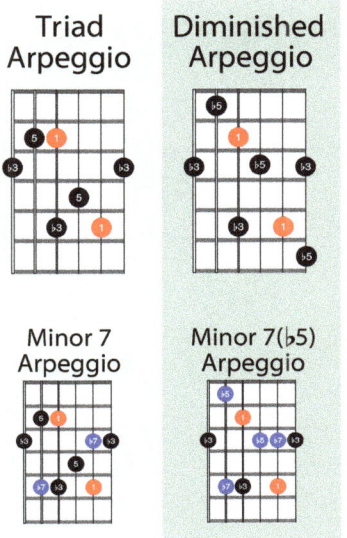

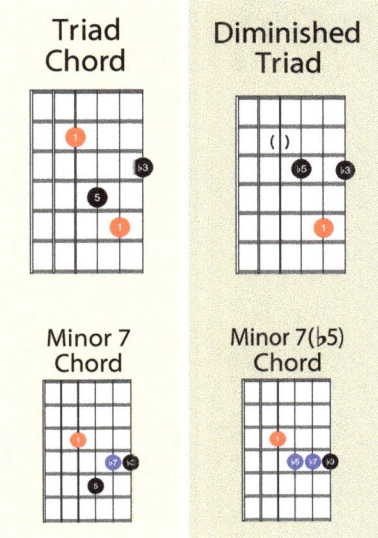

Table of Inverted Intervals

INTERVAL	→	INVERSION
Mi2		Ma7
Ma2		Mi7
Mi3		Ma6
Ma3		Mi6
P4		P5
A4		D5
D5		A4
P5		P4
Mi6		Ma3
Ma6		Mi3
Mi7		Ma2
Ma7		Mi2
P8		Unison

Shell Voicings

Pattern IV (6th string)

Major 7	Dominant 7	Minor 7	Minor 7(♭5)
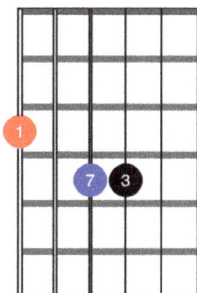	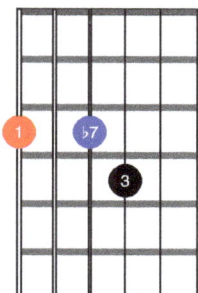	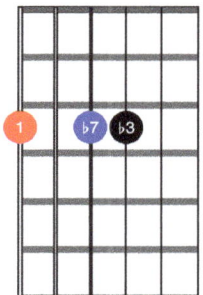	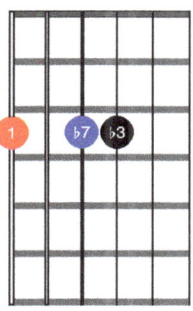

Pattern II (5th string)

Major 7	Dominant 7	Minor 7	Minor 7(♭5)
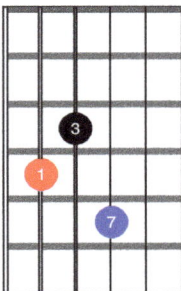	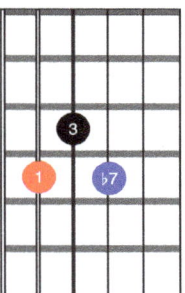	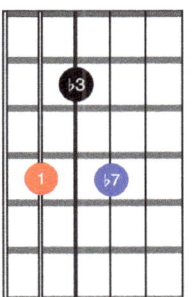	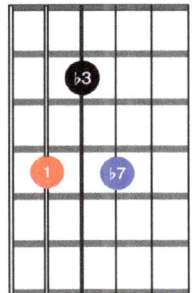

Root Map 1

Root Map 1

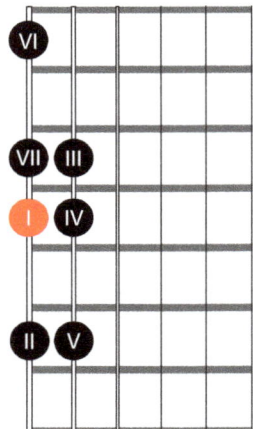

Root Map 1 Shell Voicings

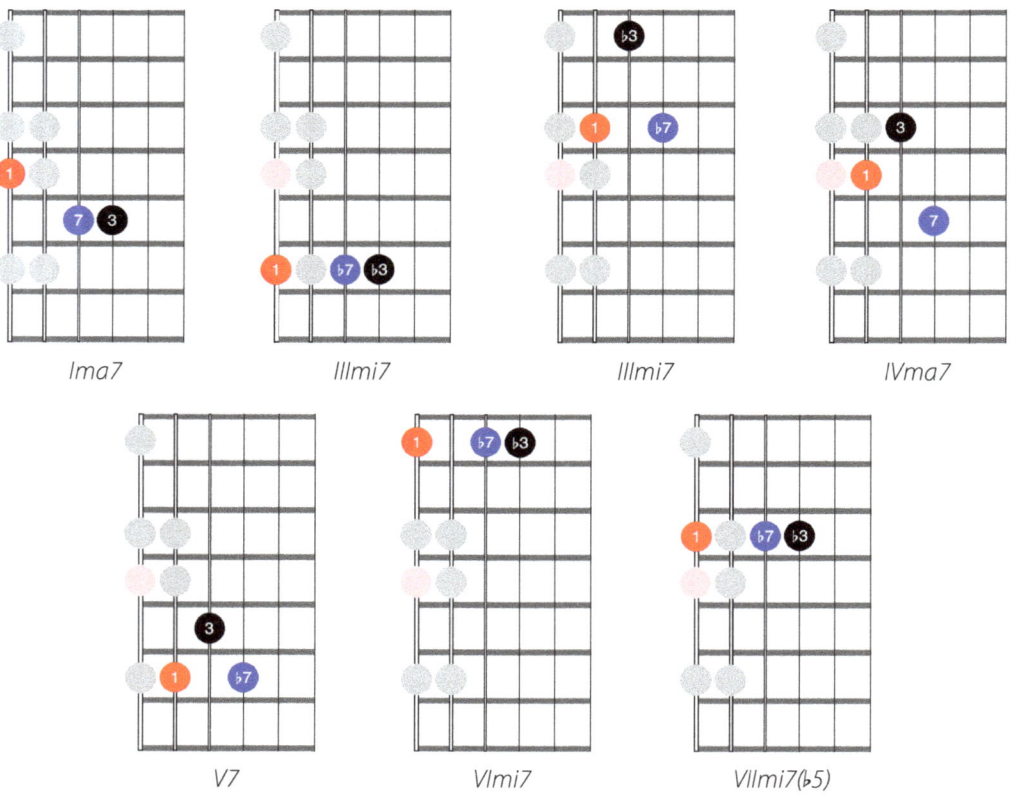

Root Map 2

Root Map 2

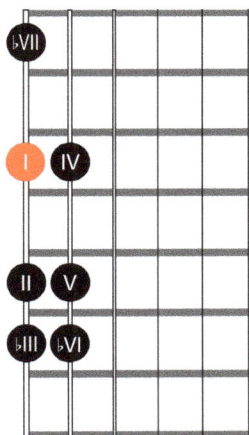

Root Map 2 Shell Voicings

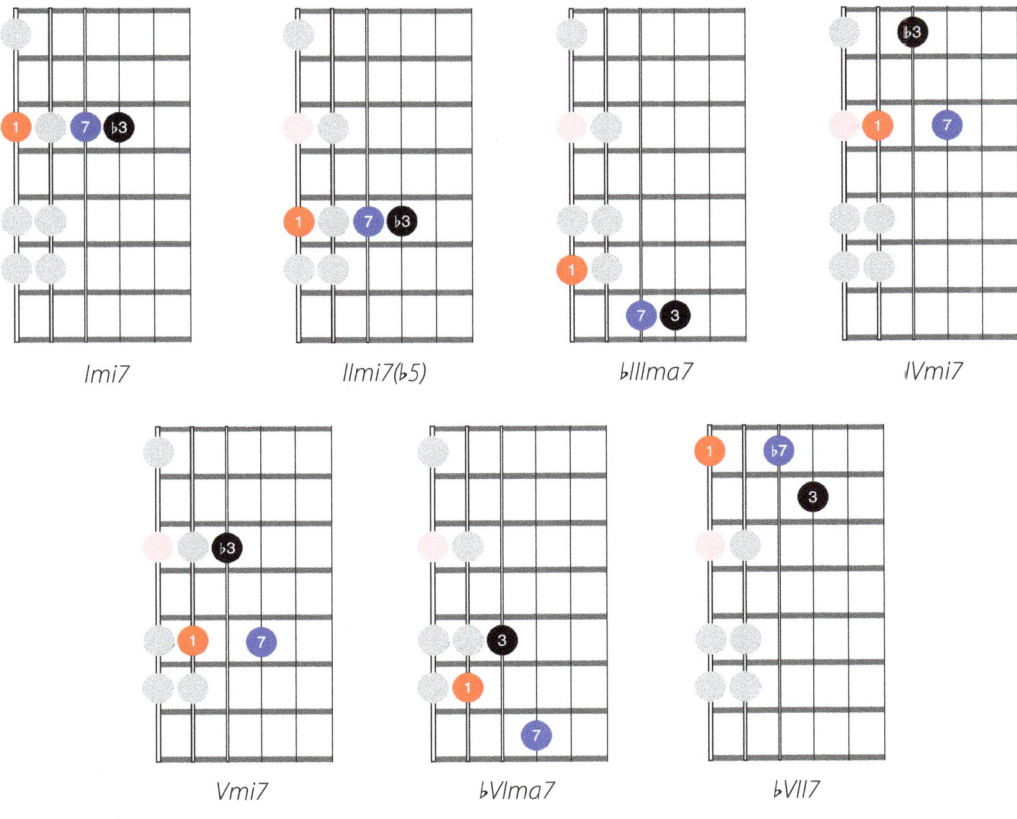

Imi7   IImi7(b5)   bIIIma7   IVmi7

Vmi7   bVIma7   bVII7

Root Map 3

Root Map 3

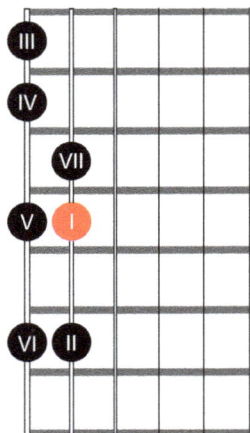

Root Map 3 Shell Voicings

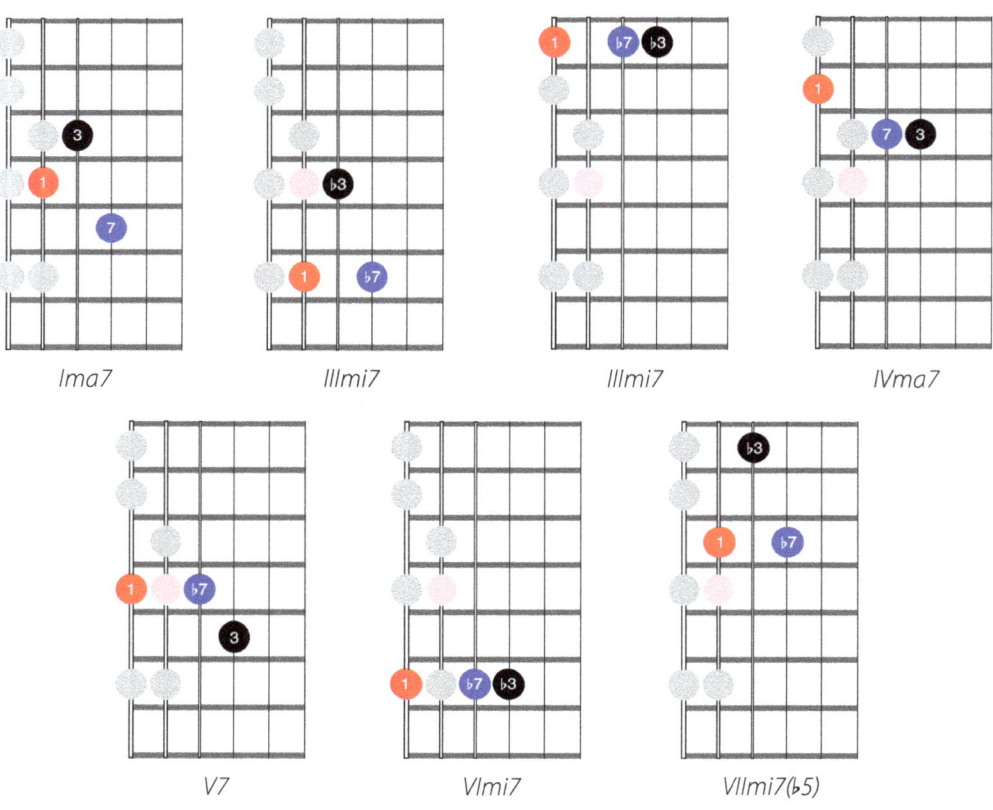

Root Map 4

Root Map 4

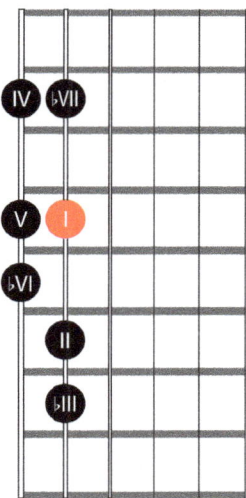

Root Map 4 Shell Voicings

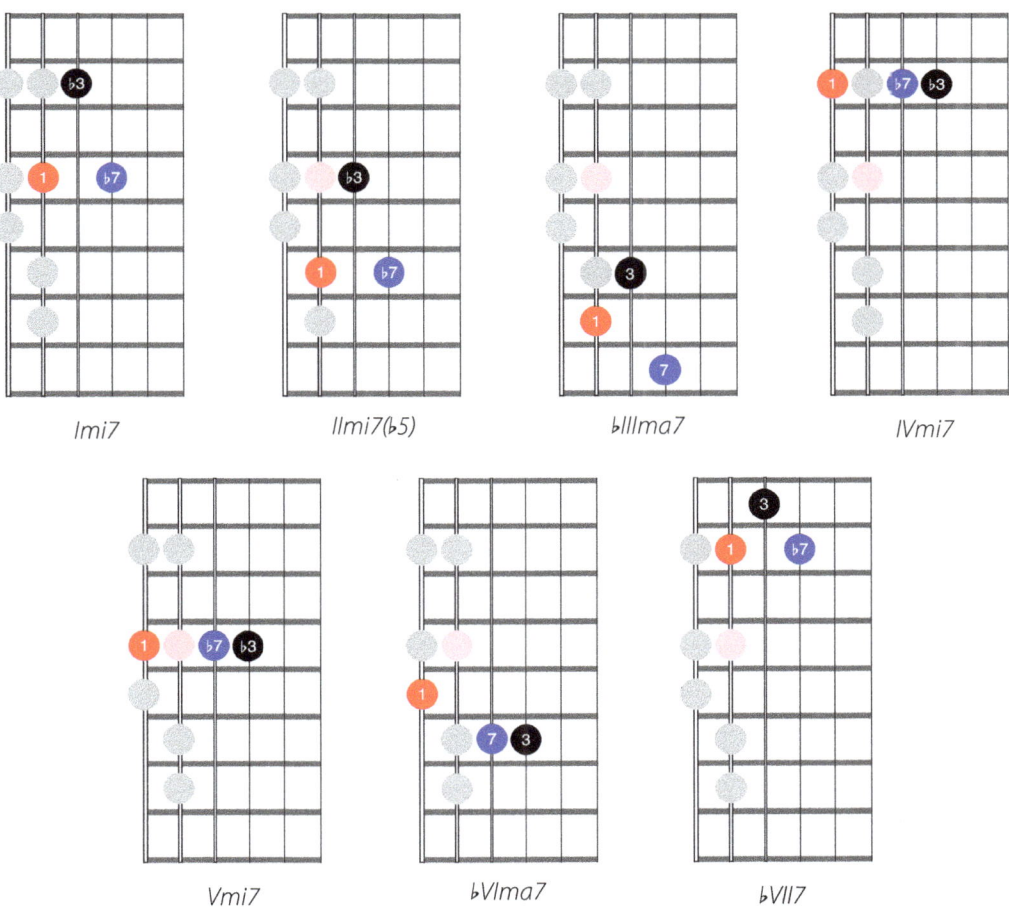

Triad In-Position Arpeggios

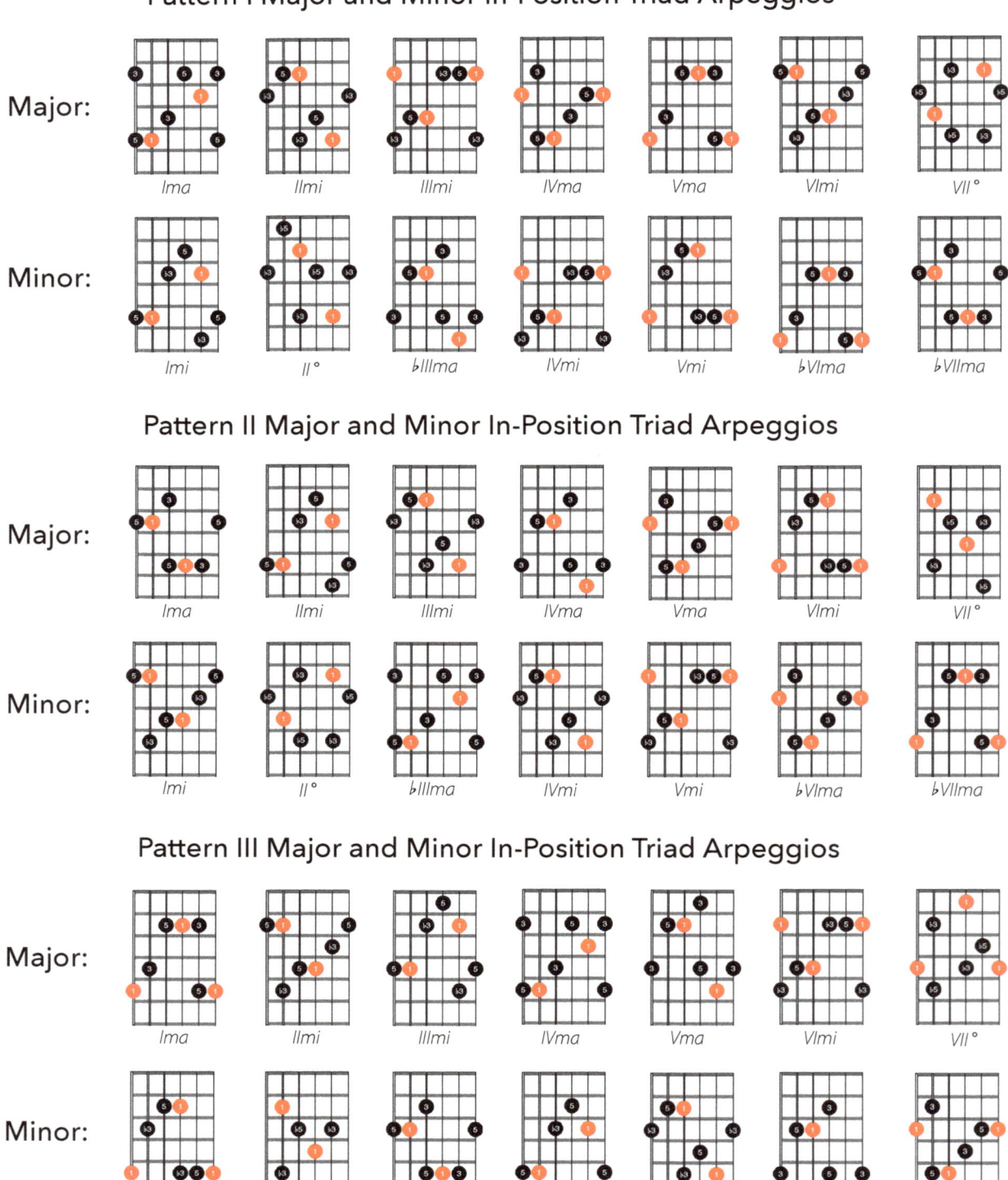

Pattern IV Major and Minor In-Position Triad Arpeggios

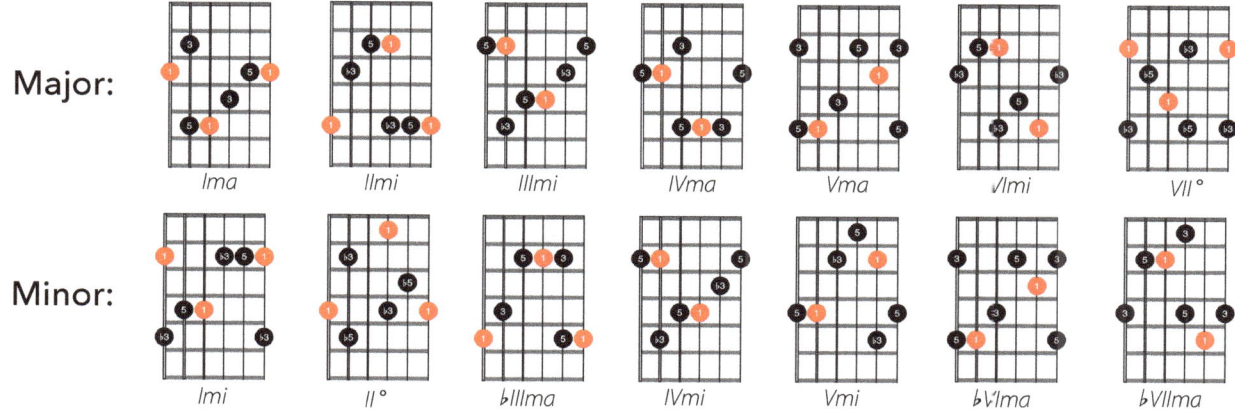

Pattern V Major and Minor In-Position Triad Arpeggios

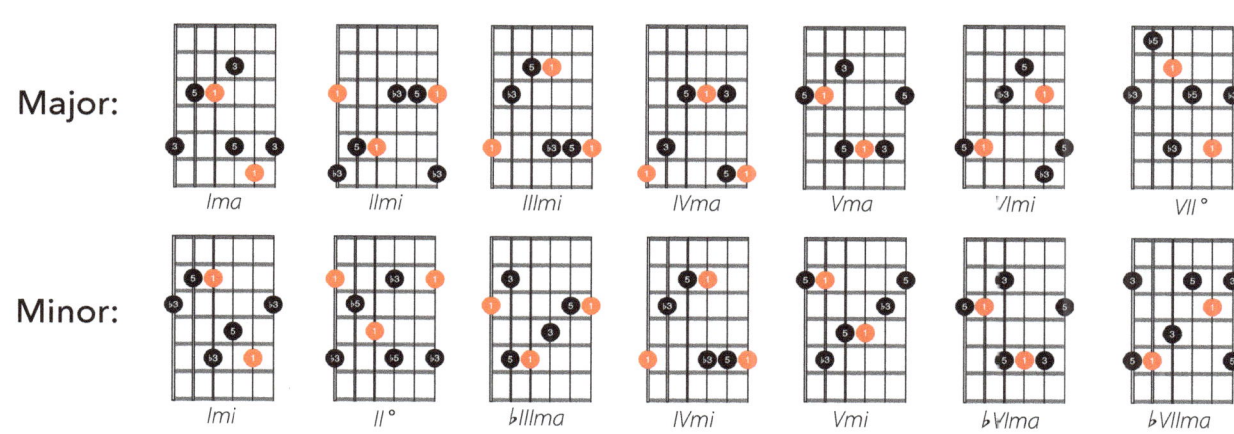

7th Chord In-Position Arpeggios

Pattern I Major and Minor In-Position 7th Chord Arpeggios

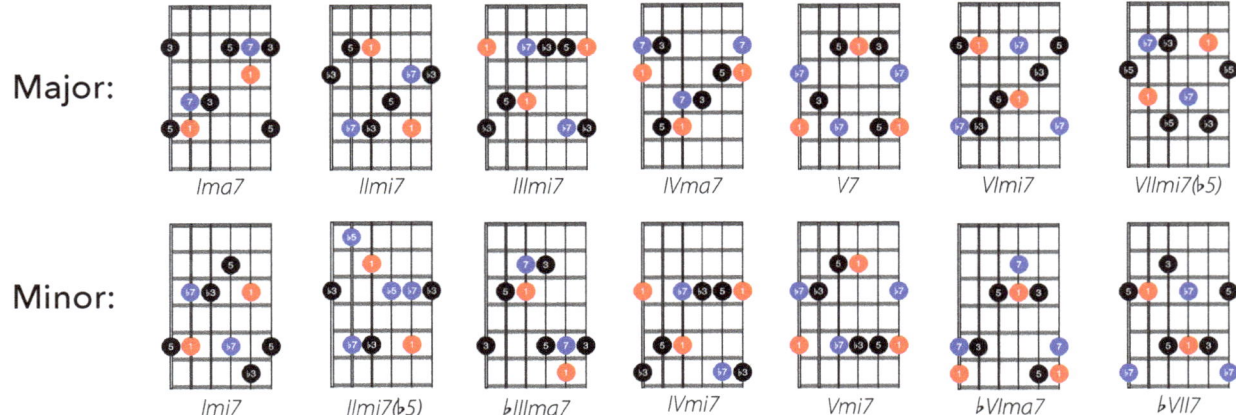

Pattern II Major and Minor In-Position 7th Chord Arpeggios

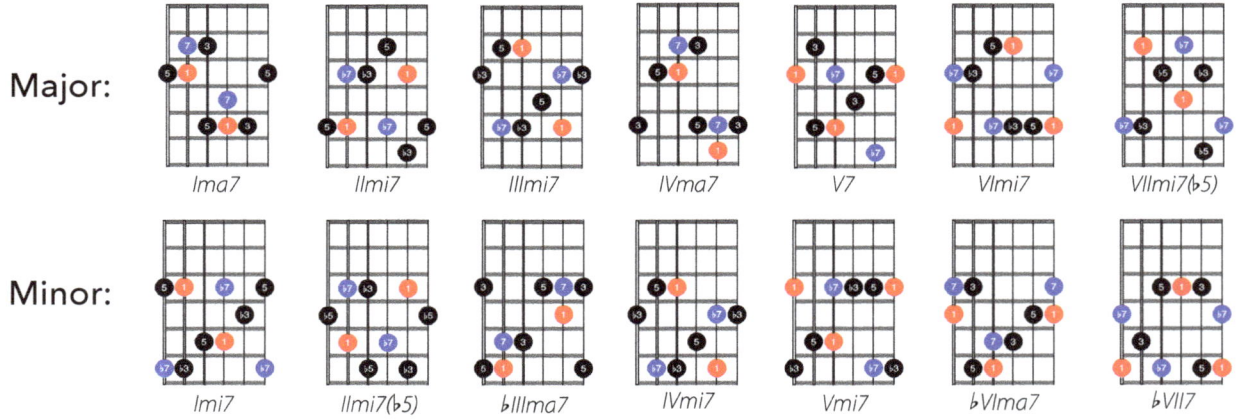

Pattern III Major and Minor In-Position 7th Chord Arpeggios

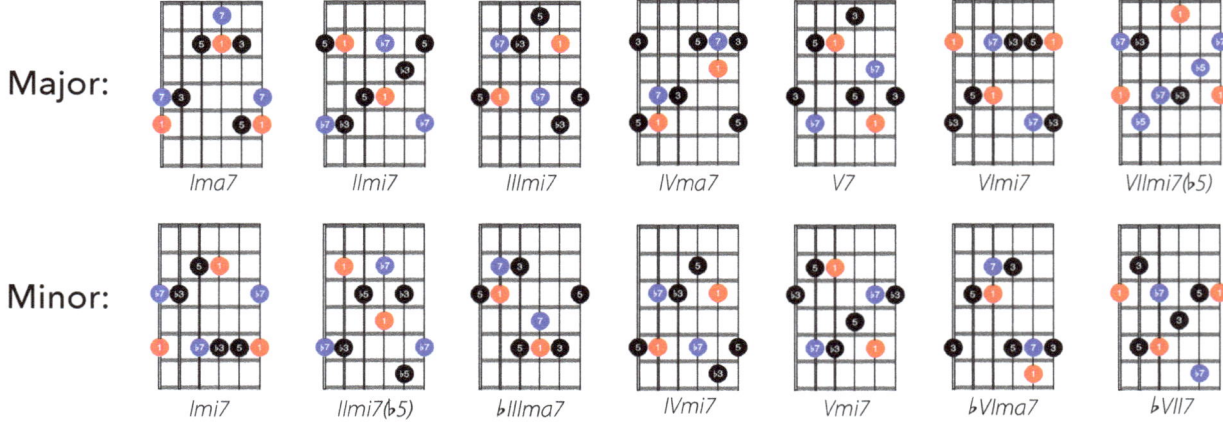

Pattern IV Major and Minor In-Position 7th Chord Arpeggios

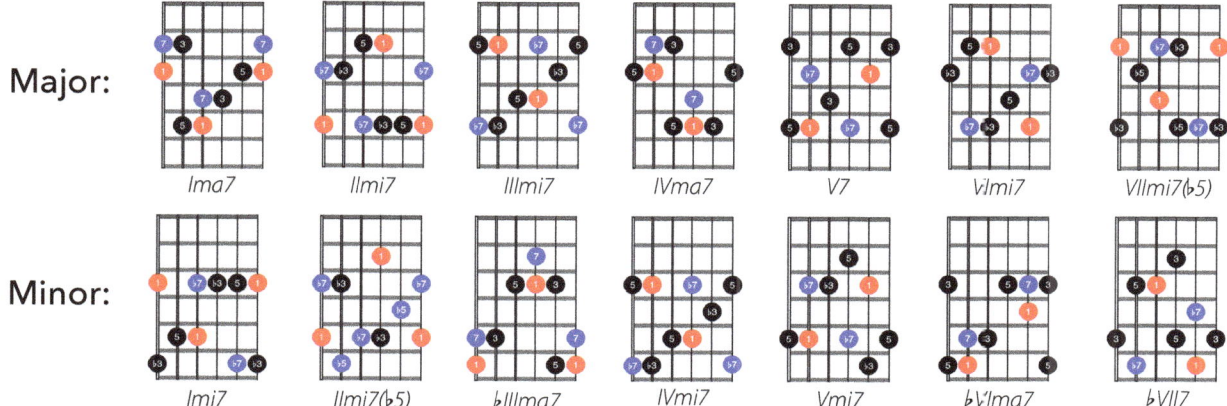

Pattern V Major and Minor In-Position 7th Chord Arpeggios

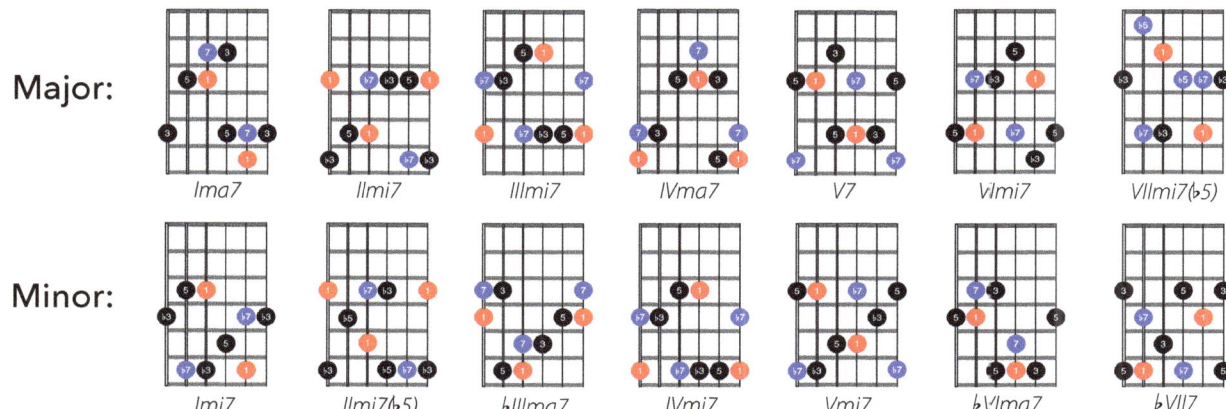

Chords

Pattern II and IV Movable / Barre Chords

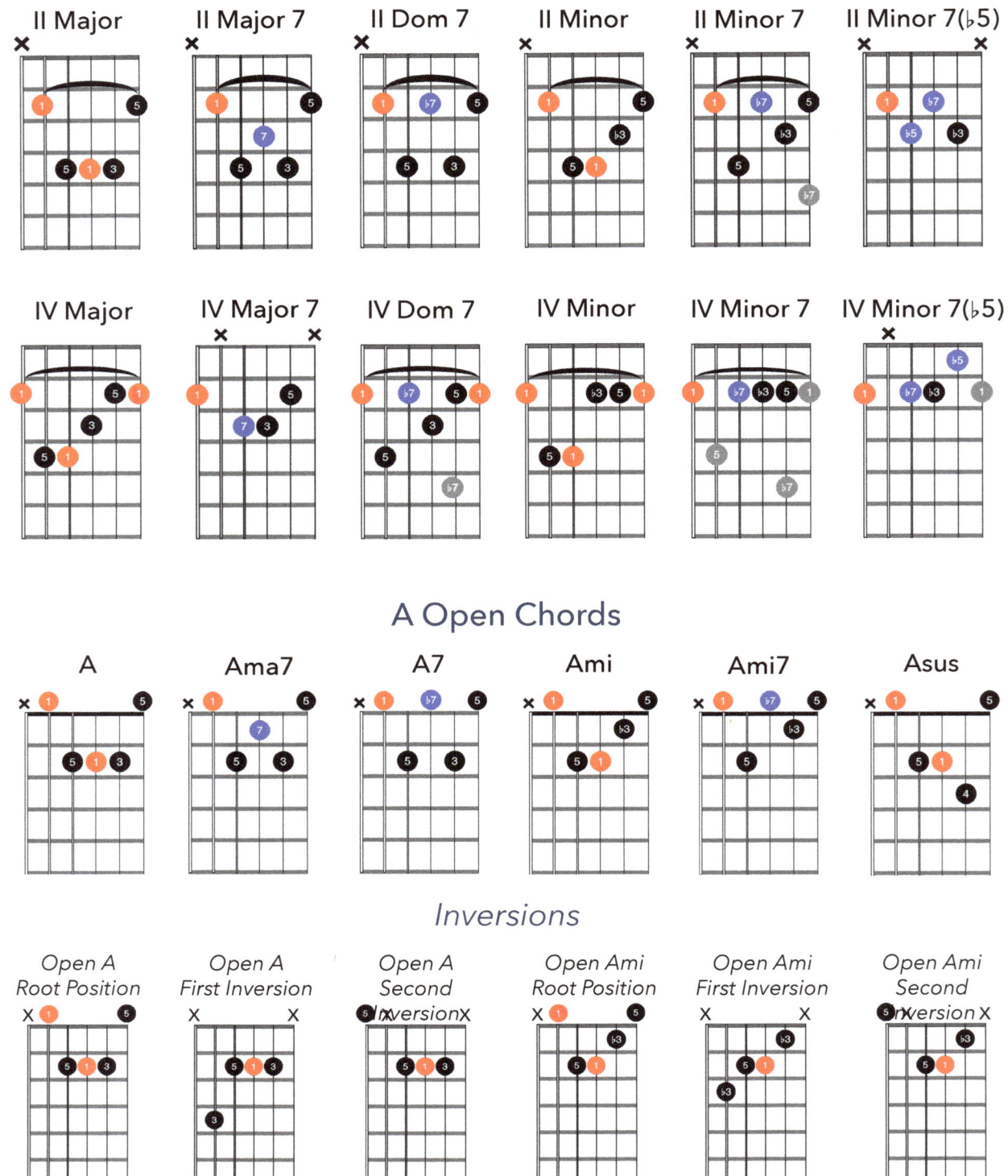

C Open Chords

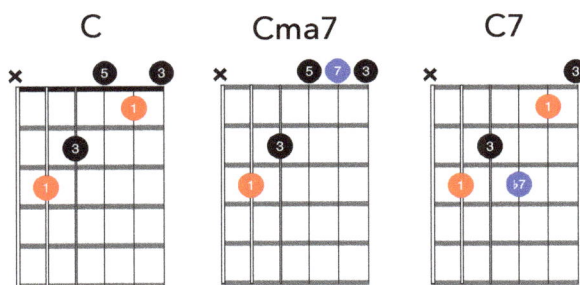
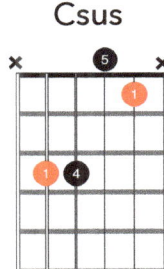

Inversions

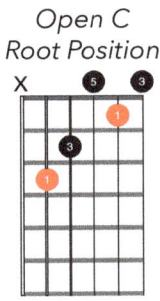
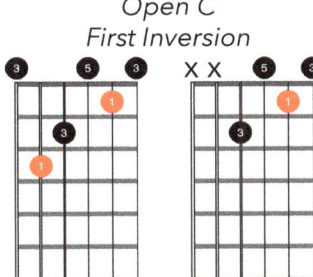
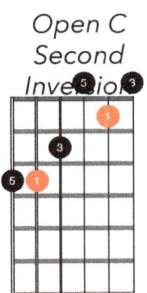

D Open Chords

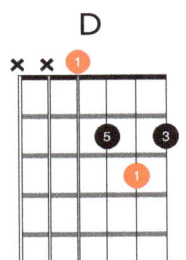
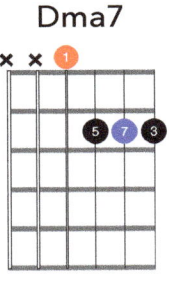
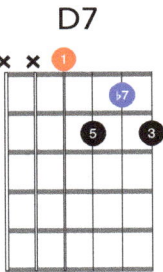
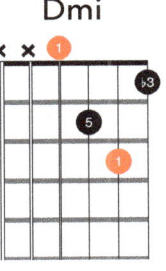
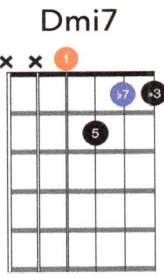
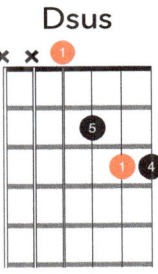

Inversions

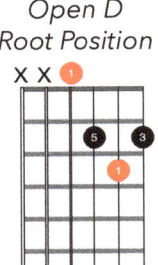
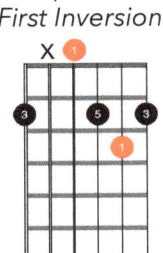
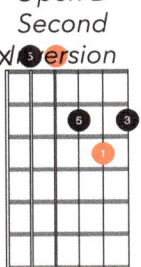
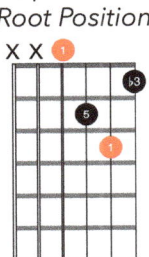
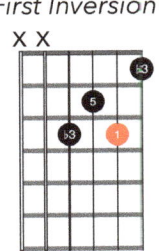
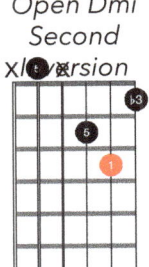

E Open Chords

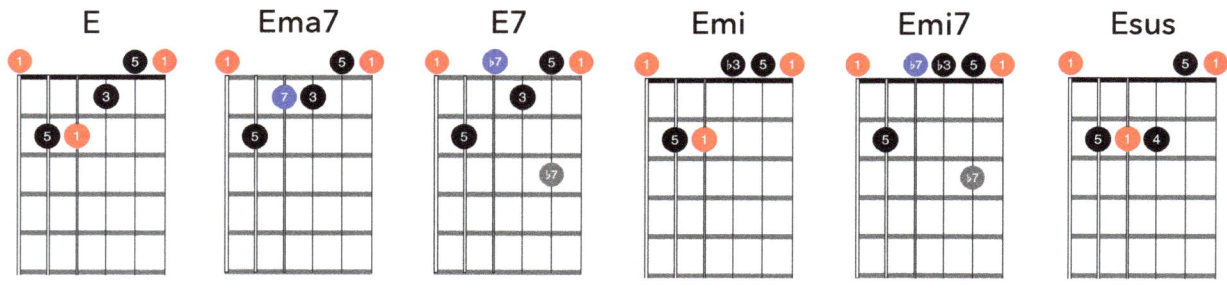

Inversions

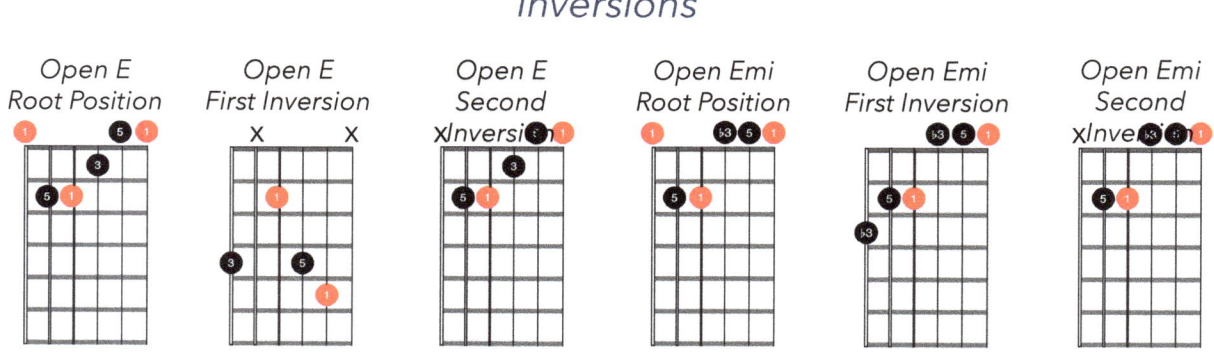

F Open Chords

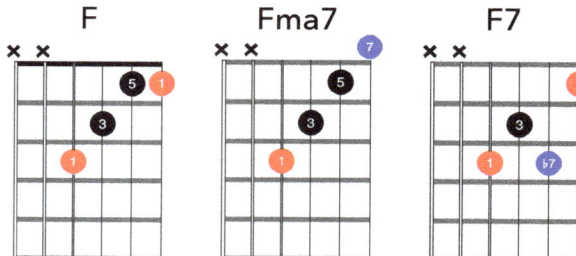

G Open Chords

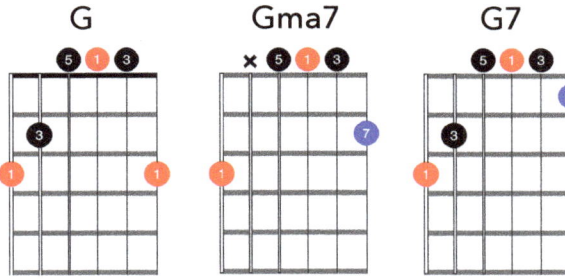
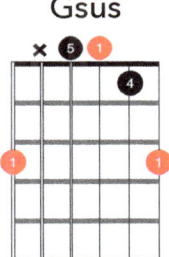

Inversions

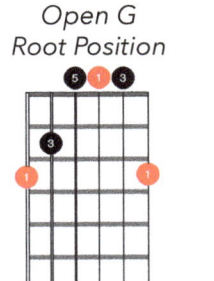
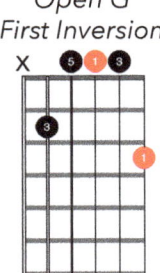
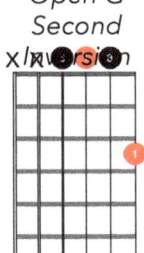

B Open Chords

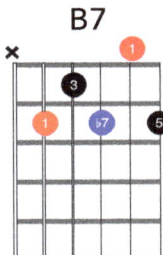

About Joe Elliott

Joe Elliott is an American guitarist, author, composer, and music educator.

Joe's professional experience as an educator includes 23 years of teaching at Musicians Institute (MI) in Hollywood, California, at the Guitar Institute of Technology (GIT). Joe has taught numerous clinics throughout the U.S. While at MI, Joe wrote and edited courses for GIT and MI's Baccalaureate programs. He spent three years as GIT Department Head and nine years as Vice President and Director of Education at Musicians Institute. He spent seven years as the Guitar Department Head and Director of Academic Administration at McNally Smith College of Music in St. Paul, Minnesota. He is currently the co-founder, CEO, and Director of Education of the guitar education website FretboardBiology.com and Music Biology, Inc.

Joe has authored several instructional books for guitar, including *An Introduction to Jazz Guitar Soloing* and *The Fretboard Biology* series of books, and has co-authored *Ear Training* with Carl Schroeder and Keith Wyatt.

Joe has released two solo guitar albums, *Joe's Place* and *Truth Serum*, as well as an instrumental country album, *Country Grit*, is currently a composer for APM Music in Los Angeles, and has composed numerous scores for television and film.